Student Study Guide
With SPSS Workbook for
Statistics for the
Behavioral Sciences

2nd Edition

Student Study Guide With SPSS Workbook for *Statistics for the Behavioral Sciences*

2nd Edition

Gregory J. Privitera

St. Bonaventure University

Los Angeles | London | New Delhi
Singapore | Washington DC

Los Angeles | London | New Delhi
Singapore | Washington DC

FOR INFORMATION:

SAGE Publications, Inc.
2455 Teller Road
Thousand Oaks, California 91320
E-mail: order@sagepub.com

SAGE Publications Ltd.
1 Oliver's Yard
55 City Road
London EC1Y 1SP
United Kingdom

SAGE Publications India Pvt. Ltd.
B 1/I 1 Mohan Cooperative Industrial Area
Mathura Road, New Delhi 110 044
India

SAGE Publications Asia-Pacific Pte. Ltd.
3 Church Street
#10-04 Samsung Hub
Singapore 049483

Copyright © 2015 by SAGE Publications, Inc.

Printed in the United States of America

ISBN 978-1-4833-5675-4

This book is printed on acid-free paper.

Acquisitions Editor: Reid Hester
Editorial Assistant: Lucy Berbeo
Production Editor: Olivia Weber-Stenis
Copy Editor: Melinda Masson
Typesetter: C&M Digitals (P) Ltd.
Proofreader: Jennifer Grubba
Cover Designer: Bryan Fishman
Marketing Manager: Shari Countryman

SUSTAINABLE FORESTRY INITIATIVE
Certified Chain of Custody
Promoting Sustainable Forestry
www.sfiprogram.org
SFI-01268
SFI label applies to text stock

14 15 16 17 18 10 9 8 7 6 5 4 3 2 1

Contents

PART V. MAKING INFERENCES ABOUT PATTERNS, FREQUENCIES, AND ORDINAL DATA

How to Use
This Study Guide

This study guide will help prepare you for exams and course materials. It can be used to help you prepare for exams and to test learning outcomes for the SPSS learning objectives. You will find many features for each chapter that meet these aims. As an overview, the contents of each chapter are as follows:

Chapter learning objectives

Chapter outline

Chapter formulas

Tips and cautions for students

Key term word searches and crossword puzzles

Practice quizzes organized by learning objective

SPSS in Focus exercises

Chapter summaries by learning objective

In addition, the answers to all word searches, crossword puzzles, and practice test questions are provided in the back matter of this study guide. Also, a General Instructions Guidebook (GIG) for using SPSS is provided in the Appendix. The GIG provides general instructions for using IBM SPSS[1] statistical software for each of the SPSS in Focus sections in the book. To give you a sense of how the contents in this study guide can help you study and test your knowledge, let's briefly look at what is included for each chapter.

Chapter Learning Objectives

The chapter learning objectives are listed on the chapter title page for each chapter in the book and are listed in this study guide as well. Learning objectives allow you to split the chapter topics into manageable units. Studying one learning objective at a time is far more manageable and

---

[1]IBM SPSS® Statistics was formerly called PASW® Statistics.

possibly less overwhelming than studying the entire chapter content at one time. In addition, the learning objectives allow professors to assign readings that are specific to the content in each chapter that they find most important or will test most heavily. The learning objectives are important inasmuch as they provide the backbone of each chapter. The learning objectives are used to organize the material covered in each chapter and organize how you can study the content in each chapter. Indeed, notice that the chapter test questions and the chapter summaries in this study guide are organized by learning objective.

Chapter Outline

An outline with a review of material covered and key terms is included with each chapter. Many students find it easier to organize their notes using an outline. Reviewing this outline can give you a good sense of where in the chapters you need to study more and where you are mastering the material. Each chapter outline lists the main headings in each chapter and gives a brief description of the material covered. The outline is a good resource for reviewing chapter material and studying for exams.

Chapter Formulas

The formulas, if any, are listed for each chapter. The formulas for each chapter are also listed in the learning objective summaries at the end of each chapter in the book. Often you will need to refer to formulas to complete assignments, compute statistics, and study for exams. The list of formulas in this study guide allows you to quickly find the formulas you need to complete your assignments or to study for exams.

Tips and Cautions for Students

The Tips and Cautions for Students sections in this study guide are aimed to bring your attention to topics in each chapter that tend to be the most difficult for students. In addition, tips are provided to help you master the difficult material. If you are having difficultly mastering material in a chapter, then refer to this section. It is likely that you are not alone and that this section will have useful tips to help you master the material.

Key Term Word Searches and Crossword Puzzles

It is important to review key terms and definitions in each chapter. In each chapter, key terms are bolded and defined. All bolded terms are then listed in the end material of each chapter. In this study guide, most key terms are included in word searches and crossword puzzles. Reviewing definitions can be boring. The crossword puzzles and word searches can make this review a little more fun and interesting. It's also a nice break from standard multiple-choice and fill-in-the-blank question formats.

Practice Quizzes Organized by Learning Objective

It is always important to study prior to an exam. It can often be just as effective—sometimes more effective—to work through practice quizzes prior to taking an exam. Quiz questions can show you where you might be misunderstanding certain material and where you are mastering the material. Three to five quiz questions are given for each learning objective in this study guide—almost 500 quiz questions in all. Completing the quiz questions will help you check your mastery of each learning objective. Because the quiz questions are given for each learning objective, you will also know immediately which sections of the chapter you are struggling with the most and which sections you are mastering. The answers to all quiz questions are given in the back of this study guide so that you can check your answers.

SPSS in Focus Exercises

SPSS in Focus sections are included in each chapter of the book to introduce you to the statistical software used by most behavioral researchers. The steps to enter, analyze, and interpret data using SPSS are described using practical research examples. This student study guide supports each SPSS in Focus section by including SPSS exercises for each chapter. The SPSS exercises in this study guide allow you to practice using SPSS and interpret output data using new research examples. A General Instructions Guidebook (GIG), provided in the back matter, provides general instructions that can be used for any example. An answer key for the SPSS exercises is not included to allow professors or instructors to use these exercises as a way of assessing your mastery of the SPSS learning objectives.

Chapter Summaries by Learning Objective

Chapter summaries are given at the end of each chapter in the book and in this study guide. The chapter summaries are organized by learning objective. This can help you quickly review learning objective material as you take the chapter quizzes. When you get a few questions wrong for a learning objective, you can then quickly refer to the chapter summary for that learning objective. Including the chapter summaries by learning objective in this study guide allows you to efficiently study chapter material.

Keep in mind that this study guide is designed to help you study and to learn the material covered in each chapter of *Statistics for the Behavioral Sciences*, 2nd edition. This student study guide supports the content in each chapter of the book by testing your retention and mastery of chapter material and allowing you to quickly review content that you are struggling with the most. The study guide provides quick references to formulas, key terms, and learning objectives in each chapter and includes assessments for the SPSS learning objectives. You will find many of the features in this study guide very useful for studying chapter content and preparing for exams. In all, this study guide was written to indubitably help you master chapter content in *Statistics for the Behavioral Sciences*, 2nd edition, and to achieve your personal goals of success in the classroom.

PART I

Introduction and Descriptive Statistics

1

Introduction to Statistics

LEARNING OBJECTIVES

After reading this chapter, you should be able to:

1. Distinguish between descriptive and inferential statistics.

2. Explain how samples and populations, as well as a sample statistic and population parameter, differ.

3. Describe three research methods commonly used in behavioral science.

4. State the four scales of measurement and provide an example for each.

5. Distinguish between variables that are qualitative or quantitative.

6. Distinguish between variables that are discrete or continuous.

7. Enter data into SPSS by placing each group in separate columns and each group in a single column (coding is required).

1.1 The Use of Statistics in Science

Statistics: A branch of mathematics used to summarize, analyze, and interpret a group of numbers or observations. The information that scientists gather is evaluated in two ways that reveal the two general types of statistics:

- Scientists organize and summarize information such that the information is meaningful to those who read about the observations scientists made in a study. This type of evaluation of information is called *descriptive statistics*.
- Scientists use information to answer a question (e.g., Is diet related to obesity?) or make an actionable decision (e.g., Should we implement a public policy change that can reduce obesity rates?). This type of evaluation of information is called *inferential statistics*.

1.2 Descriptive and Inferential Statistics

Descriptive statistics: Procedures used to summarize, organize, and make sense of a set of scores or observations. Descriptive statistics are typically presented graphically, in tabular form (in tables), or as summary statistics (single values).

   Data, or numeric measurements, are the values summarized using descriptive statistics. Presenting data in summary can clarify research findings for small and large data sets.

   Inferential statistics: Procedures used to infer or generalize observations made with samples to the larger population from which they were selected. Scientists rarely have the resources or ability to select all individuals in a *population* (all members of a group of interest). Instead, scientists select a *sample* (or subset) of those from the larger population, then use inferential statistics to identify the extent to which observations made in the sample would also be observed in the larger population from which the sample was selected.

1.3 Research Methods and Statistics

Experimental method: An experiment is any study that controls the conditions under which observations are made to isolate cause-and-effect relationships between two variables. To conduct an experiment, we must meet three requirements: *randomization, manipulation,* and *comparison.*

- *Randomization* consists of using random assignment to ensure that all participants in the study have an equal probability of being assigned to a group.

- *Manipulation* consists of creating the levels of the independent variable. Each level is a group—hence, manipulation allows us to create groups to which the participants will be randomly assigned.
- *Comparison/control* involves the use of a comparison or control group that does not receive the manipulation believed to cause changes in a dependent variable. Comparing the control group to a group that received the manipulation allows us to determine if the manipulation is actually associated with changes in the dependent variable.

Independent variable (IV): The variable that is manipulated in an experiment. By manipulating the IV, we create the different groups in a study.

Dependent variable (DV): The variable that is measured in each group or at each level of the independent variable. The dependent variable must be *operationally defined*, meaning that it is defined by the specific process or manner by which it was observed or measured.

Quasi-experimental method: A quasi-experiment is a research design that includes a quasi-independent variable and/or lacks a comparison or control group.

- A quasi-independent variable is any variable with preexisting levels. For example, if we group participants by gender (men, women), then the variable is a quasi-independent variable—the participants were men or women before the study began; hence, the researcher did not manipulate or create the gender groups in the study.

Correlational method: The measurement of pairs of scores, called data points, examines the extent to which two variables are related. No variable is manipulated to create different groups to which participants can be randomly assigned. Instead, two variables are measured for each participant, and the extent to which those variables are related is measured. Hence, correlations lack the control needed to demonstrate cause and effect.

1.4 Scales of Measurement

Scales of measurement are the rules that describe how a number was measured and the extent to which it is informative. Four scales of measurement are *nominal, ordinal, interval,* and *ratio*.

Nominal scales: Measurements where a value is used to represent something or someone.

- Nominal values are typically coded, or converted to numeric values for later statistical analysis.

Ordinal scales: Measurements where values convey order or rank alone. Ordinal scale data simply indicate that one value is greater than or less than another value.

Interval scales: Measurements with two defining principles—equidistant scales and no true zero.

- *Equidistant scales* are intervals with values that are distributed in equal units.
- A *true zero* is a scale where 0 indicates the absence of something. An interval scale lacks a true zero. Examples of scales without a true zero include rating scales, temperature, and measures of latitude and longitude.

Ratio scales: Measurements with two defining principles—equidistant scales and a true zero.

- Examples of scales with a true zero include weight, height, time, and calories.

1.5 Types of Variables for Which Data Are Measured

Continuous variables are measured along a continuum, such that they can be measured at any point beyond the decimal point. Continuous variables can be measured in whole or fractional units.

Discrete variables are measured in categories or whole units and are *not* measured along a continuum. Discrete data are not measured in fractional units.

Quantitative variables vary by amount, can be continuous or discrete, and are measured in numeric units.

Qualitative variables vary by class, can only be discrete, and are used to describe nonnumeric aspects of phenomena.

1.6 Research in Focus: Evaluating Data and Scales of Measurement

When a research study includes a qualitative variable, researchers will often also include quantitative variables because these can be more informative. For example, in their study on social networking, Jones, Blackey, Fitzgibbon, and Chew (2010) interviewed college students and recorded their qualitative responses. In addition, they measured quantitative variables by having students rate how often they used certain social software technologies. Because quantitative variables are more widely measured in the behavioral sciences, this book describes statistical procedures for quantitative variables on each scale of measurement.

1.7 SPSS in Focus: Entering and Defining Variables

SPSS can be used to enter and define variables. All variables are defined in the Variable View tab. The values recorded for each variable are listed in the Data View tab. Data can be entered by column or by row in the Data View tab.

TIPS AND CAUTIONS FOR STUDENTS

- *Dependent and independent variables:* To identify the independent variable (IV) and dependent variable (DV) in an experiment, start by determining the hypothesis that is being tested in the experiment. Then ask, what is being measured in each group to test this hypothesis? The dependent variable is typically measured in numeric units. To determine the independent variable, refer back to the groups. Determine what the researcher thinks is causing or is associated with changes in the DV. The different groups are the levels of the independent variable.

    Note that a quasi-independent variable is a variable that is preexisting. This type of variable is used in a quasi-experimental or a correlational research design. Unlike an experiment, the levels of a quasi-independent variable are preexisting, meaning that the researcher did not manipulate the levels of that variable.

- *Scales of measurement:* When determining the scale of measurement a variable is measured on, first assess whether the variable is categorical. If it is categorical, then it is likely on a nominal scale. If it is a ranked value or one that indicates only that one value is larger than another, then it is likely on an ordinal scale. Interval scale measures are typically rating scales, where participants indicate their level of agreement or opinion regarding items in a survey. To distinguish an interval scale from a ratio scale, assess whether the scale has a true zero. If 0 indicates the absence of the variable you are measuring, then it has a true zero and is on a ratio scale; if not, then it does not have a true zero and is on an interval scale.

KEY TERM WORD SEARCHES

Q	U	A	L	I	T	A	T	I	V	E	V	A	R	I	A	B	L	E	U	P	C	Q	T	M	O	X	S	P	Y	M	Q	V	J	F
S	G	W	O	S	R	J	Q	V	G	I	X	W	T	R	R	N	L	D	T	F	W	J	T	G	M	F	D	C	E	C	X	I	N	J
D	D	B	I	Y	I	Z	H	E	Q	L	N	O	I	E	A	S	B	A	D	C	Y	N	W	F	T	V	Q	L	U	U	D	H	Z	N
R	M	E	E	N	R	O	R	X	W	U	J	T	U	Y	Y	T	P	U	M	F	E	E	G	S	N	A	B	T	G	B	N	D	C	A
D	J	E	S	C	D	O	C	X	K	G	A	S	E	M	N	P	I	K	J	M	E	X	O	Q	T	A	V	V	Y	G	Q	V	W	Y	A
L	T	N	X	C	C	E	Y	O	M	J	E	N	P	R	J	G	L	O	N	X	W	U	I	A	I	A	J	P	T	B	F	T	Y	D
L	H	O	L	S	R	O	P	G	N	C	L	Y	T	U	V	V	V	G	S	M	F	S	D	R	I	W	T	V	W	U	X	K	G	S
D	J	M	B	W	T	I	Y	E	K	T	Q	U	V	I	W	A	I	X	E	C	Z	M	A	D	C	I	G	I	Y	J	Q	T	H	Y
B	O	I	I	O	T	H	P	K	N	N	I	X	E	W	T	S	L	R	K	N	A	V	X	S	I	S	K	J	S	V	D	Z	E	E
K	U	N	Q	K	G	F	U	T	E	D	U	N	U	L	S	A	O	S	D	B	T	L	Y	Z	X	S	B	G	G	T	O	B	Y	M
O	X	A	O	Z	I	F	J	H	I	I	E	M	U	A	A	C	T	I	C	N	E	Y	E	D	T	M	N	F	B	B	I	R	B	W
C	J	L	P	H	P	W	U	O	S	V	L	N	M	O	S	Z	Q	I	E	A	P	J	M	R	D	X	K	H	F	C	P	C	Y	Y
S	A	S	L	M	Q	D	D	K	N	T	E	O	T	W	U	A	D	D	V	B	L	P	C	P	L	J	C	A	L	W	D	F	S	H
P	O	C	S	A	K	D	B	Y	T	F	D	S	A	V	H	S	N	I	I	E	A	E	I	I	M	U	K	M	Q	D	C	B	I	S
O	F	A	G	N	C	M	W	J	X	N	L	R	T	N	A	E	V	U	S	U	V	E	L	E	P	E	G	S	F	Y	Y	I	U	C
X	P	L	L	C	W	S	K	L	A	R	B	R	F	A	P	R	J	A	M	C	L	A	B	E	C	O	N	Z	B	T	J	C	X	A
N	R	E	Y	T	O	W	M	R	Y	A	Z	T	B	E	T	Y	I	S	R	P	R	R	R	N	V	Y	W	L	F	U	J	B	W	L
E	W	Y	I	R	Q	D	A	J	U	B	E	J	D	V	E	I	D	A	M	I	A	E	E	I	A	X	L	W	J	X	F	J	K	E
A	X	Z	D	U	X	T	I	A	A	F	O	N	B	T	G	F	S	A	B	V	A	I	T	B	A	L	W	K	N	O	T	S	X	S
S	F	Q	Z	E	I	X	Y	N	B	S	Z	K	I	X	V	I	S	T	N	L	C	B	T	E	P	B	D	Y	L	Y	S	C	W	O
I	W	G	I	Z	S	I	H	V	G	I	K	L	I	O	V	H	Y	W	I	S	E	U	L	H	V	H	L	Y	M	E	Y	I	N	F
H	H	Y	U	E	Z	K	K	L	T	G	G	F	K	T	O	J	T	P	X	C	L	T	G	E	C	A	W	E	D	Z	L	N	Y	M
W	B	W	Y	R	F	Z	L	H	D	U	O	X	D	A	T	U	M	T	T	F	S	M	I	B	H	W	R	E	U	U	G	G	O	E
T	E	Q	F	O	W	K	M	L	P	O	P	U	L	A	T	I	O	N	P	A	R	A	M	E	T	E	R	I	B	W	D	D	K	A
X	P	J	S	N	T	H	S	Y	U	G	L	J	O	R	D	I	N	A	L	S	C	A	L	E	V	G	K	T	A	Q	B	Z	O	S
M	N	R	Y	F	G	A	W	E	G	V	B	K	D	A	W	M	M	V	S	W	C	I	Y	L	M	Y	L	I	O	B	S	U	V	U
M	C	Y	O	P	E	R	A	T	I	O	N	A	L	D	E	F	I	N	I	T	I	O	N	Z	G	O	X	L	F	H	L	D	R	R
U	Y	U	K	E	Y	E	W	J	L	A	X	C	B	F	L	A	I	Q	A	N	A	E	O	F	W	W	Z	V	N	M	S	E	X	E
D	W	I	N	F	E	R	E	N	T	I	A	L	S	T	A	T	I	S	T	I	C	S	R	P	O	F	Q	M	F	E	U	T	M	M
O	O	R	A	M	D	S	A	M	P	L	E	S	T	A	T	I	S	T	I	C	I	M	J	S	G	N	I	A	F	R	I	V	H	E
L	Z	R	O	O	G	Y	I	O	S	K	R	P	G	I	A	E	Q	U	A	S	I	I	N	D	E	P	E	N	D	E	N	T	Z	N
Q	B	S	Q	Y	N	Q	S	W	N	R	C	G	Y	L	N	B	T	H	I	X	V	G	B	V	J	E	Y	J	R	W	S	G	S	T
N	P	O	P	U	L	A	T	I	O	N	A	M	E	E	G	P	M	W	B	H	S	S	G	U	O	D	N	I	B	J	C	O	F	J
W	L	Q	V	R	A	A	B	I	L	E	E	X	P	E	R	I	M	E	N	T	A	F	L	A	J	U	K	P	X	W	A	E	W	S
X	Z	R	O	D	P	M	M	K	V	O	L	V	T	D	C	H	G	F	P	N	C	V	O	C	F	G	S	V	W	V	U	S	R	U

CODING
CONTINUOUS VARIABLE
DATA
DATUM
DEPENDENT VARIABLE
DESCRIPTIVE STATISTICS
DISCRETE VARIABLE
EXPERIMENT
INDEPENDENT VARIABLE
INFERENTIAL STATISTICS
INTERVAL SCALE
NOMINAL SCALE
OPERATIONAL DEFINITION
ORDINAL SCALE
POPULATION

POPULATION PARAMETER
QUALITATIVE VARIABLE
QUANTITATIVE VARIABLE
QUASI-INDEPENDENT
RANDOM ASSIGNMENT
RATIO SCALE
RAW SCORE
SAMPLE
SAMPLE STATISTIC
SCALES OF MEASUREMENT
SCIENCE
SCORE
STATISTICS
TRUE ZERO

CROSSWORD PUZZLES

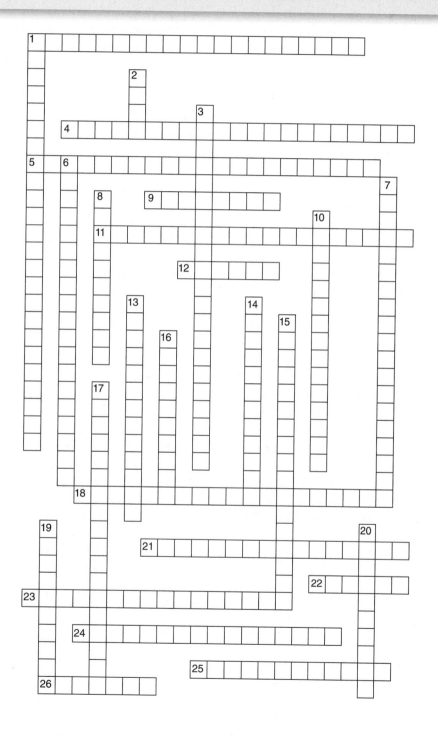

ACROSS

1 A variable that varies by amount.
4 A description of some observable event in terms of the specific process or manner by which it was observed or measured.
5 Procedures used to summarize, organize, and make sense of a set of scores or observations.
9 Describes values where the value 0 truly indicates nothing.
11 A characteristic (usually numeric) that describes a population.
12 A set of selected individuals, items, or data taken from a population of interest.
18 A variable that varies by class.
21 A scale with intervals distributed in equal units, which is characteristic of interval and ratio scales of measurement.
22 The procedure of converting a nominal value to a numeric value.
23 A variable that is measured in whole units or categories that are not distributed along a continuum.
24 A random procedure used to ensure that participants in a study have an equal chance of being assigned to a particular group or condition.
25 Measurements where values convey order or rank alone.
26 The study of phenomena, such as behavior, through strict observation, evaluation, interpretation, and theoretical explanation.

DOWN

1 A variable with levels that are not randomly assigned to participants.
2 Measurements or observations that are typically numeric (plural).
3 Procedures used to infer or generalize observations made with samples to the larger population from which they were selected.
6 Refers to how the properties of numbers can change with different uses.
7 The variable that remains unchanged or independent between conditions being observed in an experiment.
8 The set of all individuals, items, or data of interest. This is the group about which scientists will generalize.
10 A characteristic (usually numeric) that describes a sample.
13 Measurements where the values have no true zero and are equidistant.
14 Measurements where a number is assigned to represent something or someone.
15 The variable that is believed to change in the presence of the independent variable.
16 A research design in which observations are made under strictly controlled conditions that allow researchers to isolate cause-and-effect relationships between variables.
17 A variable that is measured along a continuum at any place beyond the decimal point.
19 A branch of mathematics used to summarize, analyze, and interpret a group of numbers or observations.
20 Measurements where a set of values has a true zero and the values are equidistant.

PRACTICE QUIZZES

LO 1: Distinguish between descriptive and inferential statistics.

1. The two general types of statistics are:
   a. summary; descriptive
   b. descriptive; inferential
   c. interpretive; analytical
   d. simple; complex

2. A researcher summarizes a set of data by describing the score that occurred most often. What type of statistics did the researcher use to summarize these data?
   a. descriptive
   b. inferential
   c. analytical
   d. professional

3. To study NCAA athletes at a local college, a researcher measures behavior in a portion of all athletes at the college. What type of statistics can the researcher use to draw conclusions about the behavior of all athletes at the college?
   a. descriptive
   b. parameter
   c. inferential
   d. professional

4. An instructor records the average grade on an exam in her class. What type of statistics did the instructor use to summarize exam grades in her class?
   a. descriptive
   b. parameter
   c. inferential
   d. professional

LO 2: Explain how samples and populations, as well as a sample statistic and population parameter, differ.

5. A researcher selects a _____ and uses inferential statistics to draw conclusions about the larger _____.
   a. sample; statistic
   b. parameter; population
   c. population; sample
   d. sample; population

6. A professor is interested in studying the attitudes of students in her class. She has all of the students in her class fill out a survey and records their responses. In this example, the professor:

   a. failed to identify the population of interest

   b. measured data in the sample of students

   c. measured data in the population of students

   d. did not have enough data to draw conclusions about the population of interest

7. A characteristic in a population is called a _____, whereas a characteristic in a sample is called a _____.

   a. population parameter; sample statistic

   b. sample statistic; population parameter

   c. sample parameter; population statistic

   d. population statistic; sample parameter

8. Most students selected at random to a sample are women. The characteristic that most of the sample consists of women is an example of a(n):

   a. population parameter

   b. sample statistic

   c. inferential statistic

   d. statistical anomaly

LO 3: Describe three research methods commonly used in behavioral science.

9. The research method used to demonstrate that one variable causes changes in a dependent variable is called the:

   a. experimental method

   b. quasi-experimental method

   c. correlational method

   d. investigative method

10. A researcher measures the number of hours spent studying among students living on-campus and off-campus at a local college. In this study, location (on-campus, off-campus) is the _____, and hours spent studying is the _____.

    a. independent variable; dependent variable

    b. dependent variable; independent variable

    c. quasi-independent variable; dependent variable

    d. dependent variable; quasi-independent variable

11. A researcher conducts a study that includes a quasi-independent variable and lacks a comparison group. What type of research method is described?

    a. experimental method

    b. quasi-experimental method

    c. counterintuitive method

    d. investigative method

12. The _____ is a research method in which two variables are measured for each participant, and the extent to which those variables are related is measured.

    a. experimental method

    b. quasi-experimental method

    c. correlational method

    d. investigative method

LO 4: State the four scales of measurement and provide an example for each.

13. State the scales of measurement from least to most informative:

    a. ratio, interval, ordinal, nominal

    b. nominal, ordinal, interval, ratio

    c. ordinal, interval, nominal, ratio

    d. nominal, ratio, ordinal, interval

14. A health psychologist studies food intake by recording two measures: the type of food consumed (high fat, low fat) and the number of calories consumed. Which is a nominal scale measure?

    a. the weight of the food

    b. the type of food consumed

    c. the number of calories consumed

    d. both b and c

15. An interval scale:

    a. has no true zero

    b. is distributed on an equidistant scale

    c. is the most informative scale of measurement

    d. both a and b

16. In science, researchers often go out of their way to measure variables on which scale of measurement because it is the most informative?

    a. nominal

    b. ordinal

    c. interval

    d. ratio

17. To investigate studying behavior among college students, a researcher measures the following variables: the duration of study time (in minutes per week), the number of breaks a student takes during a study session, and the time of day of studying (morning, afternoon, or night). Which is not a ratio scale of measurement?

a. duration of study time

b. number of breaks taken

c. time of day of studying

d. both b and c

LO 5: Distinguish between variables that are qualitative or quantitative.

18. A qualitative variable varies by _____; a quantitative variable varies by _____.

    a. class; amount

    b. amount; class

    c. counting; measuring

    d. measuring; counting

19. Qualitative variables tend to be on which scale of measurement?

    a. nominal

    b. ratio

    c. interval

    d. lateral

20. A researcher places a participant in a room filled with 10 strangers. To measure social behavior, he records the number of different people the participant talks to and the time (in seconds) spent talking. The number of people the participant talks to is a _____ variable; the time (in seconds) spent talking is a _____ variable.

    a. quantitative; qualitative

    b. qualitative; quantitative

    c. qualitative; qualitative

    d. quantitative; quantitative

21. A researcher records the number of times a person repeats a compulsive behavior. What type of data was measured?

    a. qualitative

    b. quantitative

LO 6: Distinguish between variables that are discrete or continuous.

22. A continuous variable:

    a. is measured along a continuum

    b. can be measured at any place beyond the decimal point

    c. can be measured in whole units or fractional units

    d. all of the above

23. A discrete variable:

   a. is measured in whole units or categories

   b. can be measured at any place beyond the decimal point

   c. can be measured in fractional units

   d. is measured along a continuum

24. A researcher places a participant in a room filled with 10 strangers. To measure social behavior, he records the number of different people the participant talks to and the time (in seconds) spent talking. The number of people the participant talks to is a _____ variable; the time (in seconds) spent talking is a _____ variable.

   a. categorical; discrete

   b. continuous; discrete

   c. discrete; continuous

   d. discrete; categorical

25. A researcher records the family relationship (brother, son, father, cousin, etc.) of the people who stay in regular contact with loved ones in a nursing home. What type of measure is family relationship?

   a. quantitative and discrete

   b. qualitative and discrete

   c. qualitative and continuous

   d. quantitative and continuous

SPSS IN FOCUS

Entering and Defining Variables

Follow the General Instructions Guidebook to complete this exercise. Also, an example for following these steps is provided in the SPSS in Focus section (Section 1.7) of the book. Complete and submit the SPSS grading template and a printout of the Data View.

Exercise 1.1: The Time It Takes to Enter Data

A researcher conducts a hypothetical study regarding the time it takes undergraduate and graduate students to enter statistical data into SPSS. After the researcher completes a hypothetical study with 20 participants, he records the time it took undergraduate and graduate students to correctly enter the data into SPSS. The time (in seconds) that it took each student to enter the data is given below. Enter these data into SPSS in two ways:

1. **Enter these data by column** using SPSS and appropriately label each group.

2. **Enter these data by row** using SPSS and appropriately code each group/label each column.

Undergraduate Student	Graduate Student
28	18
34	32
22	27
19	21
14	14
27	32
28	25
28	24
31	25
20	25

With regard to the SPSS exercise, answer the following questions:

Enter data by column:

State whether you used the Data View or Variable View to complete the following:

Naming variables

      _____

Entering the values for each variable

      _____

State the following values for the data you entered in SPSS:

The number of values entered (overall)

      _____

The number of values entered in each group

      _____

The number of groups

      _____

Enter data by row:

State whether you used the Data View or Variable View to complete the following:

Naming variables

      _____

Coding variables

      _____

Entering the values for each variable

      _____

State the following values for the data you entered in SPSS:

The number of values entered (overall)

      _____

The number of values entered in each group

      _____

The number of groups

      _____

CHAPTER SUMMARY ORGANIZED BY LEARNING OBJECTIVE

LO 1–2: Distinguish between descriptive and inferential statistics; explain how samples and populations, as well as a sample statistic and population parameter, differ.

- Statistics is a branch of mathematics used to summarize, analyze, and interpret a group of numbers or observations. Descriptive statistics are procedures used to make sense of observations by summarizing them numerically. Inferential statistics are procedures that allow researchers to infer whether observations made with samples are also likely to be observed in the population.
- A population is a set of all individuals, items, or data of interest. A characteristic that describes a population is called a population parameter. A sample is a set of individuals, items, or data selected from a population of interest. A characteristic that describes a sample is called a sample statistic.

LO 3: Describe three research methods commonly used in behavioral science.

- The experimental design uses manipulation, randomization, and comparison/control to ensure enough control to allow researchers to draw cause-and-effect conclusions. The quasi-experimental design is structured similar to an experiment but lacks randomization and/or a comparison/control group.
- The correlational method is used to measure pairs of scores for each individual and examine the relationship between the variables.

LO 4: State the four scales of measurement and provide an example for each.

- Scales of measurement identify how the properties of numbers can change with different uses. Scales are characterized by three properties: order, difference, and ratio. There are four scales of measurement: nominal, ordinal, interval, and ratio. Nominal scales are typically coded (e.g., seasons, months, sex), ordinal scales indicate order alone (e.g., rankings, grade level), interval scales have equidistant scales and no true zero (e.g., rating scale values, temperature), and ratio scales are also distributed in equal units but have a true zero (e.g., weight, height, calories).

LO 5–6: Distinguish between variables that are qualitative or quantitative; distinguish between variables that are discrete or continuous.

- A continuous variable is measured along a continuum, whereas a discrete variable is measured in whole units or categories. Hence, continuous but not discrete variables are measured at any place beyond the decimal point. A quantitative variable varies by amount, whereas a qualitative variable varies by class.

LO 7: Enter data into SPSS by placing each group in separate columns and each group in a single column (coding is required).

- SPSS can be used to enter and define variables. All variables are defined in the Variable View tab. The values recorded for each variable are listed in the Data View tab. Data can be entered by column or by row in the Data View tab. Listing data by row requires coding the variable. Variables are coded in the Variable View tab in the Values column.

2

Summarizing Data

Frequency Distributions in Tables and Graphs

LEARNING OBJECTIVES

After reading this chapter, you should be able to:

1. Construct a simple frequency distribution for grouped and ungrouped data.

2. Determine whether data should be grouped or ungrouped.

3. Identify when it is appropriate to distribute the cumulative frequency, relative frequency, relative percent, cumulative relative frequency, and cumulative percent.

4. Identify percentile points and percentile ranks in a cumulative percent distribution.

5. Construct and interpret graphs for distributions of continuous data.

6. Construct and interpret graphs for distributions of discrete data.

7. Construct frequency distributions for quantitative and categorical data using SPSS.

8. Construct histograms, bar charts, and pie charts using SPSS.

CHAPTER OUTLINE

2.1 Why Summarize Data?

Summarizing data: Summarizing data in charts, graphs, and tables makes data easier to read and interpret. One common way of summarizing data is by describing how often a value occurs in a data set.

Frequency: Describes how often a score, value, category, or interval of scores occurs in a data set.

2.2 Frequency Distributions for Grouped Data

Simple frequency distribution: A summary display for a distribution of data organized or summarized in terms of how often a category, score, or range of scores occurs.

- Simple frequency distributions can describe *ungrouped data:* how often each individual score, category, or value occurs.
- Simple frequency distributions can describe *grouped data:* how often values occur in discrete intervals.

Constructing a grouped frequency distribution:

- Find the *real range.* Subtract the smallest score in the data set from the largest score; then add 1.
  - Real range = (largest value – smallest value) + 1
- Find the *interval width.* First, determine the number of intervals in the frequency distribution—you decide the number of intervals. Then, divide the real range by the number of intervals chosen.
  - Interval width = real range/number of intervals
- Construct the frequency distribution such that:
  - Each interval has an upper and lower boundary. There should be no open intervals, such as > (greater than) or < (less than) a given value.
  - The intervals are equal width. For example, an interval width of 20 will contain 20 values in each interval.
  - No interval overlaps. This ensures that values do not occur in more than one interval.

Cumulative frequencies: The sum of the frequencies of scores across a series of values or intervals. The final cumulative frequency, if calculated for all data in a distribution, will equal the total number of values or scores in a distribution.

Relative frequency: The proportion of scores or values in each interval relative to all scores or values recorded. To find the relative frequency, we divide the frequency in a given interval by the total number of scores in the distribution.

- Relative frequency = frequency in each interval/total count or frequency
- Relative frequency is converted into *relative percent* by multiplying the proportion by 100 to obtain a percentage.

Cumulative relative frequency/cumulative percent: A cumulative relative frequency is a summary display that distributes the sum of relative frequencies across a series of intervals. A cumulative percent is a summary display that distributes the sum of relative percents across a series of intervals. A cumulative percent summary is presented from the bottom up and is called a percentile rank.

2.3 Identifying Percentile Points and Percentile Ranks

Percentile point: The value of a score on a measurement scale below which a specified percentage of scores in a distribution fall.

Percentile rank: The percentage of scores with values that fall below a specified score in a distribution. To find the percentile point in a cumulative percent distribution, follow four basic steps:

- Step 1: Identify the interval within which a specified percentile point falls.
- Step 2: Identify the real range for the interval identified.
- Step 3: Find the position of the percentile point within the interval.
- Step 4: Identify the percentile point.

2.4 SPSS in Focus: Frequency Distributions for Quantitative Data

SPSS can be used to create frequency distributions for quantitative and categorical data. Quantitative data are typically entered by column. Frequency distributions for quantitative data are created using the Analyze, then Descriptive Statistics and Frequencies, options in the menu bar.

2.5 Frequency Distributions for Ungrouped Data

Ungrouped data: The presentation of individual values, scores, or categories in a frequency distribution. Scores are not grouped into intervals—the frequency of each individual score is counted and summarized.

2.6 Research in Focus: Summarizing Demographic Information

Demographic information regarding human participants is often best summarized in a frequency table. A study by Edenborough, Jackson, Mannix, and Wilkes (2008) summarized relevant demographic information regarding the mothers in their study on child-to-mother violence in such a table. The table included the frequency of participants in different age ranges and types of households.

2.7 SPSS in Focus: Frequency Distributions for Categorical Data

SPSS can be used to create frequency distributions for quantitative and categorical data. Categorical data (which typically require coding) are entered by row. Frequency distributions for quantitative and categorical data are created using the Analyze, then Descriptive Statistics and Frequencies, options in the menu bar. Whenever the levels of a factor are coded, a Weight cases . . . option also must be selected from the menu bar.

2.8 Pictorial Frequency Distributions

Pictogram: The pictorial representation of an event, concept, object, or place using symbols and/ or illustrations.

2.9 Graphing Distributions: Continuous Data

Histogram: A graphical display used to summarize the frequency of continuous data that are distributed in numeric intervals.

- Each interval is represented by a rectangle.
- Each rectangle begins and ends at the upper and lower boundaries of each interval.
- Each rectangle touches adjacent rectangles at the upper and lower boundaries of each interval.

Frequency polygon: A dot-and-line graph used to summarize the frequency of continuous data at the midpoint of each interval.

- The midpoint of each interval is represented by a dot.
- The dots are connected by lines.

Ogive: A dot-and-line graph used to summarize the cumulative percent of continuous data at the upper boundary of each interval. The cumulative percent ranges from 0% to 100% on the *y*-axis.

Stem-and-leaf display: A graphical display that lists each individual score in the distribution, where the common digits shared by the scores are listed to the left as a "stem" and any remaining digits for each score are listed to the right as a "leaf."

- The stem-and-leaf display retains the value of each data point. The only information we lose is the order in which the data were originally obtained.

2.10 Graphing Distributions: Discrete and Categorical Data

Bar chart: A graphical display used to summarize the frequency of discrete and categorical data that are distributed in whole units or classes. Because the data are discrete, the rectangles do not touch.

Pie chart: A graphical display in the shape of a circle that is typically used to summarize the relative percent of discrete and categorical data into sectors.

2.11 Research in Focus: Frequencies and Percents

Hollands and Spence (1992, 1998) showed that participants are better able to interpret percent frequency data and percentiles when the data are presented in a pie chart than in a bar graph. Thus, it may be more effective to present proportion data or percentiles in a pie chart or ogive than in a bar graph.

2.12 SPSS in Focus: Histograms, Bar Charts, and Pie Charts

SPSS can be used to create histograms, bar charts, and pie charts. Each graph is created using the Analyze, then Descriptive Statistics and Frequencies, options in the menu bar.

CHAPTER FORMULAS

Frequencies

$$\text{Relative frequency} = \frac{\text{observed frequency}}{\text{total frequency count}}$$

$$\text{Relative percent} = \frac{\text{observed frequency}}{\text{total frequency count}} \times 100$$

TIPS AND CAUTIONS FOR STUDENTS

- *Determining interval boundaries:* The interval width is the range of values contained in each interval of a grouped frequency distribution. Suppose, for example, that a data set ranges from 0 to 99, thereby giving us a real range of 100 (99 + 1 = 100). If we want to split the data into 10 intervals, then the interval width is 10 (100/10 = 10). For an interval width of 10, the first interval would be 0 to 9. Counting 0, this is a width of 10 values. The value of 10 would then be the lowest boundary of the next interval (i.e., 10–19).

- *Cumulative frequencies:* A cumulative frequency is the sum of the frequencies above or below a certain value. To construct a cumulative frequency distribution, you can list the frequencies in each interval in one column and list a cumulative frequency column next to it. If starting from the bottom of the distribution, the first cumulative frequency will be the same as the first frequency value. For the second row, add the first cumulative frequency score to the second frequency score. For the third row, add the second cumulative frequency score to the third frequency score, and so on. The sum of the cumulative frequencies is equal to the total number of values counted.

- *Grouped or ungrouped data:* To decide how to organize a data distribution, the amount and range of the data will determine whether the data should be grouped into intervals or remain ungrouped. If you have a large range—for instance, 0 to 100 numbers—then the data should be grouped into intervals to make the data easier to read and interpret. With a smaller range of numbers, the summary display will still be clear even without grouping. If the range of values is small or the data are categorical, then the data can be presented in an ungrouped frequency distribution.

- *Graphing data:* Remember that if the data are categorical or discrete, you should choose to display them in a bar chart or a pie chart. Bar charts will most clearly show the overall shape of the distribution, and pie charts will best illustrate the proportions or percentages in each category. If the data are continuous, then they are best displayed in a histogram or frequency polygon. An ogive is used to present cumulative percents.

KEY TERM WORD SEARCHES

K	Q	M	D	D	Y	Q	K	B	R	J	R	E	L	A	T	I	V	E	P	E	R	C	E	N	T	B	B	Q	U	E
S	I	M	P	L	E	F	R	E	Q	U	E	N	C	Y	D	I	S	T	R	I	B	U	T	I	O	N	D	L	O	M
N	B	D	X	O	H	Y	Q	G	Z	U	O	P	E	N	C	L	A	S	S	E	S	C	X	A	Q	S	V	W	G	N
K	J	L	I	T	M	M	J	Q	R	C	L	A	S	S	W	I	D	T	H	P	C	F	N	X	R	D	G	E	J	P
G	P	F	N	U	M	K	E	C	D	O	K	H	M	B	Q	Q	Z	U	N	Z	F	J	Y	Z	T	D	R	K	S	M
S	H	T	R	X	P	Z	O	Z	U	L	U	S	T	Y	V	Y	H	O	I	T	C	C	N	O	B	G	C	R	Z	A
Y	H	G	J	E	A	G	E	Y	W	M	P	P	A	R	C	D	I	U	R	Q	N	O	L	V	W	X	T	K	T	M
X	A	Q	F	V	Q	D	A	W	M	T	U	R	E	N	Y	T	S	A	O	E	R	P	N	V	W	I	N	N	P	X
X	Y	U	M	F	K	U	E	X	R	P	B	L	E	D	R	D	H	W	U	U	F	S	L	X	X	S	I	G	A	I
O	I	O	A	D	R	A	E	A	U	M	E	U	A	O	D	C	E	Q	G	A	T	A	R	Z	I	O	O	Q	E	B
K	R	N	S	Z	F	E	H	N	A	N	Q	R	P	T	R	A	E	P	E	C	H	L	K	S	P	Y	P	I	V	S
O	C	Z	T	Y	S	C	Q	R	C	E	G	O	C	A	I	R	T	L	T	T	V	G	I	E	B	E	E	Y	C	U
G	X	U	I	E	E	L	G	U	R	Y	R	R	B	E	F	V	D	A	D	K	D	Y	L	E	I	Z	N	R	U	K
I	I	O	M	I	R	O	T	F	E	P	D	N	O	E	N	N	E	I	K	L	F	I	N	J	R	Y	I	E	M	P
V	Z	V	P	U	T	V	I	H	N	N	L	I	V	U	A	T	W	R	G	R	T	S	I	G	H	S	N	A	U	C
E	O	E	K	C	L	F	A	H	P	B	C	I	S	M	P	L	I	H	E	N	X	K	A	N	B	L	T	L	L	I
N	B	K	I	Z	G	A	V	L	U	M	T	Y	E	T	A	E	C	L	E	L	X	X	Y	Y	H	O	E	R	A	Q
F	P	P	G	J	Y	M	T	Y	B	A	T	T	P	V	R	B	D	C	E	O	A	M	B	P	X	W	R	A	T	J
S	Y	S	N	A	C	Y	Z	I	L	O	S	A	R	O	S	I	R	D	G	R	W	T	A	H	W	E	V	N	I	A
B	T	H	W	W	R	R	U	E	V	A	U	E	K	W	L	E	B	O	A	W	A	R	I	K	E	R	A	G	V	P
C	K	E	W	Y	W	T	R	Q	Q	E	T	N	L	V	P	Y	E	U	Q	T	G	N	P	V	T	B	L	E	E	R
C	K	O	M	O	D	N	A	U	D	N	P	X	D	G	B	T	G	R	T	R	A	Y	K	L	E	O	S	R	F	M
H	M	L	G	A	X	K	G	Y	I	K	T	E	R	A	S	N	M	O	A	I	I	O	A	M	S	U	B	O	R	Y
W	H	N	M	F	R	E	Q	U	E	N	C	Y	R	J	R	U	A	B	N	S	O	V	K	J	H	N	X	O	E	U
E	K	V	K	F	Y	Z	F	Q	X	G	I	J	V	C	F	I	C	P	P	Q	R	N	V	E	C	D	Y	Q	Q	C
I	Q	W	A	M	T	M	T	K	G	U	I	V	X	I	E	D	E	G	A	E	N	V	R	R	O	A	K	D	U	M
Q	E	E	X	B	C	U	O	T	X	Z	H	D	Q	M	A	N	Q	S	T	N	Z	L	C	Q	G	R	O	F	E	T
U	L	U	Y	G	B	L	C	D	L	O	T	Q	N	F	V	I	T	N	S	H	V	C	B	P	V	Y	R	W	N	C
A	L	U	P	P	E	R	B	O	U	N	D	A	R	Y	I	S	I	S	V	S	S	M	C	H	P	V	B	T	C	P
R	C	X	P	E	G	F	S	E	C	T	O	R	F	X	P	H	T	V	B	O	F	Y	Z	F	H	L	N	K	Y	W
X	Q	O	H	F	M	H	N	L	G	X	K	W	T	M	H	D	H	I	S	T	O	G	R	A	M	X	T	J	X	Y

BAR CHART
BAR GRAPH
CLASS WIDTH
CUMULATIVE FREQUENCY
CUMULATIVE PERCENT
CUMULATIVE RELATIVE FREQUENCY
FREQUENCY
FREQUENCY DISTRIBUTION
FREQUENCY POLYGON
GROUPED DATA
HISTOGRAM
INTERVAL
INTERVAL BOUNDARIES
INTERVAL WIDTH
LEAF
LOWER BOUNDARY
OGIVE

OPEN CLASSES
OPEN INTERVALS
OUTLIERS
PERCENTILE POINT
PERCENTILE RANK
PICTOGRAM
PIE CHART
PROPORTION
REAL RANGE
RELATIVE FREQUENCY
RELATIVE PERCENT
SECTOR
SIMPLE FREQUENCY DISTRIBUTION
STEM
STEM-AND-LEAF
UNGROUPED DATA
UPPER BOUNDARY

CROSSWORD PUZZLE

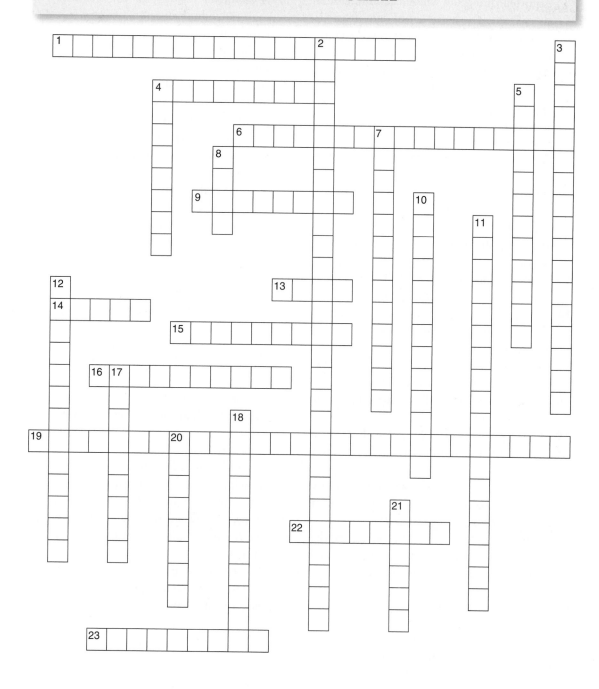

ACROSS

1   A graphical display where each individual score from an original set of data is listed. The data are organized such that the common digits shared by all scores are listed to the left, with the remaining digits for each score listed to the right.

4   A summary display that uses symbols or illustrations to represent a concept, object, place, or event.

6   A summary display that distributes the sum of relative percents across a series of intervals.

9   A graphical display used to summarize the frequency of discrete and categorical data that are distributed in whole units or classes.

13 Numbers located to the left of the vertical line in a stem-and-leaf display.

14 A dot-and-line graph used to summarize the cumulative percent of continuous data at the upper boundary of each interval.

15 The number of times or how often a category, score, or range of scores occurs.

16 A part or portion of all measured data that sums to 1.00.

19 A summary display that distributes the sum of relative frequencies across a series of intervals.

22 Extreme scores that fall substantially above or below most of the scores in a particular data set.

23 A graphical display used to summarize the frequency of continuous data that are distributed in numeric intervals.

DOWN

2   A summary display for the frequency of each individual score or category in a distribution, or the frequency of scores falling within defined groups or intervals in a distribution.

3   A summary display that distributes the proportion of scores in each interval.

4   A graphical display in the shape of a circle that is used to summarize the relative percent of discrete and categorical data into sectors.

5   An interval with no defined upper or lower boundary.

7   The range of values contained in each interval of a grouped frequency distribution.

8   Numbers located to the right of the vertical line in a stem-and-leaf display.

10 The largest value in each interval of a frequency distribution.

11 The upper and lower limits for each interval in a grouped frequency distribution.

12 The smallest value in each interval of a frequency distribution.

17 One more than the difference between the largest value and the smallest value in a data set.

18 A set of scores distributed into intervals in which the frequency of each score can fall into any given interval.

20 A discrete range of values within which the frequency of a subset of scores is contained.

21 The particular portion of a pie chart that represents the relative percent of a particular class or category.

PRACTICE QUIZZES

LO 1: Construct a simple frequency distribution for grouped and ungrouped data.

1. It is necessary to create intervals for a simple frequency distribution with what type of data?
   a. grouped data
   b. ungrouped data
   c. categorical data
   d. nominal scale data

2. If the smallest score in a distribution is 10 and the largest is 32, then what is the real range for these data?
   a. 20
   b. 21
   c. 22
   d. 23

3. If the smallest score in a distribution is 12 and the largest is 71, then what is the interval width if we create 6 intervals?
   a. 6
   b. 9.83
   c. 10
   d. 12

4. A researcher constructs the following simple frequency distribution. How many scores were recorded in this study?

Scores (x)	Frequency
12–14	8
9–11	12
6–8	4
3–5	6
0–2	10

   a. 14 scores
   b. 15 scores
   c. 40 scores
   d. not enough information

5. The lower boundaries in a frequency distribution of response times (in seconds) during a training exercise are 65, 76, 87, and 98. What is the interval width for this frequency distribution?

    a. 9

    b. 10

    c. 11

    d. 12

LO 2: Determine whether data should be grouped or ungrouped.

6. A researcher measures the following scores: 0, 2, 2, 2, 2, 2, 4, 4, 4, 4, 0, 0, 0, 0, 0, 0, 0, 2, 2, 2, 2, 2, 4, 4, 4, 4, 4, 4, 4, 4, 4, 4, 0, 2, 4, 2, 2, 4, 4, 4, 4, 4, and 0. Should these data be grouped?

    a. yes, because so many scores were measured

    b. yes, because the range of values is small

    c. no, because the data are categorical

    d. no, because the number of different scores is small

7. As a general rule, when the number of intervals needed to summarize a data set is smaller than ____, we can leave the data ungrouped.

    a. 5

    b. 10

    c. 15

    d. 20

8. Summarizing ungrouped data is especially practical for data sets with only a few different scores and for qualitative or categorical variables.

    a. true

    b. false

LO 3: Identify when it is appropriate to distribute the cumulative frequency, relative frequency, relative percent, cumulative relative frequency, and cumulative percent.

9. When we sum the frequencies across a series of intervals, the summary is called a:

    a. simple frequency distribution

    b. cumulative frequency distribution

    c. relative frequency distribution

    d. cumulative percent distribution

10. A _____ frequency distribution is often used for larger data sets where the number of frequencies in each interval could be in the thousands or millions.

    a. simple

    b. cumulative

    c. relative

    d. differential

11. A relative percent distribution is often used instead of a relative frequency distribution because:

    a. it is more appropriate

    b. it is more accurate

   c. it is more meaningful

   d. most readers find it easier to understand percentages than decimals

12. How do you convert a relative frequency to a relative percent distribution?

   a. divide each frequency by the total number of observations recorded

   b. sum the frequencies in each interval, then divide by the number of intervals

   c. no calculation is needed; a relative frequency is the same as a relative percent

   d. multiply the relative frequency by 100 at each interval

LO 4: Identify percentile points and percentile ranks in a cumulative percent distribution.

13. A _____ is a cumulative percent summary in which the ranks indicate the percent of scores at or below a given value.

   a. relative percent

   b. percentile rank

   c. relative frequency

   d. cumulative frequency

14. Which of the following is not a step to identify the percentile point in a frequency distribution?

   a. find the frequency of scores in one interval and divide by the total frequency

   b. identify the interval within which a specified percentile point falls

   c. identify the real range for the interval identified

   d. find the position of the percentile point within the interval

15. State the percentile point at the 50th percentile for a distribution with a cumulative percent distribution of 12%, 40%, 50%, 80%, and 100% at each of the following intervals: 0–2, 3–5, 6–8, 9–11, and 12–14, respectively.

   a. 7

   b. 8

   c. 9

   d. 10

LO 5: Construct and interpret graphs for distributions of continuous data.

16. Each of the following is a rule for constructing a histogram, *except:*

   a. a vertical rectangle represents each interval, and the height of the rectangle equals the frequency recorded for each interval

   b. the base of each rectangle begins and ends at the upper and lower boundaries of each interval

   c. each rectangle touches adjacent rectangles at the boundaries of each interval

   d. frequencies are plotted at the midpoints of each interval, and the line connects each plot

17. A frequency polygon is a dot-and-line graph where the dot is the _____ of each interval, and the line connects each dot.

a. lower boundary

b. midpoint

c. upper boundary

18. A researcher measures the distance (in miles) that students travel during a holiday season. What type of graph (shown below) was used to summarize these data? Is it appropriate?

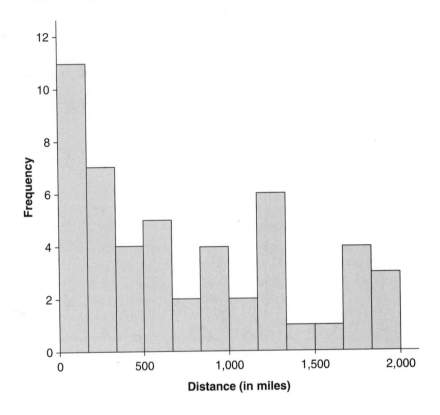

a. histogram; yes, because the data are continuous

b. histogram; yes, because the data are discrete

c. histogram; no, because the data are continuous

d. bar chart; yes, because the data are discrete

19. An ogive is used to summarize what type of frequency distribution?

a. relative percent

b. percentile rank

c. relative frequency

d. cumulative percent

LO 6: Construct and interpret graphs for distributions of discrete data.

20. A graphical display in the shape of a circle that is used to summarize the relative percent of discrete and categorical data into sectors is called a:

     a. bar chart

     b. flow chart

     c. pie chart

     d. frequency

21. A bar chart is similar to a histogram, except that in a bar chart, each rectangle _____ the adjacent rectangles at the boundaries of each interval.

     a. touches

     b. does not touch

     c. overlaps with

22. A researcher measures the number of votes submitted for each of three candidates. What type of graph (shown below) was used to summarize these data? Is it appropriate?

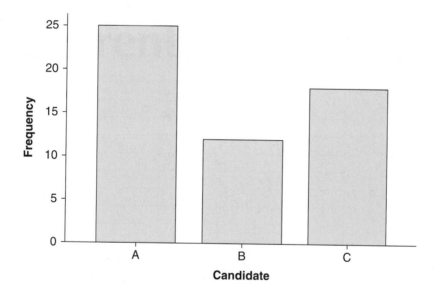

     a. bar chart; yes, because the data are continuous

     b. bar chart; yes, because the data are categorical

     c. bar chart; no, because the data are categorical

     d. histogram; yes, because the data are continuous

23. Which of the following would be most appropriate for summarizing the *relative* percent in each category for a discrete variable?

     a. frequency polygon

     b. histogram

     c. ogive

     d. pie chart

Frequency Distributions for Quantitative Data

Follow the General Instructions Guidebook to complete this exercise. Also, an example for following these steps is provided in the SPSS in Focus section (Section 2.4) of the book. Complete and submit the SPSS grading template and a printout of the output file.

Exercise 2.1: Frequency of Absences During School

A researcher wants to study behavioral problems among troubled teens. To gain a better understanding of students at the school of interest, she records the number of times that teens were absent from school during the previous academic year. The number of absences for students at this school is listed below. Enter these data and construct a frequency distribution using SPSS.

7	8	1	0
2	0	11	0
2	23	10	4
1	19	3	0
6	3	1	0
0	0	10	7
21	18	3	6
0	0	6	9
9	0	4	10
5	0	8	21
8	6	1	0
7	3	6	23
6	8	10	0
9	5	5	1
5	9	14	15
5	2	3	12
8	4	17	8
10	10	21	9
11	14	19	17
4	1	5	5
0	9	24	4
0	22	18	2
4	16	6	20
0	14	2	3
0	2	0	0

With regard to the SPSS exercise, answer the following questions:

    State the dependent variable: _____

State the following values (you can find these in the SPSS output table):

    Total number of scores entered   _____

    The score at the 50th percentile   _____

    The frequency at or above the 80th percentile   _____

    The frequency at or below the 80th percentile   _____

Explain why the frequencies at or above and at or below the 80th percentile do not sum to the total number of scores entered.

Remember that a main goal for using frequency distributions is to simplify large data sets, which makes it easier to interpret research data. That being said, how would you characterize or interpret the data displayed in the SPSS output table you created?

Follow the General Instructions Guidebook to complete this exercise. Also, an example for following these steps is provided in the SPSS in Focus section (Section 2.7) of the book. Complete and submit the SPSS grading template and a printout of the output file.

Exercise 2.2: Frequency of Texting During Class

An instructor wants to determine the types of students who text during class. To do this, he first has students complete a survey to determine whether they always (A), sometimes (S), or never (N) need to look at the keys to text—used to measure texting efficiency. Students are asked to observe a speaker during a 50-minute lecture-style class. The researcher records the category of the student (A, S, or N) if the student was observed texting in class. Enter these data and construct a frequency distribution using SPSS. We will assume that all students had their phones with them during this lecture.

A	N	S
A	S	S
S	N	S
A	S	N
S	S	N
N	S	N
N	N	N
N	N	A
S	N	N
N	N	N
N	N	N
A	A	A
N	N	N
N	N	S
N	N	A

With regard to the SPSS exercise, answer the following questions:

Answer each of the following questions about coding data in SPSS:

Are categories displayed as numbers or words in the Data View?

Are categories displayed as numbers or words in the SPSS output table?

State the dependent variable: _____

State the following values (you can find these in the SPSS output table):

Total number of scores entered   _____

The number of categories   _____

The category in the 50th percentile   _____

Remember that a main goal for using frequency distributions is to simplify large data sets, which makes it easier to interpret research data. That being said, how would you characterize or interpret the data displayed in the SPSS output table you created?

Follow the General Instructions Guidebook to complete this exercise. Also, an example for following these steps is provided in the SPSS in Focus section (Section 2.12) of the book. Complete and submit the SPSS grading template and a printout of the output file.

Exercise 2.3: Health of School Lunches

A researcher wants to determine the nutritional value of school lunches at a local school. As part of this study, the researcher reports the number of calories in each meal and summarizes this two ways.

(1) *Histogram:* The researcher reports the calories per meal. Because calories are a quantitative variable, this is summarized using a histogram. The data are given below. Construct a histogram for these data.

350	330	880
540	640	900
730	660	620
705	675	600
910	500	665
500	490	390
435	695	440
680	860	920
880	510	720
805	565	475

(2) *Bar chart and pie chart:* The researcher also summarizes the frequency of meals that are low calorie (less than 450 calories), moderate calorie (between 450 and 650 calories), and high calorie (more than 650 calories). The data given above are converted into these health categories in the table below. Because the data are now categorical, these data are summarized using a bar chart or pie chart. Compute both graphs.

High calorie	15
Moderate calorie	10
Low calorie	5

With regard to the SPSS exercise, answer the following questions:

For the histogram, state the:

Dependent variable   _____

Scale of measurement of the dependent variable   _____

For the bar chart and pie chart, state the:

Dependent variable   _____

Scale of measurement of the dependent variable   _____

Remember that a main goal for using graphs is to simplify large data sets, which makes it easier to interpret research data. That being said, how would you characterize or interpret the data displayed in the SPSS output graphs you created?

For your own reference, state which display is easiest for you to read. Please pick only one. There is no right or wrong answer here. It is simply worth recognizing the type of graphical display that makes the most sense to you.

CHAPTER SUMMARY ORGANIZED BY LEARNING OBJECTIVE

LO 1–2: Construct a simple frequency distribution for grouped and ungrouped data; determine whether data should be grouped or ungrouped.

- A frequency distribution is a summary display for a distribution of data organized or summarized in terms of how often or frequently scores occur.
- A simple frequency distribution for grouped data displays the frequency of data in intervals. Each interval is equidistant, no interval overlaps, and the degree of accuracy for each interval is the same as in the original data. This distribution can be constructed using three steps:

  Step 1: Find the real range.

  Step 2: Find the interval width.

  Step 3: Construct the frequency distribution.

- A simple frequency distribution for ungrouped data displays the frequency of categories or whole units when the number of different values collected is small. Because constructing intervals is not necessary for ungrouped data, skip straight to Step 3 to construct this frequency distribution.

LO 3: Identify when it is appropriate to distribute the cumulative frequency, relative frequency, relative percent, cumulative relative frequency, and cumulative percent.

- A cumulative frequency is a summary display that distributes the sum of frequencies across a series of intervals. You can sum from the top or the bottom depending on how you want to discuss the data. You add from the bottom up when discussing the data in terms of "less than" or "at or below" a certain value or "at most." You add from the top down when discussing the data in terms of "greater than" or "at or above" a certain value or "at least."

- A relative frequency is a summary display that distributes the proportion of scores in each interval. To compute a relative frequency, divide the frequency in each interval by the total number of scores counted. The relative frequency is reported when summarizing large data sets. To convert relative frequencies to relative percents, multiply each relative frequency by 100. Both summary displays convey the same information.

- Cumulative relative frequencies are summary displays for the sum of relative frequencies from the top down or the bottom up. These can be converted to cumulative relative percents by multiplying the cumulative relative frequency in each interval by 100. Cumulative relative percents can be distributed as percentile ranks, which indicate the percentage of scores at or below a given score.

LO 4: Identify percentile points and percentile ranks in a cumulative percent distribution.

- A cumulative percent distribution identifies percentiles, which are measures of the relative position of individuals or scores within a larger distribution. A percentile, specifically a percentile point, is the value of an individual or score within a larger distribution. The corresponding percentile of a percentile point is the percentile rank of that score.

- To find the percentile point in a cumulative percent distribution, follow four basic steps:

  Step 1: Identify the interval within which a specified percentile point falls.

  Step 2: Identify the real range for the interval identified.

  Step 3: Find the position of the percentile point within the interval.

  Step 4: Identify the percentile point.

LO 5: Construct and interpret graphs for distributions of continuous data.

- A histogram is a graphical display used to summarize the frequency of continuous data distributed in numeric intervals (grouped). Histograms are constructed by distributing the intervals along the x-axis and listing the frequencies of scores on the y-axis, with each interval connected by vertical bars or rectangles. The height of each rectangle reflects the frequency of scores in a given interval. Three rules for constructing histograms are as follows:

  Rule 1: A vertical rectangle represents each interval, and the height of the rectangle equals the frequency recorded for each interval.

  Rule 2: The base of each rectangle begins and ends at the upper and lower boundaries of each interval.

  Rule 3: Each rectangle touches adjacent rectangles at the boundaries of each interval.

- A frequency polygon is a dot-and-line graph where the dot is the midpoint of each interval, and the line connects each dot. The midpoint of an interval is distributed along the x-axis and is calculated by adding the upper and lower boundary of an interval and then dividing by 2.

- An ogive is a dot-and-line graph used to summarize the cumulative percent of continuous data at the upper boundary of each interval.
- A stem-and-leaf display is a graphical display where each individual score from an original set of data is listed. The data are organized such that the common digits shared by all scores are listed to the left (in the stem), with the remaining digits for each score listed to the right (in the leaf).

LO 6: Construct and interpret graphs for distributions of discrete data.

- Bar charts are used to summarize discrete and categorical data. Bar charts are similar to histograms, except that the bars or rectangles are separated to indicate discrete units or classes. To construct a bar chart, list the whole units or categories along the x-axis, and distribute the frequencies along the y-axis.
- A pie chart is a graphical display in the shape of a circle that is used to summarize the relative percent of discrete and categorical data into sectors. Converting proportions to a pie chart requires finding the correct angles for each slice of the pie. To find the central angles of each sector (or category), multiply each relative percent by 3.6 (100 percent × 3.6 = 360°).

LO 7–8: Construct frequency distributions for quantitative and categorical data using SPSS; construct histograms, bar charts, and pie charts using SPSS.

- SPSS can be used to create frequency distributions for quantitative and categorical data. Quantitative data are typically entered by column, whereas categorical data (which typically require coding) are entered by row. Frequency distributions for quantitative and categorical data are created using the Analyze, Descriptive Statistics, and Frequencies options in the menu bar. Whenever the levels of a variable are coded, a Weight cases . . . option must also be selected from the menu bar.

- SPSS can be used to create histograms, bar charts, and pie charts. Each graph is created using the Analyze, Descriptive Statistics, and Frequencies options in the menu bar. This option will bring up a dialog box that will allow you to identify your variable and select the Charts option that gives you the option to select bar charts, pie charts, or histograms. Select each option to see how each summary is displayed.

3

Summarizing Data

Central Tendency

LEARNING OBJECTIVES

After reading this chapter, you should be able to:

1. Distinguish between a population mean and sample mean.

2. Calculate and interpret the mean, the median, and the mode.

3. Calculate and interpret the weighted mean for two or more samples with unequal sample sizes.

4. Identify the characteristics of the mean.

5. Identify an appropriate measure of central tendency for different distributions and scales of measurement.

6. Compute the mean, the median, and the mode using SPSS.

CHAPTER OUTLINE

3.1 Introduction to Central Tendency

A *measure of central tendency* is a single score that tends to be located at or near the center of a distribution and is used to represent or describe a data set. Three common measures of central tendency are the *mean, the median,* and *the mode*.

- We use different notations for population size and sample size.
  - o Population size = N (all individuals belonging to a group of interest).
  - o Sample size = n (a subset of all individuals belonging to a group of interest).

3.2 Measures of Central Tendency

Mean: The mean is the balance point or the average value in a data distribution.

- The *mean* is calculated by taking the sum of the scores and dividing it by the population or sample size.
  - o For a population: $\mu = \dfrac{\Sigma x}{N}$.
  - o For a sample: $M = \dfrac{\Sigma x}{n}$.

Weighted mean: The weighted mean is the combined mean of two or more groups of scores in which the number of scores in each group is disproportionate or unequal.

- The weighted mean formula is $M_W = \dfrac{\Sigma(M \times n)}{\Sigma n} = \dfrac{\text{weighted sum}}{\text{combined } n}$.
  - o M = the mean for each group.
  - o n = the sample size per group.

Median: The median is the midpoint of a data distribution such that half of the scores in a distribution occur above it and half occur below it. The median is also located at the 50th percentile in a cumulative percent distribution.

- When there is an odd number of scores in the distribution (or an odd n), calculate the median by ordering the scores from least to greatest and counting in to the middle score. The number of scores above and below the median will be the same.
  - o When n is an odd number, we locate the position of the middle score using $\dfrac{n+1}{2}$ and then count in by that many scores.

- When there is an even number of scores in the distribution (or an even n), calculate the median by ordering the scores from least to greatest and average the two middle scores.
  - When n is an even number, we use $\dfrac{n+1}{2}$ to find the median position. The solution will be a .5 decimal. The middle value is the average of the two middle scores positioned above and below the median position.

Mode: The mode is the score that occurs most frequently or often in a data set. It is most commonly used with the mean or median to describe central tendency.

3.3 Characteristics of the Mean

The *mean* is calculated using every score in the distribution. For this reason, changing scores in a data set in any way can influence the value of the mean for those data. In all, there are five characteristics of the mean.

Changing an existing score: Because every score in a distribution influences the value of the mean, changing one score into another score will change the mean.

- Increasing the value of an existing score will increase the value of the mean.
- Decreasing the value of an existing score will decrease the value of the mean.

Adding a new score or removing an existing score: Adding a new score to the distribution without changing an existing score or deleting a score entirely from the distribution will change the mean as well. Depending on the value of the score that is added or removed, the mean will be affected differently.

- Adding a new score with a value greater than the mean will increase the mean.
- Adding a new score with a value less than the mean will decrease the mean.
- Removing a score with a value greater than the mean will decrease the mean.
- Removing a score with a value less than the mean will increase the mean.
- Adding or removing a value that is equal to the mean will not change the value of the mean.

Adding, subtracting, multiplying, or dividing each score by a constant: When every score in a distribution is changed by the same constant, the mean will change by that constant.

- For example, if we add a constant of 5 to each score in a distribution, then the mean will increase by 5. If we subtract this constant from all scores, then the mean will decrease by 5. Likewise, multiplying and dividing a constant will change the mean by that constant.

Summing the differences of scores from their mean: The sum of the differences of scores from their mean is zero. The mean is the balance point of a distribution, which is why the differences of scores above and below the mean cancel out (i.e., their sum is 0).

- The notation for calculating the sum of the differences of the scores from the mean is $\sum(x - M)$.

Summing the squared differences of scores from their mean: Summing the squared differences of scores from their mean will produce a minimal solution that cannot be achieved by summing the squared differences of the scores from any other value (other than the value of the mean).

- The notation for summing the squared differences of scores from their mean is $\sum(x - M)^2$.

3.4 Choosing an Appropriate Measure of Central Tendency

The choice of which measure of central tendency to use to summarize a data set largely depends on the *shape of the distribution* and the *measurement scale* of the data.

The *mean* is used to describe *normal distributions* and for data on an interval or ratio scale.

- A *normal distribution* is a distribution of data that are symmetrically distributed around the mean, the median, and the mode.
- The mean is used to describe data measured on an interval or a ratio scale as these are the only two scales in which differences between scores and the mean are informative.

The *median* is used to describe *skewed distributions* and for data measured on an ordinal scale.

- A *skewed distribution* is a distribution of data with outliers or scores that fall substantially above or below most other scores in a data set.
  - *Positively skewed:* A distribution where a few scores fall substantially above most other scores in a data set.
  - *Negatively skewed:* A distribution where a few scores fall substantially below most other scores in a data set.
- The median is used to describe ordinal scale data because values on this scale indicate direction only.

The *mode* is used to describe *modal* distributions and for data measured on a nominal scale.

- A modal distribution is a data distribution where one or more scores occur the most frequently or often.
  - *Unimodal* distributions have one mode.
  - *Bimodal* distributions have two modes.
  - *Multimodal* distributions have more than two modes.
  - *Nonmodal* distributions have no mode; instead, all scores occur at the same frequency, thus appearing graphically as a straight line.
- The mode is used to describe nominal scale data because numbers on this scale are not measured in terms of quantity or amount.

3.5 Research in Focus: Describing Central Tendency

Gulledge, Stahmann, and Wilson (2004) used the mean, median, and mode when describing data regarding types of nonsexual romantic physical contact among college students in relationships at Brigham Young University. Identifying all three measures allowed us to identify, describe, and interpret how participants in this study reported their modes of affection.

3.6 SPSS in Focus: Mean, Median, and Mode

SPSS can be used to compute the mean, the median, and the mode. Each measure of central tendency is computed using the Analyze, then Descriptive Statistics and Frequencies, options in the menu bar.

CHAPTER FORMULAS

Central Tendency

$\mu = \dfrac{\Sigma x}{N}$ (Population mean)

$M = \dfrac{\Sigma x}{n}$ (Sample mean)

$M_W = \dfrac{\Sigma (M \times n)}{\Sigma n} = \dfrac{\text{weighted sum}}{\text{combined } n}$ (Weighted mean)

TIPS AND CAUTIONS FOR STUDENTS

- *Adding or removing scores to or from the mean:* When adding or removing a score, the mean will change. When recalculating the new mean, do not forget not only to add or subtract the difference of the score from the Σx but also to add or subtract *1* from the sample size because a new score was added, or an existing score was deleted, from the original sample size.

- *Changing values and the mean:* When a value is greater than the mean and it is added to the Σx, the value of the mean will increase. However, when a value that is greater than the mean is removed from the Σx, the value of the mean will decrease. Think of individual scores as pulling the mean up or down in their direction. Thus, when a high score is added, it is pulling up the mean. Yet when a high score is removed, it no longer pulls up the mean, so the mean falls back down toward the lower scores. Thus, when a lower score is added to the Σx, it pulls the mean down (the mean decreases). When a lower score is subtracted, the mean is no longer being pulled down, so the mean increases.

- *Skewed distributions:* A positively skewed distribution will have a few values that pull the tail of a distribution toward larger values, but the majority of the scores in the body will be in the middle or lower portion of the distribution. Thus, a positively skewed distribution will have one tail that is skewed toward the larger values. A negatively skewed distribution has a few values that pull the distribution toward smaller values, but the majority of the scores in the body will be in the middle or upper portion of the distribution. Thus, a distribution with a negative skew will have one tail that is skewed toward the smaller values.

KEY TERM WORD SEARCHES

```
G U Z N K Z F Z K R K X J A C X M Z R O L Q L Y M Y J X L I Z E M L P E V Y O V
N N D S M P E R W Z Y G P X Q N K N X A B M Q H O B S F K Y K X C O K W K S D W
O I U G A U S S I A N D I S T R I B U T I O N J U B K Y E T B O Z A C M H U X B
R M E V E K W Y H Y O A D B N T C S J A G H K G J J I R R L X H P I R O J R P N
M O A V E R A G E T Z V N D V Y A R O U W I S G N P Q Y M U B F H V A D H K U K
A D D C N F Q B L T H L K J Q B I M O D A L D I S T R I B U T I O N H A C X M O
L A P P J V B S T C S R T N R D O N F H K S J D C F C V J N B L L C K L H L U R
D L B Z J L I K M Z H X C D W X D J S F E M M D T F I F A G G Q D J R D W M L G
I D X Y J Y Q D X E T P O S I T I V E L Y S K E W E D R F Q E I B K F I D Z T F
S I X G W E C D J S Y M M E T R I C A L D I S T R I B U T I O N E F T S R T I T
T S M A K E X L T W F V J G O M D O W X E G Y G S R O Z T W F O K J G T L Z M T
R T Q T L Q I Q J X E V R S R Z O N H O K V N T J W X R X Q R K Z A D R M J O Y
I R C M O Q P G I O V X G B W R A C V V P M Z G X N Y S S G T V Q P F I P Q D P
B I L C V H A U H G E F N P Y Q P B Z Q H E F N Z J S E Y Q X W C U A B O G A R
U B W E G B B O H T U A J I O T T Y W I R T Q M Q L B G G X H X K W J U P B L L
T U M N S Z T E V X E B A J E P E Q Q Z F B H G C M I J V P P Z E H K T U K D D
I T Z T R G I G L G X D O V V O U L G H X P Q Y B V C Q G P D C W J D I L V I T
O I T R E Q Z A A L F K M H S Z E L T K H X W D N S A J F F O I N S R O A F S D
N O J A C N K Z R B S V V E H H S F A I F C R J F Z S G Z J R D M O O N T B T R
M N M L T T C P P I Q H I K A F C A V T G A V B A C X Z H S Y Y D A W F I G R N
N T G T A U Q U F L T F A Q N N A A V T I Q G D C R I L N L D R F T U E O L I P
T B X E N R V G F M U H J P V K P P W Z M O Y I S Z X F Y C Z V R Y O L N R B A
E X H N G Y Y B U Z Y Q M W E Y P D V G S T N V M M L R N D U S A P G X U J U S
V F R D U P A N N W N S B E H D J S K E W E D D I S T R I B U T I O N O S A T N
W Z K E L F V Q E F O S M G T T D V D J U K S S M N G U Y D R R F Y Y U I K I K
E C H N A W A E A G C S M E H I M I L V F K N T H E I O V T T X W T N P Z S O H
T I W C R P S W N U A G R Q A U C T S M L S V M V L A F M B V I J O Y D E L N M
M A F Y D N E O G N N T Z Y A N R M X T A Z G M E X B N U H B G G A G I I P Z Q
V E E T I U O Z H D P Y I H M G M J E Y R H J H L Z N K S S D G Y O Z E F J I F
N S G L S G S F B I D M V V V U W C Y A Z I A D R I T M B K S J P P U C C Y G W
F B Y A T G A Y E H F X I L E B L B F F N F B Q X T G E B N W M S J K S X O Z X
X A Z X R S M D L H E C H H D L O O W X H E J U C Y X X M K M L Y U E K X B N E
E F I Y I T P I Z Z Z G O I E U Y N V Q E X Y Z T D M M G R N M Z R J G Q K K R
O I P U B Z L X Y G W D H D H J U S S E O E B S V I S C U M A I W I S U K W G H
P C Y C U F E G Q C J J E P W R B B K G J Y T Q N Z O N W Q J N M M L N T L C N
D B Q C T V S M F P S L I K L F G R O E B X N Q B D L N F P W C O E Q W P T M I
N A K E I N I M O B U N F M E E H U Z R W O P X B Y E W Y G P C D D Z V V O X D
R G G K O O Z L Z P H P G T L R V W X X F E X K M C G H H W L C E I Z R Q O A N
A N P D N C E Q I S A M P L E   M E A N U I D Y D U X G C Y X J A A S F E A C G
O N M I G X O Q F K E V I I U C G B R T H E M U Y E Z A U G N H I N W N M X O C
```

ARITHMETIC MEAN
AVERAGE
BELL-SHAPED DISTRIBUTION
BIMODAL DISTRIBUTION
CENTRAL TENDENCY
GAUSSIAN DISTRIBUTION
MEAN
MEDIAN
MODAL DISTRIBUTION
MODE
MULTIMODAL DISTRIBUTION
NEGATIVELY SKEWED

NORMAL DISTRIBUTION
POPULATION MEAN
POPULATION SIZE
POSITIVELY SKEWED
RECTANGULAR DISTRIBUTION
SAMPLE MEAN
SAMPLE SIZE
SKEWED DISTRIBUTION
SYMMETRICAL DISTRIBUTION
UNIMODAL DISTRIBUTION
WEIGHTED MEAN

CROSSWORD PUZZLES

ACROSS

1 A distribution of scores in which one score occurs most often or most frequently.

3 The number of individuals that constitute an entire group or population.

5 A distribution of scores in which outliers are substantially larger (toward the right tail of a graph) than most other scores.

6 A distribution of scores that includes outliers or scores that fall substantially above or below most other scores in a data set.

9 The value in a data set that occurs most often or most frequently.

10 Refers to statistical measures for locating a single score that is most representative or descriptive of all scores in a distribution.

11 The middle value of a distribution of data listed in numeric order.

13 The combined mean of two or more groups of scores in which the number of scores in each group is disproportionate or unequal.

15 The mean for a set of scores in an entire population.

16 A distribution of scores in which one or more scores occur most often or most frequently.

17 A distribution of scores in which more than two scores occur most often or most frequently.

18 A theoretical distribution with data that are symmetrically distributed around the mean, the median, and the mode.

DOWN

2 A distribution of scores in which outliers are substantially smaller (toward the left tail of a graph) than most other scores.

4 The number of individuals that constitute a subset of those selected from a larger population.

7 A distribution of scores in which two scores occur most often or most frequently.

8 The sum of a set of scores in a distribution, divided by the total number of scores summed.

12 A distribution of scores in which all scores occur at the same frequency is called a _____ modal distribution (fill in the blank).

14 The mean for a sample or a subset of scores from a population.

PRACTICE QUIZZES

LO 1: Distinguish between a population mean and sample mean.

1. Although different symbols are used to represent the number of scores in a sample and population, the computation of central tendency is _____ for samples and populations.
   a. different
   b. the same
   c. minimal
   d. summed

2. The _____ is the sum of N scores divided by N, whereas the _____ is the sum of n scores divided by n.
   a. population mean; sample mean
   b. sample mean; population mean

3. The population mean is identified by the Greek letter _____; the sample mean is identified by an italicized _____.
   a. μ; s
   b. M; μ
   c. μ; M
   d. s; M

LO 2: Calculate and interpret the mean, the median, and the mode.

4. The mean is the balance point of a distribution, which means that it is:
   a. always equal to 0
   b. not always located at the center of a distribution of scores
   c. equal to the score in the middle of a distribution of scores
   d. used to measure the extent to which objects balance

5. A researcher records the following number of mistakes made during a sports broadcast: 0, 2, 0, 5, 2, 3, 0, 8, 1, and 4. What is the mean for these data?
   a. 1.5
   b. 2.0
   c. 2.5
   d. 3.0

6. The median is:
   a. the preferred measure of central tendency when outliers are in a data set
   b. the middle value in a distribution listed in numerical order

   c. at the 50th percentile of a cumulative percent distribution

   d. all of the above

7. A researcher records the following time (in seconds) that children in a sample play with an unfamiliar toy: 12, 14, 10, 6, 8, 10, 13, 12, 4, 12, and 6. Which measure of central tendency (the mean, the median, or the mode) is largest?

   a. mean

   b. median

   c. mode

   d. all measures for central tendency are equal

8. The _____ is the value in a data set that occurs most often or most frequently.

   a. mode

   b. median

   c. mean

LO 3: Calculate and interpret the weighted mean for two or more samples with unequal sample sizes.

9. When a weighted mean is computed for two or more samples with unequal sample sizes, which value is used as the weight in the formula?

   a. M

   b. n

   c. μ

   d. N

10. A researcher records $M = 12$ in a sample of men ($n = 10$) and $M = 8$ in a sample of women ($n = 20$). What is the weighted mean for these samples?

   a. 12.0

   b. 10.33

   c. 10.0

   d. 9.33

11. The weighted mean is used to compute the mean for samples with _____ sizes.

   a. unequal

   b. equal

   c. proportional

   d. fractional

LO 4: Identify the characteristics of the mean.

12. The mean for a distribution of scores is $M = 6$. If we measure a new score equal to 10, then what will happen to the mean?

   a. the mean will increase

   b. the mean will decrease

   c. the mean will remain the same

13. The mean for a distribution of scores is $M = 3.2$. If we remove an existing score equal to 3.2, then what will happen to the mean?

    a. the mean will increase

    b. the mean will decrease

    c. the mean will remain the same

14. Which of the following will decrease the value of the mean for a distribution of scores?

    a. adding a new score above the mean

    b. deleting an existing score above the mean

    c. adding a new score equal to the mean

    d. deleting an existing score below the mean

15. A researcher measures a sample mean for five samples. The sample mean in each sample is $M = 2$, $M = 4$, $M = 5$, $M = 7$, and $M = 9$. What will the sum of the differences of scores from the mean equal in each sample?

    a. minimal

    b. equal to 0

    c. larger as the mean in the sample gets larger

    d. not enough information because the actual scores in each sample are not given

16. The sum of the squared differences of scores from their mean:

    a. is minimal

    b. is equal to 0

    c. can be any positive or negative number

LO 5: Identify an appropriate measure of central tendency for different distributions and scales of measurement.

17. The mean is used to describe:

    a. data that are normally distributed

    b. interval scale data

    c. ratio scale data

    d. all of the above

18. The mode and median can be used *with the mean* to describe data that are normally distributed.

    a. true

    b. false

19. When outliers exist in a data set, which measure of central tendency is most appropriate?

    a. the mean

    b. the median

    c. the mode

20. Why is the median appropriate for describing ordinal scale data?

    a. ordinal scale data are the only type of data that have a median

    b. ordinal scale data are always positively or negatively skewed

c. ordinal scale data convey direction only (more or less than)

d. ordinal scale data convey the same information as ratio data

21. The mode is the primary measure of central tendency to describe data on which scale of measurement?

a. nominal

b. ordinal

c. interval

d. ratio

Follow the General Instructions Guidebook to complete this exercise. Also, an example for following these steps is provided in the SPSS in Focus section (Section 3.6) of the book. Complete and submit the SPSS grading template and a printout of the output file.

Exercise 3.1: Alcohol Consumption at Local Parties I

A researcher wants to study alcohol consumption at local parties. The researcher is particularly interested in the amount of alcohol consumed at parties where untrained friends or acquaintances mix the drinks (instead of trained bartenders). For this study, a standard drink was defined as 12 oz of beer (5% vol.), 5 oz of wine (12% vol.), 1.5 oz of liquor (40% vol.), or 1.5 oz of liquor in a mixed drink (National Institute on Alcohol Abuse and Alcoholism, 2000). Below is the number of standard drinks consumed by 30 people at one local party. Compute the mean, the median, and the mode for these data.

2.4	6.6	8.2
2.3	0.5	3.2
1.4	14.2	3.5
5.4	9.3	6.4
7.5	2.0	7.9
8.2	4.4	0.9
12.1	10.0	5.4
3.2	2.8	5.4
1.1	5.6	6.3
2.0	5.0	8.8

SOURCE: National Institute on Alcohol Abuse and Alcoholism. (2000). *Tenth special report to the U.S. Congress on alcohol and health* (NIH Pub. No. 00-1583). Washington, DC: National Institutes of Health.

With regard to the SPSS exercise, answer the following questions:

State the dependent variable: _____

State the following values (from the SPSS output table):

Mean   _____

Median   _____

Mode(s)   _____

Is there more than one mode in this distribution? How does SPSS display or indicate that the distribution of scores has more than one mode?

Interpret the data displayed in the SPSS output table. Which measure of central tendency is the most appropriate statistic to summarize these data?

CHAPTER SUMMARY ORGANIZED BY LEARNING OBJECTIVE

LO 1: Distinguish between a population mean and sample mean.

- The mean for a set of scores in an entire population is called a population mean; the mean for a sample (or subset of scores from a population) is called a sample mean. Each mean is computed the same but with different notation used to identify the sample size (n) and population size (N).

LO 2: Calculate and interpret the mean, the median, and the mode.

- Measures of central tendency are statistical measures for locating a single score that is most representative or descriptive of all scores in a distribution. Three measures of central tendency are the mean, the median, and the mode.
- The mean is the sum of a set of scores divided by the total number of scores summed:

  The population mean is the sum of N scores divided by N: $\mu = \frac{\sum x}{N}$.

  The sample mean is the sum of n scores divided by n: $M = \frac{\sum x}{n}$.

- The median is the middle score in a data set that is listed in numerical order in which half of all scores fall above and half fall below its value. Unlike the mean, the value of the median is not shifted in the direction of outliers—the median is always at the center or midpoint of a data set. To find the median

position, list scores in numerical order and apply this formula:

Median position = $\frac{n+1}{2}$.

- The mode is the value in a data set that occurs most often or most frequently. The mode is often reported with the mean or the median.

LO 3: Calculate and interpret the weighted mean for two or more samples with unequal sample sizes.

- The weighted mean is the combined mean of two or more groups of scores in which the number of scores in each group is disproportionate or unequal. The formula for the weighted mean of two or more samples with unequal sample sizes is $M_w = \frac{\sum(M \times n)}{\sum n}$.

LO 4: Identify the characteristics of the mean.

- The mean has the following characteristics:
  a. Changing an existing score will change the mean.
  b. Adding a new score or removing an existing score will change the mean, unless that value equals the mean.
  c. Adding, subtracting, multiplying, or dividing each score in a distribution by a constant will cause the mean to change by that constant.
  d. The sum of the differences of scores from their mean is zero.
  e. The sum of the squared differences of scores from their mean is minimal.

LO 5: Identify an appropriate measure of central tendency for different distributions and scales of measurement.

- The *mean* is used to describe (1) data that are normally distributed and (2) interval and ratio scale data.
- The *median* is used to describe (1) data in a skewed distribution and (2) ordinal scale data.
- The *mode* is used to describe (1) any type of data with a value that occurs the most, although it is typically used together with the mean or the median, and (2) nominal scale data.

LO 6: Compute the mean, the median, and the mode using SPSS.

- SPSS can be used to compute the mean, median, and mode. Each measure of central tendency is computed using the Analyze, then Descriptive Statistics and Frequencies, options in the menu bar. These actions will bring up a dialog box that will allow you to identify the variable and select the Statistics option to select and compute the mean, the median, and the mode.

4

Summarizing Data

Variability

LEARNING OBJECTIVES

After reading this chapter, you should be able to:

1. Compute and interpret a range, interquartile range, and semi-interquartile range.

2. Compute and interpret the variance and standard deviation for a population and sample of data using the definitional formula.

3. Compute and interpret the variance and standard deviation for a population and sample of data using the computational formula.

4. Explain why the sample variance and population variance are computed differently.

5. State the characteristics of the standard deviation and explain the empirical rule.

6. Compute the range, variance, and standard deviation using SPSS.

4.1 Measuring Variability

Variability is a measure of the dispersion of scores in a distribution.

- Variability ranges from 0 to $+\infty$.
- There are three common measures of variability: the *range*, the *variance*, and the *standard deviation*.

4.2 The Range

Range: The range is a simple measure of variability and is the difference between the largest (L) and smallest (S) scores in a distribution.

- Range = $L - S$.
- The range is a good measure of variability for data sets that do not have outliers and when the number of measured scores is small.

4.3 Research in Focus: Reporting the Range

Agrawal, Madden, Buchholz, Heath, and Lynskey (2008) reported the range along with the means for five characteristics of interest. Reporting the range for each characteristic was an effective way to summarize the demographic information.

4.4 Measures of Variability: Quartiles and Interquartiles

Fractiles split data sets into equal parts. Fractiles include the *median, quartiles, deciles,* and *percentiles.*
   Quartiles split data into four equal parts. There are three steps used to locate each quartile in a data set.

- Step 1: Locate the median quartile (Q_2) for the data set.
- Step 2: Locate the median for the remaining scores below Q_2. In other words, locate the median for the bottom half of the data set. This is the upper real limit for the lower quartile (Q_1).

- Step 3: Locate the median for the remaining scores above Q_2. This is the upper real limit for the upper quartile (Q_3).
  - Once you have located each quartile, you can calculate the *interquartile range* (IQR), which is the range of the distribution of scores after the top and bottom 25% of data have been removed, or **$Q_3 - Q_1$**.
  - The *semi-interquartile range* (SIQR) measures half the distance between the cutoffs for the upper and lower quartiles of a distribution. The SIQR accounts for only half of the scores in a distribution, but outliers do not influence its value.

4.5 The Variance

Variance is a preferred measure of variability because, unlike the range or IQR, all of the scores in the distribution are used in its calculation. The variance measures the *average* squared distance or *deviation* of scores from the mean.

- *Deviation* scores refer to the difference between a score and the mean.

Population variance: Population variance is the average squared distance of the deviation scores for an entire population from their mean. This can be calculated only when every score from the population is measured.

- The population variance is symbolized as σ^2.

- $$\sigma^2 = \frac{\sum (x - \mu)^2}{N} \text{ or } \frac{SS}{N}.$$

- SS = the sum of squares and is the sum of the deviation scores from their mean.
- Population variance is calculated by first calculating the SS, then dividing the result by N, which is the size of the population.

Sample variance: Sample variance is the average squared distance of the deviation scores for a sample from the sample mean and is calculated when you have measured only a portion or sample of scores from a large population.

- The sample variance is symbolized as s^2.

- $$s^2 = \frac{\sum (x - M)^2}{n - 1} \text{ or } \frac{SS}{n - 1}.$$

- Sample variance is calculated by first calculating the SS, then dividing the result by the degrees of freedom for sample variance, or $n - 1$.

4.6 Explaining Variance for Populations and Samples

The numerator: We compute the *SS* in the numerator of the variance formula for three specific reasons.

- The sum of the difference scores from their mean equals 0.
- The sum of the squared difference scores from the mean will be a minimal solution.
- Squaring scores is corrected by taking the square root of the variance.

The denominator: To calculate the population variance, we divide the sum of squared difference scores by N. However, to calculate sample variance, we divide the sum of squared difference scores by $n - 1$. If we do not subtract 1 in the denominator, then the sample size will underestimate the population variance. Only when we divide *SS* by $n - 1$ will the sample variance be an *unbiased* estimator of the population variance.

- The degrees of freedom for sample variance are $n - 1$ because if you know the mean, then all of the scores are free to vary except for one—the last score must be a value that allows the mean to be correct.

4.7 The Computational Formula for Variance

The *definitional formula* for variance defines the *SS* in the numerator:

- Population variance definitional formula: $SS = \sum(x - \mu)^2$, where $\sigma^2 = \dfrac{SS}{N}$.
- Sample variance definitional formula: $SS = \sum(x - M)^2$, where $s^2 = \dfrac{SS}{n-1}$.

The *computational formula* is not prone to rounding errors and is calculated in such a way that the mean does not need to be computed:

- Population variance computational formula: $SS = \sum x^2 - \dfrac{(\sum x)^2}{N}$, where $\sigma^2 = \dfrac{SS}{N}$.

- Sample variance computational formula: $SS = \sum x^2 - \dfrac{(\sum x)^2}{n}$, where $s^2 = \dfrac{SS}{n-1}$.

4.8 The Standard Deviation

To compute the standard deviation, we take the square root of the variance, which is the average distance that scores deviate from their mean.

- The population standard deviation is represented as *s*.
- $\sigma = \sqrt{\sigma^2} = \sqrt{\dfrac{SS}{N}}$.
- The sample standard deviation is represented as *s* or *SD*.

- $s = \sqrt{s^2} = \sqrt{\dfrac{SS}{n-1}}$.

- To compute the standard deviation, follow two steps: (1) Calculate the variance, and (2) take the square root of the variance.

4.9 What Does the Standard Deviation Tell Us?

The standard deviation is the average distance that scores deviate from the mean. It is smaller when scores are concentrated closely around their mean and larger when scores are scattered far from their mean.

The empirical rule for data that are normally distributed encompasses the following three statements:

1. At least 68% of all scores lie within one standard deviation of the mean.

2. At least 95% of all scores lie within two standard deviations of the mean.

3. At least 99.7% of all scores lie within three standard deviations of the mean.

4.10 Characteristics of the Standard Deviation

There are four key characteristics of the population and sample standard deviation:

- The standard deviation is always positive or equal to 0. A negative standard deviation is meaningless.
- The standard deviation is the square root of the variance and, as such, is a numeric value. Thus, it is used only to describe quantitative variables.
- The standard deviation is the average distance of scores from their mean; therefore, it is most often reported with the mean.
- The value of the standard deviation is influenced by the value of every score in a distribution because all scores are included in its calculation.
  - o Adding or subtracting a constant to every value in the distribution will not change the value of the standard deviation.
  - o Multiplying or dividing a constant to every value in the distribution will change the value of the standard deviation by that constant.

4.11 SPSS in Focus: Range, Variance, and Standard Deviation

SPSS can be used to compute the range, variance, and standard deviation. Each measure of variability is computed using the Analyze, then Descriptive Statistics and Frequencies, options in the menu bar.

CHAPTER FORMULAS

Variability

Range $= L - S$

$IQR = Q_3 - Q_1$ (Interquartile range)

$SIQR = \dfrac{IQR}{2}$ (Semi-interquartile range)

$\sigma^2 = \dfrac{SS}{N}$ (Population variance)

$s^2 = \dfrac{SS}{n-1} = \dfrac{SS}{df}$ (Sample variance)

$df = n - 1$ (Degrees of freedom for sample variance)

$SS = \Sigma(x - \mu)^2$ (Definitional formula for the sum of squares in a population)

$SS = \Sigma(x - M)^2$ (Definitional formula for sum of squares in a sample)

$SS = \Sigma x^2 - \dfrac{(\Sigma x)^2}{N}$ (Computational formula for the sum of squares in a population)

$SS = \Sigma x^2 - \dfrac{(\Sigma x)^2}{N}$ (Computational formula for sum of squares in a sample)

$\sigma = \sqrt{\sigma^2} = \sqrt{\dfrac{SS}{N}}$ (Population standard deviation)

$SD = \sqrt{s^2} = \sqrt{\dfrac{SS}{n-1}} = \sqrt{\dfrac{SS}{df}}$ (Sample standard deviation)

TIPS AND CAUTIONS FOR STUDENTS

- *Range:* Note that calculations of range consider only the largest and smallest values in a data set. For this reason, the range is of limited value for data interpretation. Outliers will make the range appear very large, although the majority of the data fall within a much smaller range. For instance, if the distribution contains the scores 2, 3, 6, 8, 10, and 100, then the range is 98 (Range = 100 – 2), although only one value is larger than 10. For this reason, the range is rarely used as a primary measure of variability, particularly when outliers are in a data set.

- *Sum of squares:* When calculating sum of squares, it is important to remember to subtract each score from the mean before squaring it. The sum of squares is the sum of the deviation of scores from their mean, so you must not forget to complete these steps in this order using the definitional formula: (1) Find the mean, (2) subtract each score from the mean, (3) square each deviation, and (4) sum the squared deviations. The reason that the computational formula is easier than the definitional formula of the sum of squares is that we are not required to find the mean using the computational formula.

- *Computational* SS *and other formulas:* In this book, it is important to understand the order of operations of mathematical calculations. Knowing when to sum first or when to square first is essential for you to properly perform calculations, such as when we use the computational and definitional formulas to compute *SS*. Please read Appendix A of the book, which gives a basic math review, if you have any doubts regarding the order of mathematical operations.

KEY TERM WORD SEARCHES

U	O	V	P	E	Q	Q	J	O	P	B	O	P	C	Y	J	F	Y	S	B	V	D	I	P	O	Q	V	X	Q	G	R	J	D	S	E	H	F	T	L	T
X	J	O	E	G	F	X	C	X	Q	R	D	L	I	C	I	R	G	G	B	O	U	T	S	I	X	R	K	K	V	S	Q	T	E	E	U	R	H	Z	B
J	Q	N	Y	G	Y	C	F	B	B	W	Q	Z	M	K	F	D	P	V	V	I	N	N	S	C	X	B	J	H	O	K	B	S	M	E	W	L	A	W	N
U	F	R	Q	I	O	E	S	D	J	Y	R	C	L	D	T	V	D	V	V	I	X	S	Y	N	R	U	X	V	Q	Z	F	G	I	C	A	P	Q	X	E
S	T	A	N	D	A	R	D	D	E	V	I	A	T	I	O	N	X	D	P	X	F	X	Z	I	W	H	P	O	L	A	H	F	I	B	E	W	N	T	D
Q	T	H	X	N	E	K	T	K	A	L	N	C	Y	Y	R	X	D	Z	O	S	P	Q	K	F	J	K	P	R	A	F	X	D	N	C	X	U	N	S	J
Q	H	K	P	P	M	L	H	E	B	I	C	J	N	D	B	X	U	E	P	M	G	O	X	N	X	T	S	F	C	H	K	E	T	D	K	H	G	A	V
P	D	Z	E	C	P	A	I	B	M	M	I	D	R	A	N	G	E	H	U	N	C	W	G	I	T	H	H	V	T	U	M	W	E	X	G	E	X	M	Q
D	Z	Z	F	W	I	F	H	Q	E	I	E	M	O	P	L	L	L	F	L	D	G	A	C	L	V	D	M	N	B	D	H	C	R	X	Y	D	R	P	X
N	I	H	F	Q	R	Z	R	O	Z	C	H	E	D	I	B	K	R	D	A	X	X	O	S	D	V	S	I	D	E	J	B	K	Q	F	I	L	X	L	O
X	C	X	X	Q	I	A	K	W	W	A	F	D	K	T	C	W	L	U	T	A	F	D	F	K	N	P	W	N	V	I	N	O	U	X	N	V	F	E	U
D	I	T	F	H	C	W	E	V	G	V	M	I	Y	J	B	M	Q	Q	I	E	F	U	I	P	M	P	I	B	D	F	B	J	A	I	T	D	J	V	E
Z	Y	O	R	O	A	T	J	Z	J	E	R	A	C	X	D	T	W	W	O	Y	S	Q	L	O	L	Q	S	L	E	E	Q	C	R	M	E	Y	S	A	C
U	K	D	X	Z	L	B	L	V	U	Z	I	N	X	F	D	Z	L	F	N	N	K	K	S	P	S	M	O	H	V	F	K	P	T	S	R	W	X	R	F
Z	A	D	S	P	R	Q	B	Y	X	W	G	Q	L	V	Q	L	H	V	S	G	A	E	E	U	X	Z	E	O	H	J	B	V	I	D	Q	V	C	I	T
R	W	C	Y	C	U	U	U	D	X	F	A	U	O	Q	G	V	G	P	T	N	E	X	C	L	C	Z	A	D	Z	J	L	N	L	E	U	Z	Y	A	R
S	Q	B	X	U	L	A	N	W	D	E	K	A	W	U	S	S	J	E	A	X	B	A	X	A	I	Q	J	A	I	C	M	Z	E	G	A	S	W	N	B
U	I	K	O	Z	E	R	B	E	L	F	O	R	E	A	Y	J	B	K	N	M	J	T	E	T	J	T	U	D	Y	A	I	N	R	R	E	I	C	O
R	P	D	C	E	Z	T	I	X	V	J	W	T	R	R	Z	E	P	T	D	F	T	R	M	I	C	N	G	G	W	R	N	J	A	E	T	H	P	E	Z
B	X	W	Z	X	J	I	A	Q	P	U	P	I	Q	T	L	W	E	F	A	E	P	V	C	O	R	M	T	A	P	O	B	L	N	E	I	L	G	Z	A
Y	B	R	A	G	W	L	S	M	F	W	X	L	U	I	N	W	R	C	R	U	C	A	P	N	A	Z	C	B	F	I	C	R	G	S	L	T	E	P	H
A	K	A	L	K	T	E	E	X	L	P	X	E	A	L	U	J	C	O	D	K	A	R	I	V	W	R	P	Q	R	F	N	Y	E	O	E	C	C	J	K
A	R	V	K	Y	V	S	D	Q	O	M	U	M	R	E	W	L	E	D	D	C	F	I	D	A	S	J	N	S	F	S	M	V	S	F	R	H	H	U	Z
D	E	N	Y	C	M	M	E	Y	C	Z	S	F	T	D	Q	E	N	Z	E	Y	T	A	E	R	C	A	X	F	L	G	M	N	G	F	A	L	E	W	Z
G	E	X	Q	Y	F	K	S	A	L	T	H	R	I	E	M	Z	T	I	V	Y	J	B	C	I	O	D	K	A	S	I	S	G	Z	R	N	L	B	X	C
I	S	V	R	A	M	F	T	N	F	A	L	B	L	V	N	V	I	P	I	T	F	I	I	A	R	R	B	O	Y	X	N	X	J	E	G	D	Y	L	D
Q	N	Q	I	Q	M	H	I	H	R	S	C	H	E	I	F	G	L	M	A	C	X	L	L	N	E	X	B	W	F	C	P	N	P	E	E	Y	S	X	Z
E	U	V	I	A	X	A	M	C	W	S	K	V	C	A	P	F	E	N	T	Y	B	I	E	C	S	D	J	V	I	M	V	Q	A	D	A	I	H	G	G
A	B	A	B	S	T	O	A	I	D	W	W	T	J	T	E	D	S	Q	I	K	M	T	S	T	M	B	L	R	S	E	O	J	F	O	D	P	E	N	J
D	V	A	R	U	B	I	T	U	S	J	D	B	X	I	J	B	E	J	O	A	R	Y	E	E	E	W	L	E	Y	R	W	P	O	M	V	N	V	Q	V
P	Z	U	U	S	B	T	O	S	J	C	V	R	D	O	Y	K	T	I	N	D	J	A	F	L	T	L	R	X	Z	A	W	D	C	W	F	G	S	F	H
B	N	O	B	C	P	I	R	N	C	P	H	H	B	N	A	T	A	V	T	Z	L	V	F	S	H	D	Q	Q	D	N	N	D	W	N	R	T	T	E	Q
S	U	M	O	F	F	S	Q	U	A	R	E	S	P	R	Q	D	W	A	D	O	Q	P	K	I	O	Q	T	V	G	G	K	X	E	J	A	Q	H	E	Y
W	R	G	A	N	D	L	X	K	U	P	P	E	R	Q	U	A	R	T	I	L	E	V	O	Y	D	T	P	X	Z	E	Q	E	F	M	C	D	E	L	P
D	F	M	W	X	G	S	Z	E	N	R	U	I	Y	K	C	I	L	I	E	R	Z	U	R	A	U	G	I	K	G	Z	D	E	B	N	T	H	O	O	B
O	Q	G	F	F	L	J	L	B	U	P	B	G	W	B	Y	U	A	P	J	N	M	Q	O	M	V	L	Z	A	J	Q	H	A	K	I	J	R	O	S
E	Z	L	O	K	F	Y	L	T	I	A	X	G	C	C	T	R	F	N	O	C	A	R	J	U	M	I	C	K	N	P	R	X	N	E	L	W	E	Z	I
B	Y	H	N	E	U	N	L	B	T	G	N	N	I	E	U	M	S	C	N	P	R	B	C	D	N	Y	E	R	C	K	C	G	C	L	E	Q	M	H	G
O	V	X	W	J	K	O	W	X	Z	G	M	C	B	M	J	K	Q	E	Z	V	E	Z	G	Q	W	I	R	R	Z	K	C	S	X	O	S	X	X	Q	T
I	R	O	G	Q	Y	Y	E	Z	I	Q	W	S	A	M	P	L	E	S	T	A	N	D	A	R	D	D	E	V	I	A	T	I	O	N	K	I	S	U	Q

CHEBYSHEV'S THEOREM
DECILES
DEGREES OF FREEDOM
DEVIATION
EMPIRICAL RULE
FRACTILES
INTERQUARTILE RANGE
LOWER QUARTILE
MEDIAN
MEDIAN QUARTILE
METHOD
PERCENTILES
POPULATION STANDARD DEVIATION
POPULATION VARIANCE

QUARTILE DEVIATION
QUARTILES
RANGE
RAW SCORES
SAMPLE STANDARD DEVIATION
SAMPLE VARIANCE
SEMI-INTERQUARTILE RANGE
STANDARD DEVIATION
SUM OF SQUARES
UNBIASED ESTIMATOR
UPPER QUARTILE
VARIABILITY
VARIANCE

CROSSWORD PUZZLES

ACROSS

9 The range of a distribution of scores falling within the upper and lower quartiles of a distribution.

11 A measure of half the distance between the upper quartile and lower quartile of a distribution is called a _____-interquartile range (fill in the blank).

12 The difference between the largest value (*L*) and smallest value (*S*) in a data set.

14 A measure for the dispersion or spread of data in a distribution that ranges from 0 to $+\infty$.

15 A measure of variability for the average distance that scores in a population deviate from their mean.

DOWN

1 A measure of variability for the average squared distance that scores in a population deviate from their mean.

2 A measure of variability for the average squared distance that scores in a sample deviate from their mean.

3 A measure of variability for the average distance that scores deviate from their mean.

4 A measure of variability for the average distance that scores in a sample deviate from their mean.

5 Measures that divide a set of data into two or more equal parts.

6 Any sample statistic obtained from a randomly selected sample that equals the value of its respective population parameter on average.

7 The sum of the squared deviations of scores from their mean.

8 The difference of each score from its mean.

10 A rule that states that for any normally distributed set of data, at least 99.7% of data lie within three standard deviations of the mean, at least 95% of data lie within two standard deviations of the mean, and at least 68% of data lie within one standard deviation of the mean.

PRACTICE QUIZZES

LO 1: Compute and interpret a range, interquartile range, and semi-interquartile range.

1. A researcher measures a data set with a range equal to 12. Which of the following data sets has a range equal to 12?

    a. 2, 5, 3, 12, 8

    b. 0, 9, 3, 12, 10, 7

    c. 24, 10, 18, 26, 36

    d. 7, 13, 12, 16, 20

2. A researcher measures the following scores: 14, 12, 12, 11, 9, 9, 8, and 5. What is the range of these data?

    a. 9

    b. 4

    c. 10

    d. 14

3. A researcher measures a range equal to 12. What will the value of the interquartile range be for these same data?

    a. equal to the range

    b. greater than the range

    c. less than the range

4. A researcher measures the following data: 0, 0, 2, 4, 5, 8, 9, 11, and 12. What is the value of the median quartile?

    a. 1

    b. 5

    c. 10

    d. 12

5. A researcher computes IQR = 18. What is the semi-interquartile range for these data?

    a. 9

    b. 14

    c. 15

    d. 18

LO 2: Compute and interpret the variance and standard deviation for a population and sample of data using the definitional formula.

6. The _____ is the square root of the _____.
    a. range; interquartile range
    b. mean; median
    c. variance; standard deviation
    d. standard deviation; variance

7. Which of the following describes the calculation for the sum of squares (SS) using the definitional formula?
    a. the sum of the deviations of scores from the mean
    b. the sum of the squared deviations of scores from the mean
    c. the average distance that scores deviate from the mean
    d. the average distance that scores deviate from each other

8. How is the formula for the sample variance different from the formula for the population variance?
    a. SS is computed without squaring the deviations of scores from the mean
    b. the value for SS is placed in the denominator of the sample variance formula
    c. SS is divided by the degrees of freedom for sample variance in the denominator of the formula for sample variance
    d. none; both formulas are computed the same

LO 3: Compute and interpret the variance and standard deviation for a population and sample of data using the computational formula.

9. The denominator for sample variance is _____; the denominator for population variance is _____.
    a. N; $n - 1$
    b. $n - 1$; N
    c. df; N
    d. both b and c

10. Which value is not needed to find the SS using the computational formula?
    a. the sum of scores
    b. the sum of squared scores
    c. the mean
    d. the sample or population size

11. Compute the sample standard deviation for the following data: 2, 4, 2, 5, 8, 19, 7, 12, 13, 9, 10, 13, 15, 19, 23, 3, 20, 18, 19, and 10.

   a. 6.430

   b. 6.597

   c. 41.348

   d. 43.524

LO 4: Explain why the sample variance and the population variance are computed differently.

12. The sum of the deviation of scores from their mean is zero. To avoid this result, each deviation is _____.

   a. summed

   b. squared

   c. divided

   d. multiplied

13. Because all scores in a sample (n) are free to vary except for one, we calculate the sample variance by dividing SS by only those scores that are free to vary in a sample.

   a. true

   b. false

14. The sample variance is an unbiased estimator of the population variance when we:

   a. divide SS by $(n - 1)$

   b. divide SS by df

   c. divide SS by N

   d. both a and b

15. The sample variance is a(n) _____ when, on average, its value is equal to the value of the population variance.

   a. biased estimator

   b. unbiased estimator

LO 5: State the characteristics of the standard deviation and explain the empirical rule.

16. The standard deviation is almost always reported with which measure of central tendency?

   a. the mean

   b. the median

   c. the mode

   d. the range

17. The standard deviation is most informative for describing what type of distribution?

    a. normal distribution

    b. skewed distribution

    c. bimodal distribution

    d. nonmodal distribution

18. Suppose a normal distribution has a mean of 8 and a standard deviation of 2. What is the range of scores within which at least 95% of scores are contained?

    a. 8 to 10

    b. 4 to 12

    c. 6 to 10

    d. 6 to 8

19. Suppose that at least 68% of scores in a normal distribution fall between 7 and 10. Using the empirical rule, what is the approximate mean and standard deviation of these data?

    a. mean = 7, standard deviation = 10

    b. mean = 8.5, standard deviation = 3

    c. mean = 8.5, standard deviation = 1.5

    d. mean = 10, standard deviation = 7

20. What is the minimal number of standard deviations required to account for most of the data (i.e., more than half the data) in a normal distribution?

    a. ±0.5 SD

    b. ±1 SD

    c. ±2 SD

    d. ±3 SD

SPSS IN FOCUS

Range, Variance, and Standard Deviation

Follow the General Instructions Guidebook to complete this exercise. Also, an example for following these steps is provided in the SPSS in Focus section (Section 4.11) of the book. The example given here uses the same data as SPSS in Focus Exercise 3.1. Complete and submit the SPSS grading template and a printout of the output file.

Exercise 4.1: Alcohol Consumption at Local Parties II

A researcher wants to study alcohol consumption at local parties. The researcher is particularly interested in the amount of alcohol consumed at parties where untrained friends or acquaintances mix the drinks (instead of trained bartenders). For this study, a standard drink was defined as 12 oz of beer (5% vol.), 5 oz of wine (12% vol.), 1.5 oz of liquor (40% vol.), or 1.5 oz of liquor in a mixed drink (National Institute on Alcohol Abuse and Alcoholism, 2000). Below is the number of standard drinks consumed by 30 people at one local party. Compute the range, the variance, and the standard deviation for these data.

2.4	6.6	8.2
2.3	0.5	3.2
1.4	14.2	3.5
5.4	9.3	6.4
7.5	2.0	7.9
8.2	4.4	0.9
12.1	10.0	5.4
3.2	2.8	5.4
1.1	5.6	6.3
2.0	5.0	8.8

SOURCE: National Institute on Alcohol Abuse and Alcoholism. (2000). *Tenth special report to the U.S. Congress on alcohol and health* (NIH Pub. No. 00-1583). Washington, DC: National Institutes of Health.

With regard to the SPSS exercise, answer the following questions:

State the dependent variable: _____

State the following values (from the SPSS output table):

Sample size   _____

Range   _____

Variance   _____

Standard deviation   _____

Interpret the data displayed in the SPSS output table. Also, compute the mean using SPSS (this was computed in SPSS in Focus Exercise 3.1) and factor this in your interpretation.

CHAPTER SUMMARY ORGANIZED BY LEARNING OBJECTIVE

LO 1: Compute and interpret a range, interquartile range, and semi-interquartile range.

- The range is the difference between the largest value (L) and smallest value (S) in a data set. Although the range provides a simple measure for variability, it accounts for only two values (the largest value and smallest value) in a distribution.
- The interquartile range (IQR) is the range of a distribution of scores after the top and bottom 25% of scores in that distribution are removed.

$$IQR = Q_3 - Q_1 .$$

- The quartiles split a data set into four equal parts, each containing 25% of the data. The 25th percentile is called the lower quartile, the 50th percentile is called the median quartile, and the 75th percentile is called the upper quartile.
- The semi-interquartile range (SIQR) is used as a measure of half the distance between Q_3 and Q_1.

$$SIQR = \frac{Q_3 - Q_1}{2}, \text{ also represented as}$$

$$SIQR = \frac{IQR}{2} .$$

LO 2–3: Compute and interpret the variance and standard deviation for a population and sample of data using the definitional formula and the computational formula.

- The variance is a measure of variability for the average squared distance that scores deviate from their mean. Its value is always greater than or equal to zero. The numerator in the variance formula is the sum of squares (SS). The denominator for population variance is N; the denominator for sample variance is ($n - 1$).
- The population variance is a measure of variability for the average squared distance that scores in a population deviate from the mean:

$$\sigma^2 = \frac{\Sigma(x - \mu)^2}{N} \text{ or } \frac{SS}{N} .$$

- The sample variance is a measure of variability for the average squared distance that scores in a sample deviate from the mean:

$$s^2 = \frac{\Sigma(x - M)^2}{n - 1} \text{ or } \frac{SS}{n - 1} .$$

- The computational formula for variance is a way to calculate the population variance and sample variance without needing to compute the mean to compute SS in the numerator.

Computational formula (population):

$$SS = \Sigma x^2 - \frac{(\Sigma x)^2}{N}, \text{ where } \sigma^2 = \frac{SS}{N} .$$

Computational formula (sample):

$$SS = \Sigma x^2 - \frac{(\Sigma x)^2}{n}, \text{ where } s^2 = \frac{SS}{n-1} .$$

- The standard deviation is a measure of variability for the average distance that scores deviate from their mean and is calculated by taking the square root of the variance.

Population standard deviation:

$$\sigma = \sqrt{\sigma^2} = \sqrt{\frac{SS}{N}} \; .$$

Sample standard deviation:

$$s = \sqrt{s^2} = \sqrt{\frac{SS}{n-1}} \; .$$

LO 4: Explain why the sample variance and population variance are computed differently.

- The numerators for the sample variance and population variance do not differ. *SS* is the numerator in both formulas; only the denominators differ for two reasons. First, the sample variance is unbiased when we divide *SS* by ($n - 1$)—on average, the variance of the sample will equal the variance of the population from which the sample was selected. Second, all scores in a sample are free to vary except one when the mean is known. So we divide the *SS* by one less than the sample size, called the degrees of freedom (*df*) for sample variance.

LO 5: State the characteristics of the standard deviation and explain the empirical rule.

- The standard deviation is always positive, and it is used to describe quantitative data, typically reported with the mean, and affected by the value of each score in a distribution. Adding or subtracting the same constant to each score will not change the standard deviation. Multiplying or dividing each score using the same constant will cause the standard deviation to change by the constant.
- For normal distributions with any mean and any variance, we can make the following three statements using the empirical rule: (1) At least 68% of all scores lie within one standard deviation of the mean, (2) at least 95% of all scores lie within two standard deviations of the mean, and (3) at least 99.7% of all scores lie within three standard deviations of the mean.

LO 6: Compute the range, variance, and standard deviation using SPSS.

- SPSS can be used to compute the range, variance, and standard deviation. Each measure of variability is computed using the Analyze, Descriptive Statistics, and Frequencies options in the menu bar. These actions will bring up a dialog box that will allow you to identify the variable and select the Statistics option to select and compute the range, variance, and standard deviation.

PART II

Probability and the Foundations of Inferential Statistics

5

Probability

LEARNING OBJECTIVES

After reading this chapter, you should be able to:

1. Compute a simple probability and explain the relationship between probability and relative frequency.

2. Describe four types of relationships between multiple outcomes.

3. Define and compute Bayes's theorem for conditional outcomes.

4. Construct a probability distribution for a given random variable.

5. Compute the mean and expected value of a probability distribution.

6. Compute the variance and standard deviation of a probability distribution.

7. Compute the mean, variance, and standard deviation of a binomial probability distribution.

8. Construct a probability table and conditional probability table using SPSS.

CHAPTER OUTLINE

5.1 Introduction to Probability

Probability: The frequency or number of times an event or value occurs divided by the total number of possible outcomes. Probability, p, is used as a measure of the likelihood of the outcomes in a *random event*.

- *Random event:* An event in which the observed outcomes can vary.
- *Fixed event:* An event in which the observed outcomes do not change. Probability is unnecessary in the case of fixed events.

5.2 Calculating Probability

To calculate a probability, we need to know the sample space, which is the total number of possible outcomes. We also need to know the frequency of the outcome of interest, or how often that outcome occurs.

- The probability of an outcome occurring is represented as $p(x)$.
- The frequency of times a particular outcome occurs is represented as $f(x)$.
- The sample space is the total number of possible outcomes.
- Therefore, the probability of an outcome occurring is calculated using the following formula and steps:

$$p(x) = \frac{f(x)}{sample\ space}.$$

  - Step 1: Find the sample space.
  - Step 2: Find $f(x)$.

There are two rules that a probability outcome follows:

- Probability varies between 0 and 1.
- Probability can never be negative.

5.3 Probability and Relative Frequency

Relative frequency, defined in Chapter 2, is the probability an event or score will occur. To find the relative frequency of an event and thus the probability that it will occur, follow two steps:

- Step 1: Distribute the frequencies; sum them to find the sample space.
- Step 2: Distribute the relative frequencies.

5.4 The Relationship Between Multiple Outcomes

How we compute probabilities for multiple outcomes depends on the relationship between each outcome.

Mutually exclusive outcomes: Two outcomes are mutually exclusive when they cannot occur together. Thus, the probability they can occur together is 0.

- $P(A \cap B) = 0$; $\cap$ is the symbol for *and*.

There is also the probability that one or the other outcome occurs. Mutually exclusive outcomes follow the additive rule.

- *The additive rule:* $p(A \cup B) = p(A) + p(B)$; $\cup$ is the symbol for *or*.
  - o Using the additive rule, the probability that one or the other outcome occurs is equal to the sum of their individual probabilities.

Independent outcomes: Probabilities for different outcomes are independent when the probability of one outcome occurring does not influence the probability of a second outcome occurring. Independent outcomes follow the multiplicative rule:

- The multiplicative rule: $p(A \cap B) = p(A) \times p(B)$.
  - o Using the multiplicative rule, the probability that two outcomes occur is equal to the product of their individual probabilities.

Complementary outcomes: The probabilities of two outcomes exhaust all possible outcomes for an event: $p(A) + p(B) = 1.00$.

Conditional outcomes: When the probability of one outcome changes the probability of a second outcome, we say the second outcome is *conditional* upon the occurrence of the first outcome.

- Conditional probability statements are worded with a "given that" statement such that we ask for the probability of one outcome (A), *given that* the other outcome occurred (B).
  - o The notation for a conditional probability is $p(A/B)$.
  - o The calculation of a conditional probability is $p(A/B) = \dfrac{p(B \cap A)}{p(B)}$.

5.5 Conditional Probabilities and Bayes's Theorem

The conditional probabilities formula can be modified to be applied in research situations where we want to know the probability of obtaining certain data samples given that the parameter in a certain population is known.

- Bayes's theorem is a formula that relates the conditional and unconditional (or marginal) probabilities of two conditional outcomes that occur at random.

- The formula for Bayes's theorem is $p(\text{A}/\text{B}) = \dfrac{p(\text{B}/\text{A})\,p(\text{A})}{p(\text{B})}$.

5.6 SPSS in Focus: Probability Tables

SPSS can be used to construct probability tables for one or more variables. To construct a probability table, each variable should be coded in the Variable View tab. In the Data View tab, the combination of each level for each factor should be arranged across the rows. The corresponding frequencies for each combination of levels are then entered in the last column. Probability and conditional probability tables are created using the Analyze, Descriptive Statistics, and Crosstabs options in the menu bar.

5.7 Probability Distributions

In a random experiment, researchers are interested in the distribution of probabilities for each possible outcome of a random variable.

- A *random variable* is a variable that can lead to any number of probable outcomes in a random experiment.
- The *probability distribution* for a random variable is the distribution of probabilities for each possible outcome. The sum of probabilities for all outcomes of a random variable equals 1.00: $\sum p(x) = 1.00$.

5.8 The Mean of a Probability Distribution and Expected Value

The expected value, also called the *mathematical expectation*, for a given random variable is the expected outcome for a given variable. It is calculated by summing the products of each random outcome and the probability of its occurrence: $\mu = \sum (xp)$.

5.9 Research in Focus: When Are Risks Worth Taking?

Peter Bernstein (1998) describes in his book how people approach expectations of risk and reward. He found that people often choose against the *mathematical expectation* of an outcome and take risks on outcomes that are less probable.

5.10 The Variance and Standard Deviation of a Probability Distribution

We can also calculate the average variability of all outcomes in a probability distribution.

- The variance of a probability distribution measures the average squared distance that the outcomes of a random variable will differ from the mean of the probability distribution.
- The standard deviation of a probability distribution is a measure of the average distance that the outcomes of any random variable deviate from the mean of the probability distribution and is calculated by taking the square root of the variance.

5.11 Expected Value and the Binomial Distribution

When there are only two possible outcomes for a random variable, we can estimate the probabilities of each outcome using a binomial probability distribution. A variable with only two possible outcomes is called a bivariate random variable.

- The mean of a binomial distribution is calculated by multiplying the number of times (n) the outcome of interest occurs by the probability (p) of its occurrence: $\mu = np$.
- The variance of a binomial distribution is calculated using the following formula: $\sigma^2 = np(1-p)$ or $\sigma^2 = npq$ (q is the probability of the complementary outcome).
- The standard deviation of a binomial distribution is the square root of the variance:

$$\sigma = \sqrt{\sigma^2} = \sqrt{np(1-p)} \quad \text{or} \quad \sigma = \sqrt{\sigma^2} = \sqrt{npq} \ .$$

5.12 A Final Thought on the Likelihood of Random Behavioral Outcomes

Probability calculations are used to predict the likelihood of random outcomes. However, there are just so many factors that contribute to the likelihood of observing the behavioral outcomes that researchers study. For this reason, calculating probabilities of any type of behavior, as well as interpreting them appropriately, requires some intuition and common sense.

CHAPTER FORMULAS

Probability

$p(x) = \dfrac{f(x)}{sample\ space}$ (Simple probability)

$p(A/B) = \dfrac{p(B/A)p(A)}{p(B)}$ (Bayes's theorem)

$\mu = \Sigma(xp)$ (Mean of a probability distribution)

$\sigma^2 = \Sigma\left((x-\mu)^2 p\right)$ (Variance of a probability distribution)

$\sigma = \sqrt{\sigma^2} = \sqrt{\Sigma\left((x-\mu)^2 p\right)}$ (Standard deviation of a probability distribution)

$\sigma^2 = \left(\Sigma(x^2 p) - \mu^2\right)$ (Computing formula for variance of a probability distribution)

$\sigma = \sqrt{\sigma^2} = \sqrt{(\Sigma(x^2 p) - \mu^2)}$ (Computing formula for standard deviation of a probability distribution)

$\mu = np$ (Mean of a binomial probability distribution)

$\sigma^2 = np(1 - p)$ or $\sigma^2 = npq$ (Variance of a binomial probability distribution)

$\sigma = \sqrt{\sigma^2} = \sqrt{np(1-p)}$ or $\sigma = \sqrt{\sigma^2} = \sqrt{npq}$ (Standard deviation of a binomial probability distribution)

TIPS AND CAUTIONS FOR STUDENTS

- *Probability and frequency:* Probability is the expression of a relative frequency for a particular outcome. When we constructed frequency tables in Chapter 2, the relative frequency was the number of times a score or category occurred divided by the total sample size. The total sample size in this case was the sample space.

- *Multiple outcomes:* Notice that as the complexity of probabilities increases, we start asking about the probability of multiple outcomes or conditional outcomes. For multiple outcomes, we are asking whether one *or* another outcome occurs; we are also asking whether one *and* another outcome occurs. For conditional outcomes, we are asking whether one outcome occurs *given that* another outcome occurred. For these more complicated probability questions, replace each mathematical symbol with the word or phrase it represents to help remind you of what you are calculating.

- *Variance and the probability distribution:* The formula for the variance of a probability distribution is actually similar to the formula for variance introduced in Chapter 4. Notice that we still sum the squared deviation of scores from their mean, as we did to calculate the sum of squares in Chapter 4. In the probability distribution formula, you are merely converting each squared deviation score into a probability score before summing. Notice that you do this instead of dividing by *n*.

KEY TERM WORD SEARCHES

```
Q G Q R Z Y W U R U G J D H F V Q N C E A T H S N W G Q J Y B W L B I V J R T C
H W O H R R K R R H D I C H O T O M O U S V A R I A B L E Q N Z N C A X Z X E D
S F K T S K X C Y J L Z U Z X E F Z M U L T I P L I C A T I V E R U L E J A W L
P Z B K C J J B L W L N Q K B L U P H T I S H W O E N E V R Z W H R D G J J Q A
O A M N Z M E P V T L K T C D W S F W X V E F U W P F Y H V B K Y H F H G T W B
A X J C G O D E O G O E N T E J V S Q K G F I Z R A L L X V Q Y I U W X U C N H
L A K A H X X F C V L N D L O V V P K L F D R H S P R O B A B I L I T Y Q Q V T
W G P S E I Z G U I S T D F J U C K C U X Z A I K R H E T T S J R C E I V F S I
U M P B H S R C X I E I N V Y U T W Y E B W E F M B B A Y E S S T H E O R E M F
Y A R Y W N W R S A M P L E S P A C E R U A K J Z B S A F G K O D K V W D K M X
B R L P G C Z I R Z D A V H R T U N O K W W M A R X V Y R D E N E O K P Q V Z I
K E H A S B A B G P G T C B Q A P A P M Q T S L E H F M L P Q A P F M R R K K J
C W D K A Q R F R Y A D X O V P G I O S E S D S N O P L P K U D E B R O Q G X S
W E Q D A F M J E J N A V P G J V S Q Z E S Q W L E B V X X J D N M R B R C S B
R L R N R J J F B K U U N R V Y Q Y O G I F P Y Y J O M U W W I D J S A W E R K
A C H U H Q J T G B K F O O B S N M T M M S D A C X O J F B C T E X I B A L X N
Q T Z R V E S I E G G H V Q E K L F X I Z F X S C H E S E D B I N E D I R O C U
N B Q H A U X Q H B J K X N W V N O N L V G J Q M E N F D C D V T P H L O K W J
O P H E H H K F U H H Q E J P C A R Y G S A V N P U P O E M C E O W M I Q N C G
X H J D O W D W E G O Y S N M G X F I X E D E V E N T S P M Q L U R O T B U O U
O M T G B A Y E S S L A W O T R L U Z R C S V Q N J K O E Q H A T A W Y I V M Q
Z W Y A A V S D N U Q V P K E T L O H P X V R P J C F D K D N W C O Q D N X P P
T V M U Z V J O I W W O U D Z X V L P G V E I G P X U S I Z A D O G A I O X L A
Q I G Q P L F H I T M O K Z K G R C B R U L X P X X F D B O I Q M W R S M U E M
R R E W D A N Z M C J J T Y T I D Y F F F S I P T K I E S A D P E W Q T I M M S
O M F X R G L C V N V J C V Z M X L O G Y I L M E V W V Y J M M S S G R A F E F
B R N O M W A L V D J L T R Z B U X I O N W X B O C Z U Q N G O G Y B I L X N B
Q R L C F U F B T B V K M T I A C D X P C O W X P M T I V E Y X U Y X B D S T U
B Q A L Z V E Z T O H X E F L V E H Y C V N N S L J W E V E A M P A O U I Z A L
C L Q H J X E A F L R Z M C Q Q Y Q Z N D I A P Y J U S D C R X Q G Z T S S R S
R R S X J M N A S X I C K V R J O L I U L A I A C L Y N O V A S M J X I T Z Y G
X B E R U Z X B A R I Z M A T H E M A T I C A L E X P E C T A T I O N O R G O A
N B V R Y H Q J S V Y O Z M R E W T M V L L N G R Z L D G Z K L D R N N I A U Z
X A D D I T I V E R U L E O U K Q I W F G G D U N F W D Y W K P U C N U B O T A
Y V N C S K U W S V M U T U A L L Y E X C L U S I V E O U T C O M E S M U L C S
H B M U L T I P L I C A T I V E L A W V I V M R A N D O M E V E N T S C T O O F
H A N F Y Y K W M G H Y Y M I T L V V T N V L G H B N P B P A X A W G O I M M T
W P S W X O P O I N D E P E N D E N T O U T C O M E S N N G Z I X Z R U O S E L
O H X W K V U X F J X C G C O N D I T I O N A L O U T C O M E S W T H S N Y S F
B R Y X R T O H P T S A G G R A N D O M V A R I A B L E S B E U Z F V Z V E N X
```

ADDITIVE LAW
ADDITIVE RULE
BAYES'S LAW
BAYES'S THEOREM
BINOMIAL DISTRIBUTION
COMPLEMENTARY OUTCOMES
CONDITIONAL OUTCOMES
DEPENDENT OUTCOMES
DICHOTOMOUS VARIABLE
EXPECTED VALUE
FIXED EVENTS

INDEPENDENT OUTCOMES
MATHEMATICAL EXPECTATION
MULTIPLICATIVE LAW
MULTIPLICATIVE RULE
MUTUALLY EXCLUSIVE OUTCOMES
OUTCOME SPACE
PROBABILITY
PROBABILITY DISTRIBUTION
RANDOM EVENTS
RANDOM VARIABLES
SAMPLE SPACE

CROSSWORD PUZZLES

ACROSS

3 Any event in which the outcome observed is always the same.

9 The distribution of probabilities for each outcome of a random variable that sums to 1.00.

11 A probability relationship in which the probability of one outcome is dependent on the occurrence of the other outcome.

12 Any event in which the outcomes observed can vary.

13 A probability relationship in which the probability of one outcome does not affect the probability of the second outcome.

14 The total number of possible outcomes that can occur in a given random event.

DOWN

1 A probability relationship in which two outcomes cannot occur together.

2 A probability relationship in which the sum of the probabilities for two outcomes is 1.00.

4 The mean or average expected outcome for a given random variable.

5 A variable obtained or measured in a random experiment.

6 The frequency of times an outcome occurs divided by the total number of possible outcomes.

7 A mathematical formula that relates the conditional and marginal (unconditional) probabilities of two conditional outcomes that occur at random.

8 A rule that states that when two outcomes for a given event are independent, the probability that both outcomes occur is equal to the product of their individual probabilities.

10 A rule that states that when two outcomes for a given event are mutually exclusive, the probability that any one of these outcomes occurs is equal to the sum of their individual probabilities.

PRACTICE QUIZZES

LO 1: Compute a simple probability and explain the relationship between probability and relative frequency.

1. Probability is used to describe the likelihood of _____ events.
   a. random
   b. fixed
   c. certain
   d. all of the above

2. A school population consists of 34 first-grade, 48 second-grade, and 38 third-grade children. If we select one child at random, what is the probability that the child is in the third grade?
   a. $p = 32$
   b. $p = .03$
   c. $p = .32$
   d. $p = .38$

3. Probability can be:
   a. between 0 and 1
   b. between −1 and +1
   c. any positive value
   d. any positive or negative value

4. Suppose that a deck of 40 cards has 12 yellow cards and 28 blue cards. In this same deck of cards, 28 cards are numbered and 12 cards have shapes on them. What is the probability that one card chosen at random is numbered?
   a. $p = .15$
   b. $p = .30$
   c. $p = .35$
   d. $p = .70$

LO 2: Describe four types of relationships between multiple outcomes.

5. Which of the following is not one of the four probability relationships?
   a. independent outcomes
   b. complementary outcomes
   c. mutually exclusive outcomes
   d. individual outcomes

6. Two outcomes (A and B) are mutually exclusive when the probability of A is $p = .30$ and the probability of B is $p = .18$. Which probability is equal to 0?

   a. the probability of A or B

   b. the probability of A and B

   c. the probability of A

   d. the probability of B

7. Two outcomes (A and B) are independent when the probability of A is $p = .20$ and the probability of B is $p = .45$. What is the probability of A and B?

   a. $p = .09$

   b. $p = .20$

   c. $p = .45$

   d. $p = .65$

8. If two outcomes are complementary, then the probability of one or the other outcome occurring:

   a. is the same as the probability of one and the other outcome occurring

   b. is equal to 0

   c. is equal to 1

   d. could be any value between 0 and 1

9. A researcher selects a sample of two students from a population of 50 students at a local college. If the researcher does not replace the first participant selected before selecting a second participant, then the two outcomes are:

   a. mutually exclusive

   b. independent

   c. complementary

   d. conditional

LO 3: Define and compute Bayes's theorem for conditional outcomes.

10. A mathematical formula that relates the conditional and marginal probabilities of two conditional outcomes that occur at random is called:

    a. the multiplicative rule

    b. Bayes's theorem

    c. expected value

    d. the additive rule

11. Bayes's theorem is used to compute the probability for:

    a. mutually exclusive outcomes

    b. independent outcomes

    c. complementary outcomes

    d. conditional outcomes

12. The probability that a participant is happy is $p(H) = .55$. The probability that a participant is employed is $p(E) = .65$. The probability that a participant is employed given that he or she is happy is $p(E/H) = .73$. Using the formula for Bayes's theorem, what is the probability that a participant is happy, given that the participant is employed?

    a. $p = .73$
    b. $p = .42$
    c. $p = .62$
    d. $p = .86$

LO 4: Construct a probability distribution for a given random variable.

13. The distribution of probabilities for each outcome of a random variable is called a:

    a. probability distribution
    b. random presentation
    c. mathematical expectation
    d. conditional probability

14. What is the missing probability (A) in the probability distribution given below for the random variable, x?

x	0	1	2	3
$p(x)$	.12	.21	A	.48

    a. .02
    b. .19
    c. .81
    d. 1.00

15. In a probability distribution:

    a. the sum of all probabilities is $p = 1.00$
    b. a probability can never be negative
    c. the probabilities for all possible outcomes of a random variable are distributed
    d. all of the above

16. Based on the following probability distribution, what is the probability of obtaining an outcome of at least 3?

x	0	1	2	3	4
$p(x)$	.22	.11	.24	.31	.12

    a. .03
    b. .31
    c. .43
    d. .88

LO 5: Compute the mean and expected value of a probability distribution.

17. The mean of a probability distribution for a random variable indicates:

    a. the expected value of a random variable

    b. the outcome of a random variable that we can expect to occur on average

    c. the mathematical expectation of a random variable

    d. all of the above

18. Below is the probability distribution for the number of food pellets that are distributed from a feeder at random each day. How many food pellets can we expect an animal to receive on a given day?

Number of Pellets	2	4	6
$p(x)$	.40	.40	.20

    a. 3.6 pellets

    b. 4 pellets

    c. 0.4 pellet

    d. 4.4 pellets

19. An expected value is a long-term mean in that it is the average outcome for a random variable that is observed an infinite number of times.

    a. true

    b. false

LO 6: Compute the variance and standard deviation of a probability distribution.

20. The variance and standard deviation of a probability distribution estimate the:

    a. expected value of a random variable

    b. outcome that we can expect to occur on average

    c. distribution of all other outcomes from the mean for a random variable

    d. all of the above

21. A researcher has participants play a game in which the probabilities of obtaining reinforcement (tokens) are fixed. The probability distribution for the number of tokens participants could win playing the game is given below. What is the standard deviation for this probability distribution?

x	0	1	2	3
$p(x)$	.24	.16	.40	.20

    a. 1.0

    b. 1.06

    c. 1.12

    d. 1.56

22. What is the standard deviation for the following probability distribution of a random variable, x?

x	0	1	2
$p(x)$	.25	.50	.25

a. 0.5

b. .07

c. .71

d. 1.0

LO 7: Compute the mean, variance, and standard deviation of a binomial probability distribution.

23. The binomial probability distribution is used to distribute the probabilities for a random variable:

a. with any number of outcomes

b. that is on a ratio scale of measurement

c. with two or more nominal categories

d. with only two possible outcomes

24. A local population consists of 60% women and 40% men. If we select a sample of 20 people at random from this population, then how many women can we expect will be selected in the sample?

a. 10

b. 11

c. 12

d. 20

25. A video game is fixed such that the probability of losing is $p = .70$ for each play. What is the standard deviation for this binomial probability distribution if we play 40 times?

a. 1.0

b. 2.9

c. 5.0

d. 8.4

Follow the General Instructions Guidebook to complete this exercise. Also, an example for following these steps is provided in the SPSS in Focus section (Section 5.6) of the book. Construct a probability table and conditional probability table in SPSS for this example. Complete and submit the SPSS grading template and a printout of the output file.

Exercise 5.1: Probabilities for Type of Diet and Health

A researcher is interested in the psychological factors that control eating behavior among children. As part of this study, the researcher surveys children to determine whether they are lean/healthy or overweight and whether their diet is generally low fat or high fat. The results from this initial survey are listed below. Use the following data to construct probability distribution tables.

		Type of Diet		
		Low Fat	High Fat	Totals
Health	Lean/healthy	70	20	90
	Overweight	30	80	110
Totals		100	100	200

With regard to the SPSS exercise, answer the following questions:

Based on the table(s) shown in SPSS, state the following values:

What is the probability that a child is overweight?

What is the probability that a child consumes a high-fat diet?

What is the probability that a child is overweight and consumes a high-fat diet?

What is the probability of a child being overweight given that he or she consumes a high-fat diet?

What is the probability of a child consuming a high-fat diet given that he or she is overweight?

Are the two conditional probabilities the same or different? Explain why.

Based on your answers, provide an interpretation of these conditional probabilities.

CHAPTER SUMMARY ORGANIZED BY LEARNING OBJECTIVE

LO 1: Compute a simple probability and explain the relationship between probability and relative frequency.

- Probability (symbolized as p) is the frequency of times an outcome occurs divided by the total number of possible outcomes. Probability varies between 0 and 1 and is never negative.
- To calculate the probability of an outcome for a random variable, x, use the formula for $p(x)$, where $f(x)$ is the frequency of times an outcome occurs, and the sample space is the total number of outcomes possible:

$$p(x) = \frac{f(x)}{sample\ space}.$$

- The two steps to compute the probability formula are (1) find the sample space and (2) find $f(x)$.
- A probability is the same as a relative frequency. To find a probability using the relative frequency, we follow two steps: (1) distribute the frequencies and (2) distribute the relative frequencies.

LO 2: Describe four types of relationships between multiple outcomes.

- Four types of relationships between multiple outcomes are mutually exclusive, independent, complementary, and conditional or dependent outcomes.
- When two outcomes (A and B) are mutually exclusive, the outcomes cannot occur together, but one or the other can occur. Hence, the probability of A and B is equal to 0, and the probability of A or B is stated by the additive rule,

where $\cup$ is the symbol for *or*: $p(A \cup B)$ $= p(A) + p(B)$.
- Two outcomes (A and B) are independent when the probability of one outcome does not affect the probability of the second outcome. To compute the probability that two independent outcomes occur together, we follow the multiplicative rule, where $\cap$ is the symbol for *and*: $p(A \cap B) = p(A) \times p(B)$.
- Two outcomes (A and B) are complementary when the sum of their probabilities is equal to 1.00, so the probability of A or B is $p(A) + p(B) = 1.00$.
- Two outcomes (A and B) are conditional when the probability of one outcome is dependent on the occurrence of the other. We can compute the conditional probability of A, given that B occurred, using the following formula:

$$p(A/B) = \frac{p(B \cap A)}{p(B)}$$

LO 3: Define and compute Bayes's theorem for conditional outcomes.

- **Bayes's theorem,** or **Bayes's law,** is a mathematical formula that relates the conditional and marginal (unconditional) probabilities of two conditional outcomes that occur at random. Bayes's formula has broader applications for inferential statistics than other formulas for conditional probabilities. We can compute the conditional probability of A, given that B occurred, using Bayes's formula:

$$p(A/B) = \frac{p(B/A)\,p(A)}{p(B)}.$$

LO 4–5: Construct a probability distribution for a given random variable and compute the mean and expected value of a probability distribution.

- The probability distribution is the distribution of probabilities for each outcome of a random variable. The sum of probabilities for a probability distribution is equal to 1.
- Mathematical expectation, or expected value, is the mean, or average expected outcome, for a random variable. The expected outcome of a random variable is the sum of the products for each random outcome multiplied by the probability of its occurrence: $\mu = \Sigma(xp)$.

LO 6: Compute the variance and standard deviation of a probability distribution.

- To estimate the variance of a probability distribution, σ^2, for the outcomes of a random variable, x, compute the following formula:

$$\sigma^2 = \Sigma\left((x - \mu)^2 p\right), \text{ or}$$

$$\sigma^2 = \left(\Sigma\left(x^2 p\right) - \mu^2\right).$$

- To estimate the standard deviation of a probability distribution, s, for the outcomes of a random variable, x, take the square root of the variance: $\sigma = \sqrt{\sigma^2}$.

LO 7: Compute the mean, variance, and standard deviation of a binomial probability distribution.

- A binomial probability distribution is the distribution of probabilities for each outcome of a bivariate random variable. A bivariate or dichotomous random variable is one with only two possible outcomes.
- The mean of a binomial probability distribution is the product of the number of trials (n) and the probability of the outcome of interest on an individual trial (p):

$$\mu = np.$$

- The variance of a binomial probability distribution is

$$\sigma^2 = np(1 - p), \text{ or } \sigma^2 = npq.$$

- The standard deviation of a binomial distribution is the square root of the variance: $\sigma = \sqrt{\sigma^2}$.

LO 8: Construct a probability table and conditional probability table using SPSS.

- SPSS can be used to construct probability tables for one or more variables. To construct a probability table, each variable should be coded in the Variable View table. In the Data View tab, the combination of each level for each factor should be arranged across the rows. The corresponding frequencies for each combination of levels are then entered in the last column. Probability and conditional probability tables are created using the Analyze, Descriptive Statistics, and Crosstabs options in the menu bar. A Weight cases . . . option must also be selected from the menu bar.

6

Probability, Normal Distributions, and z Scores

LEARNING OBJECTIVES

After reading this chapter, you should be able to:

1. Identify eight characteristics of the normal distribution.

2. Define the standard normal distribution and the standard normal transformation.

3. Locate proportions of area under any normal curve above the mean, below the mean, and between two scores.

4. Locate scores in a normal distribution with a given probability.

5. Compute the normal approximation to the binomial distribution.

6. Convert raw scores to standard z scores using SPSS.

CHAPTER OUTLINE

6.1 The Normal Distribution in Behavioral Science

Behavioral data in a population tend to be normally distributed, meaning the data are symmetrically distributed around the mean, the median, and the mode, which are values at the center of the distribution. When data in the population are normally distributed, we use the *empirical rule* to determine the probability of an outcome in a research study.

6.2 Characteristics of the Normal Distribution

There are eight key characteristics that define a normal distribution.

1. *The normal distribution is mathematically defined:* An exact normal distribution is defined by a mathematical formula—however, rarely (if ever) do data fall exactly within the limits of the formula.

2. *The normal distribution is theoretical:* Because behavioral data rarely conform exactly to a normal distribution, the idea that data are normally distributed is theoretical.

3. *The mean, median, and mode are all located at the 50th percentile:* In a normal distribution, the mean, median, and mode are all located in the middle of the distribution at the 50th percentile, such that half the data fall above these measures and half fall below.

4. *The normal distribution is symmetrical:* The data in a normal distribution are equally distributed around the mean, median, and mode, making the distribution symmetrical.

5. *The mean can equal any value:* The mean of a normal distribution can be any number from positive to negative infinity.

6. *The standard deviation can equal any positive value:* The standard deviation of a normal distribution can be any positive number greater than 0.

7. *The total area under the curve of a normal distribution is equal to 1.00:* Half the area under the normal curve (or 50% of scores) falls above the mean, and half the area under the normal curve (or 50% of scores) falls below the mean. Hence, the total area under the normal curve is 1.00.

8. *The tails of a normal distribution are asymptotic:* The tails of the normal distribution are always approaching the x-axis but never touch it, allowing for the possibility of outliers in a normal distribution.

6.3 Research in Focus: The Statistical Norm

Approximately 95% of scores in a normal distribution will fall within 2 standard deviations (*SD*) of the mean. This percentage tends to be described in behavioral research as *the statistical norm*. The 5% of scores that fall outside of 2 *SD* of the mean are considered "not normal" because they fall far from the mean.

6.4 The Standard Normal Distribution

To determine the likelihood of obtaining a score in any normal distribution, researchers defined the standard normal distribution. All other normal distributions can then be converted to the standard normal distribution using the following *z* transformation formulas:

$$\text{Population } z \text{ transformation: } z = \frac{x - \mu}{\sigma}.$$

$$\text{Sample } z \text{ transformation: } z = \frac{x - M}{SD}.$$

- The standard normal distribution has a mean of 0 and a standard deviation of 1. The *z* distribution is distributed in *z*-score units along the *x*-axis.
- A *z* score is a value on the *x*-axis of the *z* distribution that specifies the distance from the mean in standard deviations.

6.5 The Unit Normal Table: A Brief Introduction

We can find the probability of obtaining a score when we know its *z* score in the standard normal distribution. The proportion of area or probability of *z* scores in the standard normal distribution is listed in the unit normal table (see Table B.1 in Appendix B of the book; also reprinted in the appendix of this study guide).

To read the *z* table, we use three columns:

- *Column A lists the z scores:* Column A in the *z* table lists only positive *z* scores. Because the *z* distribution is symmetrical, we know that a proportion associated with a *z* score above the mean is identical to that below the mean.
- *Column B lists the area between a z score and the mean:* As a *z* score is farther from the mean, the area under the curve between that *z* score and the mean increases.
- *Column C lists the area from a z score toward the tail:* As a *z* score is farther from the mean, the area under the curve between that *z* score and the tail decreases.

6.6 Locating Proportions

To locate the proportion, or probability, of a score in any normal distribution, we follow two steps:

- Step 1: Transform a raw score into a z score.
- Step 2: Locate the corresponding proportion for the z score in the unit normal table.

6.7 Locating Scores

To locate the raw score in a normal distribution based on the probability of that score occurring, we follow two steps:

- Step 1: Locate a z score associated with a given proportion in the unit normal table.
- Step 2: Transform the z score into a raw score (x).

6.8 SPSS in Focus: Converting Raw Scores to Standard z Scores

SPSS can be used to convert raw scores to standard z scores. After entering the data for a variable, we can convert raw scores to standard z scores using the Analyze, Descriptive Statistics, and Descriptives options in the menu bar. The z scores will appear in the Data View tab.

6.9 Going From Binomial to Normal

The standard normal distribution was derived from the binomial distribution. Thus, for a binomial distribution, as long as the sample size (n) is greater than or equal to 2, and as long as both np and nq (the sample size times the probability of the first outcome, p, and the sample size times the probability of the complementary outcome, q) are greater than 10, the binomial distribution will approximate a normal distribution.

6.10 The Normal Approximation to the Binomial Distribution

There are five steps to find the probability of a bivariate outcome.

- *Step 1: Check for normality:* If both np and nq are greater than 10, then the binomial distribution approximates a normal distribution.

- *Step 2: Compute the mean and standard deviation:* Compute the mean and the standard deviation of a binomial distribution using the following formulas, respectively:

$$\mu = np.$$

$$\sigma = \sqrt{npq}.$$

- *Step 3: Find the real limits:* The *real limits* for any binomial variable are the upper and lower values within which the probability of obtaining an outcome is contained. This can be defined as $x \pm 0.5$.
- *Step 4: Locate the* z *score for each real limit:* Calculate the z score for each real limit computed in Step 3.
- *Step 5: Find the proportion located within the real limits:* Find the proportion within the real limits using the unit normal table.

CHAPTER FORMULAS

z Transformations

$z = \dfrac{x - \mu}{\sigma}$ (*z* transformation for a population of scores)

$z = \dfrac{x - M}{SD}$ (*z* transformation for a sample of scores)

TIPS AND CAUTIONS FOR STUDENTS

- *Characteristics of the normal distribution:* Remember that the normal distribution is a theoretical distribution. In truth, most behavior does not exactly fit within the limits of the equation used to define the normal distribution. Instead, the behaviors we observe approximate the shape of a normal distribution. When we use inferential statistics, we will make an assumption that the populations we are interested in studying have data that are approximately normally distributed. As a general rule, as long as data in the population approximate a normal distribution, we can safely make this assumption.

- z *distribution:* Converting a score in any normal distribution to a *z* score will give you the position of that score in the standard normal distribution. The *z* score, which is a standard deviation, tells you the number of standard deviations that a score deviates from the mean in that distribution. Larger *z* scores are associated with a smaller probability of occurrence. Hence, we can use *z* scores to determine the distance that a score deviates from the mean and the probability of its occurrence.

- *Locating proportions:* When using the unit normal table to look up proportions, do not worry about whether the *z* score is negative or positive. Because the *z* distribution is symmetrical, any proportion in the positive tail of the distribution will be mirrored in the negative tail. This is why only positive values are listed in the unit normal table. Keep in mind that if the *z* score is negative, then the proportion, or area under the curve, will fall in the left or bottom half of the distribution.

```
G U I S B G G H U A G D I R Z J R O K F M M C O M S C Z C Z
J T B E Q G B Y A O Y W D E N P H B Q G Q R Z Y W U R U G J
D H F V Q N C E A T H S N W G Q J Y B W L B I V J R T C H W
O H R R K R R H N Z N C A X Z X E D S F K T S K X C Y J L Z
U Z X E F Z A W L P Z B K C J J B L W L N Q K B L U P H T I
S H W O E N E V R Z W H R D G J J Q A O A M N Z M E P V T L
K T C D W S F W X V E F U W P F Y H V Z T A B L E N B K Y H
F H G T W N O R M A L D I S T R I B U T I O N I B A X J C G
O D E O G O E N T E J V S Q K G F I Z R A L L X V Q Y I U W
X U C N H S Y M M E T R I C A L D I S T R I B U T I O N L L
A K A H X R E A L L I M I T S G X F C V L N D L V V P K L F
D R H S Q Q V T W G P S E I Z G U I S Z S C O R E S V T D F
J C K C U X G A U S S I A N D I S T R I B U T I O N S Z A I
K R H E T T S J R C E I V F S I U M P B H S R C X I E I N V
Y U W Y E B W E F M B Y A R Y W N W R U A K J Z B S A F G K
O K V W D K M X B R L P G C Z I R Z D A V H R T U N K W W M
A R X V Y R D E N O K Q V Z I K E H A S B A B G P G T C B Q
A P A P Q T S L E H F M L P Q F M R K K J C W D K A Q R F R
Y A D X O V P G I O S S D S N O P L P K U B R Q G X S W E Q
S T A N D A R D N O R M A L T R A N S F O R M A T I O N F R
D A F M J E J N A V P G J V S Q Z E Q W L E B V X X J M R R
C S B R L R N R J J F B K U U N R V Y Q Y O G I F Y Y J O M
U W W J S W E R K A C H U H Q J T G B K F O O B S N M T M M
U N I T N O R M A L T A B L E H V S D C X O J F B C X I A L
X N Q T Z R V E S I E G G H V Q E K L F X I Z F X S H E S E
D B E D R O R B E L L S H A P E D D I S T R I B U T I O N J
C D Z T R A N S F O R M A T I O N U N B Q H A U X Q H B J K
X N W V N O N L V G J Q M N F D C D P H O K W J O P H E H H
K S T A N D A R D N O R M A L D I S T R I B U T I O N B J F
U H H Q E J P C A R Y G S A V N P U O E M C W M Q N G X H J
```

BELL-SHAPED DISTRIBUTION

GAUSSIAN DISTRIBUTION

NORMAL DISTRIBUTION

REAL LIMITS

STANDARD NORMAL DISTRIBUTION

STANDARD NORMAL TRANSFORMATION

SYMMETRICAL DISTRIBUTION

UNIT NORMAL TABLE

Z SCORES

Z TABLE

Z TRANSFORMATION

CROSSWORD PUZZLES

ACROSS

5 A formula used to convert any normal distribution with any mean and any variance to a standard normal distribution with a mean equal to 0 and a standard deviation equal to 1.

6 The upper and lower values within which the probability for obtaining the outcome of a binomial variable is contained.

7 A value on the x-axis of a standard normal distribution.

8 A theoretical distribution with data that are symmetrically distributed around the mean, the median, and the mode.

DOWN

1 A normal distribution with a mean equal to 0 and a standard deviation equal to 1.

2 A different name for the standard normal distribution.

3 A different name for the standard normal transformation.

4 A type of probability distribution table displaying a list of z scores and the corresponding probabilities associated with each z score listed.

PRACTICE QUIZZES

LO 1: Identify eight characteristics of the normal distribution.

1. A theoretical distribution in which scores are symmetrically distributed above and below the mean, the median, and the mode at the center of the distribution is called a:

   a. normal distribution

   b. fixed distribution

   c. skewed distribution

   d. bimodal distribution

2. The mean, the median, and the mode are located _____ of a normal distribution.

   a. at the extremes

   b. at the 50th percentile

   c. in the upper tail

   d. in different locations

3. The distribution of data above the mean in a normal distribution is the same as the distribution of data below the mean. Hence, the normal distribution is:

   a. disproportional

   b. skewed

   c. asymptotic

   d. symmetrical

4. The tails of the normal distribution are always approaching the x-axis but never touch it. Hence, the normal distribution is:

   a. disproportional

   b. symmetrical

   c. asymptotic

   d. skewed

5. Which of the following statements about the normal distribution is true?

   a. the mean can equal any value

   b. the standard deviation can equal any positive value

   c. the total area under the normal curve is equal to 1.0

   d. all of the above

LO 2: Define the standard normal distribution and the standard normal transformation.

6. A normal distribution with a mean of 0 and a standard deviation of 1 is called a:

   a. small normal distribution

   b. minimal normal distribution

   c. standard normal distribution

   d. centered normal distribution

7. A normal distribution has a mean of 10 and a standard deviation of 2. What is the z score for $x = 13$?

   a. 0.7

   b. 1.5

   c. 3.0

   d. 13

8. A normal distribution has a mean of 7.5 and a variance of 4. What is the z score for $x = 9.5$?

   a. 0.5

   b. 1.0

   c. 1.5

   d. 2.0

LO 3: Locate proportions of area under any normal curve above the mean, below the mean, and between two scores.

9. A normal distribution has a mean equal to 3.4. What is the probability of a score above the mean?

   a. 0

   b. 0.5

   c. 1.0

   d. not enough information

10. The unit normal table does not have negative z scores listed. Why?

   a. because it is not possible to observe negative z scores

   b. because negative z scores become positive when computed using a z transformation

   c. because a normal distribution is symmetrical, so proportions above and below the mean at any given z score are the same

   d. because probabilities are negative for negative z scores, so probabilities do not have meaning when z scores are negative

11. A normal distribution has a mean equal to 10 and a standard deviation equal to 2. Which outcome is more probable?

    a. obtaining a score between 10 and 12

    b. obtaining a score between 11 and 13

    c. none; they are equally probable

12. A normal distribution of quiz scores has a mean equal to 6 and a variance equal to 1.5. Which outcome is more probable?

    a. scoring above a 3.8 on this quiz

    b. scoring below an 8.2 on this quiz

    c. none; they are equally probable

13. A researcher gives two practice exams, with scores normally distributed on each exam. If Exam 1 is distributed as 71 ± 9.2 ($M ± SD$) and Exam 2 is distributed as 75 ± 4.8 ($M ± SD$), then on which exam is a score of 80 more likely?

    a. Exam 1

    b. Exam 2

    c. none; a score of 80 is equally likely

LO 4: Locate scores in a normal distribution with a given probability.

14. A normal distribution has a mean equal to 4.6 and a standard deviation equal to 1.4. What score is the cutoff for the top 10% of this distribution?

    a. .10

    b. 1.28

    c. 6.00

    d. 6.39

15. When computing a z transformation to find a score at a given probability for a distribution with a given mean and standard deviation, which value in the z-transformation formula is a variable (i.e., which value is unknown)?

    a. z

    b. M

    c. x

    d. SD

16. A normal distribution of memory recall scores has a mean equal to 12 items recalled and a standard deviation equal to 2.3. If Participant A scores a 16.6 and Participant B scores a 15.2, then which participant scored in the top 10% on this memory recall test?

    a. Participant A

    b. Participant B

    c. none; they both failed to score in the top 10%

    d. both; they both scored in the top 10%

17. A normal distribution has a mean equal to 10 and a standard deviation equal to 1. What is the z-score cutoff for the top and bottom 2.5% of this distribution?

    a. ±1.28

    b. ±1.96

    c. ±1.645

    d. ±10.96

LO 5: Compute the normal approximation to the binomial distribution.

18. The normal distribution was derived from the _____ distribution.

    a. skewed

    b. bimodal

    c. binomial

    d. standard

19. Suppose we select a sample from a population of children in which an equal number of children live with or without their biological parents. We select a sample of 50 children. What is the probability that 30 children in this sample will be children who live with their biological parents? *Hint:* Use the normal approximation to the binomial distribution, where p and q equal .50.

    a. .0414

    b. .414

    c. .50

20. Suppose that 10% of students earn an A in a statistics course. Using this percentage, what is the probability that exactly 25 students in a random sample of 200 students will earn an A in a statistics course? *Hint:* Use the normal approximation to the binomial distribution, where $p = .10$ (the probability that a student earns an A) and $q = .90$ (the probability that a student does not earn an A).

    a. .48

    b. .048

    c. .10

    d. .90

Follow the General Instructions Guidebook to complete this exercise. Also, an example for following these steps is provided in the SPSS in Focus section (Section 6.8) of the book. Complete and submit the SPSS grading template and a printout of the output file.

Exercise 6.1: Standardizing Participant Reactions

A researcher has participants read a vignette that describes a person making inappropriate remarks toward a colleague at work, and then they are asked to complete a survey. Lower total scores on the survey indicate more negative impressions of the person described in the vignette; higher total scores indicate more positive impressions. Convert the following data to *z* scores to determine who scored above, below, and at the mean in this sample.

18	19	8	20
12	14	12	25
17	14	8	14
8	14	20	14
23	9	16	15
7	17	14	11
10	21	14	19
10	7	18	8
12	11	5	10
25	8	19	14

With regard to the SPSS exercise, answer the following questions:

Based on the table shown in SPSS, state the following values for the original data:

    Sample size   _____

    Minimum score   _____

    Maximum score   _____

    Mean score   _____

    Standard deviation   _____

Based on the *z* scores listed in the *z*-scores column (Data View), state the following values:

    Minimum *z* score   _____

    Maximum *z* score   _____

    Mean *z* score   _____

State how many scores were:

    Above the mean   _____

    Below the mean   _____

    Equal to the mean   _____

CHAPTER SUMMARY ORGANIZED BY LEARNING OBJECTIVE

LO 1: Identify eight characteristics of the normal distribution.

- The normal distribution is a theoretical distribution in which scores are symmetrically distributed above and below the mean, the median, and the mode at the center of the distribution.
- Eight characteristics of a normal distribution are as follows:

  1. The normal distribution is mathematically defined.
  2. The normal distribution is theoretical.
  3. The mean, the median, and the mode are all located at the 50th percentile.
  4. The normal distribution is symmetrical.
  5. The mean can equal any value.
  6. The standard deviation can equal any positive value.
  7. The total area under the curve of a normal distribution is equal to 1.00.
  8. The tails of a normal distribution are asymptotic.

LO 2: Define the standard normal distribution and the standard normal transformation.

- The standard normal distribution, or z distribution, is a normal distribution with a mean equal to 0 and a standard deviation equal to 1. The standard normal distribution is distributed in z score units along the x-axis.
- The standard normal transformation, or z transformation, is an equation that converts any normal distribution with any mean and any positive standard deviation into a standard normal distribution with a mean equal to 0 and a standard deviation equal to 1:

  For a population: $z = \dfrac{x - \mu}{\sigma}$.

  For a sample: $z = \dfrac{x - M}{SD}$.

- The probabilities of z scores in a standard normal distribution are listed in the unit normal table in Table B.1 in Appendix B.

LO 3: Locate proportions of area under any normal curve above the mean, below the mean, and between two scores.

- To locate the proportion, and therefore probabilities, for scores in any normal distribution, we follow two steps:

  Step 1: Transform a raw score (x) into a z score.

  Step 2: Locate the corresponding proportion for the z score in the unit normal table.

LO 4: Locate scores in a normal distribution with a given probability.

- To locate scores that fall within a given proportion, or probability, we follow two steps:

  Step 1: Locate a z score associated with a given proportion in the unit normal table.

  Step 2: Transform the z score into a raw score (x).

LO 5: Compute the normal approximation to the binomial distribution.

- It is appropriate to use the normal distribution to approximate or estimate binomial probabilities when $np > 10$ and $nq > 10$.
- To use the normal approximation to estimate probabilities in a binomial distribution, follow five steps:

Step 1: Check for normality.

Step 2: Compute the mean and standard deviation.

Step 3: Find the real limits.

Step 4: Locate the *z* score for each real limit.

Step 5: Find the proportion located within the real limits.

LO 6: Convert raw scores to standard *z* scores using SPSS.

- SPSS can be used to convert raw scores to standard *z* scores. After entering the data for each variable, raw scores are converted to standard *z* scores using the Analyze, Descriptive Statistics, and Descriptives options in the menu bar. These actions will allow you to select the "Save standardized values as variables" option to convert raw scores to standard *z* scores.

7

Probability and Sampling Distributions

LEARNING OBJECTIVES

After reading this chapter, you should be able to:

1. Define sampling distribution.

2. Compare theoretical and experimental sampling strategies.

3. Identify three characteristics of the sampling distribution of the sample mean.

4. Calculate the mean and standard error of a sampling distribution of the sample mean and draw the shape of this distribution.

5. Identify three characteristics of the sampling distribution of the sample variance.

6. Explain the relationship between standard error, standard deviation, and sample size.

7. Compute z transformations for the sampling distribution of the sample mean.

8. Summarize the standard error of the mean in APA format.

9. Compute the estimate for the standard error of the mean using SPSS.

7.1 Selecting Samples From Populations

In inferential statistics, researchers select a sample or portion of data from a larger population to learn more about characteristics in a population. The mean and the variance of a population tend to be of considerable interest to researchers. For this reason, it is important to understand how sample statistics (e.g., the sample mean and the variance) are related to population parameters (e.g., the population mean and the variance). To determine how samples are related to populations, we use sampling distributions of the mean and the variance for all possible samples of a given size (*n*) from a population.

Sampling and conditional probabilities: To ensure that the probability of selecting each participant is the same, participants must be replaced after each selection before selecting again from the population.

- *Sampling without replacement:* A method of sampling in which each participant selected is *not* replaced before the next selection.
- *Sampling with replacement:* A method of sampling in which each participant selected *is* replaced before the next selection. This ensures that the probability of each selection is the same and is the basis for statistical theory.

7.2 Selecting a Sample: Who's In and Who's Out?

It is important to develop a *sample design* once you have designated a population of interest to study. A sample design is a plan for how individuals in a population of interest will be selected. Two questions must be asked when creating a sample design:

1. Does the order of selecting participants matter?

2. Do we replace each selection before the next draw?

Sampling strategy: The basis for statistical theory: The type of sampling used to develop statistical theory requires that the answer to the two questions be yes.

- *Order matters:* If two participants (A and B) are selected from a population, then selecting Participant A first, then B, is regarded as a different sample than selecting Participant B first, then A.
- *Sample with replacement:* This means that the same participant can be selected two or more times in a sample because we replace each selection before making another selection.

Sampling strategy: Most used in behavioral research: The type of sampling used in behavioral research typically requires that the answer to the two questions be no.

- *Order does not matter:* Selecting Participant A, then B, is regarded as the same sample as selecting Participant B, then A.
- *Sample without replacement:* This means that the same participant can never be sampled twice. For example, in a population of three people (A, B, and C), if we select samples of size 2, then samples of AA, BB, and CC from the population are not possible.

7.3 Sampling Distributions: The Mean

We can use theoretical sampling to construct a sampling distribution of the mean for samples of a given size to determine how well a sample mean estimates the value of an unknown population mean.

- *Unbiased estimator:* On average, the sample mean is equal to the population mean—hence, the sample mean is an unbiased estimator of the population mean.
- *Central limit theorem:* The sampling distribution of all possible sample means of a given size is normally distributed, regardless of the distribution of the scores in the population.
- *Minimum variance:* The variance of a sampling distribution of the mean is the smallest possible variance. The standard deviation of a sampling distribution is called the *standard error of the mean.*
  - Standard error of the mean (*SEM*): The standard deviation of a sampling distribution of sample means. It is the standard error or distance that sample mean values deviate from the value of the population mean.

7.4 Sampling Distributions: The Variance

We can use theoretical sampling to construct a sampling distribution of the variance for samples of a given size to determine how well the sample variance estimates the value of an unknown population variance.

For each sample selected, the sample variance is computed by dividing the sum of squares (*SS*) by $n - 1$.

- *Unbiased estimator:* The mean of the sampling distribution of the sample variance is equal to the population variance on average—the sample variance is an unbiased estimator of the population variance when we divide *SS* by $n - 1$ to compute sample variance.
- *Skewed distribution rule:* The sampling distribution of the sample variance is positively skewed, regardless of the distribution of scores in the population.
- *No minimum variance:* The sampling distribution of the sample variance does not have minimum variance because sample variances can vary far from the actual population variance.

7.5 The Standard Error of the Mean

The *standard error of the mean* is the standard deviation for a sampling distribution of sample means:

$$\sigma_M = \sqrt{\frac{\sigma^2}{n}} = \frac{\sigma}{\sqrt{n}}.$$

Sampling error: The extent to which sample means selected from the same population differ from one another. This difference, which occurs by chance, is measured by the standard error of the mean.

We follow three steps to construct a sampling distribution:

- Identify the mean of the sampling distribution.
- Compute the standard error of the mean (*SEM*).
- Distribute the possible sample means 3 *SEM* above and below the mean.

7.6 Factors That Decrease Standard Error

The following key factors decrease the standard error of the mean.

- As the population standard deviation decreases, the standard error decreases.
- *The law of large numbers:* As the sample size increases, the standard error decreases.

7.7 SPSS in Focus: Estimating the Standard Error of the Mean

SPSS can be used to compute the standard error of the mean. An estimate of the standard error is computed using the Analyze, Descriptive Statistics, and Descriptives options in the menu bar. These actions will bring up a dialog box that will allow you to identify the variable, select Options, and choose the S.E. mean option to compute an estimate for the standard error.

We estimate the standard error by substituting the sample standard deviation in place of the population standard deviation in the formula for standard error, as shown in the following formula. SPSS does this automatically.

$$s_M = \frac{s}{\sqrt{n}}.$$

7.8 APA in Focus: Reporting the Standard Error

The *Publication Manual of the American Psychological Association* (American Psychological Association, 2009) recommends any combination of three ways to report the standard error. The *SEM* can be reported directly in the text, in a table, or in a figure.

7.9 Standard Normal Transformations With Sampling Distributions

Because the sampling distribution approximates a normal distribution, we can find the probability of obtaining a sample mean using the standard normal distribution by applying the z transformation.

- Step 1: Transform a sample mean (M) into a z score using the following formula:

$$z = \frac{M - \mu}{\sigma_M}.$$

- Step 2: Locate the corresponding proportion for the z score in the unit normal table.

CHAPTER FORMULAS

z Transformations

$z = \dfrac{M - \mu}{\sigma_M}$ (*z* transformation for a distribution of sample means)

Standard Error

$\sigma_M = \sqrt{\dfrac{\sigma^2}{n}} = \dfrac{\sigma}{\sqrt{n}}$ (Standard error of the mean)

TIPS AND CAUTIONS FOR STUDENTS

- *The sampling distribution:* Sampling distributions are used to determine how samples selected from a given population are related to parameters in the population. To construct a sampling distribution of the mean, for example, we select all possible samples of a given size from a given population of interest. So we are selecting a population of sample means and not individual scores. With larger samples, we get better estimates of the population mean because we basically have more information or data. In a sampling distribution, this means that the distribution of possible sample means we could select from a population is closer to the actual population mean on average, which is why increasing the sample size reduces the standard error.

- *Standard error:* Standard error is calculated by examining the differences of each sample mean from the population mean in a sampling distribution. Notice that the population mean is the mean of a sampling distribution. The variance (and therefore standard deviation) in the population will affect the standard error of the mean because the population standard deviation is used in the formula to compute standard error. Hence, the standard error will be smaller for populations with a smaller standard deviation compared to populations with a larger standard deviation.

- *Standard normal transformations and the sampling distribution:* Note that the standard error is part of the equation to transform a sample mean into a *z* score. Therefore, it makes sense to find the standard error first before trying to calculate a *z* transformation. Once you compute the standard error, it becomes a matter of simply substituting values into the equation.

KEY TERM WORD SEARCHES

S	A	M	P	L	E	D	E	S	I	G	N	X	J	L	E	K	H	M	D	C	X	D	S	P	A	D	X	J	U
J	Z	C	O	M	L	H	R	T	E	H	X	S	W	L	R	M	L	N	Z	A	Z	X	T	F	D	X	V	N	X
K	E	U	A	U	I	L	A	W	O	F	L	A	R	G	E	N	U	M	B	E	R	S	A	S	K	R	L	J	R
P	X	D	N	R	D	E	G	K	A	S	A	D	O	J	J	T	K	B	I	I	I	Q	T	A	I	I	Z	S	M
W	Y	O	Z	H	V	W	P	W	N	H	U	O	Y	T	U	V	W	H	P	K	R	A	Y	M	A	R	I	A	G
H	K	T	I	D	E	R	J	M	L	S	T	H	S	U	N	F	C	G	U	K	P	V	X	P	B	P	J	M	C
F	X	Q	O	G	M	C	Q	H	L	U	Z	Q	X	P	G	J	C	C	Z	X	Q	D	U	L	D	Q	G	P	Y
Q	U	M	M	V	H	U	E	P	E	O	V	E	M	V	B	M	B	L	D	Q	W	U	I	I	V	R	U	L	C
M	N	Q	L	B	C	U	L	N	Z	O	Z	V	Y	Z	R	W	H	K	S	O	Y	P	E	N	D	I	C	I	J
S	B	N	B	K	D	I	A	R	T	A	F	I	D	C	M	A	S	N	G	B	R	C	L	G	U	R	P	N	K
Q	I	X	W	I	F	X	Q	H	Z	R	S	B	Y	P	L	R	U	H	Z	M	O	D	H	W	N	P	F	G	C
Y	A	U	M	Z	A	Y	G	S	U	S	A	R	C	V	V	H	S	W	D	T	Y	U	X	I	K	Q	W	E	V
M	S	Z	G	L	C	S	K	K	Q	C	Z	L	W	V	A	U	U	F	U	S	A	S	M	T	E	R	V	R	H
E	E	N	O	L	F	D	E	J	Q	D	L	H	L	M	I	Q	H	S	E	T	I	W	A	H	Y	I	D	R	P
C	D	B	K	E	J	I	U	D	K	E	Y	X	V	I	F	W	W	M	F	X	J	N	S	O	C	R	S	O	Z
H	E	K	W	Z	G	B	O	L	E	W	D	B	Z	L	M	T	D	M	C	E	S	K	X	U	W	P	M	R	J
V	S	F	P	Q	W	Q	Z	R	E	S	B	X	Y	K	X	I	W	I	K	J	T	U	M	T	D	Q	F	T	A
P	T	H	K	I	C	I	O	K	P	K	T	W	Z	U	Z	M	T	C	I	G	S	F	O	R	G	R	V	C	M
P	I	C	R	X	C	C	J	P	G	J	O	I	J	C	S	J	N	T	U	N	A	I	P	E	H	T	S	D	M
K	M	A	L	X	A	O	G	P	S	L	S	S	M	I	U	P	F	S	H	D	N	Z	E	P	V	C	B	X	T
V	A	T	X	F	V	Z	T	Q	R	I	E	J	I	A	A	D	M	A	X	E	U	C	E	L	S	D	K	R	D
E	T	E	H	L	E	K	A	G	T	M	S	M	Q	T	T	Y	S	C	H	A	O	J	V	A	V	A	S	Z	Y
G	O	V	O	P	A	N	O	S	U	P	I	F	D	U	I	O	B	G	Q	U	N	R	H	C	D	C	M	D	L
J	R	I	I	R	I	O	M	G	D	E	R	D	M	E	Y	X	R	Y	J	J	X	D	E	E	A	X	T	G	F
Y	F	L	Q	A	P	Y	S	T	A	N	D	A	R	D	E	R	R	O	R	O	F	T	H	E	M	E	A	N	A
F	S	C	M	O	E	F	J	D	G	T	T	X	Q	E	K	D	E	P	O	J	C	U	D	E	M	D	I	C	I
P	K	D	Q	A	P	Y	M	P	R	X	A	T	N	V	C	P	D	G	Q	V	I	C	B	N	X	B	H	C	Y
Z	G	G	B	X	U	S	D	D	S	H	S	R	U	M	G	P	V	V	H	R	N	C	C	T	M	C	G	I	B
H	C	I	V	O	S	A	M	P	L	I	N	G	D	I	S	T	R	I	B	U	T	I	O	N	X	Q	K	R	Y
W	T	C	Z	T	C	S	A	M	P	L	I	N	G	W	I	T	H	R	E	P	L	A	C	E	M	E	N	T	M

BIASED ESTIMATOR

CENTRAL LIMIT THEOREM

LAW OF LARGE NUMBERS

SAMPLE DESIGN

SAMPLING DISTRIBUTION

SAMPLING ERROR

SAMPLING WITH REPLACEMENT

SAMPLING WITHOUT REPLACEMENT

STANDARD ERROR OF THE MEAN

UNBIASED ESTIMATOR

CROSSWORD PUZZLES

ACROSS

1 A method for sampling, where each participant or item selected is replaced before the next selection.

3 The extent to which sample means selected from the same population differ from one another.

7 A theorem that states that regardless of the distribution of scores in a population, the sampling distribution of sample means selected from that population will be approximately normally distributed.

8 The standard deviation of a sampling distribution of sample means.

DOWN

1 A method of sampling, where each participant or item selected is not replaced before the next selection.

2 A distribution of all sample means or sample variances that could be obtained in samples of a given size from the same population.

4 A law that states that increasing the number of observations or the sample size in a study will decrease the standard error.

5 A specific plan or protocol for how individuals will be selected or sampled from a population of interest.

6 A sample statistic that equals the value of the population parameter on average.

PRACTICE QUIZZES

LO 1: Define sampling distribution.

1. A distribution of all possible sample means that could be obtained in samples of a given size from the same population is called a:

    a. normal distribution

    b. sampling distribution

    c. binomial distribution

    d. skewed distribution

2. We can determine the probability of obtaining a sample mean from a population with a given population mean by using a:

    a. predictive distribution

    b. bimodal distribution

    c. sampling distribution

    d. population distribution

3. A sampling distribution:

    a. can be used to determine the likelihood of obtaining outcomes in a sample from a given population

    b. of the sample mean is approximately normally distributed

    c. of the sample variance is approximately positively skewed

    d. all of the above

LO 2: Compare theoretical and experimental sampling strategies.

4. Theoretical sampling is the basis for _____; experimental sampling is most used in _____.

    a. statistical theory; behavioral research

    b. behavioral research; statistical theory

    c. behavioral research; behavioral research

    d. statistical theory; statistical theory

5. A researcher samples from a hypothetical population of four people (A, B, C, D). Which of the following samples of size two ($n = 2$) can be selected from this population using theoretical sampling?

    a. Person A and Person A

    b. Person B and Person B

    c. Person A and Person D

    d. all of the above

6. A researcher samples from a hypothetical population of four people (A, B, C, D). Which of the following samples of size two ($n = 2$) can be selected from this population using experimental sampling?

   a. Person A and Person A

   b. Person B and Person B

   c. Person A and Person D

   d. all of the above

7. How many samples of size 4 can be selected from a population of six people using theoretical sampling?

   a. 4

   b. 15

   c. 1,296

   d. 4,096

8. How many samples of size 4 can be selected from a population of six people using experimental sampling?

   a. 4

   b. 15

   c. 1,296

   d. 4,096

LO 3: Identify three characteristics of the sampling distribution of the sample mean.

9. Values in a sampling distribution of the sample mean:

   a. are approximately normally distributed

   b. are always equal to the population mean

   c. can never be negative

   d. both a and c

10. The sample mean is an unbiased estimator of the population mean. What does this mean?

    a. the sampling distribution of the mean is approximately normally distributed

    b. a randomly selected sample mean equals the population mean on average

    c. the sample mean and the population mean are both estimates

    d. both a and b

11. The concept of the _____ explains that the sampling distribution of the sample mean is approximately normally distributed, regardless of the distribution in the population.

    a. unbiased estimator

    b. conditional probability

    c. random sampling

    d. central limit theorem

LO 4: Calculate the mean and standard error of a sampling distribution of the sample mean and draw the shape of this distribution.

12. Which of the following is the approximate shape of the sampling distribution of the sample mean?

    a.

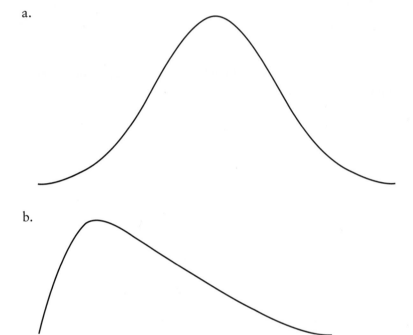

    b.

13. A researcher selects a sample of 25 participants from a population with a standard deviation equal to 5. What is the standard error of the mean for the sampling distribution?

    a. 0.2

    b. 1

    c. 5

    d. 25

14. A researcher selects a sample of 25 participants from a population with a mean of 20 and a standard deviation of 10. What is the range of values for the sample mean that fall within 1 standard error of the mean in a sampling distribution?

    a. 16 to 24

    b. 21 to 29

    c. 18 to 22

    d. 18.5 to 21.5

15. The range of values for the sample mean that fall within 1 standard error of the mean in a sampling distribution is $M = 39$ to $M = 43$. What is the mean of the sampling distribution, and what is the standard error?

    a. mean = 41, standard error = 2

    b. mean = 39 or 43, standard error = 4

c. mean = 41, standard error = 4

d. the mean and the standard error are unknown

LO 5: Identify three characteristics of the sampling distribution of the sample variance.

16. Which of the following is the approximate shape of the sampling distribution of the sample variance?

a.

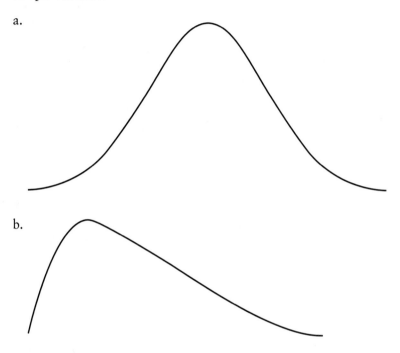

b.

17. The sample variance is an unbiased estimator of the population variance when:

a. *SS* is divided by *N*

b. *SS* is divided by (*n* – 1)

c. *SS* is divided by *df*

d. both b and c

18. Which of the following is *not* a characteristic of the sampling distribution of the sample variance?

a. the sample variance is an unbiased estimator when *SS* is divided by *df*

b. the sampling distribution of the sample variance is approximately positively skewed

c. the sample variance has minimum variance when *SS* is divided by *n*

d. the sample variance has minimum variance when *SS* is divided by *df*

LO 6: Explain the relationship between standard error, standard deviation, and sample size.

19. The standard error of the mean is:

a. the standard deviation for a sampling distribution

b. a measure of the distance that sample means deviate from the population mean

    c. equal to the population standard deviation divided by the square root of the sample size

    d. all of the above

20. Researcher A selects a sample of 20 participants. Researcher B selects a sample of 30 participants. If both samples were selected from the same population, then which researcher selected a sample associated with a larger standard error?

    a. Researcher A

    b. Researcher B

    c. the standard error is the same in both samples

21. Two researchers select samples of the same size. Researcher A selects a sample from a population with a standard deviation equal to 10. Researcher B selects a sample from a population with a standard deviation equal to 20. Which researcher selected a sample associated with a larger standard error?

    a. Researcher A

    b. Researcher B

    c. the standard error is the same in both samples

LO 7: Compute z transformations for the sampling distribution of the sample mean.

22. A researcher selects a sample of nine participants from a population with a mean equal to 10 and a standard deviation equal to 3. What is the z score for selecting a sample mean equal to 7.0 from this population?

    a. +3.00

    b. −3.00

    c. +1.00

    d. −1.00

23. A researcher selects a sample of nine participants from a population with a mean equal to 10 and a standard deviation equal to 3. What is the probability of selecting a sample mean of 7.0 or less from this population?

    a. .0013

    b. .4987

    c. .9987

    d. 1.00

24. A researcher selects a sample of 36 participants from a population with a mean equal to 101 and a standard deviation equal to 9. What is the probability of selecting a sample mean of 104 or greater from this population?

    a. less than .0001

    b. .3707

    c. .4772

    d. .0228

LO 8: Summarize the standard error of the mean in APA format.

25. The standard error of the mean can be reported in a research journal:

    a. in the text of an article

    b. in a table

    c. in a graph

    d. any of the above

26. An article states that a sample of 10 rat subjects took 12 ± 2.3 ($M \pm SEM$) seconds to complete a radial arm maze. Which value is the standard error of the mean?

    a. 10

    b. 12

    c. 2.3

    d. the standard error of the mean is not given

27. A researcher states that a sample of 26 parents spent 112 ± 22.3 ($M \pm SEM$) dollars on their children during the holiday season. Which value is the standard error of the mean?

    a. 22.3

    b. 26

    c. 112

    d. the standard error of the mean is not given

SPSS IN FOCUS

Estimating the Standard Error of the Mean

Follow the General Instructions Guidebook to complete this exercise. Also, an example for following these steps is provided in the SPSS in Focus section (Section 7.7) of the book. Complete and submit the SPSS grading template and a printout of the output file.

Exercise 7.1: The Estimated Standard Error of Exam Grades

A professor gives students a final exam for one of her statistics in psychology courses. She records grades out of 100 points, where higher scores indicate better performance. Use SPSS to estimate the standard error for this distribution of exam grades.

80	86	90	74
92	87	96	79
56	88	87	96
70	70	83	100
76	73	84	48
77	76	80	55
73	93	74	90
82	79	78	84
88	100	67	79
83	55	72	81
60	82	73	60
100	75	86	68
98	82	89	70
45	90	97	74
65	90	93	96
69	66	60	100
94	94	56	90
100	84	81	82
73	100	90	72
81	60	78	96

With regard to the SPSS exercise, answer the following questions:

Based on the table shown in SPSS, state the following values for the original data (labeled as *statistic* in the SPSS output table):

Sample size   _____

Minimum score   _____

Maximum score   _____

Mean score   _____

Standard deviation   _____

Based on the table shown in SPSS, state the following values for the sampling distribution:

Mean   _____

Standard error   _____

Draw the sampling distribution 3 *SEM* above and below the mean for this example.

CHAPTER SUMMARY ORGANIZED BY LEARNING OBJECTIVE

LO 1: Define sampling distribution.

- A sampling distribution is a distribution of all sample means or sample variances that could be obtained in samples of a given size from the same population.

LO 2: Compare theoretical and experimental sampling strategies.

- The theoretical sampling strategy is a sampling method in which we sample with replacement and the order in which a participant is selected matters.
- Sampling with replacement is a method of sampling in which each participant or item selected is replaced before the next draw.
- The experimental sampling strategy is a sampling method in which we sample without replacement and the order in which a participant is selected does not matter.
- Sampling without replacement is a method of sampling in which each participant or item selected is not replaced before the next draw.

LO 3–4: Identify three characteristics of the sampling distribution of the sample mean; calculate the mean and standard error of a sampling distribution of the sample mean and draw the shape of this distribution.

- The sample mean has the following three characteristics:

  a. The sample mean is an unbiased estimator. On average, the sample mean we obtain in a randomly selected sample will equal the value of the population mean.

  b. A distribution of sample means follows the central limit theorem. Regardless of the shape of the distribution in a population, the distribution of sample means selected at random from the population will approach the shape of a normal distribution, as the number of samples in the sampling distribution increases.

  c. A distribution of sample means has minimum variance. The sampling distribution of the mean will vary minimally from the value of the population mean.

- The variance of the sampling distribution of sample means equals the population variance divided by the sample size:

$$\sigma_M^2 = \frac{\sigma^2}{n}.$$

- The standard error of the mean is the standard deviation of the sampling distribution of the sample means. It is the square root of the variance:

$$\sigma_M = \sqrt{\sigma_M^2} = \sqrt{\frac{\sigma^2}{n}} = \frac{\sigma}{\sqrt{n}}.$$

LO 5: Identify three characteristics of the sampling distribution of the sample variance.

- The sample variance has the following characteristics:

a. The sample variance is an unbiased estimator. On average, the sample variance we obtain in a randomly selected sample will equal the value of the population variance when we divide *SS* by *df*.

b. A distribution of sample variances follows the skewed distribution rule. Regardless of the distribution of scores in a population, the sampling distribution of sample variances selected at random from that population will approach the shape of a positively skewed distribution, as the number of samples in the sampling distribution increases.

c. A distribution of sample variances has no minimum variance, meaning that this distribution will not vary minimally from the value of the population variance when we divide *SS* by *df*.

LO 6: Explain the relationship between standard error, standard deviation, and sample size.

- As the population standard deviation (σ) increases, standard error increases. Hence, the farther scores in a population deviate from the mean in a population, the farther possible sample means can deviate from the value of the population mean.
- As the sample size (n) increases, standard error decreases. Hence, the more data you collect, the closer your estimate of the value of the population mean. This relationship is explained by the law of large numbers.

LO 7: Compute z transformations for the sampling distribution of the sample mean.

- Using the notation for sample means, the z transformation formula can be stated as follows:

$$z = \frac{M - \mu_M}{\sigma_M} \text{ or } z = \frac{M - \mu}{\sigma_M}.$$

- To locate the proportion of area, and therefore probabilities, of sample means in any sampling distribution, we follow two steps:

  Step 1: Transform a sample mean (M) into a z score.

  Step 2: Locate the corresponding proportion for the z score in the unit normal table.

LO 8: Summarize the standard error of the mean in APA format.

- The standard error is most often reported in the text, in a table, or in a graph. When data are reported in the text or in a table, they are usually reported with the value of the mean. In a graph, the standard error is displayed as a vertical bar extending above and below each mean plot or mean bar.

LO 9: Compute the estimate for the standard error of the mean using SPSS.

- SPSS can be used to compute an estimate of the standard error of the mean. An estimate for the standard error is computed using the Analyze, Descriptive Statistics, and Descriptives options in the menu bar. These actions will bring up a dialog box that will allow you to identify your variable, select Options, and choose the S.E. mean option to compute an estimate of the standard error.

PART III

Making Inferences About One or Two Means

8

Hypothesis Testing: Significance, Effect Size, and Power

LEARNING OBJECTIVES

After reading this chapter, you should be able to:

1. Identify the four steps of hypothesis testing.

2. Define null hypothesis, alternative hypothesis, level of significance, test statistic, p value, and statistical significance.

3. Define Type I error and Type II error, and identify the type of error that researchers control.

4. Calculate the one-sample z test and interpret the results.

5. Distinguish between a one-tailed test and a two-tailed test, and explain why a Type III error is possible only with one-tailed tests.

6. Elucidate effect size and compute a Cohen's d for the one-sample z test.

7. Define *power* and identify six factors that influence power.

8. Summarize the results of a one-sample z test in American Psychological Association (APA) format.

CHAPTER OUTLINE

8.1 Inferential Statistics and Hypothesis Testing

In inferential statistics, we use sample means to estimate the population mean. On average, we expect the value of a sample mean to equal the value of the population mean. The larger the difference between the sample mean and the population mean, the less probable it is that the population mean is correct.

- *Hypothesis:* A statement or proposed explanation for an observation, a phenomenon, or a scientific problem that can be tested using the research method. A hypothesis is often a statement about the value for a parameter in a population.
- *Hypothesis testing or significance testing:* A method for testing a claim or hypothesis about a parameter in a population, using data measured in a sample. We use hypothesis testing to determine the probability that a sample statistic would be selected from a population if the hypothesis regarding the population mean were true.

8.2 Four Steps to Hypothesis Testing

The four steps to hypothesis testing can be further described and elaborated upon.

Step 1: State the hypotheses: Begin by stating the *null* and *alternative hypotheses.*

- Null hypothesis (H_0): A statement about the population parameter that is assumed to be true. In hypothesis testing, we test whether this value should be retained or rejected.
- Alternative hypothesis (H_1): A statement that contradicts the null hypothesis by stating that the value of the parameter is less than, greater than, or not equal to the value stated in the null hypothesis.

Step 2: Set the criteria for a decision: To determine whether the null hypothesis should be retained or rejected, we first set criteria for making a decision about the null hypothesis. To do this, we state the *level of significance* for a test, which is typically set at .05 for behavioral research.

- In behavioral science, the significance level is typically set at .05 (or 5%). When the probability of obtaining a sample mean would be less than 5% if the null hypothesis were true, we decide to reject the value stated in the null hypothesis.

Step 3: Compute the test statistic: We use a test statistic to evaluate the likelihood of obtaining a sample mean of a certain value if the null hypothesis is correct. The test statistic tells us the number of standard deviations by which the sample mean deviates from the population mean stated in the null hypothesis.

Step 4: Make a decision: We use the value of the test statistic to make a decision regarding the null hypothesis. We base the decision on the probability of obtaining the sample mean, given that the null hypothesis is true.

- If the probability of obtaining the sample mean would be less than or equal to 5% if the null hypothesis were true, then we reject the null hypothesis.
- If the probability of obtaining the sample mean would be greater than 5% if the null hypothesis were true, then we retain the null hypothesis.
- The probability of obtaining a particular sample mean is stated as a *p* value, which varies between 0 and 1. We compare the *p* value to the criteria set in Step 2. If the null hypothesis is rejected, then the criterion or *p* value was less than or equal to .05 and the test statistic reached *statistical significance*.

8.3 Hypothesis Testing and Sampling Distributions

To calculate a test statistic and make a decision regarding the null hypothesis, we need to know the population mean and the standard error of the mean. This allows us to calculate a *z* score for the sample mean and to identify the probability of its occurrence in the *z* table (see Table B.1 in Appendix B of the book; also reprinted in the appendix of this study guide).

8.4 Making a Decision: Types of Error

The decision regarding the null hypothesis can be correct or incorrect. There are four possible decision alternatives regarding the truth or falsity of the decision made.

1. Decide to retain the null hypothesis correctly.
   - The null hypothesis is correct, and we correctly decide to retain the null hypothesis. This result is called a *null finding*.

2. Decide to retain the null hypothesis incorrectly.
   - Type II error (β): The null hypothesis is false, but we incorrectly made the decision to retain the null hypothesis.

3. Decide to reject the null hypothesis correctly.
   - Significant result: The null hypothesis is false, and we correctly decide to reject the null hypothesis. This is called the *power* of the decision-making process.

4. Decide to reject the null hypothesis incorrectly.
   - Type I error (α): The null hypothesis is true, but we incorrectly made the decision to reject the null hypothesis. Researchers control for this type of error by stating an alpha level. An alpha (α) level is the level of significance or criterion for a hypothesis test.

8.5 Testing for Significance: Examples Using the z Test

The one-sample z test: A statistical procedure used to test hypotheses concerning a mean in a single population with a known variance. To conduct a z test, we need to evaluate one of three alternative hypotheses, which are described in Step 1.

- We follow the four steps to hypothesis testing to compute the one-sample z test:
    - *Step 1: State the hypotheses.* State the null hypothesis and the alternative hypothesis. For nondirectional tests, the alternative hypothesis is stated as not equal to ($\neq$) the value stated in the null hypothesis. For directional tests, the alternative hypothesis is stated as greater than (>) or less than (<) the value stated in the null hypothesis.
    - *Step 2: Set the criteria for a decision.* If the level of significance is .05, then α = .05. The rejection region is in the tail of the z distribution. For a nondirectional test, we split the alpha level (α = .05) into two tails. For a directional test, we place the rejection region in only the upper or lower tail.
    - *Step 3: Compute the test statistic.* The test statistic is known as the z *statistic* or *obtained value*. We compare the obtained value to the critical value(s). The formula of the test statistic for a one-sample z test is

$$z_{\text{obt}} = \frac{M - \mu}{\sigma_M}, \text{ where } \sigma_M = \frac{\sigma}{\sqrt{n}}.$$

    - *Step 4: Make a decision.* Reject the null hypothesis if the obtained value exceeds either critical value; otherwise, retain the null hypothesis.

- *Type III errors:* For one-tailed tests, a Type III error can occur when we retain the null hypothesis, not because the effect did not exist, but because we placed the rejection region in the wrong tail.

8.6 Research in Focus: Directional Versus Nondirectional Tests

Kruger and Savitsky (2006) showed participants two results: one for a one-tailed test at a .05 level of significance and another for a two-tailed test at a .10 level of significance. In this study, participants were more convinced by the results of a significant one-tailed test than by the results of a significant two-tailed test, although the criterion or critical value in the upper tail was the same. The one-tailed test was significant because it was associated with greater power to detect an effect. However, because a one-tailed test increases the likelihood that we will reject the null hypothesis, it is important that we can justify that an outcome can occur in only one direction, which can be difficult. For this reason, most studies in behavioral research are two-tailed tests.

8.7 Measuring the Size of an Effect: Cohen's *d*

Hypothesis testing is used to determine whether an effect exists in the population, but it does not tell you the size of the effect. Instead, different measures are used to determine effect size.

- *Effect size:* A statistical measure of the size of an effect in a population.

Cohen's d: A measure of effect size in terms of the number of standard deviations that an effect shifted above or below the population mean stated in the null hypothesis. The formula for Cohen's *d* is as follows:

$$\text{Cohen's } d = \frac{M - \mu}{\sigma}.$$

- Cohen's *d* effect size conventions are standardized rules for identifying small, medium, or large effect sizes. The sign of *d* only indicates that an effect is greater than or less than the hypothesized population mean. The following rules are stated by the effect size conventions for interpreting the size of an effect:
  - Small: $d < 0.2$
  - Medium: $0.2 < d < 0.8$
  - Large: $d > 0.8$

8.8 Effect Size, Power, and Sample Size

The relationship between effect size and power is such that as effect size increases, power increases. In other words, the larger a difference between the sample mean and the hypothesized population mean stated in the null hypothesis, the more likely we are to reject the null hypothesis. Also, the relationship between sample size and power is such that increasing sample size will increase power.

8.9 Additional Factors That Increase Power

Along with increasing effect size and sample size, to increase power (the likelihood of rejecting the null hypothesis), you can increase the *alpha level*.

Decreasing the beta (β; the likelihood of committing a Type II error) will increase alpha and thus increase power. Decreasing the population standard deviation and standard error will also increase power.

8.10 SPSS in Focus: A Preview for Chapters 9 to 18

There is no (direct) way to compute a z test in SPSS, likely because it is not a common statistical test in the behavioral sciences. However, SPSS can be used to compute all other hypothesis tests taught in this book.

8.11 APA in Focus: Reporting the Test Statistic and Effect Size

To report the result of a one-sample z test, we report the test statistic, p value, and effect size of a hypothesis test. You are not required to report the exact p value, although it is recommended. Instead, you can report the p value as being greater than or less than .05, .01, or .001. Finally, it is recommended that you include a figure or a table to illustrate a significant effect and its effect size.

CHAPTER FORMULAS

The z Test and Effect Size

$z_{obt} = \dfrac{M - \mu}{\sigma_M}$ (Test statistic for the one-sample z test)

$d = \dfrac{M - \mu}{\sigma}$ (Cohen's d effect size measure for the one-sample z test)

TIPS AND CAUTIONS FOR STUDENTS

- *Setting criteria and the empirical rule:* Because about 95% of all sample means in a sampling distribution fall within two standard deviations of the population mean, the remaining 5% are divided into the two tails of the distribution. In a normal distribution, we determined that exactly 5% of sample means fall ±1.96 standard deviations from the mean. Thus, there is a 2.5% probability that we will select a sample mean above 1.96 *SD* from the population mean, and there is a 2.5% probability that we will select a sample mean below 1.96 *SD* from the population mean.

   When the probability of selecting a sample mean is less than 5%, we will decide to reject the null hypothesis in hypothesis testing. Note that there is still some probability that the null hypothesis is correct, but it is so unlikely (less than 5%) that we choose to reject it. The alternative hypothesis, then, is not necessarily correct—it is essentially the best remaining hypothesis or alternative to the null hypothesis.

- *Effect size and Cohen's* d: Cohen's d indicates the number of standard deviations that an effect shifts in the population. The sample standard deviation is used as an estimate of the population standard deviation, which is unknown. Note that Cohen's d uses the sample standard deviation in the denominator of the formula, and not sample size, which is why the value of Cohen's d (effect size) is not affected by changes in sample size.

KEY TERM WORD SEARCHES

```
M K D F Y D K S G Y C W F Y W I D D U T C D G E P W L I S W U N D R H C W E
L R C S S I W S B B U N T R X H W E I D Y P C S B W L K I Z S E U Y V C Z D
R M R B J U K M O U R V C D Q W V D U S G W O K Q W W L G T T W Z D Y R N P
A K P U U O T M B H A F T I U C J U B H X V X H L N Y Y N T A S T R S I I N
C F G A I F Y T U G J K C N R Q M I W A F S F N I J G Q I V T S E J Q T I X
G G O W I M W J D A R A X A K K G D F L J V C U X S Y R F B I P S C A I L Q
B N W H D U E V A W P P F V K J W G P T P D G N O V L I I W S X T R K C G G
C O A A W N O C D I B V N U F S F S W E O H F J J N L H C J T O S L Z A G W
M K L U Q M Q V O W H A D L G I C T S R P F Q Z E J J F A X I T R G R L I U
C D P W M O C A P S B L B A L G X F B N E F Q E Q V D F N I C H N C F V X W
V K H N D F B F A P U U N Q S N Z M O A X I X F I H R R C M A J B B M A R X
U O A Y B M X C S X R E Y U K I S F L T J R Z F N D D S E T L N J E F L Y F
F I J C S N J H F A W B T P G F P X Z I O M O E R M G D T J S U B J O U E A
F T H Z W N O P H V B B K Z K I N P G V N X D C E W J Q E S I L J T Z E F Z
A I U D F V V N C U T S S Z P C E M K E D M V T P P T U S W G L R B E S V D
O P D O K H H U D S H H U P K A V M U H E D G F V E H F T H N H E P F B G M
D C B Z Z F Y D P I D P I J T N D W S Y F E Y H N B M X I X I Y Q Z H K V K
U C O G D F P S Q L R P I F A C O Y W P K D J O D Y K H N Y F P L R F D J A
Y T T T U F O U N A Q E Z P T E J Y W O L I Z U Y O D B G G I O L K U Q V M
A P H K Q P T L R H U S C B X D S P J T Q X Z P N F W D F O C T M U R N H J
L D S O Q J H I E I J T J T K E O H S H Q A J R T C T X R G A H G D M S Y V
X Y Z K H Y E T J F O C F B I H E Q E E A I V W I V T I V E N E Q N M L H M
X C P K X L S E E M E D A T L O L G M S B L T B S B F V Q V C S D C P C U U
T O M T H Q I S C H L X H E R V N F V I C J H C A J D E U L E I J B Q H U H
U H V K J J S T T G H R E Q E P O A L S W K J Q J U S T U N U S P S R P Z A
J E F Z A R T S I P M J G L V P U R L R D L F O P Q I O Z R A M B O O A I R
S N U G G I E T O Z R D Y Y Z N E Y U T F Y B R D B N D Y R L K N Y W O Q A
L S A P T B S A N I O J D U B P R I B V E T F G E D N J H D P V P U X E L S
P D I Y O M T T R O E T X K R N H M N G I S K P T T H N N B T L D F S T R L
R R C L H T I I E U E F F E C T S I Z E F P T G O H Y P O T H E S I S L J T
V W Z R C P N S G G K I S I B E T A E R R O R S Y I U K M T D B O E R F V F
A F N O U I G T I O U L E V E L O F S I G N I F I C A N C E E H X U R F T T
B P L I C Z D I O C M J H V L Z S T A T I S T I C C N W E C P A U R X C S Q
Z N R L A S G C N A K A Y T I C W B X S D D I R E C T I O N A L T E S T S C
G Z G R K S R C Y F Y C D N S R D M M R M Q B V S N X L T M E S T E Y L Q T
V G S I Q B B H W L A Q Z J P G G N F E N E M H Y P B F J Z P H B J R F Z D
A Z T K R M K C M U D N Y L G M F R T L K A Z W Y W V T P P S K G D M F L D
N Z W W C G C V A E A O E Z M O O B T A I N E D V A L U E P T A Z W M U R R
```

ALPHA

ALTERNATIVE HYPOTHESIS

BETA ERROR

COHEN'S *D*

CRITICAL VALUES

DIRECTIONAL TESTS

EFFECT

EFFECT SIZE

HYPOTHESIS

HYPOTHESIS TESTING

LEVEL OF SIGNIFICANCE

NONDIRECTIONAL TESTS

NULL HYPOTHESIS

OBTAINED VALUE

POWER

P VALUE

REJECTION REGION

SIGNIFICANCE

SIGNIFICANCE TESTING

STATISTICAL SIGNIFICANCE

TEST STATISTIC

Z STATISTIC

Z TEST

CROSSWORD PUZZLES

ACROSS

1 A statement about a population parameter, such as the population mean, that is assumed to be true.

4 The region beyond a critical value in a hypothesis test.

6 For a single sample, this is the difference between a sample mean and the population mean stated in the null hypothesis.

7 The value of a test statistic.

14 Hypothesis tests where the alternative hypothesis is stated as not equal to ($\neq$) a value stated in the null hypothesis.

16 A cutoff value that defines the boundaries beyond which 5% or less of sample means can be obtained if the null hypothesis is true.

17 A statement that directly contradicts a null hypothesis.

18 A mathematical formula that allows researchers to determine the likelihood or probability of obtaining sample outcomes if the null hypothesis were true.

DOWN

2 A method for testing a claim or hypothesis about a parameter in a population, using data measured in a sample.

3 A criterion of judgment upon which a decision is made regarding the value stated in a null hypothesis.

5 The level of significance or criterion for a hypothesis test.

8 Hypothesis tests where the alternative hypothesis is stated as greater than (>) or less than (<) a value stated in the null hypothesis.

9 A term that describes a decision made concerning a value stated in the null hypothesis.

10 A statistical measure for the size of an effect in a population.

11 An inferential statistic used to determine the number of standard deviations in a standard normal distribution that a sample mean deviates from the population mean stated in the null hypothesis.

12 A measure of effect size in terms of the number of standard deviations that mean scores shifted above or below the population mean stated by the null hypothesis.

13 The probability of rejecting a false null hypothesis.

15 The probability of obtaining a sample outcome, given that the value stated in the null hypothesis is true.

PRACTICE QUIZZES

LO 1: Identify the four steps of hypothesis testing.

1. A method for testing a claim or hypothesis about a parameter in a population, using data measured in a sample, is called:
   a. the central limit theorem
   b. hypothesis testing
   c. significance testing
   d. both b and c

2. In which step of hypothesis testing do we state a hypothesis about a parameter in a population of interest?
   a. state the hypotheses
   b. set the criteria for a decision
   c. compute the test statistic
   d. make a decision

3. In which step of hypothesis testing do we state the criteria for making a decision?
   a. state the hypotheses
   b. set the criteria for a decision
   c. compute the test statistic
   d. make a decision

4. In which step of hypothesis testing do we state that we retain or reject the null hypothesis?
   a. state the hypotheses
   b. set the criteria for a decision
   c. compute the test statistic
   d. make a decision

5. In which step of hypothesis testing do we analyze the likelihood of a sample outcome, if the population mean stated by the null hypothesis is true?
   a. state the hypotheses
   b. set the criteria for a decision
   c. compute the test statistic
   d. make a decision

LO 2: Define null hypothesis, alternative hypothesis, level of significance, test statistic, p value, and statistical significance.

6. The _____ hypothesis is a statement about a population parameter, such as the population mean, that is assumed to be true.

   a. null

   b. alternative

   c. true

   d. false

7. A researcher hypothesizes that parents read to their children less than the recommended 30 minutes each day. The alternative hypothesis should be:

   a. mean time that parents spend reading to their children is equal to 30 minutes

   b. mean time that parents spend reading to their children is greater than 30 minutes

   c. mean time that parents spend reading to their children is less than 30 minutes

   d. mean time that parents spend reading to their children is not equal to 30 minutes

8. A researcher sets the following criterion: When the probability of obtaining a sample mean would be less than 5% if the null hypothesis were true, we reject the value stated in the null hypothesis. What is the 5% criterion called?

   a. the sample mean

   b. the test statistic

   c. the p value

   d. the level of significance

9. A researcher computes a test statistic and determines that the probability of obtaining a sample mean, given that the value stated in the null hypothesis is true, is .02. The .02 refers to what value?

   a. the value of the sample mean

   b. the value of the test statistic

   c. the p value

   d. the level of significance

10. When a decision is to reject the null hypothesis, the result is:

    a. significant

    b. not significant

LO 3: Define Type I error and Type II error, and identify the type of error that researchers control.

11. A researcher incorrectly decides to retain a null hypothesis that is actually false. The researcher has committed a:

    a. Type I error

    b. Type II error

c. Type III error

d. all of the above

12. A researcher incorrectly decides to reject a null hypothesis that is actually true. The researcher has committed a:

a. Type I error

b. Type II error

c. Type III error

d. all of the above

13. The level of significance for a hypothesis test is:

a. the probability of incorrectly rejecting the null hypothesis

b. the probability of committing a Type I error

c. the alpha level

d. all of the above

14. Researchers state an alpha level, thereby directly controlling for which type of error?

a. Type I error

b. Type II error

c. Type III error

d. all of the above

LO 4: Calculate the one-sample z test and interpret the results.

15. A statistical procedure used to test hypotheses concerning the mean in a single population with a known variance is called a:

a. one-sample z test

b. level of significance

c. null hypothesis

d. test statistic

16. A researcher conducts a one-sample z test at a .05 level of significance. If the rejection region is placed in both tails, then what are the critical values for this hypothesis test?

a. ±1.645

b. ±1.96

c. ±2.58

d. ±3.30

17. The average employee at a packaging company can package 650 ± 80 ($\mu \pm \sigma$) units of product per hour. In a sample of 16 employees, the company finds that employees actually package 700 ± 20 ($M \pm SD$) units of product per hour. Using a one-sample z test at a .05

level of significance, did employees package significantly more product than the average for the company?

    a. Retain the null hypothesis. Employees failed to package more units of product than the average for the company.

    b. Reject the null hypothesis. Employees packaged fewer units of product than the average for the company.

    c. Retain the null hypothesis. Employees packaged fewer units of product than the average for the company.

    d. Reject the null hypothesis. Employees packaged more units of product than the average for the company.

18. A researcher obtains $z = 1.68$ using a one-sample z test. What is the decision for the hypothesis test at a .05 level of significance?

    a. retain the null

    b. reject the null

    c. it depends on whether the test is one-tailed or two-tailed

LO 5: Distinguish between a one-tailed test and a two-tailed test, and explain why a Type III error is possible only with one-tailed tests.

19. A researcher computes a one-sample z test. If the test is a nondirectional hypothesis test, then the critical value is placed in:

    a. the upper tail of the standard normal distribution

    b. the lower tail of the standard normal distribution

    c. both tails of the standard normal distribution

    d. no tails of the standard normal distribution

20. The alternative hypothesis for a lower-tail critical test is given as a _____; the alternative hypothesis for an upper-tail critical test is given as a _____.

    a. "less than" statement; "less than" statement

    b. "less than" statement; "greater than" statement

    c. "greater than" statement; "less than" statement

    d. "greater than" statement; "greater than" statement

21. A Type III error is only possible when we conduct:

    a. one-tailed tests

    b. two-tailed tests

    c. nondirectional tests

    d. both a and c

22. A one-tailed test should be used only when we can justify that an outcome can _____ occur in one direction.

    a. mostly

    b. probably

    c. rarely

    d. only

LO 6: Elucidate effect size and compute a Cohen's *d* for the one-sample *z* test.

23. A statistical measure of the size of an effect in a population is called:

    a. statistical significance

    b. effect size

    c. power

    d. all of the above

24. Measures of effect size allow researchers to describe:

    a. statistical significance

    b. how far scores shifted in the population

    c. the percent of variance that can be explained by a given variable

    d. both b and c

25. A researcher found that the mean difference between a sample mean and a population mean was 3.2 points. If the population standard deviation equals 6.4 points, then what is the effect size for this mean difference using Cohen's *d*?

    a. $d = 0.50$

    b. $d = 2.00$

    c. $d = 3.20$

    d. not possible to know because the level of significance is not given

26. Using Cohen's effect size conventions, what is the size of an effect when Cohen's *d* equals 0.82?

    a. small

    b. medium

    c. large

LO 7: Define *power* and identify six factors that influence power.

27. The power in hypothesis testing is:

    a. the probability of rejecting a false null hypothesis

    b. the probability of rejecting a null hypothesis that is not true

    c. the probability that a randomly selected sample will show that the null hypothesis is false when the null hypothesis is in fact false

    d. all of the above

28. Which of the following will increase the power to detect an effect?

    a. increase the sample size

    b. increase the standard error

    c. decrease effect size

    d. all of the above

29. Which of the following will increase the power to detect an effect when it is decreased?

    a. sample size

    b. standard error

    c. effect size

    d. alpha level

30. A researcher selects two samples from the same population. Sample A is $n = 20$ and Sample B is $n = 40$. Which sample has greater power to detect an effect?

    a. Sample A

    b. Sample B

    c. none; the power will be the same in both samples

LO 8: Summarize the results of a one-sample z test in American Psychological Association (APA) format.

31. To report the results of a z test, which of the following is not reported?

    a. the test statistic

    b. the p value

    c. the effect size

    d. the critical values

32. A researcher reports that intelligence scores were higher than the mean in the population, $z = 1.645, p = .05$ $(d = 0.14)$. Was this a one-tailed test or a two-tailed test?

    a. one-tailed test because the p value is equal to .05

    b. two-tailed test because the p value is equal to .05

    c. it could be a one- or a two-tailed test

33. A researcher reports the following result for a one-sample z test at a .05 level of significance: $z = 1.88, p = .06$ $(d = 0.25)$. Is this result significant?

    a. yes, the decision is to reject the null hypothesis

    b. no, the decision is to retain the null hypothesis

    c. yes, because the effect size is large

    d. no, because the effect size is small

CHAPTER SUMMARY ORGANIZED BY LEARNING OBJECTIVE

LO 1: **Identify the four steps of hypothesis testing.**

- Hypothesis testing, or significance testing, is a method of testing a claim or hypothesis about a parameter in a population, using data measured in a sample. In this method, we test a hypothesis by determining the likelihood that a sample statistic would be selected if the hypothesis regarding the population parameter were true. The four steps of hypothesis testing are as follows:

  - Step 1: State the hypotheses.
  - Step 2: Set the criteria for a decision.
  - Step 3: Compute the test statistic.
  - Step 4: Make a decision.

LO 2: **Define null hypothesis, alternative hypothesis, level of significance, test statistic, p value, and statistical significance.**

- The null hypothesis (H_0) is a statement about a population parameter, such as the population mean, that is assumed to be true.
- The alternative hypothesis (H_1) is a statement that directly contradicts a null hypothesis by stating that the actual value of a population parameter, such as the mean, is less than, greater than, or not equal to the value stated in the null hypothesis.
- Level of significance is a criterion of judgment upon which a decision is made regarding the value stated in a null hypothesis. The criterion is based on the probability of obtaining a statistic measured in a sample if the value stated in the null hypothesis were true.
- The test statistic is a mathematical formula that allows researchers to determine the likelihood or probability of obtaining sample outcomes if the null hypothesis were true. The value of a test statistic can be used to make inferences concerning the value of a population parameter stated in the null hypothesis.
- A p value is the probability of obtaining a sample outcome, given that the value stated in the null hypothesis is true. The p value of a sample outcome is compared to the level of significance.
- Significance, or statistical significance, describes a decision made concerning a value stated in the null hypothesis. When a null hypothesis is rejected, a result is significant. When a null hypothesis is retained, a result is not significant.

LO 3: **Define Type I error and Type II error, and identify the type of error that researchers control.**

- We can decide to retain or reject a null hypothesis, and this decision can be correct or incorrect. Two types of errors in hypothesis testing are called Type I and Type II errors.
- A Type I error is the probability of rejecting a null hypothesis that is actually true. The probability of this type of error is determined by the researcher and stated as the level of significance or alpha level for a hypothesis test.
- A Type II error is the probability of retaining a null hypothesis that is actually false.

LO 4: Calculate the one-sample z test and interpret the results.

- The one-sample z test is a statistical procedure used to test hypotheses concerning the mean in a single population with a known variance. The test statistic for this hypothesis test is

$$z_{obt} = \frac{M-\mu}{\sigma_M}, \text{ where } \sigma_M = \frac{\sigma}{\sqrt{n}}.$$

- Critical values, which mark the cutoffs for the rejection region, can be identified for any level of significance. The value of the test statistic is compared to the critical values. When the value of a test statistic exceeds a critical value, we reject the null hypothesis; otherwise, we retain the null hypothesis.

LO 5: Distinguish between a one-tailed test and two-tailed test, and explain why a Type III error is possible only with one-tailed tests.

- Nondirectional (two-tailed) tests are hypothesis tests in which the alternative hypothesis is stated as *not equal to* ($\neq$) a value stated in the null hypothesis. So we are interested in any alternative to the null hypothesis.
- Directional (one-tailed) tests are hypothesis tests in which the alternative hypothesis is stated as *greater than* (>) or *less than* (<) a value stated in the null hypothesis. So we are interested in a specific alternative to the null hypothesis.
- A Type III error is a type of error possible with one-tailed tests in which a result would have been significant in one tail, but the researcher retains the null hypothesis because the rejection region was placed in the wrong or opposite tail.

LO 6: Elucidate effect size and compute a Cohen's d for the one-sample z test.

- Effect size is a statistical measure of the size of an observed effect in a population, which allows researchers to describe how far scores shifted in the population, or the percent of variance that can be explained by a given variable.
- Cohen's d is used to measure how far scores shifted in a population and is computed using the following formula:

$$\text{Cohen's } d = \frac{M-\mu}{\sigma}.$$

- To interpret the size of an effect, we refer to Cohen's effect size conventions, which are standard rules for identifying small, medium, and large effects based on typical findings in behavioral research. These conventions are given in Table 8.6.

LO 7: Define *power* and identify six factors that influence power.

- In hypothesis testing, power is the probability that a sample selected at random will show that the null hypothesis is false when the null hypothesis is indeed false.
- To increase the power of detecting an effect in a given population:
  a. Increase effect size (d), sample size (n), and alpha (α).
  b. Decrease beta error (β), population standard deviation (σ), and standard error (σ_M).

LO 8: Summarize the results of a one-sample z test in American Psychological Association (APA) format.

- To report the results of a z test, we report the test statistic, p value, and effect size of a hypothesis test. In addition, a figure or table can be used to summarize the means and standard error or standard deviation measured in a study.

9

Testing Means

One-Sample and Two-Independent-Sample t *Tests*

LEARNING OBJECTIVES

After reading this chapter, you should be able to:

1. Explain why a t distribution is associated with $n - 1$ degrees of freedom and describe the information that is conveyed by the t statistic.

2. Calculate the degrees of freedom for a one-sample t test and a two-independent-sample t test and locate critical values in the t table.

3. Identify the assumptions for the one-sample t test.

4. Compute a one-sample t test and interpret the results.

5. Compute effect size and proportion of variance for a one-sample t test.

6. Identify the assumptions for the two-independent-sample t test.

7. Compute a two-independent-sample t test and interpret the results.

8. Compute effect size and proportion of variance for a two-independent-sample t test.

9. Summarize the results of a one-sample t test and a two-independent-sample t test in APA format.

10. Compute a one-sample t test and a two-independent-sample t test using SPSS.

CHAPTER OUTLINE

9.1 Going From z to t

To compute the z statistic, the population mean and variance must be known. However, we rarely know the population variance of the behaviors that researchers measure. Therefore, an alternative test statistic is used for situations in which we do not know the population standard deviation and thus cannot calculate standard error. To compute this test statistic, we substitute the population variance with the sample variance in the formula for calculating the standard error. We make this substitution because the sample variance is an unbiased estimator of the population variance. The substituted formula, called the *estimated standard error* (s_M), is as follows:

$$s_M = \sqrt{\frac{s^2}{n}} = \frac{SD}{\sqrt{n}} .$$

The test statistic for a one-sample t test that uses the estimated standard error of the mean in the denominator is called the t *statistic*. The formula is as follows:

$$t_{obt} = \frac{M - \mu}{s_M}, \text{ where } s_M = \frac{SD}{\sqrt{n}} .$$

- To make decisions using this test statistic, we use a t distribution, which is similar to a z distribution, except that it has more variability in the tails due to the sample variance being an estimate of the population variance.

9.2 The Degrees of Freedom

The t distribution is associated with the same degrees of freedom as sample variance. As the sample size increases, the sample variance will more closely estimate the population variance, and thus, the t distribution will change in shape to reflect less variability in the tails.

- The degrees of freedom for the t distribution are equal to the degrees of freedom for the sample variance: $df = n - 1$.

9.3 Reading the t Table

We use the t distribution to locate critical values that can be compared to the value we obtain using the test statistic. To use the t table, you must know the sample size (n), the alpha level (α), and the location of the rejection regions (i.e., two-tailed or one-tailed test). Note that you use the *df* to locate the critical values for the hypothesis test.

9.4 One-Sample *t* Test

The one-sample *t* test is computed to test hypotheses concerning a single group mean selected from a population with an unknown variance. It is used in place of the *z* statistic for cases in which the population variance is not known. We make three assumptions to compute the one-sample *t* test:

1. *Normality.* We assume that the population sampled has a normal distribution, particularly for samples less than 30 ($n < 30$).

2. *Random sampling.* We assume the measured data are from a sample selected using a random sampling procedure.

3. *Independence.* We assume that each outcome or observation is independent, meaning that one outcome does not influence another. Specifically, outcomes are independent when the probability of one outcome has no effect on the probability of another outcome.

Once these three assumptions are met, we use the four steps to hypothesis testing to conduct the one-sample *t* test.

- *Step 1: State the hypotheses.* State the null and alternative hypotheses.
- *Step 2: Set the criteria for a decision.* The level of significance is typically equal to .05. Refer to the *t* table to find the critical values (see Table B.2 in Appendix B of the book; also reprinted in the appendix of this study guide).
- *Step 3: Compute the test statistic:* $t_{\text{obt}} = \dfrac{M - \mu}{s_M}$, where $s_M = \dfrac{SD}{\sqrt{n}}$.
- *Step 4: Make a decision.* Decide to retain or reject the null hypothesis.

9.5 Effect Size for the One-Sample *t* Test

To determine the size of an effect, we can compute an estimated Cohen's *d*, which is a measure of proportion of variance.

Estimated Cohen's d: When the population standard deviation is unknown, we substitute the sample standard deviation in the formula for Cohen's *d*.

- Estimated Cohen's $d = \dfrac{M - \mu}{SD}$.
- *Proportion of variance* is a measure of effect size for the proportion of variance that can be accounted for by a treatment, which is any unique characteristic of a sample or any

unique way that a researcher treats a sample. The proportion of variance estimates how much of the variability in a dependent variable can be accounted for by the treatment.

○ Proportion of variance = $\dfrac{\text{variability explained}}{\text{total variability}}$.

Eta-squared (η^2): A measure of proportion of variance that can be described in a single equation based on the result of a *t* test.

$$\eta^2 = \frac{t^2}{t^2 + df} \, .$$

Omega-squared (ω^2): To compute omega-squared, we subtract 1 in the numerator to correct for the tendency of eta-squared to overestimate the size of an effect. Omega-squared is a more conservative estimate than is eta-squared.

$$\omega^2 = \frac{t^2 - 1}{t^2 + df} \, .$$

9.6 SPSS in Focus: One-Sample *t* Test

SPSS can be used to compute a one-sample *t* test using the Analyze, Compare Means, and One-Sample T Test options in the menu bar.

9.7 Two-Independent-Sample *t* Test

In the behavioral sciences, we often study differences between two groups or populations. In these studies, researchers measure two sample means and compare differences between them. In this research situation, the two-independent-sample *t* test is performed to test for differences between two population means, where the variability in one or both populations is unknown.

To perform the two-independent-sample *t* test, we make four assumptions:

1. *Normality.* We assume that each population sampled has a normal distribution, particularly for samples less than 30 ($n < 30$).

2. *Random sampling.* We assume the measured data are from samples selected using a random sampling procedure.

3. *Independence.* We assume that each outcome or observation is independent, meaning that one outcome does not influence another. Specifically, outcomes are independent when the probability of one outcome has no effect on the probability of another outcome.

4. *Equal variances*. We assume the population variances equal one another. This assumption is typically satisfied when the larger sample variance is not greater than two times the smaller sample variance.

Once these four assumptions are met, we use the four steps to hypothesis testing to conduct the two-independent-sample *t* test.

- *Step 1: State the hypotheses*. State the null and alternative hypotheses.
- *Step 2: Set the criteria for a decision*. The level of significance is typically equal to .05. Refer to the *t* table to find the critical values (see Table B.2 in Appendix B of the book; also reprinted in the appendix of this study guide).
  - To find the degrees of freedom for two samples and thus be able to find the appropriate critical values in the *t* table, we sum the degrees of freedom for each group or sample.
- *Step 3: Compute the test statistic*: $t_{\text{obt}} = \dfrac{(M_1 - M_2) - (\mu_1 - \mu_2)}{s_{M_1 - M_2}}$, where $s_{M_1 - M_2} = \sqrt{\dfrac{s_p^2}{n_1} + \dfrac{s_p^2}{n_2}}$

  and $s_p^2 = \dfrac{s_1^2(df_1) + s_2^2(df_2)}{df_1 + df_2}$.

  - The estimated standard error for the difference is an estimate of the standard error or standard distance that mean differences deviate from the mean difference stated in the null hypothesis. Note that to calculate the estimated standard error for the difference, you must first compute the pooled sample variance.
- *Step 4: Make a decision*. Decide whether to retain or reject the null hypothesis.

9.8 Effect Size for the Two-Independent-Sample *t* Test

We can select from three measures of effect size for the two-independent-sample *t* test: estimated Cohen's *d*, eta-squared, and omega-squared.

Estimated Cohen's d: To calculate estimated Cohen's *d* for the two-independent-sample *t* test, we place the difference between the two sample means in the numerator and the pooled sample standard deviation in the denominator.

$$\text{Estimated Cohen's } d = \frac{M_1 - M_2}{\sqrt{s_p^2}}.$$

The formula for eta-squared is the same for all *t* tests: $\eta^2 = \dfrac{t^2}{t^2 + df}$.

The formula for omega-squared is the same for all *t* tests: $\omega^2 = \dfrac{t^2 - 1}{t^2 + df}$.

9.9 SPSS in Focus: Two-Independent-Sample *t* Test

SPSS can be used to compute a two-independent-sample *t* test using the Analyze, Compare Means, and Independent-Samples T Test options in the menu bar.

9.10 APA in Focus: Reporting the *t* Statistic and Effect Size

When reporting the results of a *t* test, we include the value of the test statistic, the degrees of freedom, and the *p* value. The effect size should also be reported. In addition, a figure or a table is often used to summarize the means and standard error or standard deviations measured in a study. Although this information can be included in the written results of the study, it is often more concise to do so in a table or a figure.

CHAPTER FORMULAS

The One-Sample and Two-Independent-Sample t Tests

One-Sample t Test

$t_{obt} = \dfrac{M - \mu}{s_M}$ (Test statistic for the one-sample t test)

$s_M = \sqrt{\dfrac{s^2}{n}}$ (Estimated standard error)

$df = n - 1$ (Degrees of freedom for the one-sample t test)

Two-Independent-Sample t Test

$t_{obt} = \dfrac{(M_1 - M_2) - (\mu_1 - \mu_2)}{s_{M_1 - M_2}}$ (Test statistic for the two-independent-sample t test)

$s_{M_1 - M_2} = \sqrt{\dfrac{s_p^2}{n_1} + \dfrac{s_p^2}{n_2}}$ (Estimated standard error for the difference)

$s_p^2 = \dfrac{s_1^2(df_1) + s_2^2(df_2)}{df_1 + df_2}$ (Pooled sample variance for unequal sample sizes)

$df = (n_1 - 1) + (n_2 - 1)$ (Degrees of freedom for the two-independent-sample t test)

Effect Size

$d = \dfrac{M - \mu}{SD}$ (Estimated Cohen's d for the one-sample t test)

$d = \dfrac{M_1 - M_2}{\sqrt{s_p^2}}$ (Estimated Cohen's d for the two-independent-sample t test)

$\eta^2 = \dfrac{t^2}{t^2 + df}$ (Eta-squared estimate of proportion of variance; used for all t tests)

$\omega^2 = \dfrac{t^2 - 1}{t^2 + df}$ (Omega-squared estimate of proportion of variance; used for all t tests)

TIPS AND CAUTIONS FOR STUDENTS

- *The* t *table:* When using the *t* table to find critical values, note that the critical values for a two-tailed test at a .05 level of significance are the same as the critical values for a one-tailed test at a .025 level of significance. This is because a two-tailed test at a .05 level of significance splits that alpha level such that $\alpha = .025$ in each tail. As a general rule, you will find the same critical values for one-tailed tests that are half the level of significance of two-tailed tests. Also, notice that as the degrees of freedom increase, the critical values decrease. The larger degrees of freedom reflect a larger sample size, which is why the critical values decrease as the degrees of freedom increase.

- *Computing the* t *statistic:* To compute the test statistic, break down the formula into its individual calculations. For the one-sample *t* test, compute the estimated standard error, and then compute the test statistic formula. For the two-independent-sample *t* test, compute the pooled sample variance, then the estimated standard error for the difference, and then the test statistic formula. Breaking the test statistic into individual calculations will make it a lot easier to compute and likely reduce possible mathematical errors in your calculations.

KEY TERM WORD SEARCHES

I	S	D	F	V	F	D	E	G	R	E	E	S	O	F	F	R	E	E	D	O	M	X	M	I
I	J	J	U	E	E	B	M	A	S	O	C	E	G	W	N	S	F	J	M	W	X	G	J	B
B	V	O	S	S	P	S	N	Z	A	E	T	J	D	X	Q	Y	E	Y	A	Y	K	O	M	V
E	F	A	C	T	P	M	T	T	S	Z	H	C	Z	I	H	Z	N	U	K	T	E	O	K	B
A	M	M	K	I	U	P	K	I	I	X	X	V	V	G	W	Q	O	P	A	D	B	F	P	H
E	K	M	H	M	E	P	J	Z	M	Q	E	P	G	Z	T	E	S	N	S	I	U	W	O	I
K	T	B	K	A	H	D	C	K	I	A	Z	E	K	D	I	T	V	A	F	S	G	F	O	B
G	O	L	R	T	S	H	P	W	M	S	T	X	A	X	F	E	X	X	C	T	B	Z	L	T
A	B	N	Y	E	Q	Q	A	F	C	Q	Z	E	I	S	I	L	P	Q	X	R	S	J	E	O
D	S	S	H	D	P	R	L	Z	H	F	Z	L	D	W	S	Z	F	F	R	I	H	U	D	B
B	E	S	C	S	M	F	M	J	F	R	L	P	O	C	Z	E	T	X	G	B	T	X	S	T
G	R	F	R	T	S	Z	C	F	D	P	S	C	F	X	O	I	D	R	Q	U	B	F	A	A
B	V	C	H	A	G	H	V	P	L	M	R	Z	B	Z	M	H	U	A	P	T	J	A	M	I
C	E	K	A	N	J	U	M	P	F	S	F	W	N	D	W	B	E	R	U	I	Z	Y	P	N
J	D	W	K	D	R	T	L	Q	Q	D	T	D	H	N	H	Q	Z	N	V	O	B	T	L	E
N	T	S	Q	A	X	F	P	D	V	F	X	V	Z	B	Q	Z	D	S	S	N	S	H	E	D
X	D	V	L	R	X	T	S	T	A	T	I	S	T	I	C	M	P	Y	I	D	F	N	V	X
G	P	B	L	D	E	R	G	M	M	D	H	U	L	F	Y	E	F	X	I	M	Q	G	A	C
U	V	J	Y	E	G	D	I	G	H	Y	I	I	R	F	X	Q	M	I	W	F	G	X	R	D
Q	I	K	F	R	N	K	S	L	X	A	Q	D	V	G	B	G	K	C	E	F	V	J	I	M
D	O	T	G	R	P	L	Z	Q	T	R	E	A	T	M	E	N	T	B	V	Q	E	B	A	N
B	P	X	O	O	W	A	I	R	N	J	R	O	F	X	T	A	B	I	G	W	H	R	N	U
E	D	Z	X	R	J	P	I	E	B	A	S	J	M	H	Q	Z	I	E	L	B	J	P	C	A
F	C	W	A	Z	T	I	X	E	G	K	V	S	K	W	C	Y	C	E	E	P	O	M	E	O
G	T	K	J	C	Y	S	W	Q	L	P	C	U	V	M	O	P	W	D	V	M	Y	R	O	F

DEGREES OF FREEDOM

ESTIMATED COHEN'S *D*

ESTIMATED STANDARD ERROR

POOLED SAMPLE VARIANCE

T DISTRIBUTION

T OBSERVED

T OBTAINED

T STATISTIC

TREATMENT

CROSSWORD PUZZLES

ACROSS

1 Any unique characteristic of a sample or any unique way that a researcher treats a sample.

3 A normal-like distribution with greater variability in the tails because the sample variance is substituted for the population variance to estimate the standard error in this distribution.

4 A measure of effect size in terms of the number of standard deviations that mean scores shift above or below the population mean stated by the null hypothesis.

6 An inferential statistic used to determine the number of standard deviations in a *t* distribution that a sample mean deviates from the mean value or mean difference stated in the null hypothesis.

7 An estimate of the standard deviation of a sampling distribution of mean differences between two sample means.

9 A measure of effect size in terms of the proportion or percentage of variability in a dependent variable that can be explained or accounted for by a treatment.

10 The combined sample variance of two samples.

DOWN

2 An estimate of the standard deviation of a sampling distribution of sample means selected from a population with an unknown variance.

5 A statistical procedure used to test hypotheses concerning the mean in a single population with an unknown variance is called a _____-sample *t* test (fill in the blank).

8 A statistical procedure used to test hypotheses concerning the difference between two population means in which the variance in one or both populations is unknown is called a _____-independent-sample *t* test (fill in the blank).

PRACTICE QUIZZES

LO 1: Explain why a t distribution is associated with $n - 1$ degrees of freedom and describe the information that is conveyed by the t statistic.

1. Why does the t distribution have greater variability in the tails of the distribution compared to a normal distribution?

   a. because the t distribution is positively skewed

   b. because the sample variance is substituted for the population variance to estimate the standard error in this distribution

   c. because the normal distribution is negatively skewed compared to the t distribution

   d. it does not; the t distribution is the same as a normal distribution

2. What are the degrees of freedom for a t distribution?

   a. none

   b. N

   c. n

   d. $n - 1$

3. Which of the following best explains why the t distribution is associated with $n - 1$ degrees of freedom?

   a. As sample size increases, the sample variance more closely estimates the population variance, thereby changing the shape of the t distribution (the tails approach the x-axis quicker). For this reason, a t distribution is associated with the same degrees of freedom as sample variance.

   b. As population size increases, the population variance is reduced, thereby making the shape of the t distribution less variable. For this reason, a t distribution is associated with the same degrees of freedom as the population variance.

   c. The t distribution is one unit smaller than a normal distribution. Therefore, a t distribution is associated with $n - 1$ degrees of freedom.

   d. The sample size is typically associated with one person whose data we would prefer not to include in the data analyses. Therefore, a t distribution is associated with $n - 1$ degrees of freedom.

4. The t statistic is an inferential statistic used to determine the number of standard deviations in a t distribution that a sample mean deviates from:

   a. a t statistic stated in the null hypothesis

   b. a population mean or mean difference stated in the null hypothesis

   c. a sample mean value or mean difference stated in the null hypothesis

   d. the sample standard deviation

LO 2: Calculate the degrees of freedom for a one-sample *t* test and a two-independent-sample *t* test and locate critical values in the *t* table.

5. A researcher conducts a one-sample *t* test with a sample of 12 participants. What are the degrees of freedom for this hypothesis test?

    a. 10

    b. 11

    c. 12

    d. 13

6. A researcher conducts a two-independent-sample *t* test with a sample of 24 participants, where 12 participants are observed in each group. What are the degrees of freedom for this hypothesis test?

    a. 22

    b. 23

    c. 24

    d. 25

7. A researcher conducts a one-sample *t* test. What are the critical values for a two-tailed hypothesis test at a .05 level of significance when $df = 14$?

    a. 1.761

    b. 1.771

    c. 2.145

    d. 2.160

8. A researcher conducts a two-independent-sample *t* test. What are the critical values for a two-tailed hypothesis test at a .05 level of significance when $n = 14$ participants in each group?

    a. 2.179

    b. 2.145

    c. 2.048

    d. 2.056

LO 3: Identify the assumptions for the one-sample *t* test.

9. A statistical procedure used to test hypotheses concerning the mean in a single population with an unknown variance is called the:

    a. one-sample *t* test

    b. two-independent-sample *t* test

10. Which of the following is an assumption of the one-sample *t* test?

    a. the sample data are normally distributed

    b. participants were randomly sampled from the population

    c. different participants were observed in two or more groups

    d. all of the above

11. The one-sample *t* test can be computed only when:

    a. the same participants are repeatedly observed in a group

    b. the sample is selected from a population with a known variance

    c. the size of the sample is larger than the size of the population

    d. the population being sampled from is normally distributed

LO 4: Compute a one-sample *t* test and interpret the results.

12. Suppose a researcher selects a sample of 16 participants from a population with an unknown variance and records the following data: 4.5 ± 2.0 (*M* ± *SD*). If the null hypothesis is that the population mean equals 0, then what is the decision for a one-sample *t* test at a .05 level of significance (two-tailed test)?

    a. reject the null hypothesis

    b. retain the null hypothesis

13. A sample of 25 mothers rated how important they thought patience was for being a good mother. Women reported an average rating of 1.1 ± 1.0 (*M* ± *SD*) on a rating scale from –3 (*not important at all*) to +3 (*very important*). If the null hypothesis is that the rating equals 0, then test whether or not women find patience important at a .05 level of significance (two-tailed test).

    a. women rated patience as being significantly important, $t(24) = 5.50$, $p < .05$

    b. women did not rate patience as being important, $t(24) = 0.22$, $p > .05$

    c. women rated patience as being significantly important, $t(25) = 5.50$, $p < .05$

    d. women did not rate patience as being important, $t(25) = 0.22$, $p > .05$

14. In a sample of 26 participants, a researcher reports the following result for a one-sample *t* test: $t(25) = 1.907$, $p < .05$. If this is a two-tailed test at a .05 level of significance, then what *must* be incorrect with this result?

    a. the degrees of freedom

    b. the value of the test statistic

    c. the level of significance

    d. the *p* value

15. A researcher selects a sample of 28 participants and conducts a one-sample *t* test at a .05 level of significance. What is the smallest value that the test statistic could be for this test to result in a decision to reject the null hypothesis using a two-tailed test?

    a. 1.701

    b. 1.703

    c. 2.052

    d. 2.048

LO 5: Compute effect size and proportion of variance for a one-sample *t* test.

16. What value is placed in the denominator of the formula for estimated Cohen's *d* for the one-sample *t* test?

    a. the standard error

    b. the estimated standard error

    c. the population standard deviation

    d. the sample standard deviation

17. Sample 1 has a standard deviation of 4.0 and Sample 2 has a standard deviation of 2.0. If the mean difference between the sample mean and population mean is 5.0 for both samples, then which sample will have the larger effect size using the estimated Cohen's *d* formula?

    a. Sample 1

    b. Sample 2

    c. the effect size will be the same in both samples

18. A researcher computes the following test statistic for a one-sample *t* test: $t(12) = 3.425$, $p < .05$. What is the proportion of variance for this test using the formula for eta-squared?

    a. .49

    b. .47

    c. .45

    d. not enough information

19. A researcher computes the following test statistic for a one-sample *t* test, $t(16) = 2.900$, $p < .05$. What is the proportion of variance for this test using the formula for omega-squared?

    a. .34

    b. .32

    c. .30

    d. not enough information

LO 6: Identify the assumptions for the two-independent-sample *t* test.

20. A statistical procedure used to test hypotheses concerning the difference between two population means, where the variance in one or both populations is unknown, is called the:

    a. one-sample *t* test

    b. two-independent-sample *t* test

21. Which of the following is an assumption of the two-independent-sample *t* test?

    a. the data in the population are positively skewed

    b. participants were randomly sampled from the population

    c. different participants were observed in two or more groups

    d. all of the above

22. The two-independent-sample t test can only be computed when:

   a. the same participants are repeatedly observed in a group

   b. the sample is selected from a population with a known variance

   c. the size of the sample is larger than the size of the population

   d. different participants are observed one time in each group

LO 7: Compute a two-independent-sample t test and interpret the results.

23. Suppose a researcher observes 16 participants assigned to an experimental group ($n = 16$) and 16 assigned to a control group ($n = 16$). Scores in the experimental group are 32 ± 8 ($M ± SD$); scores in the control group are 32 ± 12 ($M ± SD$). If the null hypothesis is that the mean difference equals 0, then what is the decision for a two-independent-sample t test at a .05 level of significance?

   a. reject the null hypothesis

   b. retain the null hypothesis

   c. not enough information

24. Participants who own a home ($n = 16$) or rent a home ($n = 16$) are asked to rate how concerned they are regarding the current state of the economy on a scale from –3 (*not concerned at all*) to +3 (*very concerned*). Mean ratings for homeowners are –1.8 ± 0.6 ($M ± SD$); mean ratings for renters are 0.6 ± 0.4 ($M ± SD$). If the null hypothesis is that the mean difference in ratings is 0, then test whether there is a difference in ratings at a .05 level of significance (two-tailed test).

   a. reject the null hypothesis

   b. retain the null hypothesis

   c. not enough information

25. A researcher compares the mean difference between two groups with 15 students in each group and reports the following result for a two-independent-sample t test: $t(29) = 3.52$, $p < .05$. If this is a two-tailed test at a .05 level of significance, then what must be incorrect with this result?

   a. the degrees of freedom

   b. the value of the test statistic

   c. the level of significance

   d. the p value

26. A researcher selects a sample of 30 participants, randomly assigned to one of two groups. She conducts a two-independent-sample t test at a .05 level of significance. What is the smallest value that the test statistic could be for this test to result in a decision to reject the null hypothesis using a two-tailed test?

   a. 2.052

   b. 2.042

    c. 2.045

    d. 2.048

LO 8: Compute effect size and proportion of variance for a two-independent-sample *t* test.

27. What value is placed in the denominator of the formula for the estimated Cohen's *d* for the two-independent-sample *t* test?

    a. estimated standard error

    b. population standard deviation

    c. pooled sample standard deviation

    d. estimated standard error for the difference

28. A researcher selects two samples of equal size and computes a mean difference of 1.0 between the two sample means. If the pooled sample variance is 4.0, then what is the effect size using the estimated Cohen's *d* formula?

    a. 0.25

    b. 0.50

    c. 1.40

    d. not enough information

29. A researcher computes the following test statistic for a two-independent-sample *t* test: $t(28) = 2.97$, $p < .05$. What is the proportion of variance for this test using the formula for eta-squared?

    a. .21

    b. .24

    c. .27

    d. not enough information

30. A researcher computes the following test statistic for a two-independent-sample *t* test: $t(22) = 3.14$, $p < .05$. What is the proportion of variance for this test using the formula for omega-squared?

    a. .28

    b. .31

    c. .34

    d. not enough information

LO 9: Summarize the results of a one-sample *t* test and a two-independent-sample *t* test in APA format.

31. To report the results of a *t* test, which of the following is not reported?

    a. the test statistic

    b. the *p* value

    c. the degrees of freedom

    d. the critical values

32. A researcher reports that stress levels among nurses are higher compared to stress levels in the general population, $t(40) = 1.684$, $p = .05$ ($d = 0.09$). Was this a one-tailed test or a two-tailed test?

    a. one-tailed test because the p value is equal to .05

    b. two-tailed test because the p value is equal to .05

    c. it could be a one- or a two-tailed test

33. A researcher reports the following result for a t test at a .05 level of significance: $t(40) = 3.02$, $p < .05$ ($d = 0.22$). Is this result significant?

    a. no, the p value is less than 5%

    b. yes, but only for a one-sample t test

    c. yes, but only for a two-independent-sample t test

    d. yes, for both a one-sample and a two-independent-sample t test

SPSS IN FOCUS

One-Sample *t* Test

Follow the General Instructions Guidebook to complete this exercise. Also, an example for following these steps is provided in the SPSS in Focus section (Section 9.6) of the book. Complete and submit the SPSS grading template and a printout of the output file.

Exercise 9.1: Change in Mood Following a Romantic Movie Clip

A researcher asks participants to watch a short romantic movie clip. The movie clip depicts a romantic scene ending with two long-lost lovers embracing in a kiss. After the short romantic movie clip, participants are asked to indicate how the romantic movie clip has affected their mood on a bipolar scale ranging from –3 (*much worse mood*) to +3 (*much better mood*), with 0 indicating no change in mood. The results are given below. It was assumed that the average participant would give a rating of 0 if there were no change in mood. Test whether or not participants reported a significant change in mood at a .05 level of significance using a two-tailed test.

–3	–2	–3
0	–1	–2
–2	–1	2
0	0	–3
–2	0	–3
–2	–1	0
–3	–1	–2
–1	–2	0
–1	0	0
–1	–2	–3
0	–3	–3
0	–3	–2

With regard to the SPSS exercise, answer the following questions:

Based on the table shown in SPSS, state the following values for the sample:

Sample size   _____

Sample mean   _____

Sample standard deviation   _____

Estimated standard error   _____ (labeled *Std. Error Mean*)

Based on the table shown in SPSS, state the following values associated with the test statistic:

Mean difference   _____

t obtained (*t*)   _____

Degrees of freedom (*df*)   _____

Significance (2-tailed)   _____

Based on the value of the test statistic, what is the decision for a one-sample *t* test? (Circle one)

Retain the null hypothesis   Reject the null hypothesis

Compute Cohen's *d* and state the size of the effect as small, medium, or large. (Show your work.) In a sentence, also state the number of standard deviations that scores have shifted in the population. *Note:* The tables in SPSS give you all the data you need to compute effect size.

Compute proportion of variance using eta-squared or omega-squared, and state the size of the effect as small, medium, or large. (Show your work.) In a sentence, also state the proportion of variance in the dependent variable that can be explained by the factor. The tables in SPSS give you all the information you need to compute proportion of variance.

SPSS IN FOCUS

Two-Independent-Sample *t* Test

Follow the General Instructions Guidebook to complete this exercise. Also, an example for following these steps is provided in the SPSS in Focus section (Section 9.9) of the book. Complete and submit the SPSS grading template and a printout of the output file.

Exercise 9.2: Sitting Down to Measure Attraction

A researcher has individuals sit in a "waiting area" prior to participating in a study. In the waiting area is an attractive or unattractive woman sitting in one of the chairs. In fact, the same woman is present in the waiting area and manipulated to look either attractive or unattractive (relatively speaking). The woman is a confederate in the study, meaning that, unbeknownst to participants, she is a co-researcher in the study. Participants are asked to sit in the waiting area until called upon. One group waits in the room with the attractive confederate; the second group waits in the room with the unattractive confederate. The distance (in feet) that participants sit from the confederate is used as a measure of attraction. It was hypothesized that participants would sit closer (in feet) to the attractive versus unattractive confederate. Given the following data, test this hypothesis at a .05 level of significance using a two-tailed test.

Attractiveness of Confederate	
Attractive	Unattractive
1.3	6.8
2.2	5.7
3.5	4.9
0.7	8.5
2.3	9.2
2.1	8.4
4.0	6.7
6.0	4.3
2.3	1.3
5.8	6.3
6.8	8.8
5.3	9.2
8.4	5.7
3.5	7.3
0.4	2.6
7.9	2.1
8.2	6.0
1.6	3.4

With regard to the SPSS exercise, answer the following questions:

Based on the table shown in SPSS, state the following values for each group. Make sure you label a group name for each group in each column in the space provided:

	Group 1:	Group 2:
	_____	_____
Sample size	_____	_____
Sample mean	_____	_____
Sample standard deviation	_____	_____
Estimated standard error	_____	_____

Based on the table shown in SPSS, state the following values associated with the test statistic (assume equal variances):

Mean difference   _____

t obtained   _____

Degrees of freedom   _____

Significance   _____

Estimated standard error for the difference   _____

Based on the value of the test statistic, what is the decision for a two-independent-sample t test? (Circle one)

Retain the null hypothesis   Reject the null hypothesis

Compute Cohen's d and state the size of the effect as small, medium, or large. (Show your work.) In a sentence, also state the number of standard deviations that scores have shifted in the population. *Note:* The tables in SPSS give you all the data you need to compute effect size.

Compute proportion of variance using eta-squared or omega-squared, and state the size of the effect as small, medium, or large. (Show your work.) In a sentence, also state the proportion of variance in the dependent variable that can be explained by the levels of the factor. *Note:* The tables in SPSS give you all the information you need to compute proportion of variance.

CHAPTER SUMMARY ORGANIZED BY LEARNING OBJECTIVE

LO 1: Explain why a *t* distribution is associated with $n - 1$ degrees of freedom and describe the information that is conveyed by the *t* statistic.

- The *t* distribution is a normal-like distribution with greater variability in the tails than a normal distribution because the sample variance is substituted for the population variance to estimate the standard error in this distribution.
- The *t* distribution is a sampling distribution for *t* statistic values that are computed using the sample variance to estimate the population variance in the formula. As sample size increases, the sample variance more closely estimates the population variance. The result is that there is less variability in the tails of a *t* distribution as the sample size increases. Each *t* distribution is associated with the same degrees of freedom as sample variance for a given sample: $df = n - 1$.
- The *t* statistic is an inferential statistic used to determine the number of standard deviations in a *t* distribution that a sample mean deviates from the mean value or mean difference stated in the null hypothesis.

LO 2: Calculate the degrees of freedom for a one-sample *t* test and a two-independent-sample *t* test and locate critical values in the *t* table.

- The degrees of freedom for a *t* distribution are equal to the degrees of freedom for sample variance: $n - 1$. As the degrees of freedom increase, the tails of the corresponding *t* distribution change, and sample outcomes in the tails become less likely.

- The degrees of freedom for a one-sample *t* test are $(n - 1)$; the degrees of freedom for a two-independent-sample *t* test are $(n_1 - 1) + (n_2 - 1)$.

LO 3–4: Identify the assumptions for the one-sample *t* test; compute a one-sample *t* test and interpret the results.

- We compute a one-sample *t* test to compare a mean value measured in a sample to a known value in the population. It is specifically used to test hypotheses concerning a single population mean from a population with an unknown variance. We make three assumptions for this test: normality, random sampling, and independence.
- The larger the value of the test statistic, the less likely a sample mean would be to occur if the null hypothesis were true, and the more likely we are to reject the null hypothesis. The test statistic for a one-sample *t* test is the difference between the sample mean and population mean, divided by the estimated standard error:

$$t_{obt} = \frac{M - \mu}{s_M}, \text{where } s_M = \frac{SD}{\sqrt{n}}.$$

- The estimated standard error is an estimate of the standard deviation of a sampling distribution of sample means. It is an estimate of the standard error or standard distance that sample means can be expected to deviate from the value of the population mean stated in the null hypothesis.

LO 5: Compute effect size and proportion of variance for a one-sample t test.

- Effect size measures the size of an observed difference in a population. For the one-sample t test, this measure estimates how far, or how many standard deviations, an effect shifts in a population. The formula for estimated Cohen's d for the one-sample t test is

$$d = \frac{M - \mu}{SD}.$$

- Proportion of variance is a measure of effect size in terms of the proportion or percent of variability in a dependent variable that can be explained by a treatment. In hypothesis testing, a treatment is considered any unique characteristic of a sample or any unique way that a researcher treats a sample. Two measures of proportion of variance are computed in the same way for all t tests:

Using eta-squared: $\eta^2 = \dfrac{t^2}{t^2 + df}.$

Using omega-squared: $\omega^2 = \dfrac{t^2 - 1}{t^2 + df}.$

LO 6–7: Identify the assumptions for the two-independent-sample t test; compute a two-independent-sample t test and interpret the results.

- We compute a two-independent-sample t test to compare the mean difference between two groups. This test is specifically used to test hypotheses concerning the difference between two population means from one or two populations with unknown variances. We make four assumptions for this test: normality, random sampling, independence, and equal variances.

- The larger the value of the test statistic, the less likely a sample mean would be to occur if the null hypothesis were true, and the more likely we are to reject the null hypothesis. The test statistic for a two-independent-sample t test is the mean difference between two samples minus the mean difference stated in the null hypothesis, divided by the estimated standard error for the difference:

$$t_{\text{obt}} = \frac{(M_1 - M_2) - (\mu_1 - \mu_2)}{s_{M_1 - M_2}}, \text{ where}$$

$$s_{M_1 - M_2} = \sqrt{\frac{s_p^2}{n_1} + \frac{s_p^2}{n_2}},$$

and $s_p^2 = \dfrac{s_1^2(df_1) + s_2^2(df_2)}{df_1 + df_2}.$

- The estimated standard error for the difference is an estimate of the standard deviation of a sampling distribution of mean differences between two sample means. It is an estimate of the standard error or distance that mean differences can deviate from the mean difference stated in the null hypothesis.

LO 8: Compute effect size and proportion of variance for a two-independent-sample t test.

- Estimated Cohen's d can be used to estimate effect size for the two-independent-sample t test. This measure estimates how far, or how many standard deviations, an observed mean difference is shifted in one or two populations. The formula for estimated Cohen's d for the two-independent-sample t test is

$$\frac{M_1 - M_2}{\sqrt{s_p^2}}.$$

- The computation and interpretation of proportion of variance are the same for all *t* tests.

LO 9: Summarize the results of a one-sample *t* test and a two-independent-sample *t* test in APA format.

- To report the results of a one-sample *t* test and a two-independent-sample *t* test, state the test statistic, degrees of freedom, *p* value, and effect size. In addition, a figure or table is often used to summarize the means and standard error or standard deviations measured in a study. While this information can be included in the written report, it is often more concise to include it in a table or figure.

LO 10: Compute a one-sample *t* test and a two-independent-sample *t* test using SPSS.

- SPSS can be used to compute a one-sample *t* test using the Analyze, Compare Means, and One-Sample T Test options in the menu bar. These actions will display a dialog box that allows you to identify the variable, enter the comparison or null hypothesis value for the test, and run the test.
- SPSS can be used to compute a two-independent-sample *t* test using the Analyze, Compare Means, and Independent-Samples T Test options in the menu bar. These actions will display a dialog box that allows you to identify the groups and run the test.

10

Testing Means

The Related-Samples t *Test*

LEARNING OBJECTIVES

After reading this chapter, you should be able to:

1. Describe two types of research designs used when we select related samples.

2. Explain why difference scores are computed for the related-samples *t* test.

3. Calculate the degrees of freedom for a related-samples *t* test and locate critical values in the *t* table.

4. Identify the assumptions for the related-samples *t* test.

5. Compute a related-samples *t* test and interpret the results.

6. Compute effect size and proportion of variance for a related-samples *t* test.

7. State three advantages for selecting related samples.

8. Summarize the results of a related-samples *t* test in APA format.

9. Compute a related-samples *t* test using SPSS.

CHAPTER OUTLINE

10.1 Related and Independent Samples

In a *related* or *dependent* sample, participants in each group are observed in more than one group or matched on common characteristics. Note that this type of design takes many different forms, broadly categorized as the repeated-measures design and the matched-pairs design.

Repeated-measures design: A research design in which the same participants are observed in each sample. Two types of repeated-measures designs are the pre-post design and the within-subjects design.

- *Pre-post design:* Researchers measure a dependent variable for participants before (pre) and after (post) a treatment.
- *Within-subjects design:* Researchers observe the same participants across many groups or treatments but not necessarily before and after a treatment.

Matched-pairs design: A research design in which participants are selected and then matched, experimentally or naturally, based on common characteristics or traits.

- Participants can be matched experimentally by manipulating the traits upon which the participants are matched.
- Participants can be matched through *natural occurrence* based on preexisting traits.

10.2 Introduction to the Related-Samples *t* Test

For related-samples designs, we use a related-samples *t* test to compare difference scores in a sample to those stated for a population in the null hypothesis.

- *Related-samples* t *test:* A statistical procedure used to test hypotheses concerning two related samples selected from populations in which the variance in one or both populations is unknown.
  - *Difference scores* are obtained by subtracting pairs of scores for each participant. Computing difference scores eliminates the between-persons source of error, which is included only when different participants are observed in each group. Because the same participants are observed in each group using the related-samples design, we can eliminate this source of error.
  - *Error:* Any unexplained difference that cannot be attributed to having different groups or treatments.

The test statistic: As with other test statistics, mean differences are placed in the numerator, and standard error is placed in the denominator. The formula for the test statistic for the related-samples *t* test is as follows:

$$t_{obt} = \frac{M_D - \mu_D}{s_{MD}} \text{, where } s_{MD} = \sqrt{\frac{s_D^2}{n_D}} = \frac{s_D}{\sqrt{n_D}}.$$

- *Degrees of freedom:* The degrees of freedom equal the number of difference scores minus 1.

$$df = n_D - 1.$$

Assumptions of the Related-Samples *t* Test

- *Normality.* We assume that the population sampled from is normally distributed, particularly for samples less than 30 ($n < 30$).
- *Independence within groups.* Although the samples are related between groups, we assume that different participants are observed within each group or treatment.

10.3 The Related-Samples *t* Test: Repeated-Measures Design

Once these two assumptions are met, we use the four steps to hypothesis testing to conduct the related-samples *t* test.

- *Step 1: State the hypotheses.* We state the null and alternative hypotheses regarding the population of difference scores. For example, we could state the following for a non-directional test:

$$H_0: \mu_D = 0.$$

$$H_1: \mu_D \neq 0.$$

- *Step 2: Set the criteria for a decision.* The level of significance is typically equal to .05. We still refer to the *t* table to find the critical values (see Table B.2 in Appendix B of the book; also reprinted in the appendix of this study guide).
- *Step 3: Compute the test statistic.* We compute (1) the mean, variance, and standard deviation for difference scores; (2) the estimated standard error for difference scores; and then (3) the following test statistic:

$$t_{obt} = \frac{M_D - \mu_D}{s_{MD}} \text{, where } s_{MD} = \frac{s_D}{\sqrt{n_D}}.$$

- *Step 4: Make a decision.* Compare the obtained value to the critical value to make a decision to retain or reject the null hypothesis.

10.4 SPSS in Focus: The Related-Samples *t* Test

SPSS can be used to compute a related-samples *t* test by using the Analyze, Compare Means, and Paired-Samples T Test options in the menu bar.

10.5 The Related-Samples *t* Test: Matched-Pairs Design

The procedures and test statistic formula for the related-samples *t* test are the same regardless of whether we use the matched-pairs or the repeated-measures design.

10.6 Measuring Effect Size for the Related-Samples *t* Test

There are three measures of effect size for the related-samples *t* test: estimated Cohen's *d*, eta-squared, and omega-squared.

Estimated Cohen's d: We calculate the mean difference between two samples in the numerator and the standard deviation of the difference scores in the denominator.

$$\text{Estimated Cohen's } d = \frac{M_D}{s_D}.$$

The formula for eta-squared is the same for all *t* tests: $\eta^2 = \dfrac{t^2}{t^2 + df}$.

The formula for omega-squared is the same for all *t* tests: $\omega^2 = \dfrac{t^2 - 1}{t^2 + df}$.

10.7 Advantages for Selecting Related Samples

There are three key advantages for selecting related samples compared to selecting independent samples in behavioral research:

- It can be more practical in that selecting related samples may provide a better way to test your hypotheses, particularly when researchers must observe changes in behavior or development over time or between matched pairs of participants.
- Selecting related samples minimizes standard error. Computing difference scores prior to computing the test statistic eliminates the between-persons source of error, which reduces the estimate of standard error.

- Selecting related samples increases power. It follows from the second advantage that reducing the estimate of standard error will increase the value of the test statistic, thereby increasing power.

10.8 APA in Focus: Reporting the *t* Statistic and Effect Size for Related Samples

To summarize a related-samples *t* test, we report the test statistic, degrees of freedom, and *p* value. In addition, you should summarize the means and the standard error or the standard deviations measured in the study in a figure, in a table, or in the main text.

CHAPTER FORMULAS

The Related-Samples t Test

Related-Samples t Test

$$t_{obt} = \frac{M_D - \mu_D}{s_{M_D}} \quad \text{(Test statistic for the related-samples } t \text{ test)}$$

$$s_{M_D} = \sqrt{\frac{s_D^2}{n_D}} = \frac{s_D}{\sqrt{n_D}} \quad \text{(Estimated standard error for difference scores)}$$

$$df = n_D - 1 \quad \text{(Degrees of freedom for the related-samples } t \text{ test)}$$

Effect Size

$$d = \frac{M_D}{s_D} \quad \text{(Estimated Cohen's } d \text{ for the related-samples } t \text{ test)}$$

$$\eta^2 = \frac{t^2}{t^2 + df} \quad \text{(Eta-squared estimate of proportion of variance; used for all } t \text{ tests)}$$

$$\omega^2 = \frac{t^2 - 1}{t^2 + df} \quad \text{(Omega-squared estimate of proportion of variance; used for all } t \text{ tests)}$$

TIPS AND CAUTIONS FOR STUDENTS

- *The test statistic:* For the related-samples t test, we compute difference scores by subtracting participant scores to eliminate the between-persons error that is associated with observing different participants in each group. Because the same participants are observed in each group using the related-samples design, we can eliminate this source of error. The result is that the estimate of standard error will be smaller and the related-samples t test will have greater power to detect an effect. Again, we do this only when we use the related-samples design.

- *Degrees of freedom:* The degrees of freedom (df) for the related-samples t test are similar to those for a one-sample t test. Using a one-sample t test, we have one column of participant scores. Using the related-samples t test, we have one column of difference scores—hence, the degrees of freedom are the number of difference scores minus 1: $n_D - 1$.

- *Advantages for related samples:* Remember that we compute difference scores before computing the related-samples t test. This reduces the standard error compared to the standard error we would have computed using the original two columns of participant scores. By reducing standard error, we increase the power of the design (i.e., we are more likely to detect an effect or difference between groups).

KEY TERM WORD SEARCHES

T	W	I	T	H	I	N	S	U	B	J	E	C	T	S	D	E	S	I	G	N	C	S	M	L	R	V	G	Q	V
V	F	Y	D	N	F	R	E	P	E	A	T	E	D	M	E	A	S	U	R	E	S	D	E	S	I	G	N	Z	A
Z	E	M	D	O	E	M	E	F	N	N	T	C	Y	G	M	Y	Q	Y	X	N	C	D	R	C	X	K	Z	Q	B
G	Q	Z	T	V	D	V	P	O	Y	X	O	R	O	H	X	D	C	E	S	P	I	G	H	E	P	S	W	A	U
A	Q	T	M	M	I	N	D	H	X	M	T	I	E	C	K	X	J	S	B	J	Y	U	F	N	A	T	R	K	I
U	Y	M	A	J	F	B	Z	V	U	O	A	H	D	L	C	A	D	Q	G	I	V	Q	F	K	X	P	C	F	T
B	V	G	T	A	F	X	C	B	F	J	I	T	L	K	A	H	C	O	C	V	K	Y	H	Y	R	P	H	S	Y
B	F	X	C	X	E	J	J	E	H	X	A	O	C	N	K	T	A	A	U	U	H	V	X	O	O	Q	I	B	E
D	X	V	H	K	R	F	Z	I	Z	B	V	I	L	H	Z	B	E	F	A	E	O	O	I	Z	X	H	D	W	H
M	U	J	E	N	E	P	P	W	E	F	G	L	N	U	E	P	F	D	L	Z	E	R	R	O	R	E	M	J	H
T	S	O	D	J	N	B	T	T	F	F	Q	S	O	Y	N	D	N	P	S	N	G	T	P	V	W	Z	O	R	U
Z	C	O	S	Y	C	C	Q	N	Z	S	C	V	D	N	V	C	P	Z	Z	A	Q	S	Z	W	C	R	W	L	Y
T	T	M	U	X	E	T	Z	S	H	U	Q	Q	H	N	C	A	Y	A	U	L	M	T	K	S	Y	N	W	W	I
V	R	Y	B	C	S	X	L	R	M	E	W	T	D	N	V	I	V	L	I	G	A	P	L	I	R	C	Q	Y	X
H	F	C	J	Y	C	B	F	V	G	Q	A	K	E	E	A	J	X	F	Y	R	V	I	L	F	H	L	Z	C	X
Y	L	X	E	P	O	B	N	E	G	F	T	A	P	G	P	P	K	Z	B	N	S	W	U	E	Y	R	L	X	D
G	J	W	C	R	R	T	K	R	L	I	C	F	D	T	X	E	F	C	V	D	Y	D	G	I	F	H	Y	J	K
J	D	T	E	E	O	E	E	F	N	O	U	U	E	I	M	N	U	C	P	H	D	E	K	H	F	D	I	U
Z	V	T	S	P	S	E	O	V	H	Z	L	J	H	X	W	D	Y	D	Z	Q	F	D	L	S	X	N	Q	E	E
T	A	V	D	O	D	Z	C	E	A	L	U	F	J	M	I	A	Y	M	E	E	W	C	N	E	I	T	D	F	K
R	A	Z	E	S	X	W	M	E	O	A	V	V	M	Z	J	F	G	M	C	N	Y	P	M	H	F	G	F	Y	S
Q	O	R	S	T	A	Z	W	Q	O	L	D	A	N	X	T	F	Y	I	E	D	T	Z	F	N	X	G	N	R	R
F	P	Y	I	D	R	E	L	A	T	E	D	S	A	M	P	L	E	S	T	T	E	S	T	H	G	I	J	F	V
U	Y	E	G	E	V	Q	X	Z	V	Y	W	L	X	B	G	Y	E	E	K	O	Z	A	A	B	Z	N	D	Q	Y
K	J	I	N	S	Q	A	Q	B	I	F	P	T	Y	O	A	I	I	E	D	U	P	V	Z	M	S	M	B	F	K
K	U	T	U	I	Z	Q	R	Z	M	Q	N	I	V	U	V	S	B	J	L	G	V	N	Q	S	P	X	V	T	N
U	L	Q	T	G	W	P	V	G	R	N	M	Q	C	G	P	O	S	V	V	I	Z	U	C	Y	I	L	B	U	J
W	T	C	V	N	D	X	E	E	B	Z	Q	T	Z	O	D	F	O	S	I	A	F	Z	X	W	B	N	E	T	T
R	M	H	I	N	D	E	P	E	N	D	E	N	T	S	A	M	P	L	E	V	V	U	L	J	Y	L	Q	L	N
F	B	K	M	M	A	T	C	H	E	D	S	A	M	P	L	E	S	D	E	S	I	G	N	Y	X	T	E	C	I

DEPENDENT SAMPLE

DIFFERENCE SCORES

ERROR

INDEPENDENT SAMPLE

MATCHED-PAIRS DESIGN

MATCHED-SAMPLES DESIGN

MATCHED-SUBJECTS DESIGN

PRE-POST DESIGN

RELATED SAMPLE

RELATED-SAMPLES *T* TEST

REPEATED-MEASURES DESIGN

WITHIN-SUBJECTS DESIGN

CROSSWORD PUZZLES

ACROSS

9 A research design in which the same participants are observed in each sample.

DOWN

1 A statistical procedure used to test hypotheses concerning two related samples selected from populations in which the variance in one or both populations is unknown.

2 Scores that are obtained by subtracting paired scores for two related samples.

3 A type of repeated-measures design in which researchers observe the same participants across many treatments but not necessarily before and after a treatment.

4 A type of sample in which participants in each group or sample are related.

5 A type of repeated-measures design in which researchers measure a dependent variable for participants before and after a treatment.

6 A research design in which participants are selected and then matched, experimentally or naturally, based on common characteristics or traits.

7 A type of sample in which participants in each group or sample are unrelated in that they are observed once in only one sample.

8 A term that refers to any unexplained difference that cannot be attributed to, or caused by, having different treatments.

PRACTICE QUIZZES

LO 1: Describe two types of research designs used when we select related samples.

1. A researcher observes the same group of participants in the morning and again at night. What type of research design did the researcher use?

    a. repeated-measures design

    b. matched-pairs design

2. A researcher compares differences in personality traits among pairs of identical twins. What type of research design did the researcher use?

    a. repeated-measures design

    b. matched-pairs design

3. Which of the following is a type of repeated-measures design?

    a. pre-post design

    b. within-subjects design

    c. matched-pairs design

    d. both a and b

4. A researcher wants to study differences in mood due to listening to music. Before conducting the study, she has participants report how often they listen to music (in minutes) per week. Participants were matched based on their responses, and differences in mood between matched pairs of participants were computed. What type of strategy was used to match participants?

    a. matching through experimental manipulation

    b. matching through natural occurrence

    c. both a and b

LO 2: Explain why difference scores are computed for the related-samples t test.

5. Scores that are obtained by subtracting paired scores for two related samples are called:

    a. raw scores

    b. repeated scores

    c. difference scores

    d. bivariate scores

6. An advantage of computing difference scores in the related-samples t test is that it:

    a. reduces variability

    b. reduces standard error

    c. increases power

    d. all of the above

7. Difference scores are computed _____ we compute the test statistic for the related-samples *t* test.

a. after

b. before

LO 3: Calculate the degrees of freedom for a related-samples *t* test and locate critical values in the *t* table.

8. The degrees of freedom for the related-samples *t* test are:

a. the number of samples minus 1

b. the number of total scores minus 1

c. the number of difference scores minus 1

d. the number of groups minus 1

9. A group of 20 participants is observed two times. The related-samples *t* test for this study will have a degree(s) of freedom equal to:

a. 1

b. 18

c. 19

d. 20

10. A group of 18 participants is observed two times. The critical values for a two-tailed related-samples *t* test at a .05 level of significance are:

a. ±1.734

b. ±2.110

c. ±2.101

d. ±1.740

LO 4: Identify the assumptions for the related-samples *t* test.

11. A statistical procedure used to test hypotheses concerning two related samples selected from populations in which the variance in one or both populations is unknown is called a:

a. one-sample *t* test

b. two-independent-sample *t* test

c. related-samples *t* test

12. Which of the following is an assumption of the related-samples *t* test?

a. the population of difference scores is normally distributed

b. participants were randomly assigned to one of two groups

c. different participants were observed in each of two groups

d. all of the above

13. The related-samples *t* test can be computed when:

    a. the same participants are observed two times or in two groups

    b. the sample is selected from two or more populations

    c. different participants are observed in each group

    d. the same participants are observed in three or more groups

LO 5: Compute a related-samples *t* test and interpret the results.

14. A researcher measures scores in two groups ($n = 12$ in each group) with $M_1 = 9.8$ and $M_2 = 4.8$. In this study, the estimated standard error for difference scores is 2.0. What is the decision for a related-samples *t* test using a two-tailed test at a .05 level of significance?

    a. reject the null hypothesis

    b. retain the null hypothesis

    c. not enough information

15. Using a repeated-measures design, Researcher A computes the following test statistic, $t(22) = 1.980$, and decides to reject the null hypothesis. Using a matched-pairs design, Researcher B computes the same test statistic, $t(22) = 1.980$, but decides to retain the null hypothesis. Which of the following can explain why this occurred?

    a. the repeated-measures design is a more powerful design than the matched-pairs design

    b. Researcher A computed a one-tailed test; Researcher B computed a two-tailed test

    c. Researcher B computed a one-tailed test; Researcher A computed a two-tailed test

    d. both b and c could be true

16. A researcher computes a related-samples *t* test using the following data: $M_1 = 16$, $M_2 = 13$, $s_D = 8.0$, and $n_D = 16$. What is the value of the test statistic using these data if the null hypothesis is that there is no mean difference?

    a. $t(15) = 1.50$

    b. $t(14) = 1.50$

    c. $t(15) = 6.00$

    d. $t(14) = 6.00$

17. Two researchers (A and B) measure the same mean difference between two related groups using the same sample size. The only difference is that the estimated standard error for difference scores is larger for the data of Researcher A than for the data of Researcher B. Which researcher will compute a larger test statistic for a related-samples *t* test?

    a. Researcher A

    b. Researcher B

    c. the test statistic will be the same for both researchers

LO 6: Compute effect size and proportion of variance for a related-samples *t* test.

18. What value is placed in the denominator of the formula for estimated Cohen's d for the related-samples t test?

    a. estimated standard error

    b. population standard deviation

    c. the standard deviation of the difference scores

    d. the estimated standard error for the difference scores

19. A researcher selects two related samples with a mean difference of 6.3. If the standard deviation of the difference scores is 7.2, then what is the effect size using the estimated Cohen's d formula?

    a. 6.30

    b. 1.14

    c. 0.88

    d. not enough information

20. A researcher computes the following test statistic for a related-samples t test: $t(28) = 2.97$, $p < .05$. What is the proportion of variance for this test using the formula for eta-squared?

    a. .21

    b. .27

    c. .24

    d. not enough information

21. A researcher computes the following test statistic for a related-samples t test: $t(22) = 3.14$, $p < .05$. What is the proportion of variance for this test using the formula for omega-squared?

    a. .28

    b. .31

    c. .34

    d. not enough information

LO 7: State three advantages for selecting related samples.

22. Three advantages for selecting related samples include each of the following, *except*:

    a. it can be more practical

    b. it minimizes the estimate for standard error

    c. it increases power

    d. it decreases the likelihood of a Type I error

23. How does selecting related samples increase the power to detect an effect?

    a. by increasing the likelihood of a Type I error

    b. by increasing the estimate for standard error

    c. by reducing the estimate for standard error

    d. by decreasing the likelihood of a Type I error

24. How does selecting related samples minimize the estimate for standard error?

    a. it changes the level of significance for a hypothesis test

    b. it eliminates the between-persons source of error

    c. it decreases the likelihood of a Type I error

    d. both a and b

LO 8: Summarize the results of a related-samples *t* test in APA format.

25. Which of the following is reported only with a related-samples *t* test and not for any other type of *t* test?

    a. the test statistic

    b. the *p* value

    c. the degrees of freedom

    d. none of the above; the same information is reported for all *t* tests

26. The sample means and the standard error or the standard deviations measured in the study can be reported in:

    a. a figure

    b. a table

    c. the main text

    d. all of the above

27. A researcher reports the following result for a related-samples *t* test at a .05 level of significance: $t(40) = 3.02$, $p < .05$ ($d = 0.20$). Is this result significant?

    a. no, because the *p* value is less than 5%

    b. yes, because the *p* value is less than 5%

    c. no, because the effect size is small

    d. yes, because the effect size is large

Follow the General Instructions Guidebook to complete this exercise. Also, an example for following these steps is provided in the SPSS in Focus section (Section 10.4) of the book. Complete and submit the SPSS grading template and a printout of the output file.

Exercise 10.1: Enhancing Recall With Color

A researcher wants to test whether color can influence recall of words in a list. To test this, the researcher displays 20 words on a computer screen. Ten words are in color, and 10 words are in black. All words are presented on a white background. Participants are given one minute to view the list, and then the list is taken away and participants are allowed one additional minute to write down as many words as they can recall. The researcher records the number of colored versus black words accurately recalled. The results are given below. Test whether the color of words in the list influenced recall at a .05 level of significance using a two-tailed test.

Participant	Type of Word	
	Color	Black
1	7	4
2	8	4
3	4	6
4	6	4
5	4	6
6	8	2
7	6	3
8	7	3
9	5	6
10	6	9
11	4	5
12	6	7
13	5	5
14	8	3
15	9	0
16	10	0
17	6	8
18	4	6
19	2	6
20	8	4
21	6	2
22	4	1

With regard to the SPSS exercise, answer the following questions:

Based on the table shown in SPSS, state the following values for each group. Make sure you label a group name for each group in the space provided:

	Group 1:	Group 2:
	_____	_____
Sample size	_____	_____
Sample mean	_____	_____
Sample standard deviation	_____	_____
Estimated standard error	_____	_____

Based on the table shown in SPSS, state the following values associated with the difference scores:

Mean difference	_____
Standard deviation	_____
Estimated standard error for difference scores	_____

Based on the values you have summarized thus far, what value is the numerator of the test statistic? What value is the denominator of the test statistic?

Based on the table shown in SPSS, state the following values associated with the test statistic:

t obtained (*t*)	_____
Degrees of freedom (*df*)	_____
Significance (2-tailed)	_____

Based on the value of the test statistic, what is the decision for a related-samples *t* test? (Circle one)

Retain the null hypothesis   Reject the null hypothesis

Compute Cohen's *d* and state the size of the effect as small, medium, or large. (Show your work.) In a sentence, also state the number of standard deviations that scores have shifted in the population. *Note:* The tables in SPSS give you all the data you need to compute effect size.

Compute proportion of variance using eta-squared or omega-squared, and state the size of the effect as small, medium, or large. (Show your work.) In a sentence, also state the proportion of variance in the dependent variable that can be explained by the levels of the factor. *Note:* The tables in SPSS give you all the information you need to compute proportion of variance.

CHAPTER SUMMARY ORGANIZED BY LEARNING OBJECTIVE

LO 1: Describe two types of research designs used when we select related samples.

- In a related sample, participants are related. Participants can be related in one of two ways: They are observed in more than one group (a repeated-measures design), or they are matched, experimentally or naturally, based on common characteristics or traits (a matched-pairs design).
- The repeated-measures design is a research design in which the same participants are observed in each treatment. Two types of repeated-measures designs are the pre-post design and the within-subjects design.
- The matched-pairs design is a research design in which participants are selected, then matched, experimentally or naturally, based on common characteristics or traits.

LO 2: Explain why difference scores are computed for the related-samples t test.

- To test the null hypothesis, we state the mean difference between paired scores in the population and compare this to the difference between paired scores in a sample. A related-samples t test is different from a two-independent-sample t test in that we first find the difference between the paired scores and then compute the test statistic. The difference between two scores in a pair is called a difference score.
- Computing difference scores eliminates between-persons error. This error is associated with differences associated with observing different participants in each group or treatment. Because we

observe the same (or matched) participants in each treatment, not different participants, we can eliminate this source of error before computing the test statistic. Removing this error reduces the value of the estimate of standard error, which increases the power to detect an effect.

LO 3–5: Calculate the degrees of freedom for a related-samples t test and locate critical values in the t table; identify the assumptions for the related-samples t test; compute a related-samples t test and interpret the results.

- The related-samples t test is a statistical procedure used to test hypotheses concerning two related samples selected from related populations in which the variance in one or both populations is unknown.
- The degrees of freedom for a related samples t test is the number of difference scores minus 1: $df = (n_D - 1)$.
- To compute a related-samples t test, we assume normality and independence within groups. The test statistic for a related-samples t test concerning the difference between two related samples is as follows:

$$t_{obt} = \frac{M_D - \mu_D}{s_{MD}}, \text{ where } s_{MD} = \frac{s_D}{\sqrt{n_D}}.$$

LO 6: Compute effect size and proportion of variance for a related-samples t test.

- Estimated Cohen's d is the most popular estimate of effect size used with the t test. It is a measure of effect size in terms of the number of standard deviations

205

that mean difference scores shifted above or below the population mean difference stated in the null hypothesis. To compute estimated Cohen's d with two related samples, divide the mean difference (M_D) between two samples by the standard deviation of the difference scores (s_D):

$$d = \frac{M_D}{s_D}.$$

- Another measure of effect size is proportion of variance. Specifically, this is an estimate of the proportion of variance in the dependent variable that can be explained by a treatment. Two measures of proportion of variance for the related-samples t test are eta-squared and omega-squared. These measures are computed in the same way for all t tests:

Using eta-squared: $\eta^2 = \frac{t^2}{t^2 + df}$.

Using omega-squared: $\omega^2 = \frac{t^2 - 1}{t^2 + df}$.

LO 7: **State three advantages for selecting related samples.**

- Three advantages for selecting related samples are that selecting related samples (1) can be more practical, (2) reduces standard error, and (3) increases power.

LO 8: **Summarize the results of a related-samples t test in APA format.**

- To report the results of a related-samples t test, state the test statistic, the degrees of freedom, the p value, and the effect size. In addition, summarize the means and the standard error or the standard deviations measured in the study in a figure or a table or in the text. Finally, note that the type of t test computed is reported in a data analysis section that precedes the results section, where the statistics are reported.

LO 9: **Compute a related-samples t test using SPSS.**

- SPSS can be used to compute a related-samples t test using the Analyze, Compare Means, and Paired-Samples T Test options in the menu bar. These actions will display a dialog box that allows you to identify the groups and run the test.

11

Estimation and Confidence Intervals

LEARNING OBJECTIVES

After reading this chapter, you should be able to:

1. Describe the process of estimation and identify two types of estimation.

2. Distinguish between significance testing and estimation.

3. Compute confidence intervals for the one-sample z test.

4. Compute confidence intervals for the one-sample t test.

5. Compute confidence intervals for the two-independent-sample t test.

6. Compute confidence intervals for the related-samples t test.

7. Distinguish between the certainty and precision of an interval estimate.

8. Summarize confidence intervals for the z test and t tests in APA format.

9. Compute confidence intervals for the one-sample, two-independent-sample, and related-samples t tests using SPSS.

11.1 Point Estimation and Interval Estimation

We can learn about the mean or mean difference in a population without testing a null hypothesis. An alternative way to learn about the mean or mean difference in a population, called *estimation*, is to set limits for the population parameter within which it is likely to be contained.

Estimation: A statistical procedure in which a sample statistic is used to estimate the value of an unknown population parameter. To use estimation, we select a sample, measure a sample mean or mean difference, and then use that measurement to estimate the value of a parameter.

- *Point estimation:* The use of a sample statistic (e.g., a sample mean) to estimate a population parameter (e.g., a population mean). The point estimate is an unbiased estimator of the population mean. However, we have little certainty that the sample mean equals the population mean.
- *Interval estimation:* A statistical procedure in which a sample of data is used to find the interval or range of possible values within which a population parameter is likely to be contained.
  - o *Confidence interval:* The range of possible values within which the population mean is contained.
  - o *Level of confidence:* The likelihood that an interval estimate contains the population mean.
  - o *Confidence limits:* The upper and lower boundaries of a confidence interval.

11.2 The Process of Estimation

In estimation, we use the sample mean as a point estimate and the standard error to find the range of sample means within which the population mean is likely to be contained (the interval estimate).

- A population mean is estimated as the point estimate plus or minus the interval estimate.

In all, we follow three steps to estimate the value of a population mean using a point estimate and an interval estimate. Point and interval estimates can be computed as an alternative to the z test and the t tests taught in Chapters 8 to 10.

- Step 1: Compute the sample mean and standard error.
- Step 2: Choose the level of confidence and find the critical values at that level of confidence.
- Step 3: Compute the estimation formula to find the confidence limits.

11.3 Estimation for the One-Sample z Test

Instead of calculating a one-sample z test in cases when we know the population mean and the variance, we can use estimation to estimate the limits within which a population mean is likely to be contained.

Estimation formula for the one-sample z: $M \pm z(\sigma_M)$.

Step 1: Compute the sample mean and standard error.

- Standard error: $\sigma_M = \dfrac{\sigma}{\sqrt{n}}$.

Step 2: Choose the level of confidence and find the critical values.
- In this step, first determine the level of confidence for the interval, and then find the critical values. The critical values are listed in the unit normal table (see Table B.1 in Appendix B of the book; also reprinted in the appendix of this study guide).

Step 3: Compute the estimation formula to find the confidence limits.

- *Upper confidence limit:* The largest possible value of a population parameter in a confidence interval within a specified level of confidence. To find the upper confidence limit: $M + z(\sigma_M)$.
- *Lower confidence limit:* The smallest possible value of a population parameter in a confidence interval within a specified level of confidence. To find the lower confidence limit: $M - z(\sigma_M)$.

Confidence intervals and hypothesis testing: If the value stated by the null hypothesis falls inside the confidence interval, the decision is to retain the null hypothesis. If the value stated by the null hypothesis falls outside the confidence interval, the decision is to reject the null hypothesis.

Effect Size for Confidence Intervals

The effect size for a confidence interval is a range where the lower effect size estimate is calculated as the difference between the null hypothesis and the lower confidence limit, and the upper effect size estimate is calculated as the difference between the null hypothesis and the upper confidence limit.

11.4, 11.6, and 11.8: Estimation for the One-Sample, Two-Independent-Sample, and Related-Samples t Tests

We can also use estimation as an alternative to the t tests, in cases when we do not know the population variance. There are estimation formulas for each type of t test, and each is summarized here.

Step 1: Compute the sample mean and the estimate of standard error.

- Estimate of standard error:

$$s_M = \frac{SD}{\sqrt{n}} \text{ for the one-sample } t \text{ test.}$$

$$s_{M_1-M_2} = \sqrt{\frac{s_P^2}{n_1} + \frac{s_P^2}{n_2}} \text{ for the two-independent-sample } t \text{ test.}$$

$$s_{MD} = \sqrt{\frac{s_D^2}{n_D}} = \frac{s_D}{\sqrt{n_D}} \text{ for the related-samples } t \text{ test.}$$

Step 2: Choose the level of confidence and find the critical values.

- In this step, first determine the level of confidence for the interval, and then find the critical values. The critical values are listed in the t table for each type of t test (see Table B.2 in Appendix B of the book; also reprinted in the appendix of this study guide).

Step 3: Compute the estimation formula to find the confidence limits.

Estimation formula for the one-sample t test: $M \pm t(s_M)$

Estimation formula for the two-independent-sample t test: $M_1 - M_2 \pm t(s_{M_1-M_2})$

Estimation formula for the related-samples t test: $M_D \pm t(s_{MD})$

11.5, 11.7, and 11.9 SPSS in Focus: Confidence Intervals for the One-Sample, Two-Independent-Sample, and Related-Samples t Tests

To compute a confidence interval for a one-sample t test, follow the steps for computing the one-sample t test given in Chapter 9 of the book (p. 276), and select Options in the dialog box in Steps 3 to 5. This action will display an additional dialog box that will allow you to choose any confidence interval.

To compute the confidence interval for a two-independent-sample t test, follow the steps for computing the two-independent-sample t test given in Chapter 9 of the book (p. 287), and select Options in the dialog box in Steps 4 to 6. This action will display an additional dialog box that will allow you to choose any confidence interval.

To compute the confidence interval for a related-samples t test, follow the steps for computing the related-samples t test given in Chapter 10 of the book (p. 307), and select Options in the dialog box in Steps 3 to 4. This action will display an additional dialog box that will allow you to choose any confidence interval.

11.10 Characteristics of Estimation: Precision and Certainty

There are two key characteristics related to interpreting confidence intervals: the *precision* and the *certainty* of the confidence interval.

- *Precision:* The smaller the range of the interval, the more precise the estimate.
  - Decreasing the level of confidence increases the precision of an estimate.
- *Certainty:* The larger the level of confidence, the more certain the estimate.
  - Increasing the level of confidence increases the certainty of the estimate.

11.11 APA in Focus: Reporting Confidence Intervals

To report estimation, we state the level of confidence, the point estimate, and the interval estimate of each confidence interval.

CHAPTER FORMULAS

Estimation

$M \pm z(\sigma_M)$ (The estimation formula for a one-sample z test)

$M \pm t(s_M)$ (The estimation formula for a one-sample t test)

$M_1 - M_2 \pm t(s_{M_1 - M_2})$ (The estimation formula for a two-independent-sample t test)

$M_D \pm t(s_{MD})$ (The estimation formula for a related-samples t test)

TIPS AND CAUTIONS FOR STUDENTS

- *Estimation:* Estimation makes use of the confidence interval to determine the range of possible values that may contain the actual population mean. The range of the confidence interval is determined by the standard error and the critical value, which is determined by the alpha level. Therefore, just as we used the alpha level to find critical values using hypothesis testing, we also use critical values to determine the confidence interval, or range of possible values, for the population mean within a specified level of confidence. Keep in mind that the level of confidence in estimation directly relates to the alpha level for a hypothesis test.

- *Precision and certainty:* The two key characteristics of confidence intervals, precision and certainty, are related in that to increase one means we must decrease the other. To have more *precision* and thus a narrower confidence interval, we must reduce the certainty of the estimate. Likewise, to be more certain, we must give up precision (i.e., the confidence interval is widened). Because of this give-and-take relationship, the certainty and precision of a confidence interval are characteristics that we try to balance.

KEY TERM WORD SEARCHES

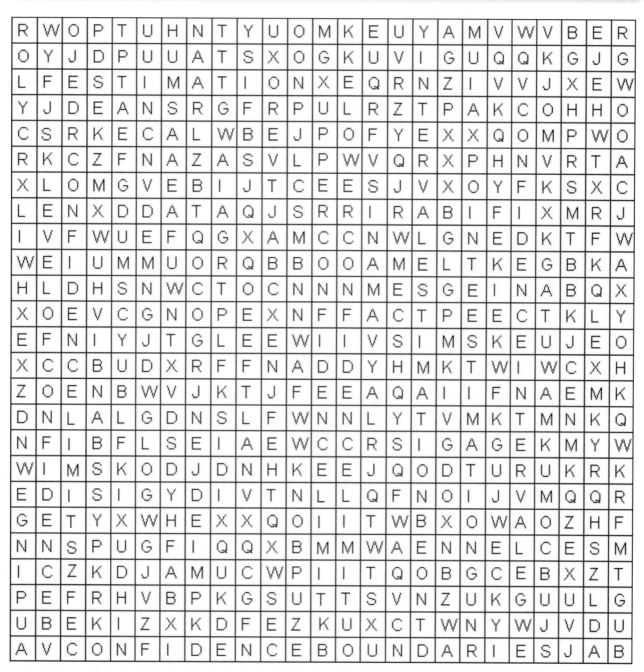

R	W	O	P	T	U	H	N	T	Y	U	O	M	K	E	U	Y	A	M	V	W	V	B	E	R
O	Y	J	D	P	U	U	A	T	S	X	O	G	K	U	V	I	G	U	Q	Q	K	G	J	G
L	F	E	S	T	I	M	A	T	I	O	N	X	E	Q	R	N	Z	I	V	V	J	X	E	W
Y	J	D	E	A	N	S	R	G	F	R	P	U	L	R	Z	T	P	A	K	C	O	H	H	O
C	S	R	K	E	C	A	L	W	B	E	J	P	O	F	Y	E	X	X	Q	O	M	P	W	O
R	K	C	Z	F	N	A	Z	A	S	V	L	P	W	V	Q	R	X	P	H	N	V	R	T	A
X	L	O	M	G	V	E	B	I	J	T	C	E	E	S	J	V	X	O	Y	F	K	S	X	C
L	E	N	X	D	D	A	T	A	Q	J	S	R	R	I	R	A	B	I	F	I	X	M	R	J
I	V	F	W	U	E	F	Q	G	X	A	M	C	C	N	W	L	G	N	E	D	K	T	F	W
W	E	I	U	M	M	U	O	R	Q	B	B	O	O	A	M	E	L	T	K	E	G	B	K	A
H	L	D	H	S	N	W	C	T	O	C	N	N	N	M	E	S	G	E	I	N	A	B	Q	X
X	O	E	V	C	G	N	O	P	E	N	F	F	A	C	T	P	E	E	C	T	K	L	Y
E	F	N	I	Y	J	T	G	L	E	E	W	I	I	V	S	I	M	S	K	E	U	J	E	O
X	C	C	B	U	D	X	R	F	F	N	A	D	D	Y	H	M	K	T	W	I	W	C	X	H
Z	O	E	N	B	W	V	J	K	T	J	F	E	E	A	Q	A	I	I	F	N	A	E	M	K
D	N	L	A	G	D	N	S	L	F	W	N	N	L	Y	T	V	M	K	T	M	N	K	Q
N	F	I	B	F	L	S	E	I	A	E	W	C	C	R	S	I	G	A	G	E	K	M	Y	W
W	I	M	S	K	O	D	J	D	N	H	K	E	E	J	Q	O	D	T	U	R	U	K	R	K
E	D	I	S	I	G	Y	D	I	V	T	N	L	L	Q	F	N	O	I	J	V	M	Q	Q	R
G	E	T	Y	X	W	H	E	X	X	Q	O	I	I	T	W	B	X	O	W	A	O	Z	H	F
N	N	S	P	U	G	F	I	Q	Q	X	B	M	M	W	A	E	N	N	E	L	C	E	S	M
I	C	Z	K	D	J	A	M	U	C	W	P	I	I	T	Q	O	B	G	C	E	B	X	Z	T
P	E	F	R	H	V	B	P	K	G	S	U	T	T	S	V	N	Z	U	K	G	U	U	L	G
U	B	E	K	I	Z	X	K	D	F	E	Z	K	U	X	C	T	W	N	Y	W	J	V	D	U
A	V	C	O	N	F	I	D	E	N	C	E	B	O	U	N	D	A	R	I	E	S	J	A	B

CONFIDENCE BOUNDARIES	ESTIMATION	LOWER CONFIDENCE LIMIT
CONFIDENCE INTERVAL	INTERVAL ESTIMATION	POINT ESTIMATION
CONFIDENCE LIMITS	LEVEL OF CONFIDENCE	UPPER CONFIDENCE LIMIT

CROSSWORD PUZZLES

ACROSS

2 The use of a sample statistic to estimate a population parameter.

4 The largest possible value of a population parameter in a confidence interval with a specified level of confidence.

5 The upper and lower boundaries of a confidence interval given within a specified level of confidence.

6 A statistical procedure in which a sample of data is used to find the interval or range of possible values within which a population parameter is likely to be contained.

7 The interval or range of possible values within which an unknown population parameter is likely to be contained.

8 The probability or likelihood that an interval estimate will contain an unknown population parameter.

DOWN

1 The smallest possible value of a population parameter in a confidence interval with a specified level of confidence.

3 A statistical procedure in which a sample statistic is used to estimate the value of an unknown population parameter.

PRACTICE QUIZZES

LO 1: Describe the process of estimation and identify two types of estimation.

1. A statistical procedure in which a sample statistic is used to estimate the value of an unknown population parameter is called:

   a. hypothesis testing

   b. significance testing

   c. estimation

   d. both a and b

2. Which of the following is a type of estimation?

   a. point estimation

   b. interval estimation

   c. approximation estimation

   d. both a and b

3. Which type of estimation identifies an interval or range of possible values within which a population parameter is likely to be contained?

   a. point estimation

   b. interval estimation

4. Which type of estimation uses the sample mean to estimate the value of a population mean?

   a. point estimation

   b. interval estimation

LO 2: Distinguish between significance testing and estimation.

5. In hypothesis testing, a decision is to reject the null hypothesis when:

   a. the null hypothesis value is contained within the confidence limits

   b. the confidence interval is more precise but less certain

   c. the null hypothesis value is outside the confidence limits

   d. the confidence interval is less precise but more certain

6. In hypothesis testing, a decision is to retain the null hypothesis when:

   a. the null hypothesis value is contained within the confidence limits

   b. the confidence interval is more precise but less certain

   c. the null hypothesis value is outside the confidence limits

   d. the confidence interval is less precise but more certain

216

7. The process of estimation is different from hypothesis testing in that:

   a. estimation does not require that a decision be made regarding a null hypothesis

   b. estimation, but not hypothesis testing, is used to learn more about the value of a population mean

   c. the sample mean is measured when using estimation but not hypothesis testing

   d. estimation, but not hypothesis testing, requires that a null hypothesis be stated

8. A researcher measures a 95% CI of 12 to 16. If the null hypothesis is that the mean value is 10, then what is the effect size for this confidence interval?

   a. none; effect size is not informative with a CI

   b. scores shifted 2 to 6 points in the population

   c. scores shifted 12 to 16 points in the population

   d. scores shifted 4 to 6 points in the population

LO 3: Compute confidence intervals for the one-sample z test.

9. What is the estimation formula for the one-sample z test?

   a. $M \pm z(\sigma_M)$

   b. $M \pm t(s_M)$

   c. $M_D \pm t(s_{MD})$

   d. $M_1 - M_2 \pm t(s_{M_1 - M_2})$

10. A sample of scores is normally distributed with $M = 12$ and standard error = 5. What are the upper and lower 95% confidence limits for a one-sample z test?

    a. 7 to 17

    b. 3.8 to 20.2

    c. 2.2 to 21.8

    d. 10.04 to 13.96

11. A sample of scores is normally distributed with $M = 3.5$ and standard error = 1.3. What are the upper and lower 90% confidence limits for a one-sample z test?

    a. 1.3 to 3.5

    b. 1.0 to 6.0

    c. 2.2 to 4.8

    d. 1.4 to 5.6

LO 4: Compute confidence intervals for the one-sample t test.

12. What is the estimation formula for the one-sample t test?

    a. $M \pm z(\sigma_M)$

    b. $M \pm t(s_M)$

   c. $M_D \pm t(s_{MD})$

   d. $M_1 - M_2 \pm t(s_{M_1 - M_2})$

13. A sample of 20 scores is normally distributed with $M = 10$ and $s_M = 2$. What are the upper and lower 80% confidence limits for a one-sample t test?

   a. 6.5 to 13.5

   b. 7.3 to 12.7

   c. 8 to 12

   d. 5.8 to 15. 2

14. A sample of 16 scores is normally distributed with $M = 14.8$ and $s_M = 3$. What are the upper and lower 95% confidence limits for a one-sample t test?

   a. 8.4 to 21.2

   b. 11.8 to 17.8

   c. 9.6 to 21.0

   d. 10.8 to 18.8

LO 5: Compute confidence intervals for the two-independent-sample t test.

15. What is the estimation formula for the two-independent-sample t test?

   a. $M \pm z(\sigma_M)$

   b. $M \pm t(s_M)$

   c. $M_D \pm t(s_{MD})$

   d. $M_1 - M_2 \pm t(s_{M_1 - M_2})$

16. A researcher selects a sample and assigns participants to one of two groups. Scores in each group are normally distributed with $M_1 = 35$ ($n_1 = 10$), $M_2 = 23$ ($n_2 = 10$), and $s_{M1-M2} = 1.8$. What are the upper and lower 95% confidence limits for a two-independent-sample t test?

   a. 6.2 to 13.8

   b. 8.2 to 15.8

   c. 10.2 to 13.8

   d. 23 to 35

17. A researcher selects a sample and assigns participants to one of two groups. Scores in each group are normally distributed with $M_1 = 20$ ($n_1 = 14$), $M_2 = 18$ ($n_2 = 18$), and $s_{M1-M2} = 0.9$. What are the upper and lower 95% confidence limits for a two-independent-sample t test?

   a. 17.2 to 20.8

   b. 1.1 to 2.9

   c. 0.2 to 3.8

   d. 18 to 20

LO 6: Compute confidence intervals for the related-samples t test.

18. What is the estimation formula for the related-samples t test?

   a. $M \pm z(\sigma_M)$

   b. $M \pm t(s_M)$

   c. $M_D \pm t(s_{MD})$

   d. $M_1 - M_2 \pm t(s_{M_1 - M_2})$

19. A sample of 20 difference scores is normally distributed with $M_D = 10$ and $s_{MD} = 2$. What are the upper and lower 80% confidence limits for a related-samples t test?

   a. 6.5 to 13.5

   b. 7.3 to 12.7

   c. 8 to 12

   d. 5.8 to 15. 2

20. A sample of 16 difference scores is normally distributed with $M_D = 14.8$ and $s_{MD} = 3$. What are the upper and lower 95% confidence limits for a related-samples t test?

   a. 10.8 to 18.8

   b. 11.8 to 17.8

   c. 9.6 to 21.0

   d. 8.4 to 21.2

LO 7: Distinguish between the certainty and precision of an interval estimate.

21. The _____ of an estimate is determined by the range of the confidence interval.

   a. precision

   b. certainty

   c. significance

   d. null hypothesis

22. The _____ of an estimate is determined by the level of confidence.

   a. precision

   b. significance

   c. certainty

   d. null hypothesis

23. Researcher A calculated an 80% CI and Researcher B calculated a 95% CI for the same data. Which researcher calculated the more precise estimate?

   a. Researcher A

   b. Researcher B

   c. none; both CIs are equally precise

24. Researcher A calculated a point estimate and Researcher B calculated an interval estimate for the same data. Which researcher calculated the more certain estimate?

    a. Researcher A

    b. Researcher B

    c. none; both CIs are equally precise

LO 8: Summarize confidence intervals for the z test and t tests in APA format.

25. Which of the following is not reported with a confidence interval?

    a. the level of confidence

    b. the point estimate

    c. the interval estimate

    d. the p value

26. The sample means and the standard error or the standard deviations measured in a study can be reported in:

    a. a figure

    b. a table

    c. the main text

    d. all of the above

27. A researcher reports the following confidence interval: 95% CI, 5.5 to 9.5. What is the value of the point estimate for this confidence interval?

    a. 5.5

    b. 7.5

    c. 9.5

    d. not enough information

Follow the General Instructions Guidebook to complete this exercise. Also, an example for following these steps is provided in the SPSS in Focus section (Section 11.5) of the book. *Note:* You must compute a one-sample *t* test to obtain the confidence intervals for this test. Complete and submit the SPSS grading template and a printout of the output file.

Exercise 11.1: Mixing Aromatherapy With Studying

A researcher knows that aromatherapy can relieve stress but wants to determine whether it can also enhance focus. To test this, the researcher selected a sample of students whose grades were below the class mean of 77. Prior to a final exam, these students studied individually in a small library room where a lavender scent was present. If students in this group scored significantly above the class average on this final exam, then this was taken as evidence that the lavender scent enhanced focus. Compute the 95% confidence interval for the following data.

90	83	90
56	82	88
79	74	93
75	73	60
76	78	80
77	89	85
88	68	86
82	99	90
70	70	76
80	77	69
94	81	98
50	78	85
98	84	84
60	88	89
68	70	90

With regard to the SPSS exercise, answer the following questions:

Based on the table shown in SPSS, state the following values for the sample:

Sample size _____

Sample mean _____

Sample standard deviation _____

Estimated standard error _____

Based on the table shown in SPSS, state the following values associated with the test statistic and confidence intervals:

Mean difference _____

t obtained (t) _____

Degrees of freedom (df) _____

Significance (2-tailed) _____

95% lower confidence interval _____

95% upper confidence interval _____

Based on the value of the test statistic, what is the decision for a one-sample t test? (Circle one)

Retain the null hypothesis   Reject the null hypothesis

What is the point estimate for this example?

State the confidence interval in APA format for the actual data (not the difference scores, which SPSS uses to construct the confidence interval [CI]). Based on the null hypothesis that $\mu = 77$, does the confidence interval confirm your decision? Explain.

If the decision of the hypothesis test was to reject the null hypothesis, state (in words) the size of the effect in the population.

Confidence Intervals for the Two-Independent-Sample *t* Test

Follow the General Instructions Guidebook to complete this exercise. Also, an example for following these steps is provided in the SPSS in Focus section (Section 11.7) of the book. *Note:* You must compute a two-independent-sample *t* test to obtain the confidence intervals for this test. Complete and submit the SPSS grading template and a printout of the output file.

Exercise 11.2: Counting Calories in a Dining Hall

A researcher notes that women tend to be more conscientious eaters, meaning that they tend to pay more attention to the nutritional value of the foods they consume. He hypothesized that because women are more conscientious eaters, this may also mean that they tend to eat healthier. To test this, he observed male and female college students eating at a campus dining hall at a local college. He recorded each food they ate and how much of it they ate. He then determined the number of calories in that meal that came from fat. It was assumed that the fewer calories in a meal that came from fat, the healthier the meal. The data (number of calories from fat) are given by sex. Compute the 95% confidence interval for these data.

Sex	
Men	Women
158	30
110	38
140	49
78	95
69	86
100	50
86	48
75	18
21	42
28	45
64	82
104	63
153	32
92	35
12	22

With regard to the SPSS exercise, answer the following questions:

Based on the table shown in SPSS, state the following values for each group. Make sure you label a group name for each group in each column in the space provided:

	Group 1:	Group 2:
	_____	_____
Sample size	_____	_____
Sample mean	_____	_____
Sample standard deviation	_____	_____
Estimated standard error	_____	_____

Based on the table shown in SPSS, state the following values associated with the test statistic and confidence intervals (assume equal variances):

Mean difference	_____
t obtained	_____
Degrees of freedom	_____
Significance	_____
Estimated standard error for the difference	_____
95% lower confidence interval	_____
95% upper confidence interval	_____

Based on the value of the test statistic, what is the decision for a two-independent-sample t test? (Circle one)

Retain the null hypothesis　　　　　　　　　　　　　　　　Reject the null hypothesis

What is the point estimate for this example?

State the confidence interval in APA format. Based on the null hypothesis that $\mu_1 - \mu_2 = 0$, does the confidence interval confirm your decision? Explain.

If the decision of the hypothesis test was to reject the null hypothesis, state (in words) the size of the effect in the population.

SPSS IN FOCUS

Confidence Intervals for the Related-Samples *t* Test

Follow the General Instructions Guidebook to complete this exercise. Also, an example for following these steps is provided in the SPSS in Focus section (Section 11.9) of the book. *Note:* You must compute a related-samples *t* test to obtain the confidence intervals for this test. Complete and submit the SPSS grading template and a printout of the output file.

Exercise 11.3: Driving While Thinking You Are Intoxicated

A researcher hypothesized that thinking that one is intoxicated can significantly influence driving accuracy. To test this hypothesis, he brought in adult college students who were at least 21 years of age for a "social" where they drank water. After four glasses of water, they were given a driving test, and the number of cones knocked down during the test was recorded. The next day, the researcher brought the students in for another "social" where nonalcoholic drinks were served, although students were told that the drinks contained alcohol. After four drinks, the students were again given a driving test, and the number of cones knocked down during the test was recorded. It was hypothesized that students would knock down more cones after thinking they drank alcohol. The following table shows the number of cones knocked down after each type of drink. Compute the 95% confidence interval for these data.

Type of Drink	
Water	Nonalcoholic
0	0
1	0
1	2
2	3
0	1
3	2
1	3
0	0
0	1
2	0
1	0
0	3
0	2
2	0
0	0
1	2
1	1
0	1

With regard to the SPSS exercise, answer the following questions:

Based on the table shown in SPSS, state the following values for each group (given in the top table of the output screen). Make sure you label a group name for each group in the space provided:

	Group 1:	Group 2:
	_____	_____
Sample size	_____	_____
Sample mean	_____	_____
Sample standard deviation	_____	_____
Estimated standard error	_____	_____

Based on the table shown in SPSS, state the following values associated with the difference scores:

Mean difference   _____

Standard deviation   _____

Estimated standard error for difference scores   _____

Based on the table shown in SPSS, state the following values associated with the test statistic and confidence intervals:

t obtained (t)   _____

Degrees of freedom (df)   _____

Significance (2-tailed)   _____

95% lower confidence interval   _____

95% upper confidence interval   _____

Based on the value of the test statistic, what is the decision for the related-samples t test? (Circle one)

Retain the null hypothesis   Reject the null hypothesis

What is the point estimate for this example?

State the confidence interval in APA format. Based on the null hypothesis that $\mu_D = 0$, does the confidence interval confirm your decision? Explain.

If the decision of the hypothesis test was to reject the null hypothesis, state (in words) the size of the effect in the population.

CHAPTER SUMMARY ORGANIZED BY LEARNING OBJECTIVE

LO 1: Describe the process of estimation and identify two types of estimation.

- Estimation is a statistical procedure in which a sample statistic is used to estimate the value of an unknown population parameter. Two types of estimation are point estimation and interval estimation.
- Point estimation is the use of a sample statistic (e.g., a sample mean) to estimate the value of a population parameter (e.g., a population mean).
- Interval estimation is a statistical procedure in which a sample of data is used to find the interval or range of possible values within which a population parameter is likely to be contained.
- In research studies that use estimation, we report the sample mean (a point estimate) and the interval within which a population mean is likely to be contained (an interval estimate).

LO 2: Distinguish between significance testing and estimation.

- Estimation does not require that we state a null hypothesis and decide whether or not it should be rejected. We use estimation to measure the mean or mean difference in a sample, as we did in hypothesis testing, but instead of making a decision regarding a null hypothesis, we identify the limits within which the population mean or mean difference is likely to be contained.
- The decision for a hypothesis test can be determined by comparing the value stated in the null hypothesis to the confidence limits for a confidence interval. When the value stated in the null hypothesis is outside the confidence limits, the decision is to reject the null hypothesis. When the value stated in the null hypothesis is inside the confidence limits, the decision is to retain the null hypothesis.
- The effect size of a confidence interval can be determined when the value stated in the null hypothesis is outside the confidence limits. The effect size is a range in which the lower effect size estimate is the difference between the value stated in the null hypothesis and the lower confidence limit; the upper effect size estimate is the difference between the value stated in the null hypothesis and the upper confidence limit. The effect size for a confidence interval is interpreted in terms of a shift in the population.

LO 3–6: Compute confidence intervals for the one-sample z test, the one-sample t test, the two-independent-sample t test, and the related-samples t test.

- The three steps to estimation are as follows:

  Step 1: Compute the sample mean and standard error.

  Step 2: Choose the level of confidence and find the critical values at that level of confidence.

  Step 3: Compute the estimation formula to find the confidence limits.

- The estimation formula for the one-sample z test is $M \pm z(\sigma_M)$.

- The estimation formula for each t test is as follows:

  One-sample t test: $M \pm t(s_M)$.

  Two-independent-sample t test: $M_1 - M_2 \pm t(s_{M_1-M_2})$.

  Related-samples t test: $M_D \pm t(s_{MD})$.

LO 7: Distinguish between the certainty and precision of an interval estimate.

- The precision of an estimate is determined by the range of the confidence interval. The certainty of an estimate is determined by the level of confidence.
- To be more certain that an interval contains a population parameter, we must typically give up precision.

LO 8: Summarize confidence intervals for the z test and t tests in APA format.

- To report the results of estimation in scientific journals, state the level of confidence, point estimate, and interval estimate of the confidence interval. In addition, the sample means, the standard error, and the standard deviations can be summarized in a figure or table or in the main text.

LO 9: Compute confidence intervals for the one-sample, two-independent-sample, and related-samples t tests using SPSS.

- To compute the confidence interval for a one-sample t test, follow the steps for computing the one-sample t test given in Chapter 9, and select Options in the dialog box in Steps 3 to 5. This action will display an additional dialog box that will allow you to choose any level of confidence.
- To compute the confidence interval for a two-independent-sample t test, follow the steps for computing the two-independent-sample t test given in Chapter 9, and select Options in the dialog box in Steps 4 to 6. This action will display an additional dialog box that will allow you to choose any level of confidence.
- To compute the confidence interval for a related-samples t test, follow the steps for computing the related-samples t test given in Chapter 10, and select Options in the dialog box in Steps 3 to 4. This action will display an additional dialog box that will allow you to choose any level of confidence.

PART IV

Making Inferences About the Variability of Two or More Means

12

Analysis of Variance

One-Way Between-Subjects Design

LEARNING OBJECTIVES

After reading this chapter, you should be able to:

1. Define the one-way between-subjects ANOVA and identify each source of variation in this statistical procedure.

2. Calculate the degrees of freedom for the one-way between-subjects ANOVA and locate critical values in the F table.

3. Identify the assumptions for the one-way between-subjects ANOVA.

4. Compute the one-way between-subjects ANOVA and interpret the results.

5. Compute the Fisher's LSD and Tukey's HSD post hoc tests and identify which test is most powerful.

6. Compute proportion of variance for the one-way between-subjects ANOVA.

7. Summarize the results of the one-way between-subjects ANOVA in APA format.

8. Compute the one-way between-subjects ANOVA and select an appropriate post hoc test using SPSS.

CHAPTER OUTLINE

12.1 Increasing *k*: A Shift to Analyzing Variance

Analysis of variance (ANOVA) is a statistical procedure used to test hypotheses for one or more factors concerning the variance among two or more group means ($k \geq 2$), where the variance in one or more populations is unknown.

- *k* is the *levels of the factor* or the number of groups in a study.
- The term *factor* is used to describe both independent and quasi-independent variables.

12.2 An Introduction to Analysis of Variance

The type of ANOVA we use depends on the number of factors being tested and how the participants are observed across the levels of each factor.

Identifying the type of ANOVA: We can use several types of ANOVAs to test differences between groups.

- The *way* of the ANOVA indicates the number of factors being tested. A one-way ANOVA has one factor, a two-way ANOVA has two factors, and so on.
- The *subjects* term in an ANOVA indicates how participants were observed. A between-subjects ANOVA indicates that different participants are observed in each group; a within-subjects ANOVA indicates that the same participants are observed across groups.

Two ways to select independent samples: One method of selecting samples using the between-subjects design is to select participants from two or more populations. This method is used in quasi-experiments. A second method is to select participants from a single population, then randomly assign them to groups. This method is used for experiments because it allows participants from a single population to be randomly assigned to each group in a study.

Changes in notation. There are several different notations for an ANOVA than for a *z* test or a *t* test.

- *n* = the number of participants in each level or group, *not* the number of participants in a sample.
- *N* = the number of total participants in a study, *not* the number of individuals in a population.
- *k* = the number of levels of a factor (i.e., the number of groups in a study).
  - When *n* is equal in each group: $N = k \times n$.

12.3 Sources of Variation and the Test Statistic

A one-way ANOVA is used to analyze the variance of one factor with two or more levels. There are two sources of variation we measure using the one-way between-subjects ANOVA. Between-groups variation is the variability attributed to differences between group means; within-groups variation is the variability attributed to differences in participant scores in each group. This within-groups variation is an estimate of error and is placed in the denominator of the test statistic.

The test statistic is the variance or mean square between groups divided by the variance or mean square error: $F_{obt} = \dfrac{MS_{BG}}{MS_E}$.

The test statistic is used to determine whether the variance attributed to differences between group means is significantly larger than the variability we can expect by chance (i.e., error). Specifically, the test statistic is used to determine how large or disproportional the differences are between group means compared to the variance we would expect to occur by chance.

- To make a decision using the ANOVA, we use a positively skewed F distribution, which is derived from a sampling distribution of F ratios.

12.4 Degrees of Freedom

For a one-way between-subjects ANOVA, $df_T = N - 1$. However, the degrees of freedom must be split for each source of variation in the ANOVA: one for the between-groups variation (numerator) and one for the within-groups variation (denominator).

- Degrees of freedom between groups (df_{BG}): $k - 1$.
- Degrees of freedom within groups or error (df_E): $N - k$.

F *table:* The F table lists the critical values for the F distributions at a .01 and .05 level of significance, with the .01 values bolded (see Table B.3 in Appendix B of the book; also reprinted in the appendix of this study guide). To locate the critical values, find the degrees of freedom between groups or numerator listed in the columns and the degrees of freedom within groups (error) or denominator listed in the rows. Critical values are given at the intersection of the rows and columns in the table.

12.5 The One-Way Between-Subjects ANOVA

We make four assumptions to compute the one-way between-subjects ANOVA.

1. *Normality.* We assume the data in the population being sampled are normally distributed, especially for smaller sample sizes.

2. *Random sampling.* We assume the data were sampled using a random sampling procedure.

3. *Independence.* We assume the probabilities of each measured outcome are independent and equal.

4. *Homogeneity of variance.* We assume the variance in each population is equal to that of the others. Violating this assumption will increase the likelihood of committing a Type I error.

   o To compute this test, there must be an equal sample size (n) in each group. With larger samples, this requirement is less critical.

Once these four assumptions are met, we use the four steps of hypothesis testing to conduct the one-way between-subjects ANOVA.

Step 1: State the hypotheses. The null hypothesis states that group means will not vary in the population, whereas the alternative hypothesis states that group means in the population do vary.

$$H_0: \sigma^2_{\mu} = 0$$

$$H_1: \sigma^2_{\mu} > 0$$

Step 2: Set the criteria for a decision. The level of significance is typically equal to .05. We will refer to the F table to find the critical values (see Table B.3 in Appendix B of the book; also reprinted in the appendix of this study guide). To find the critical values, we need to know the degrees of freedom between groups ($k - 1$) and the degrees of freedom error ($N - k$).

Step 3: Compute the test statistic. To compute the test statistic, we calculate the variance or mean square for each source of variation and make the following calculations: preliminary, intermediate, the sums of squares (SS), and then the F statistic. Each calculation to find the SS is summarized in Table 12.8 in Chapter 12 of the book. The following table lists the formulas for completing the F table.

Source of Variation	SS	df	MS	F_{obt}
Between groups		$k - 1$	$\dfrac{SS_{BG}}{df_{BG}}$	$\dfrac{MS_{BG}}{MS_{E}}$
Within groups (error)		$N - k$	$\dfrac{SS_{E}}{df_{E}}$	
Total		$N - 1$		

Step 4: Make a decision. Compare the obtained value to the critical value to make a decision to retain or reject the null hypothesis.

A decision to reject the null hypothesis indicates that the group means in at least one pair significantly differ from one another, but we do not yet know which pair or pairs of means differ. To determine this, we compute post hoc tests by making all pairwise comparisons for each pair of group means.

12.6 What Is the Next Step?

A significant ANOVA indicates that at least one pair of group means significantly differs. To determine which pairs differ, we compute post hoc tests or "after-the-fact" tests. These tests analyze differences for all possible pairs of group means, called pairwise comparisons. With only two groups ($k = 2$), post hoc tests are not needed because only one pair of group means can be compared. With more than two groups ($k > 2$), multiple comparisons must be made, so post hoc tests are necessary.

12.7 Post Hoc Comparisons

Post hoc tests control for the *experimentwise alpha* level by ensuring that the overall likelihood of a Type I error for all pairwise comparisons is .05.

A variety of post hoc tests can be used to make pairwise comparisons. The two described here are Fisher's least significant difference (LSD) and Tukey's honestly significant difference (HSD) tests.

Fisher's Least Significant Difference (LSD) Test

Fisher's LSD is the most liberal of the post hoc tests and thus has high power to detect an effect or mean difference between two groups.

- Step 1: Compute the test statistic for each pair of group means by subtracting the smallest from the largest group mean for each comparison. This will give you a difference score for each pair of group means you are testing.
- Step 2: Find a critical value for each pairwise comparison using the following formula:

$$\text{Fisher's LSD: } t_\alpha \sqrt{MS_E \left(\frac{1}{n_1} + \frac{1}{n_2} \right)}.$$

- Step 3: Compare the test statistic for each pairwise comparison to the critical value. If the test statistic is larger than the critical value, then we reject the null hypothesis and conclude that the pair of group means significantly differs; otherwise, we retain the null hypothesis.

Tukey's Honestly Significant Difference (HSD) Test

Tukey's HSD test is a more conservative post hoc test and thus has less power than Fisher's LSD to detect an effect or mean difference between two groups.

- Step 1: Compute the test statistic for each pair of group means by subtracting the smallest from the largest group mean for each comparison. This will give you a difference score for each pair of group means you are testing.

- Step 2: Compute the critical value for each pairwise comparison using the following formula:

$$\text{Tukey's HSD: } q_\alpha \sqrt{\frac{MS_E}{n}} \ .$$

  o q is the studentized range statistic and is listed in the studentized range statistic table (see Table B.4 in Appendix B of the book; also reprinted in the appendix of this study guide). We will need to know the value of df_E and the real range r, which is equal to the number of groups in a study.

- Step 3: Compare the test statistic for each pairwise comparison to the critical value. If the test statistic is larger than the critical value, then we reject the null hypothesis and conclude that the pair of group means significantly differs; otherwise, we retain the null hypothesis.

12.8 SPSS in Focus: The One-Way Between-Subjects ANOVA

- SPSS can be used to compute the one-way between-subjects ANOVA. The one-way between-subjects ANOVA is computed using one of two commands:
  o Using the One-Way ANOVA command, select the Analyze, Compare Means, and One-Way ANOVA options in the menu bar. These actions will display a dialog box that allows you to identify the variables, choose an appropriate post hoc test, and run the analysis.
  o Using the GLM Univariate command, select the Analyze, General Linear Model, and Univariate options in the menu bar. These actions will display a dialog box that allows you to identify the variables, choose an appropriate post hoc test, measure observed power, and run the analysis.

12.9 Measuring Effect Size

We can determine the size of an effect in the population by computing proportion of variance. The two measures of proportion of variance are eta-squared and omega-squared.

- Proportion of variance is described as the proportion of variance in the dependent variable that can be accounted for by the levels of the factor.

Eta-Squared (η^2 or R^2)

When eta-squared is used with ANOVA, it is represented as R^2.

$$R^2 = \eta^2 = \frac{SS_{BG}}{SS_T} \ .$$

Omega-Squared (ω^2)

Omega-squared has two advantages over eta-squared when used with an ANOVA.

1. It corrects for the size of error by including MS_E in the formula.

2. It corrects for the number of groups by including df_{BG} in the formula.

The formula for omega-squared is

$$\omega^2 = \frac{SS_{BG} - df_{BG}(MS_E)}{SS_T + MS_E}.$$

12.10 APA in Focus: Reporting the *F* Statistic, Significance, and Effect Size

To summarize the results of a one-way between-subjects ANOVA, we report the test statistic, the degrees of freedom, and the p value. We also report the effect size for significant analyses. You can summarize the means and the standard error or the standard deviations measured in a study in a figure, in a table, or in the main text of the article. To report the results of a post hoc test, identify which post hoc test you computed and the p value for significant results.

CHAPTER FORMULAS

One-Way Between-Subjects Analysis of Variance

Between-Subjects Design

$F_{obt} = \dfrac{MS_{BG}}{MS_E}$ (Test statistic for the one-way between-subjects ANOVA)

$MS = \dfrac{SS}{df}$ (Mean square for each source of variation; used for all ANOVA tests)

$df_{BG} = k - 1$ (Degrees of freedom between groups)

$df_E = N - k$ (Degrees of freedom error)

$df_T = N - 1$ (Degrees of freedom total)

Effect Size (Between-Subjects Design)

$R^2 = \eta^2 = \dfrac{SS_{BG}}{SS_T}$ (Eta-squared estimate for proportion of variance)

$\omega^2 = \dfrac{SS_{BG} - df_{BG}(MS_E)}{SS_T + MS_E}$ (Omega-squared estimate for proportion of variance)

Post Hoc Tests

$t_\alpha \sqrt{MS_E \left(\dfrac{1}{n_1} + \dfrac{1}{n_2} \right)}$ (Fisher's LSD formula)

$q_\alpha \sqrt{\dfrac{MS_E}{n}}$ (Tukey's HSD formula)

TIPS AND CAUTIONS FOR STUDENTS

- *Changes in notation:* Take the time to get familiar with the new notation used with an analysis of variance (ANOVA). The term n now refers to the number of participants in each group, and N refers to the total number of participants in a study. We will also begin using k to refer to the number of groups or levels of the factor. The need to change notation comes from the fact that the factor can have any number of levels. This is more complex than with the t tests, where we had two groups at most. Hence, although this change may seem petty now, you will find it makes the summary of statistical procedures much simpler as we continue to increase the complexity of design.

- *The hypotheses and the test statistic:* Now that we are stating hypotheses in terms of variance, the decision is based on the positively skewed F distribution. The rejection region is always placed in the upper tail. When finding critical values, you only need to keep track of the degrees of freedom for each source of variation and the alpha level. In addition, because variance is never negative, the test statistic will never be negative. If you obtain a negative value of the test statistic, you made a mathematical error and should recalculate the test statistic.

- *Degrees of freedom, sum of squares, and variance:* An analysis of variance is just that—steps we follow to compute the variance. Although the analyses are more involved, we are still computing a variance: We calculate SS and df for each source of variation. Using these values, we then compute the variance (or mean square) of each source of variation by dividing SS by df, just as was introduced in Chapter 4 for variance.

KEY TERM WORD SEARCHES

K	B	P	N	U	A	E	Z	O	Z	W	A	V	K	G	E	Z	Q	Z	T	G	A	B	L	E	P	E	Y	K	D
X	E	X	F	B	O	Z	Z	N	U	I	E	H	Q	E	K	F	L	A	V	F	F	I	F	U	L	J	D	N	Y
K	T	Y	Q	C	U	W	B	E	Z	V	U	V	G	E	F	I	V	M	P	W	Q	F	T	O	I	S	E	U	R
S	W	D	U	R	L	M	A	W	J	J	O	E	V	H	J	G	Q	G	Z	Y	B	D	X	Z	Z	U	G	W	T
O	E	R	K	H	K	Q	C	A	J	W	A	C	K	U	D	V	Y	G	I	T	P	H	Z	C	H	I	U	T	C
U	E	R	T	D	Q	V	X	Y	E	Y	P	H	R	Z	G	T	F	E	Z	K	Q	D	P	O	E	Y	P	H	Z
R	N	S	R	A	H	R	P	B	U	P	U	D	C	K	U	V	Y	G	I	T	P	B	S	Z	I	P	A	Z	R
C	S	N	L	P	W	S	F	E	S	F	G	A	E	F	D	I	S	T	R	I	B	U	T	I	O	N	I	P	E
E	U	J	U	L	I	E	X	T	N	T	A	N	N	C	W	G	C	S	T	J	R	K	U	Y	I	Z	R	C	D
O	B	B	R	C	T	M	G	W	H	F	A	D	Z	A	F	B	J	C	V	G	B	I	D	T	E	H	W	B	C
F	J	U	L	W	H	R	Y	E	X	B	F	T	L	P	L	B	F	T	U	B	K	G	E	S	I	Z	I	X	B
V	E	A	I	R	I	N	L	E	J	Q	P	U	I	V	C	Y	Y	X	Q	P	P	I	N	I	B	T	S	U	M
A	C	I	W	C	N	M	Z	N	X	M	L	Z	C	S	F	S	S	L	N	Z	K	M	T	S	P	V	E	U	G
R	T	D	U	W	G	K	V	S	Q	J	Z	X	D	G	T	O	A	I	U	L	Y	J	I	S	C	I	C	V	Z
I	S	T	E	F	R	C	P	U	Y	W	J	E	Y	R	B	I	T	I	S	Q	P	C	Z	V	B	Z	O	F	B
A	D	M	W	M	O	F	Z	B	Z	N	J	W	T	L	K	D	C	A	S	O	F	S	E	B	L	D	M	O	Z
T	E	H	W	Y	U	B	C	J	U	I	U	Q	G	H	V	U	S	R	J	P	F	K	D	Y	I	Z	P	I	F
I	S	F	Q	Q	P	H	X	E	P	J	J	U	Q	W	Q	C	F	Z	O	D	W	V	R	F	O	F	A	M	E
O	I	P	I	I	V	A	V	C	O	D	Q	N	V	O	Q	B	R	H	L	V	K	K	A	H	M	Q	R	Z	E
N	G	P	M	J	A	B	G	T	S	B	D	K	C	T	B	B	H	Z	X	O	G	D	N	R	C	B	I	C	L
G	N	D	I	G	R	S	B	S	T	U	E	Y	F	F	O	B	T	A	I	N	E	D	G	Z	I	N	S	P	E
N	A	S	N	M	I	B	J	A	H	M	R	D	O	I	Q	G	D	V	N	W	A	I	E	O	Y	A	O	B	E
J	A	A	V	O	A	Z	I	N	O	G	E	T	N	L	D	H	J	B	F	T	Q	J	Z	X	V	S	N	Z	O
G	H	I	X	R	B	Z	R	O	C	O	B	S	E	R	V	E	D	P	O	W	E	R	J	C	O	E	S	C	L
G	V	M	J	X	I	J	O	V	T	C	U	A	O	D	U	V	O	X	P	C	H	O	I	V	Z	T	A	X	E
G	C	N	U	A	L	S	F	A	E	Q	Y	Y	E	Z	C	N	G	P	E	O	R	E	N	C	C	B	B	A	H
Q	C	K	W	T	I	J	Z	L	S	D	L	P	A	Z	V	X	E	W	Q	T	Q	A	T	H	S	Q	L	B	V
K	E	A	M	S	T	A	L	S	T	P	N	O	C	L	P	D	K	V	A	E	O	W	H	J	F	L	H	L	A
N	I	K	T	L	Y	R	O	T	S	O	Y	K	D	I	Z	J	I	R	I	O	I	A	X	J	L	S	M	W	E
O	B	Z	O	E	G	A	Y	R	G	D	V	R	T	B	O	L	K	X	W	P	N	Y	R	X	X	Z	L	C	D

ANALYSIS OF VARIANCE

BETWEEN-SUBJECTS DESIGN

F DISTRIBUTION

F OBTAINED

OBSERVED POWER

ONE-WAY BETWEEN-SUBJECTS ANOVA

PAIRWISE COMPARISONS

POST HOC TESTS

SOURCE OF VARIATION

STUDENTIZED RANGE STATISTIC

WITHIN-GROUP VARIABILITY

CROSSWORD PUZZLES

ACROSS

1 The number of groups or different ways that an independent or quasi-independent variable is observed.

3 A statistical procedure computed following a significant ANOVA to determine which pair or pairs of group means significantly differ.

9 The variation attributed to mean differences between groups.

15 The degrees of freedom associated with the variance for the group means in the numerator of the test statistic.

16 Any variation that can be measured in a study.

17 A statistical procedure used to test hypotheses for one or more factors concerning the variance among two or more group means ($k \geq 2$), where the variance in one or more populations is unknown.

DOWN

2 The alpha level on at least one test when multiple tests are conducted on the same data.

4 A research design in which we select independent samples, meaning that different participants are observed at each level of a factor.

5 The variance attributed to differences within each group. It is the denominator for the test statistic.

6 The degrees of freedom associated with the error variance in the denominator.

7 A positively skewed distribution derived from a sampling distribution of F ratios.

8 The variation attributed to mean differences within each group.

10 A statistic used to determine critical values for comparing pairs of means at a given range.

11 The variance attributed to differences between group means.

12 A statistical comparison for the difference between two group means.

13 A type of post hoc or retrospective power analysis that is used to estimate the likelihood of detecting a population effect, assuming that the observed results in a study reflect a true effect in the population.

14 The test statistic for an ANOVA.

PRACTICE QUIZZES

LO 1: Define the one-way between-subjects ANOVA and identify each source of variation in this statistical procedure.

1. A statistical procedure used to test hypotheses for one factor with two or more levels concerning the variance among group means, where different participants are observed at each level of a factor, is called the:

   a. two-independent-sample t test

   b. one-way between-subjects ANOVA

   c. two-way between-subjects ANOVA

   d. one-sample t test

2. The one-way between-subjects ANOVA is used when different participants are assigned to _____ group(s).

   a. one

   b. two

   c. two or more

   d. zero

3. Which of the following is a source of variation in the one-way between-subjects ANOVA?

   a. within-subjects variation

   b. between-subjects variation

   c. between-groups variation

   d. both b and c

4. Variation attributed to mean differences among participant scores within each group is called:

   a. within-groups variation

   b. within-subjects variation

   c. between-groups variation

   d. both a and b

5. The source of variation that cannot be attributed to or caused by having different groups is called:

   a. within-groups variation

   b. error variation

   c. between-groups variation

   d. both a and b

LO 2: Calculate the degrees of freedom for the one-way between-subjects ANOVA and locate critical values in the F table.

6. What is the degrees of freedom numerator for a study with $n = 12$ in each of four groups?

   a. 3

   b. 4

   c. 32

   d. 36

7. What is the degrees of freedom denominator for a study with $n = 10$ in each of three groups?

   a. 2

   b. 7

   c. 27

   d. 30

8. What is the critical value for a study with 2 and 27 degrees of freedom at a .05 level of significance?

   a. 3.32

   b. 3.35

   c. 5.49

   d. the critical value is not listed in the F table

9. What is the critical value for F in a study with $n = 12$ in each of two groups at a .05 level of significance?

   a. 3.89

   b. 3.40

   c. 4.28

   d. 4.30

LO 3: Identify the assumptions for the one-way between-subjects ANOVA.

10. Homogeneity of variance refers to the assumption that:

    a. data in the population or populations being sampled from are normally distributed

    b. the variance of scores in each population is equal

    c. the probabilities of each measured outcome in a study are independent

    d. the data were selected using a random sampling procedure

11. Which of the following is an assumption of the one-way between-subjects ANOVA?

    a. normality

    b. random sampling

  c. homogeneity of variance

  d. all of the above

12. Violating the assumption of homogeneity of variance can:

  a. inflate the value of the variance in the numerator of the test statistic

  b. increase the likelihood of committing a Type I error

  c. increase the likelihood of retaining the null hypothesis

  d. both a and b

LO 4: Compute the one-way between-subjects ANOVA and interpret the results.

13. A researcher randomly assigned 33 adults to observe a short video clip depicting a person preparing a low-, moderate-, or high-fat meal. Participants rated how likely they would be to consume the meal. If $SS_{BG} = 30$ and $SS_E = 104$, then what was the decision at a .05 level of significance?

  a. reject the null hypothesis

  b. retain the null hypothesis

  c. not enough information

14. A researcher conducts two studies on social influence. In Study 1, 24 participants are randomly assigned to one of three situations. An equal number of participants are assigned to each situation. Study 2 is similar except that $k = 3$ and $n = 8$. If $SS_{BG} = 28$ and $SS_E = 42$ in both studies, then in which study will the decision be to reject the null hypothesis at a .05 level of significance?

  a. Study 1

  b. Study 2

  c. both

  d. none

15. A researcher conducts two studies. In Study 1, 30 participants are randomly assigned to one of three groups. An equal number of participants are assigned to each group. Study 2 is similar except that $k = 4$ and $n = 10$ in each group. If $F_{obt} = 2.98$ in both studies, then in which study will the decision be to reject the null hypothesis at a .05 level of significance?

  a. Study 1

  b. Study 2

  c. both

  d. none

16. A researcher computes the following one-way between-subjects ANOVA table for a study where $k = 4$ and $n = 12$. State the decision at a .05 level of significance. (*Hint:* Complete the table first.)

Source of Variation	SS	df	MS	F
Between groups	120			
Within groups (error)				
Total	780			

a. reject the null hypothesis

b. retain the null hypothesis

c. not enough information

17. A researcher computes the following one-way between-subjects ANOVA table. State the decision at a .05 level of significance. (*Hint:* Complete the table first.)

Source of Variation	SS	df	MS	F
Between groups	1.96	2		
Within groups (error)			0.26	
Total	8.20			

a. reject the null hypothesis

b. retain the null hypothesis

c. not enough information

LO 5: Compute the Fisher's LSD and Tukey's HSD post hoc tests, and identify which test is most powerful.

18. Which post hoc test is associated with the greatest power to detect an effect?

a. Tukey's HSD test

b. Fisher's LSD test

c. one-way between-subjects test

19. A researcher had participants engage in a conversation with a confederate who was dressed in casual, informal, or formal clothes. A one-way between-subjects ANOVA showed that duration of eye contact in the conversation significantly varied by type of dress. If the mean duration of eye contact (in seconds) in each group was 14 (casual), 10 (informal), and 20 (formal), then which pairwise comparison for the difference between two groups must be significant?

a. the casual and formal groups

b. the casual and informal groups

c. the formal and informal groups

d. all the groups must be significantly different

20. A researcher computes a significant one-way between-subjects ANOVA with 10 participants in each group and $MS_E = 32.4$ and $df_E = 27$. What is the critical value for Fisher's LSD at a .05 level of significance for each pairwise comparison?

a. 2.6

b. 5.2

    c. 13.3

    d. not enough information

21. A researcher computes a significant one-way between-subjects ANOVA with eight participants in each of four groups and $MS_E = 18.1$ and $df_E = 28$. What is the critical value for Tukey's HSD at a .05 level of significance for each pairwise comparison?

    a. 6.7

    b. 5.3

    c. 4.4

    d. 5.8

LO 6: Compute proportion of variance for the one-way between-subjects ANOVA.

22. Which measure of proportion of variance is the most conservative estimate?

    a. eta-squared

    b. omega-squared

23. A researcher conducts two studies. The sum of squares between groups is larger in Study 1 compared with Study 2; the sum of squares total is smaller in Study 1 compared with Study 2. In which study will eta-squared be smaller?

    a. Study 1

    b. Study 2

    c. the value will be the same in both studies

24. A researcher conducts a study using the one-way between-subjects ANOVA. She computes $SS_{BG} = 180$ and $SS_E = 520$. What is the effect size for this test using eta-squared?

    a. .31

    b. .28

    c. .35

    d. .26

25. What is omega-squared using the values given in the F table for a one-way between-subjects ANOVA?

Source of Variation	SS	df	MS	F
Between groups	2.3	2	1.2	5.2*
Within groups (error)	4.9	21	0.23	
Total	7.2			

    a. .21

    b. .23

    c. .25

    d. .28

LO 7: Summarize the results of the one-way between-subjects ANOVA in APA format.

26. To report the results of the one-way between-subjects ANOVA, which of the following is reported?

    a. the test statistic

    b. the p value

    c. the degrees of freedom numerator and denominator

    d. all of the above

27. A researcher reports that alertness in the classroom varies by the intensity of lighting in the room, $F(3, 36) = 3.96$, $p < .05$. How many light intensity groups were observed in this study?

    a. 1

    b. 2

    c. 3

    d. 4

28. Using a between-subjects design, a researcher reports that emotional responses varied by the type of stressor in a controlled environment, $F(4, 55) = 6.01$, $p < .05$. How many participants were observed in this study?

    a. 12

    b. 55

    c. 59

    d. 60

SPSS IN FOCUS

The One-Way Between-Subjects ANOVA

Follow the General Instructions Guidebook to complete this exercise. Also, an example for following these steps is provided in the SPSS in Focus section (Section 12.8) of the book. Complete and submit the SPSS grading template and a printout of the output file.

Exercise 12.1: Reinforcing Behavior in the Workplace

A local business is having difficulty keeping its office workers on task at work. To help improve this situation, the owner asks a psychologist to provide consultation. The psychologist notes that the company mostly uses punishment to keep employees on task (for example, by docking pay or firing employees for not being on task). The psychologist proposes that employees would stay on task more if the company put more emphasis on reinforcing employees for staying on task (rather than simply punishing them for getting off task). To test this, the researcher randomly assigns employees to one of three groups. In one group, the employees meet as a group at the start of their shift, at which time the researcher praises them for the things they did well (group reinforcement). In the second group, this feedback is provided individually to each employee at the start of his or her shift (individual reinforcement). In the third control group, employees do not receive any type of reinforcement (no reinforcement). The amount of time spent on task (in minutes) during the last 2 hours of work is recorded. Given the following data, test whether time spent on task varied by type of reinforcement at a .05 level of significance.

Type of Reinforcement			Type of Reinforcement		
Group	Individual	None	Group	Individual	None
55	87	76	59	100	92
43	95	59	60	66	34
100	48	43	110	60	56
105	32	46	100	76	45
95	103	60	92	60	82
93	99	88	108	65	94
50	108	90	84	85	80
83	110	30	75	97	50
86	112	65	60	91	40

With regard to the SPSS exercise, answer the following questions:

Based on the output shown in SPSS, complete the following F table:

Sources of Variation	SS	df	MS	F Statistic	Sig.
Between groups					
Error					
Total					

Based on the value of the test statistic, what is the decision for the one-way between-subjects ANOVA? (Circle one)

Retain the null hypothesis   Reject the null hypothesis

Based on the F table you just completed, state the following values:

Total sample size   _____

Sample size per group   _____

Number of groups (k)   _____

Degrees of freedom numerator   _____

Degrees of freedom denominator   _____

Significance   _____

Based on your decision, is it appropriate to conduct a post hoc test? Explain. Note: If it is not necessary to conduct a post hoc test, then stop here.

Based on the SPSS output table, state each pair of means that significantly differed using Fisher's LSD post hoc test. *Hint:* SPSS places an asterisk in the "Mean Difference" column of the output table to indicate statistical significance.

Compute proportion of variance using eta-squared or omega-squared, and state the size of the effect as small, medium, or large. (Show your work.) In a sentence, also state the proportion of variance in the dependent variable that can be explained by the levels of the factor. Note: The tables in SPSS give you all the information you need to compute proportion of variance.

State the conclusion for this test in APA format. Make sure you summarize the test statistic, the effect size, and each significant post hoc comparison. Provide an interpretation for the statistics you report.

CHAPTER SUMMARY ORGANIZED BY LEARNING OBJECTIVE

LO 1: Define the one-way between-subjects ANOVA and identify each source of variation in this statistical procedure.

- An analysis of variance (ANOVA) is a statistical procedure used to test hypotheses for one or more factors concerning the variance among two or more group means, where the variance in one or more populations is unknown.
- The one-way between-subjects ANOVA is a statistical procedure used to test hypotheses for one factor with two or more levels concerning the variance among means. This test is used when different participants are observed in each group and the variance in any one population is unknown.
- A source of variation is any variation that can be measured in a study. In the one-way between-subjects ANOVA, there are two sources of variation: variation attributed to differences between group means and variation attributed to error.
- Between-groups variation is variance attributed to differences between group means.
- Within-groups variation is variance attributed to differences within each group. This is a source of error because it is variability that is not associated with mean differences between groups.

LO 2: Calculate the degrees of freedom for the one-way between-subjects ANOVA and locate critical values in the F table.

- The degrees of freedom for a one-way between-subjects ANOVA are the following:

  ○ Degrees of freedom between groups are the degrees of freedom for the variance of the group means. They are equal to the number of groups minus 1: $df_{BG} = k - 1$.

  ○ Degrees of freedom within groups or degrees of freedom error are the degrees of freedom for the variance attributed to error. They are equal to the total sample size minus the number of groups: $df_E = N - k$.

LO 3–4: Identify the assumptions for the one-way between-subjects ANOVA; compute the one-way between-subjects ANOVA and interpret the results.

- Four assumptions for the one-way between-subjects ANOVA are normality, random sampling, independence, and homogeneity of variance.
- The test statistic for the one-way ANOVA is $F_{obt} = \dfrac{MS_{BG}}{MS_E}$. The test statistic is computed as the mean square (or variance) between groups divided by the mean square (or variance) within groups.
- The steps for conducting a one-way between-subjects ANOVA are as follows: Step 1: State the hypotheses.

  Step 2: Set the criteria for a decision.

  Step 3: Compute the test statistic.

  Stage 1: Preliminary calculations.

  Stage 2: Intermediate calculations.

  Stage 3: Computing the SS for each source of variation.

  Stage 4: Completing the F table.

  Step 4: Make a decision.

LO 5: Compute the Fisher's LSD and Tukey's HSD post hoc tests and identify which test is most powerful.

- A post hoc test is a statistical procedure computed following a significant ANOVA to determine which pair or pairs of group means significantly differ. These tests are necessary when $k > 2$ because multiple comparisons are needed. When $k = 2$, the two means must significantly differ; this is the only comparison.

- A pairwise comparison is a statistical comparison for the difference between two group means. A post hoc test evaluates all possible pairwise comparisons for an ANOVA with any number of groups.

- To compute the Fisher's LSD and Tukey's HSD post hoc tests, follow three steps (only Step 2 is different for each test):

  Step 1: Compute the test statistic for each pairwise comparison.

  Step 2: Compute the critical value for each pairwise comparison.

  Step 3: Make a decision to retain or reject the null hypothesis for each pairwise comparison.

- All post hoc tests control for experimentwise alpha when multiple pairwise comparisons are made on the same data. The formulas for two post hoc tests, Fisher's LSD and Tukey's HSD, are given here from most to least powerful:

$$\text{Fisher's LSD: } t_{\alpha}\sqrt{MS_E\left(\frac{1}{n_1}+\frac{1}{n_2}\right)}$$

$$\text{Tukey's HSD: } q_{\alpha}\sqrt{\frac{MS_E}{n}}$$

LO 6: Compute proportion of variance for the one-way between-subjects ANOVA.

- Proportion of variance estimates how much of the variability in the dependent variable can be accounted for by the levels of the factor. Two measures of proportion of variance are eta-squared (η^2 or R^2) and omega-squared (ω^2). The formula for each measure is as follows:

$$R^2 = \eta^2 = \frac{SS_{BG}}{SS_T};$$

$$\omega^2 = \frac{SS_{BG} - df_{BG}(MS_E)}{SS_T + MS_E}.$$

LO 7: Summarize the results of the one-way between-subjects ANOVA in APA format.

- To summarize a one-way between-subjects ANOVA test, we report the test statistic, degrees of freedom, and p value. You should also report the effect size for significant analyses. The means and standard error or standard deviations measured in a study can be summarized in a figure or table or in the main text. To report the results of a post hoc test, you must identify which post hoc test you computed and the p value for significant results.

LO 8: Compute the one-way between-subjects ANOVA and select an appropriate post hoc test using SPSS.

- SPSS can be used to compute the one-way between-subjects ANOVA. The one-way between-subjects ANOVA test is computed using one of two commands:
  ○ Using the One-Way ANOVA command: Select the Analyze, Compare Means, and One-Way ANOVA options in the menu bar. These actions will display a dialog box that allows you to identify the variables, choose an appropriate post hoc test, and run the analysis.

o Using the GLM Univariate command: Select the Analyze, General Linear Model, and Univariate options in the menu bar. These actions will display a dialog box that allows you to identify the variables, choose an appropriate post hoc test, measure observed power, and run the analysis.

13

Analysis of Variance

One-Way Within-Subjects (Repeated-Measures) Design

LEARNING OBJECTIVES

After reading this chapter, you should be able to:

1. Define the one-way within-subjects ANOVA and identify each source of variation in this statistical procedure.

2. Calculate the degrees of freedom for the one-way within-subjects ANOVA and locate critical values in the *F* table.

3. Identify the assumptions for the one-way within-subjects ANOVA.

4. Compute the one-way within-subjects ANOVA and interpret the results.

5. Compute the Bonferroni procedure and explain why it is appropriate to use following a significant one-way within-subjects ANOVA.

6. Compute proportion of variance for the one-way within-subjects ANOVA.

7. Explain how the consistency of changes in the dependent variable across groups influences the power of a one-way within-subjects ANOVA.

8. Summarize the results of the one-way within-subjects ANOVA in APA format.

9. Compute the one-way within-subjects ANOVA and select an appropriate post hoc test using SPSS.

CHAPTER OUTLINE

13.1 Observing the Same Participants Across Groups

Many research studies require that we observe the same participants at each level of one factor with two or more levels. These types of research studies use the within-subjects design (introduced in Chapter 10 of the book).

The One-Way Within-Subjects ANOVA

The one-way within-subjects (or repeated-measures) analysis of variance (ANOVA) is a statistical procedure used to test hypotheses for one factor with two or more levels concerning the variance among group means. This test is used when the same participants are observed at each level of a factor and the variance in any one population is unknown.

- Using the within-subjects design, n subjects are observed k times.

Selecting Related Samples: The Within-Subjects Design

To select participants using the within-subjects design, participants are selected from a single population and are observed at each level of one factor.

13.2 Sources of Variation and the Test Statistic

There are three sources of variation using the one-way within-subjects ANOVA. Between-groups variation is the variability attributed to differences between group means, between-persons variation is the variability attributed to differences between person means averaged across groups, and within-groups variation is the variability associated with differences in participant scores in each group. The within-groups variation is placed in the denominator of the test statistic.

The test statistic is the variance or mean square between groups divided by the variance or mean square error (within-groups variation only): $F_{\text{obt}} = \dfrac{MS_{\text{BG}}}{MS_{\text{E}}}$

Error Variation

There are two sources of error using the one-way within-subjects ANOVA: between-persons and within-groups variation. However, using a within-subjects design, the same, not different, participants are observed in each group. Hence, the individual differences in participant characteristics are the same in each group—because the same participants are observed in each group. In a within-subjects design, then, we can assume that any differences in the characteristics of participants across groups are the same. For this reason, between-persons variation can be measured and then removed from the error term in the denominator of the test statistic, leaving only within-groups variation as the error term in the denominator of the test statistic.

13.3 Degrees of Freedom

The degrees of freedom for the one-way within-subjects ANOVA are split into three calculations: one for each source of variation.

- Degrees of freedom between groups: $df_{\text{BG}} = k - 1$.
- Degrees of freedom between persons: $df_{\text{BP}} = n - 1$.
- Degrees of freedom error: $df_{\text{E}} = (k - 1)(n - 1)$.

13.4 The One-Way Within-Subjects ANOVA

We make four assumptions to compute the one-way within-subjects ANOVA:

- *Normality.* We assume the data in the population we sample from are normally distributed, especially for small sample sizes.
- *Independence within groups.* We assume that participants within groups are independently observed, although not between groups.
- *Homogeneity of variance.* We assume that the variance in each population is equal to that of the others.
- *Homogeneity of covariance.* We assume that participant scores in each group are related because the same participants are observed in each group.
  - The assumptions of homogeneity of variance and homogeneity of covariance are called *sphericity.* If we violate sphericity, the likelihood of committing a Type I error will increase.

Once these four assumptions are met, we use the four steps of hypothesis testing to conduct the one-way within-subjects ANOVA.

Step 1: State the hypotheses. The null hypothesis states that group means will not vary in the population. The alternative hypothesis states that group means in the population do vary.

$$H_0: \sigma_\mu^2 = 0$$

$$H_1: \sigma_\mu^2 > 0$$

Step 2: Set the criteria for a decision. The level of significance is typically equal to .05. We refer to the F table to find the critical values (see Table B.3 in Appendix B of the book; also reprinted in the appendix of this study guide). To find the critical values, we need to know the degrees of freedom between groups, the degrees of freedom between persons, and the degrees of freedom error.

Step 3: Compute the test statistic. To compute the test statistic, we have to calculate the variance or mean square for each source of variation, and we make the following calculations: preliminary, intermediate, the sums of squares (*SS*), and then the *F* statistic. Each calculation to find *SS* is summarized in Table 13.6 in Chapter 13 of the book. The following table lists the formulas for completing the *F* table.

Source of Variation	SS	df	MS	F_{obt}
Between groups		$k - 1$	$\dfrac{SS_{BG}}{df_{BG}}$	$\dfrac{MS_{BG}}{MS_E}$
Between persons		$n - 1$	$\dfrac{SS_{BP}}{df_{BP}}$	
Within groups (error)		$(k - 1)(n - 1)$	$\dfrac{SS_E}{df_E}$	
Total		$(kn - 1)$		

Step 4: Make a decision. Compare the obtained value to the critical value to make a decision to retain or reject the null hypothesis.

A decision to reject the null hypothesis indicates that the group means in at least one pair significantly differ, but we do not yet know which pair or pairs of means differ. To determine this, we compute post hoc tests by making all pairwise comparisons for each pair of group means.

13.5 Post Hoc Comparisons: Bonferroni Procedure

Post hoc tests control for experimentwise alpha by ensuring that the overall likelihood of a Type I error for all pairwise comparisons is .05. The post hoc tests introduced in Chapter 12 of the book are better adapted for a one-way between-subjects ANOVA. The Bonferroni procedure, on the other hand, is suitable for a within-subjects design.

The *Bonferroni procedure* adjusts the alpha level for each test, called the testwise alpha, such that the experimentwise alpha equals .05.

$$\text{Testwise alpha} = \frac{\text{experimentwise alpha}}{\text{total number of pairwise comparisons}}.$$

To use the Bonferroni procedure, we follow two steps:

- Step 1: Calculate the testwise alpha and find the critical values.
  - ○ Compute the testwise alpha level.
  - ○ Locate the critical values. To find critical values, we look in the *t* table for a two-tailed test at an alpha level that is the same as the testwise alpha with a degrees of freedom equal to *n* − 1 (see Table B.2 in Appendix B of the book; also reprinted in the appendix of this study guide).

- Step 2: Compute a related-samples *t* test for each pairwise comparison and make a decision to retain or reject the null hypothesis. The test statistic for the related-samples *t* test is given here and defined in Chapter 10 of the book:

$$t_{\text{obt}} = \frac{M_{\text{D}} - \mu_{\text{D}}}{s_{M_{\text{D}}}}.$$

13.6 SPSS in Focus: The One-Way Within-Subjects ANOVA

SPSS can be used to compute the one-way within-subjects ANOVA. The one-way within-subjects ANOVA is computed using the Analyze, General Linear Model, and Repeated Measures options in the menu bar.

13.7 Measuring Effect Size

When we use a within-subjects design, we can determine the size of an effect in the population by computing a partial proportion of variance. Two measures of partial proportion of variance are partial eta-squared and partial omega-squared.

- Partial proportion of variance is described as the proportion of variance in the dependent variable that can be accounted for by the levels of the factor.

Partial eta-squared (η_{P}^2): To compute the partial eta-squared, we remove the sum of squares between persons from the total sum of squares in the denominator.

$$\eta_{\text{P}}^2 = \frac{SS_{\text{BG}}}{SS_{\text{T}} - SS_{\text{BP}}}.$$

or

$$\eta_{\text{P}}^2 = \frac{SS_{\text{BG}}}{SS_{\text{BG}} + SS_{\text{E}}}.$$

Partial omega-squared (ω_P^2): Partial omega-squared has two advantages over partial eta-squared when used with an ANOVA.

1. It corrects for the size of error by including MS_E in the formula.

2. It corrects for the number of groups by including df_{BG} in the formula.

To compute partial omega-squared, we remove the sum of squares between persons from the sum of squares total in the denominator.

$$\omega_P^2 = \frac{SS_{BG} - df_{BG}(MS_E)}{(SS_T - SS_{BP}) + MS_E}.$$

or

$$\omega_P^2 = \frac{SS_{BG} - df_{BG}(MS_E)}{(SS_{BG} + SS_E) + MS_E}.$$

13.8 The Within-Subjects Design: Consistency and Power

The one-way within-subjects ANOVA has greater power than a one-way between-subjects ANOVA only when participant responding is consistent between groups.

- *Consistency:* The extent to which a dependent variable changes in a predictable pattern across groups. When changes in the dependent variable are consistent across groups, most of the error variation is attributed to the between-persons source of variation, which is the source of variation that is removed from the error term in the denominator of the test statistic.

Because consistency increases power, we can state three rules for the power of a one-way within-subjects ANOVA.

1. As SS_{BP} increases, power increases.

2. As SS_E decreases, power increases.

3. As MS_{BP} decreases, power increases.

13.9 APA in Focus: Reporting the *F* Statistic, Significance, and Effect Size

To summarize a one-way within-subjects ANOVA, we report the test statistic, the degrees of freedom, and the *p* value. The effect size for significant analyses should also be reported. The means and the standard error or the standard deviations measured in a study can be summarized in a figure, in a table, or in the main text. To report the results of a post hoc test, identify which post hoc test was computed and the *p* value for significant results.

CHAPTER FORMULAS

One-Way Within-Subjects Analysis of Variance

Within-Subjects Design

$F_{obt} = \dfrac{MS_{BG}}{MS_E}$ (Test statistic for the one-way within-subjects ANOVA)

$df_{BG} = k - 1$ (Degrees of freedom between groups)

$df_{BP} = n - 1$ (Degrees of freedom between persons)

$df_E = (k - 1)(n - 1)$ (Degrees of freedom error)

$df_T = (kn) - 1$ (Degrees of freedom total)

Effect Size (Within-Subjects Design)

$\eta_P^2 = \dfrac{SS_{BG}}{SS_T - SS_{BP}}$ (Partial eta-squared)

$\omega_P^2 = \dfrac{SS_{BG} - df_{BG}(MS_E)}{(SS_T - SS_{BP}) + MS_E}$ (Partial omega-squared)

TIPS AND CAUTIONS FOR STUDENTS

- *Sources of variance:* The one-way within-subjects ANOVA is unique in that it is used when the same participants are observed across two or more groups. When the same participants are observed in each group, we can eliminate the between-persons variation, just as we did for the related-samples *t* test. Do not be confused by having to calculate *SS* and *df* for the between-persons variation. We are only making that calculation so that we can remove it from the error term in the denominator (i.e., mean square error). By reducing error, we increase the power to detect an effect, just as we did for the related-samples *t* test in Chapter 10 of the book.

- *Consistency:* Remember that the one-way within-subjects ANOVA has greater power to detect an effect compared to the one-way between-subjects ANOVA only when changes in the dependent variable are consistent across groups. You can think of consistency in terms of overlap. If scores are 1, 2, and 3 in Group A and 5, 6, and 7 in Group B, then the scores do not overlap—scores in Group A are obviously different from those in Group B. However, if the scores are 1, 2, and 3 in Group A and 2, 4, and 3 in Group B, then the scores do overlap—specifically, scores of 2 and 3 are in both groups. This reflects low consistency and decreases the power to detect an effect.

- *Preliminary and intermediate calculations:* It is important to organize the calculations you make to compute the test statistic. You can make a chart and print blank copies of each problem you have to compute. The chart can include spaces for information such as means, *n*, and sums of scores. It should have areas for the preliminary and intermediate calculations, as well as a separate area for the *F* table itself. Keep your calculations organized, and you will likely make fewer mistakes and have a better understanding of how to perform the calculations.

KEY TERM WORD SEARCHES

```
L J U C G J E U G Y A W D Q K S T J H O E U F H C E E R E K M H B U Y Y
R Y I H A J Y Z M I D Q B H Z L L C L T R D N Z T B E N P V M T E C F S
T U K C H F F U S Z Z O C J F Z A E I E G N L I E F V V J D A P T A K J
N F A J V G N W K O A M C D K W M O U A M G J C S W L J W R S K W Z D T
W Z Z Q J B Q K D W I S T S Y H O A G J X H W Y T N J W Q F R D E B J J
G K W V O E S J B C M T D S R Y K E J T T W P D W B C A F A E L E T H J
K L N K S N W N Z V E J E K R E S V N U I P N Q I G V T E N J X N R T M
T I F K Z L E M F T A L T W S J A H J X Y Z T X S U G O Z S Z Q P Y M Q
S Q J Z H V B W H C V M F M Z A U N C N T U M Z E L K D L M U F E D C Z
C D C A B A O V A Q X Y K P T O Y X M N K S W F A Q X O D J P M R W S J
F K V Y U L C Y X Y D P B A V J W O X S P S G G L X L C M W F G S E A F
B J J T A C A L L U W S Q O X S T M B P D C R Z P D X M S Z F T O R Z P
V Y L Z D N U R D G L I N H X E U C S F O W D K H K G V N J B F N S D T
B S Z H U I N U L Y L N T P Q P O F D B L K S S A O B T I A L Q S X O I
U G E E M I J S T K E Y W H R F Y U W C Q R I I Q A K G A A M J V V B W
F U J K J S V S S R H N P E I C C B Q T V X Q M X E U G H I F K A P D C
R W V O L E G Y Z R B M V B Y N X L S C F Z O I M G P L N J M G R S K N
M G H N F O O Z R V V R Y E J L S U S M X C D N J H V S S P M K I J C H
O S Q Y M N Q A X N Q P Q H E X S U O F M K J S Y F K W W J E K A M P Q
P R U W F Z H C F A S S E L O R T W B E P X F Z S S C R U Q S C T E Z Z
R N D W I G F I D R F N F K I S L N H J Z T K R C D C H M M N Y I N S E
U A O X N Y K P B I M F W G M X H P X A E G G W A S G Y S V Q T O R U B
Q H E O Z J P E J I P Y F A A O G I Q S Y C N E N E H A R T K P N V K V
Q E T S P N K B X N K U A X R G K K A C C D T C Q J S J X L Y T Y U N J
K W V N T C H X Q R D J G C Z M A E U I S M B S D J X E N P Y U S Q H Q
M V L W R Y V F M L N A L G Y Y Y O A E R X U R A E V X U H S W M B P Q
M S B E T W E E N P E R S O N S P G D A D N W N N N A Q Q I L Y O R Z G
Q D Z O B U S V A A Y T O A Y V Q U X U A D Q D X D O B V J Z F P S Q W
Y P B B G L R W M P G B P J Q H U T E F M M W R X S W V M A V I A Y D A
G O S R J I H E O Q C L L T R L W O K K M T K E N O F V A R G F D M J K
T B C V W E I H A V H K S I J L M N T O M E O D U D L M H Z L Z Y C J Y
K U T O F E M K I F E M N H V T P T V X O M Y A T T V Z P V Z I I J J Z
R T Z N K A T F X Q R Y F M R J F G L J X V S U M I M V N X V H C D H D
S S B E T W E E N P E R S O N S M H Z Q F L X V G A J C V Q N X B M D B
X Z C V A E A B N Y S A U O U X I S T Z V N O Q V I S R S Y X A U T E E
F I Z M F K K W N Z P U D F B E T W E E N P E R S O N S J N A S E F S D
```

BETWEEN-PERSONS VARIATION

DF BETWEEN PERSONS

MS BETWEEN PERSONS

ONE-WAY WITHIN-SUBJECTS ANOVA

SS BETWEEN PERSONS

TESTWISE ALPHA

263

CROSSWORD PUZZLES

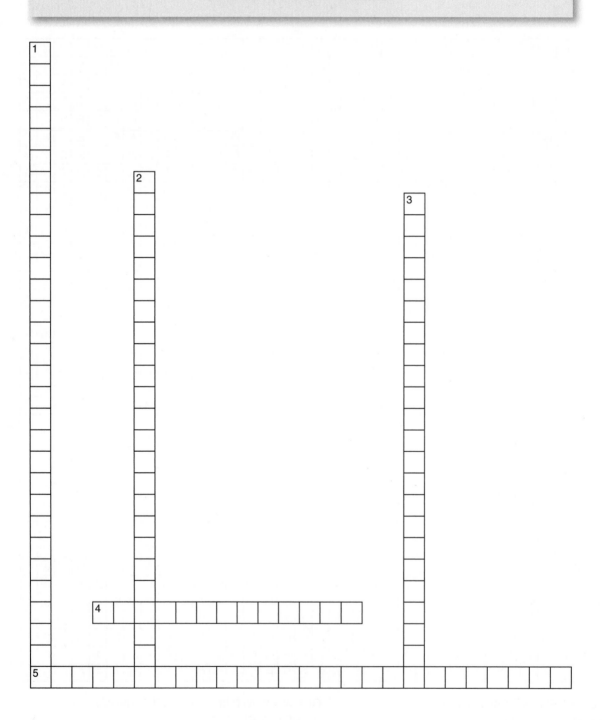

ACROSS

4 The alpha level, or probability of committing a Type I error, for each test or pairwise comparison made on the same data.

5 The sum of squares attributed to variability in participant scores across groups.

DOWN

1 The degrees of freedom associated with the variance of person means averaged across groups.

2 A measure for the variance attributed to differences in scores between persons.

3 The variance attributed to differences between person means averaged across groups.

PRACTICE QUIZZES

LO 1: Define the one-way within-subjects ANOVA and identify each source of variation in this statistical procedure.

1. A statistical procedure used to test hypotheses for one factor with two or more levels concerning the variance among group means, where the same participants are observed at each level of a factor, is called the:

   a. one-way within-subjects ANOVA

   b. one-way between-subjects ANOVA

   c. two-way between-subjects ANOVA

   d. two-way within-subjects ANOVA

2. A one-way within-subjects ANOVA is used when the same participants are observed in _____ group(s).

   a. one

   b. two

   c. two or more

   d. zero

3. Which of the following is a source of variation in the one-way within-subjects ANOVA but not in the one-way between-subjects ANOVA?

   a. within-groups variation

   b. between-persons variation

   c. between-groups variation

   d. both a and b

4. Variation attributed to differences between person means averaged across groups is called:

   a. within-groups variation

   b. between-persons variation

   c. between-groups variation

   d. within-subjects variation

5. The source of variation that cannot be attributed to or caused by having different groups is called:

   a. within-groups variation

   b. error variation

   c. between-persons variation

   d. all of the above

LO 2: Calculate the degrees of freedom for the one-way within-subjects ANOVA and locate critical values in the *F* table.

6. What are the degrees of freedom between persons for a study with $n = 12$ participants observed in four groups?

   a. 3

   b. 4

   c. 11

   d. 12

7. What are the degrees of freedom within groups (error) for a one-way within-subjects ANOVA with $n = 10$ participants observed in three groups?

   a. 9

   b. 18

   c. 29

   d. 30

8. What is the critical value for a study with 2 (between groups) and 27 (error) degrees of freedom at a .05 level of significance?

   a. 3.32

   b. 3.35

   c. 5.49

   d. the critical value is not listed in the *F* table

9. What is the critical value for the following test for between-group differences using the data given in the table at a .05 level of significance?

Source of Variation	SS	df	MS	F_{obt}
Between groups	32	2	16	8.00
Between persons	12	6	2	
Within groups (error)	24	12	2	
Total	68	20		

   a. 3.89

   b. 3.40

   c. 4.28

   d. 6.93

LO 3: Identify the assumptions for the one-way within-subjects ANOVA.

10. Homogeneity of covariance refers to the assumption that:

    a. participant scores in each group are related because the same participants are observed across or between groups

    b. the data were selected using a random sampling procedure

    c. the probabilities of each measured outcome in a study are independent

    d. data in the population being sampled from are normally distributed

11. Which of the following is an assumption of the one-way within-subjects ANOVA but not the one-way between-subjects ANOVA?

    a. normality

    b. random sampling

    c. homogeneity of variance

    d. homogeneity of covariance

12. The assumptions of homogeneity of variance and homogeneity of covariance are often called the:

    a. assumption of convenience

    b. assumption of sphericity

    c. assumption of participants

    d. assumption of complexity

LO 4: Compute the one-way within-subjects ANOVA and interpret the results.

13. A researcher observes 14 adults in each of three groups and computes a one-way within-subjects ANOVA. If $SS_{BG} = 30$ and $SS_E = 104$, then what was the decision at a .05 level of significance?

    a. reject the null hypothesis

    b. retain the null hypothesis

    c. not enough information

14. A researcher conducts two studies on memory. In Study 1, eight participants observed each of three visual clips and recorded how many items from each clip they could recall. Study 2 was again $n = 8$, but participants viewed each of four video clips in this study. If $SS_{BG} = 32$ and $SS_E = 110$ in both studies, then in which study is the value of mean square error the largest?

    a. Study 1

    b. Study 2

    c. both; the test statistics are the same value

15. A researcher conducts two studies. In Study 1, 10 participants are observed in each of three groups. Study 2 is similar except $n = 10$ participants are observed in each of four groups. If $F_{obt} = 3.25$ in both studies, then in which study will the decision be to reject the null hypothesis at a .05 level of significance?

a. Study 1

b. Study 2

c. both

d. none

16. A researcher computes the following one-way within-subjects ANOVA table for a study where $k = 4$ and $n = 12$. State the decision at a .05 level of significance. (*Hint:* Complete the table first.)

Source of Variation	SS	df	MS	F_{obt}
Between groups	60			
Between persons				
Within groups (error)	198			
Total				

a. reject the null hypothesis

b. retain the null hypothesis

c. not enough information

17. A researcher computes the following one-way between-subjects ANOVA table. State the decision at a .05 level of significance. (*Hint:* Complete the table first.)

Source of Variation	SS	df	MS	F_{obt}
Between groups	120	4		
Between persons		15		
Within groups (error)	900			
Total				

a. reject the null hypothesis

b. retain the null hypothesis

c. not enough information

LO 5: Compute the Bonferroni procedure and explain why it is appropriate to use following a significant one-way within-subjects ANOVA.

18. The Bonferroni procedure adjusts the alpha level, or probability of committing a Type I error, for each test, thereby controlling for:

a. the total number of comparisons

b. the p value for each test

c. the testwise alpha level

d. the value of mean square error

19. To compute the Bonferroni procedure, we divide _____ by the total number of pairwise comparisons.

    a. experimentwise alpha

    b. the p value for each test

    c. testwise alpha

    d. mean square error

20. Following a significant one-way within-subjects ANOVA, we find that we need to make three additional pairwise comparisons. What is the testwise alpha level if we want to ensure that the experimentwise alpha level is .05?

    a. .02

    b. .05

    c. .15

    d. depends on the value of mean square error

LO 6: Compute proportion of variance for the one-way within-subjects ANOVA.

21. Which measure of proportion of variance tends to overestimate the size of an effect?

    a. partial eta-squared

    b. partial omega-squared

22. A researcher conducts two studies. The sum of squares between groups is smaller in Study 1 compared with Study 2; the sum of squares total is larger in Study 1 compared with Study 2. If the sum of squares between persons is equal in both studies, then in which study will partial eta-squared be smaller?

    a. Study 1

    b. Study 2

    c. the value will be the same in both studies

23. A researcher conducts a study using the one-way within-subjects ANOVA. He computes SS_{BG} = 180, SS_{BP} = 20, and SS_T = 520. What is the effect size for this test using partial eta-squared?

    a. .31

    b. .34

    c. .36

    d. .39

24. What is partial omega-squared using the values given in the F table for a one-way between-subjects ANOVA?

Source of Variation	SS	df	MS	F_{obt}
Between groups	180	3	60	6.0*
Between persons	88	11	8	
Within groups (error)	330	33	10	
Total	598			

a. .23

b. .25

c. .27

d. .29

LO 7: Explain how the consistency of changes in the dependent variable across groups influences the power of a one-way within-subjects ANOVA.

25. The within-subjects design is associated with more power to detect an effect than the between-subjects design because:

    a. there is more error variation in the within-subjects design compared to the between-subjects design

    b. we add a between-persons source of variation to the within-subjects sign, thereby making it more likely that we will detect this error

    c. we remove some of the error in the denominator of the test statistic—specifically, the between-persons error is removed

    d. both a and b

26. The within-subjects design has greater power than the between-subjects design when:

    a. changes in the dependent variable are not consistent

    b. changes in the dependent variable are consistent

    c. changes in the independent variable are consistent

    d. changes in the independent variable are not consistent

27. Which of the following changes will increase power?

    a. the sum of squares between persons increases

    b. the sum of squares error decreases

    c. the mean of square error decreases

    d. all of the above

28. Which table shows more consistent responding?

TABLE 1		
Groups		
A	B	C
2	1	5
4	6	2
2	3	3
5	3	2
3	5	5

TABLE 2		
Groups		
A	B	C
0	2	5
2	4	7
4	6	9
2	4	7
3	5	8

a. Table 1

b. Table 2

LO 8: Summarize the results of the one-way within-subjects ANOVA in APA format.

29. To report the results of the one-way within-subjects ANOVA, which of the following is not reported?

    a. the test statistic

    b. the p value

    c. the degrees of freedom between persons

    d. the degrees of freedom between groups

30. A researcher reports that the effectiveness of behavioral therapy varies depending on how long the sessions lasted, $F(3, 36) = 3.96, p < .05$. Assuming this is a within-subjects design, how many participants were observed in this study?

    a. 11

    b. 12

    c. 13

    d. 14

31. A researcher reports that cultural stereotypes varied by the type of situation a participant experienced, $F(4, 40) = 2.89$. Is the p value less than .05 for this test?

    a. yes, because the critical value is smaller than 2.89

    b. yes, because the critical value is larger than 2.89

    c. no, because the critical value is smaller than 2.89

    d. no, because the critical value is larger than 2.89

SPSS IN FOCUS

The One-Way Within-Subjects ANOVA

Follow the General Instructions Guidebook to complete this exercise. Also, an example for following these steps is provided in the SPSS in Focus section (Section 13.6) of the book. Complete and submit the SPSS grading template and a printout of the output file.

Exercise 13.1: Getting Children to Like Toys

A researcher notices that many products sold in the United States depict famous people or characters. To determine whether this actually influences how much children like these products, the researcher gave children a block of wood. On the top of the block of wood was a sticker of a superhero, a parent, a teacher, or no person at all (just a plain colored sticker). Children were allowed to handle each block of wood for 2 minutes and then were asked to rate how much they liked each block of wood on a pictorial scale similar to the one shown on the next page (adapted from Bradley & Lang, 1994). These types of scales are typically used with children because faces are familiar to them. Higher ratings indicated greater liking. Given the following data, test whether liking for the block of wood varied by the type of sticker at a .05 level of significance.

Type of Reinforcement			
Superhero	Parent	Teacher	None
4	5	5	3
3	5	4	1
4	4	5	3
4	4	5	5
5	3	4	5
5	4	3	3
4	5	5	1
3	4	3	1
4	2	4	3
5	4	3	4
4	5	4	3
5	4	3	4
4	4	5	1
5	5	4	5

An example of a pictorial scale for liking used with children:

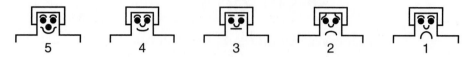

SOURCE: Bradley, M. M., & Lang, P. J. (1994). Measuring emotion: The Self-Assessment Manikin and the semantic differential. *Journal of Behavior Therapy & Experimental Psychiatry, 25,* 49–59.

With regard to the SPSS exercise, answer the following questions:

Based on the output given in SPSS, complete the following F table (assume sphericity):

Sources of Variation	SS	df	MS	F Statistic	Sig.
Between groups					
Error					
Total					

Based on the value of the test statistic, what is the decision for the one-way within-subjects ANOVA? (Circle one)

Retain the null hypothesis   Reject the null hypothesis

Based on the table, the sum of squares error is _____. Is this the total error in this study? If not, then what additional source of error is omitted?

Based on the F table you just completed, state the following values:

Sample size (n)   _____

Number of groups (k)   _____

Degrees of freedom numerator   _____

Degrees of freedom denominator   _____

Significance   _____

Based on your decision, is it appropriate to conduct a post hoc test? Explain. *Note:* If it is not necessary to conduct a post hoc test, then stop here.

Based on the SPSS output table, state each pair of means that significantly differed using Fisher's LSD post hoc test. *Hint:* SPSS places an asterisk in the "Mean Difference" column of the output table to indicate statistical significance.

Compute proportion of variance using eta-squared or omega-squared, and state the size of the effect as small, medium, or large. (Show your work.) In a sentence, also state the proportion of variance in the dependent variable that can be explained by the levels of the factor. Note: SPSS does not give the value of the sum of squares between persons (SS_{BP}) in a one-way within-subjects ANOVA. To find this value, you need to reanalyze the data as a one-way between-subjects ANOVA. The sum of squares total (SS_T) for that test (given in the output) is also the sum of squares total for the one-way within-subjects ANOVA. To find SS_{BP}, subtract SS_T (for the between-subjects test) from SS_E (for the within-subjects test).

State the conclusion for this test in APA format. Make sure you summarize the test statistic, the effect size, and each significant post hoc comparison. Provide an interpretation for the statistics you report.

CHAPTER SUMMARY ORGANIZED BY LEARNING OBJECTIVE

LO 1: Define the one-way within-subjects ANOVA and identify each source of variation in this statistical procedure.

- The one-way within-subjects (repeated-measures) ANOVA is a statistical procedure used to test hypotheses for one factor with two or more levels concerning the variance among group means. This test is used when the same participants are observed in each group.

- In the one-way within-subjects ANOVA, we measure three sources of variation: between-groups, within-groups, and between-persons variation. The between-groups and within-groups sources of variation are the same as those described in Chapter 12.

- Between-persons variation is the variance attributed to differences between person means averaged across groups. Because the same participants are observed across groups, this source of variation is removed from the error term in the denominator of the test statistic.

LO 2: Calculate the degrees of freedom for the one-way within-subjects ANOVA and locate critical values in the *F* table.

- The degrees of freedom for a one-way within-subjects ANOVA are as follows:

  o The degrees of freedom between groups are the degrees of freedom associated with the variance of group means: $df_{BG} = k - 1$.

  o The degrees of freedom between persons are the degrees of freedom associated with the variance of person means averaged across groups: $df_{BP} = n - 1$.

  o The degrees of freedom error is the variance associated with differences within each group: $df_E = (k - 1)(n - 1)$.

LO 3–4: Identify the assumptions for the one-way within-subjects ANOVA; compute the one-way within-subjects ANOVA and interpret the results.

- Four assumptions for the one-way within-subjects ANOVA are normality, independence within groups, homogeneity of variance, and homogeneity of covariance.

- The test statistic for the one-way ANOVA is $F_{obt} = \dfrac{MS_{BG}}{MS_E}$.

- The steps to conduct a one-way within-subjects ANOVA are as follows:
  Step 1: State the hypotheses.

  Step 2: Set the criteria for a decision.

  Step 3: Compute the test statistic.

    Stage 1: Preliminary calculations.

    Stage 2: Intermediate calculations.

    Stage 3: Computing *SS* for each source of variation.

    Stage 4: Completing the *F* table.

  Step 4: Make a decision.

LO 5: Compute the Bonferroni procedure and explain why it is appropriate to use following a significant one-way within-subjects ANOVA.

- A Bonferroni procedure is used to control for testwise alpha, which is the alpha level, or the probability of committing a Type I error, for each pairwise comparison made on the same data. The calculation for testwise alpha is

$$\text{Testwise alpha} = \frac{\text{experimentwise alpha}}{\text{total number of pairwise comparisons}}.$$

- The Bonferroni procedure is appropriate following a significant one-way within-subjects ANOVA because it allows us to use a hypothesis test that is adapted for within-subjects comparisons, such as the related-samples t test, to make pairwise comparisons. We follow two steps to complete the Bonferroni procedure using related-samples t tests:

  Step 1: Calculate the testwise alpha and find the critical values.

  Step 2: Compute a related-samples t test for each pairwise comparison and make a decision to retain or reject the null hypothesis.

LO 6: Compute proportion of variance for the one-way within-subjects ANOVA.

- Proportion of variance measures how much of the variability in the dependent variable can be accounted for by the levels of the factor. Two measures of proportion of variance using the within-subjects design are partial eta-squared (η^2_P) and partial omega-squared (ω^2_P). To compute each measure, we partial out the between-persons variation before computing effect size. The formula for each estimate is

$$\eta^2_P = \frac{SS_{BG}}{SS_T - SS_{BP}} \text{ or } \eta^2_P = \frac{SS_{BG}}{SS_{BG} + SS_E}.$$

$$\omega^2_P = \frac{SS_{BG} - df_{BG}(MS_E)}{(SS_T - SS_{BP}) + MS_E} \text{ or } \omega^2_P = \frac{SS_{BG} - df_{BG}(MS_E)}{(SS_{BG} + SS_E) + MS_E}.$$

LO 7: Explain how the consistency of changes in the dependent variable across groups influences the power of a one-way within-subjects ANOVA.

- Consistency refers to the extent to which the dependent measure changes in an identifiable or predictable pattern across groups. As consistency increases, the power to detect an effect also increases. Increased consistency increases the value of SS_{BP} and decreases the value of SS_E and MS_E.

LO 8: Summarize the results of the one-way within-subjects ANOVA in APA format.

- To summarize the one-way within-subjects ANOVA, we report the test statistic, the degrees of freedom, and the p value. The effect size for significant analyses should also be reported. The means and the standard error or standard deviations measured in a study can be summarized in a figure or table or in the main text. To report the results of a post hoc test, identify which post hoc test was computed and the p value for significant results.

LO 9: Compute the one-way within-subjects ANOVA and select an appropriate post hoc test using SPSS.

- SPSS can be used to compute the one-way within-subjects ANOVA using the Analyze, General Linear Model, and Repeated Measures options in the menu bar. These actions will display a dialog box that allows you to identify the variables, choose an appropriate post hoc test, and run the analysis.

14

Analysis of Variance

Two-Way Between-Subjects Factorial Design

LEARNING OBJECTIVES

After reading this chapter, you should be able to:

1. Describe how the complexity of the two-way ANOVA differs from that of the *t* tests and one-way ANOVAs.

2. List the three types of factorial designs for the two-way ANOVA.

3. Define and explain the following terms: *cell*, *main effect*, and *interaction*.

4. Identify the assumptions and list the order of interpretation for outcomes in the two-way between-subjects ANOVA.

5. Calculate the degrees of freedom for the two-way between-subjects ANOVA and locate critical values in the *F* table.

6. Compute the two-way between-subjects ANOVA and interpret the results.

7. Identify when it is appropriate to compute simple main effect tests and analyze a significant interaction.

8. Compute proportion of variance for the two-way between-subjects ANOVA.

9. Summarize the results of the two-way between-subjects ANOVA in APA format.

10. Compute the two-way between-subjects ANOVA using SPSS.

CHAPTER OUTLINE

14.1 Observing Two Factors at the Same Time

To this point, the complexity of statistical design has varied in two ways:

- We changed the levels of one factor. In Chapters 9 and 10, we described tests for differences within one group and between two groups or levels of one factor. In Chapters 12 and 13, we described tests for the variance of more than two groups or levels of one factor.
- We changed how participants were observed. In Chapters 9 and 12, we described tests in which different participants were observed in each group or at each level of one factor (between-subjects design). In Chapters 10 and 13, we described tests in which the same participants were observed in each group or across the levels of one factor (within-subjects design).

Using the two-way analysis of variance (ANOVA), we add a factor to the design. There are two reasons we typically include a second factor in a design: to answer a hypothesis or to control for threats to *validity*—the extent to which we demonstrate the effect we claim to be demonstrating.

14.2 New Terminology and Notation

The factorial design is a research design in which participants are observed across the levels of two or more factors. When we cross the levels of two factors, the two-way ANOVA is the statistical procedure used to test hypotheses. This test is used when the variance in any one population is unknown.

- In a two-way ANOVA, a letter identifies each factor (Factor A, Factor B), and a multiplication sign is used to separate the factors, such that an A-by-B ANOVA is notated as an A × B ANOVA.
- More often, the levels of each factor are identified numerically. Thus, if Factor A has three levels and Factor B has two levels, the A × B ANOVA would instead be notated as a 3 × 2 ANOVA.
- There is special notation to refer to the levels of each factor when a research design with two factors is summarized in a table. The levels of Factor A are symbolized as p, and the levels of Factor B are symbolized as q.
- Each cell in a table summary will be a combination of one level from each factor. To determine the number of cells in a two-way ANOVA, we multiply the levels of each factor:
  o Total number of cells = pq.

- A complete factorial design is where each level of each factor is combined, such that participants are observed in each cell.
  - o In this chapter, we introduce an ANOVA for when it is a complete factorial design.

14.3 Designs for the Two-Way ANOVA

There are three types of designs for the two-way ANOVA, depending on whether a between-subjects factor or a within-subjects factor is observed.

1. *The 2-between or between-subjects design.* Using this design, both factors are between-subjects factors.
   - o Different participants are observed in each cell created by combining the levels of two factors. The total number of participants equals *npq*.
2. *The 1-between 1-within or mixed design.* Using this design, different participants are observed at each level of the between-subjects factor, and the same participants are observed across the levels of the within-subjects factor.
   - o The total number of participants equals the sample size per cell (*n*) multiplied by the number of levels for the between-subjects factor.
3. *The 2-within or within-subjects design.* Using this design, both factors are within-subjects factors.
   - o The same participants are observed in each cell created by combining the levels of two factors. The total number of participants equals the sample size per cell (*n*).

14.4 Describing Variability: Main Effects and Interactions

When examining the two-way between-subjects ANOVA, four sources of variation can be measured.

Sources of Variability

- The variation of group means across the levels of Factor A
- The variation of group means across the levels of Factor B
  - o Sources of variation associated with differences in group means across the levels of a single factor are called main effects.
- The variation of cell means associated with the combination of levels for each factor
  - o The source of variation associated with differences in cell means (the group means at each combination of levels for two factors) is called an interaction.
- Within-groups variation or error is variation associated with differences in participants' scores in each group. This source of error is placed in the denominator of the test statistic.

Using a two-way between-subjects ANOVA, we could observe up to two main effects (one for each factor) and one interaction (for the combination of levels of the two factors). In all, we compute three hypothesis tests: one for each possible effect.

Testing Main Effects

The hypothesis test for each main effect determines whether group means vary significantly across the levels of a single factor. The variance attributed to the factor is placed in the numerator, and the error variance is placed in the denominator.

$$F_A = \frac{\text{variance of group means for Factor A}}{\text{variance attributed to error}} = \frac{MS_A}{MS_E}.$$

$$F_B = \frac{\text{variance of group means for Factor B}}{\text{variance attributed to error}} = \frac{MS_B}{MS_E}.$$

A significant main effect indicates that the dependent variable changes across the levels of a single factor, regardless of the levels of the second factor.

Testing the Interaction

The hypothesis test for the A × B interaction identifies whether group means (in the cells of a summary table) at each level of one factor significantly vary across the levels of the second factor. The variance attributed to the cell means is placed in the numerator, and the error variance is placed in the denominator.

$$F_{A \times B} = \frac{\text{variance of cell means}}{\text{variance attributed to error}} = \frac{MS_{A \times B}}{MS_E}.$$

- The pattern of an interaction can be more obvious when graphed. To graph the interaction, we plot the cell means for each combination of factors. When the distance between the two lines changes or is not parallel, this indicates that there is a possible interaction.

Outcomes and Order of Interpretation

A significant interaction indicates that changes across the levels of one factor depend on which level of a second factor you look at. Hence, if an interaction is significant, then you should typically analyze that result before looking at main effects.

14.5 The Two-Way Between-Subjects ANOVA

We make four assumptions to compute the two-way between-subjects ANOVA:

- *Normality.* We assume the data in the population, or populations being sampled, are normally distributed, especially for smaller sample sizes.
- *Random sampling.* We assume the data were sampled using a random sampling procedure.
- *Independence.* We assume the probabilities of each measured outcome are independent and equal.
- *Homogeneity of variance.* We assume the variance in each population is equal to that in the others. Violating this assumption can increase the likelihood of committing a Type I error.

Once these four assumptions are met, we use the four steps of hypothesis testing to conduct the two-way between-subjects ANOVA.

Step 1: State the hypotheses. The null hypothesis states that group means for Factor A, Factor B, and the levels of both factors combined do not vary in the population. The alternative hypothesis states that group means do vary in the population.

$$H_0: \sigma^2_{\mu's} = 0 \,.$$

$$H_1: \sigma^2_{\mu's} > 0 \,.$$

Step 2: Set the criteria for a decision. The level of significance is typically equal to .05. We will refer to the F table to find the critical values (see Table B.3 in Appendix B of the book; also reprinted in the appendix of this study guide). To find the critical values, we need to know the following degrees of freedom:

- The degrees of freedom for Factor A are $df_A = p - 1$.
- The degrees of freedom for Factor B are $df_B = q - 1$.
- The degrees of freedom for the A × B interaction are $df_{A \times B} = (p - 1)(q - 1)$.
- The degrees of freedom for the error are $df_E = pq(n - 1)$.

Step 3: Compute the test statistic. To compute the test statistic, we have to calculate the variance or mean square for each source of variation and make the following calculations: preliminary, intermediate, sums of squares (*SS*), and then the F statistic. Each calculation to find *SS* is summarized in Table 14.14 in Chapter 14 of the book. The following table lists the formulas for completing the F table.

Source of Variation	SS	df	MS	F
Factor A		$p - 1$	$\dfrac{SS_A}{df_A}$	$F_A = \dfrac{MS_A}{MS_E}$
Factor B		$q - 1$	$\dfrac{SS_B}{df_B}$	$F_B = \dfrac{MS_B}{MS_E}$
A × B		$(p-1)(q-1)$	$\dfrac{SS_{A\times B}}{df_{A\times B}}$	$F_{A\times B} = \dfrac{MS_{A\times B}}{MS_E}$
Error (within groups)		$pq(n-1)$	$\dfrac{SS_E}{df_E}$	
Total		$npq - 1$		

Step 4: Make a decision. We make a decision for each hypothesis test: one for each main effect and one for the interaction. For each hypothesis test, we compare the obtained value to the critical value to make a decision to retain or reject the null hypothesis.

When the interaction is significant, we compute simple main effect tests. When the main effects are significant, we compute post hoc tests.

14.6 Analyzing Main Effects and Interactions

To analyze a significant interaction, we compute simple main effect tests.

- Simple main effect tests are hypothesis tests used to analyze a significant interaction by comparing the main effects of one factor at each level of a second factor.

Interactions: Simple Main Effect Tests

Follow three steps to analyze an interaction:

1. Choose how to describe the data. We can analyze the data in one of two ways:
   - Compare cell means for Factor A at each level of Factor B.
   - Compare cell means for Factor B at each level of Factor A.

2. Compute simple main effect tests.
   - Analyze group means at each level of one factor. When more than two group means are analyzed, use the one-way between-subjects ANOVA to analyze the simple main effects.

3. Compute pairwise comparisons.

- o When $k > 2$, compute pairwise comparisons for the significant simple main effects found in Step 2. Tukey's honestly significant difference (HSD) test is the preferable option because it is more conservative, although Fisher's least significant difference (LSD) test will be the more powerful option. Both post hoc tests are appropriate.

Main Effects: Pairwise Comparisons

Compute pairwise comparisons to analyze differences between pairs of group means for each significant main effect. To do this, we skip straight to Step 3 for the steps given to analyze a significant interaction.

14.7 Measuring Effect Size

We can determine the size of an effect in the population by computing proportion of variance. The two measures of proportion of variance are eta-squared and omega-squared.

- Proportion of variance is described as the proportion of variance in the dependent variable that can be accounted for by the levels of the factor.

Eta-Squared (η^2 or R^2)

Eta-squared can be computed for each main effect and the interaction using the following formulas given for each effect:

$$\eta_A^2 = \frac{SS_A}{SS_T}$$

$$\eta_B^2 = \frac{SS_B}{SS_T}$$

$$\eta_{A \times B}^2 = \frac{SS_{A \times B}}{SS_T}$$

Omega-Squared (ω^2)

Omega-squared can be computed for each main effect and the interaction. It is less biased than eta-squared for two reasons:

1. It corrects for the size of error by including MS_E in the formula.

2. It corrects for the number of cells by including the df for the main effect or interaction in the formula.

The formulas for each effect using omega-squared are as follows:

$$\omega_A^2 = \frac{SS_A - df_A(MS_E)}{SS_T + MS_E}$$

$$\omega_B^2 = \frac{SS_B - df_B(MS_E)}{SS_T + MS_E}$$

$$\omega_{A \times B}^2 = \frac{SS_{A \times B} - df_{A \times B}(MS_E)}{SS_T + MS_E}$$

14.8 SPSS in Focus: The Two-Way Between-Subjects ANOVA

SPSS can be used to compute the two-way between-subjects ANOVA using the Analyze, General Linear Model, and Univariate options in the menu bar. These actions will display a dialog box that allows you to identify the variables, choose an appropriate post hoc test for the main effects, and run the analysis. SPSS does not perform simple main effect tests by default. If a significant interaction is obtained, then you must reorganize the data and conduct these tests separately.

14.9 APA in Focus: Reporting Main Effects, Interactions, and Effect Size

To summarize any type of two-way ANOVA, we report the test statistic, the degrees of freedom, and the p value for each significant main effect and interaction. The effect size should also be reported for each significant hypothesis test and for the simple main effect tests. To report the results of a post hoc test, identify the name of the post hoc test used and the p value for the test. The means and the standard error or the standard deviations measured in a study can be summarized in a figure, in a table, or in the main text.

CHAPTER FORMULAS

Two-Way Between-Subjects Analysis of Variance

Between-Subjects Design

$F_A = \dfrac{MS_A}{MS_E}$ (Test statistic for the main effect of Factor A)

$F_B = \dfrac{MS_B}{MS_E}$ (Test statistic for the main effect of Factor B)

$F_{A \times B} = \dfrac{MS_{A \times B}}{MS_E}$ (Test statistic for the A × B interaction)

$df_A = p - 1$ (Degrees of freedom for Factor A)

$df_B = q - 1$ (Degrees of freedom for Factor B)

$df_{A \times B} = (p - 1)(q - 1)$ (Degrees of freedom for the A × B interaction)

$df_E = pq(n - 1)$ (Degrees of freedom error)

$df_T = npq - 1$ (Degrees of freedom total)

Effect Size (Two-Way Between-Subjects ANOVA)

$\eta_A^2 = \dfrac{SS_A}{SS_T}$, $\eta_B^2 = \dfrac{SS_B}{SS_T}$ (Eta-squared for main effects)

$\eta_{A \times B}^2 = \dfrac{SS_{A \times B}}{SS_T}$ (Eta-squared for the interaction)

$\omega_A^2 = \dfrac{SS_A - df_A(MS_E)}{SS_T + MS_E}$, $\omega_B^2 = \dfrac{SS_B - df_B(MS_E)}{SS_T + MS_E}$ (Omega-squared for main effects)

$\omega_{A \times B}^2 = \dfrac{SS_{A \times B} - df_{A \times B}(MS_E)}{SS_T + MS_E}$ (Omega-squared for the interaction)

TIPS AND CAUTIONS FOR STUDENTS

- *Validity:* You will likely hear the term *validity* to describe research design. Validity is the extent to which we are demonstrating what we claim to be demonstrating. Any time a factor can threaten the validity of a result, the most straightforward thing to do is to include that factor in the design. By adding the factor in the design, we can be more confident that if we still observe the same result, then we are in fact demonstrating the effect we claim to be demonstrating.

- *A × B between-subjects ANOVA:* To simplify the notation of the two-way ANOVA, we label the factors alphabetically (e.g., A × B ANOVA), then refer to the levels of each factor in the design (e.g., 3 × 2 ANOVA). Notice that we immediately know the number of groups by multiplying the levels of each factor, as indicated in the notation for the design. For example, a 3 × 2 design has six groups. Because each number indicates the levels of a factor, we also know that the levels for two factors were observed, so this notation is rather informative.

- F *table:* The F table is an important summary table for the calculations you make to compute an ANOVA. Before you begin to compute the test statistic, make sure you print an F table and have it in front of you. The degrees of freedom should be the first values you enter into the F table because you can find these with only a few calculations. The best way to get better is to practice. Complete the end-of-chapter problems if you are still struggling. Answers are given for even-numbered problems in Appendix C of the book.

KEY TERM WORD SEARCHES

H	W	J	B	G	E	F	D	U	K	M	I	X	E	D	D	E	S	I	G	N	J	J	E	E	L	R	S	A	S
E	V	G	I	N	T	E	R	A	C	T	I	O	N	O	D	N	L	X	I	C	G	M	G	Z	Z	Z	A	S	N
D	J	D	J	G	F	F	W	J	O	Y	T	I	Q	I	X	W	B	Z	T	T	V	Q	J	V	D	S	I	D	J
F	E	K	Z	E	W	I	B	L	M	A	I	Y	R	C	S	Y	O	T	U	D	J	C	Y	A	H	Z	S	N	A
H	G	N	X	B	M	E	T	J	P	J	L	M	O	V	I	P	Z	K	U	D	O	K	H	B	J	Y	E	U	G
G	E	W	C	A	M	I	H	U	L	F	M	L	W	E	M	X	F	F	K	I	R	U	H	E	J	A	X	E	O
Z	P	I	Z	W	O	T	G	G	E	X	O	G	I	Z	P	T	D	G	B	J	M	Z	Y	T	W	Y	Q	F	C
Z	Q	T	M	A	Z	X	D	F	T	W	X	J	S	U	L	W	J	Y	R	P	Y	Z	Q	W	I	B	Y	B	M
J	O	H	N	G	A	O	Y	F	E	Q	J	K	X	X	E	O	Y	G	G	G	A	K	A	E	T	E	M	B	A
U	O	I	G	Z	O	H	I	Z	F	Q	O	D	X	G	M	W	Y	M	T	W	P	H	Q	E	H	T	H	Z	I
H	W	N	L	Z	L	J	S	Z	A	F	X	P	H	U	A	A	Y	Z	A	Z	Q	X	Q	N	I	W	T	V	N
U	A	S	S	H	T	N	D	V	C	T	W	U	U	H	I	Y	K	O	P	V	Z	H	R	S	N	E	J	F	E
I	Z	U	E	O	U	W	Q	Q	T	T	Q	G	L	B	N	A	L	H	D	P	E	V	K	U	S	E	E	T	F
M	Z	B	R	O	M	K	U	X	O	J	C	M	O	S	E	N	S	D	F	T	H	E	D	B	U	N	C	E	F
N	W	J	I	C	I	R	J	C	R	V	Y	B	O	M	F	O	E	X	F	K	F	V	V	J	B	S	G	E	E
Y	M	E	T	O	A	K	L	O	I	F	B	Q	I	L	F	V	V	F	J	C	C	N	G	E	J	U	G	O	C
N	D	C	G	Y	H	N	W	Y	A	H	H	X	J	X	E	A	V	I	T	R	Z	R	H	C	E	B	S	A	T
Y	D	T	S	C	Z	A	D	S	L	H	A	Y	K	Z	C	K	Q	H	B	C	Y	R	G	T	C	J	T	J	B
L	C	S	X	K	B	I	L	O	D	P	Y	V	M	E	T	J	C	G	F	N	V	U	O	S	T	E	Z	C	X
L	N	D	W	R	M	P	W	S	E	P	L	G	P	S	T	Q	E	P	Z	V	H	S	K	D	S	C	Z	E	O
M	M	E	F	V	W	K	V	M	S	F	J	O	R	J	E	O	J	V	V	R	W	I	K	E	F	T	G	L	O
J	Q	S	B	Y	V	Y	H	G	I	M	M	Z	J	F	S	G	U	A	I	U	Z	B	G	S	A	S	E	L	Z
U	B	I	Q	Z	L	A	N	Q	G	E	G	X	V	F	T	V	M	Z	N	Y	C	B	F	I	C	F	K	E	D
P	B	G	R	O	O	K	E	I	N	E	R	G	W	F	S	Z	V	F	Y	V	U	C	I	G	T	A	L	P	E
V	U	N	M	D	D	C	U	J	C	W	N	K	K	I	X	Z	B	T	C	O	Q	O	O	N	O	C	P	U	O
C	W	B	D	J	P	C	U	E	U	L	N	S	U	Y	A	A	F	B	X	W	A	R	O	R	R	T	K	W	Y
T	B	J	A	U	U	B	P	G	Z	Y	A	G	Z	K	L	T	U	S	G	Y	V	H	H	V	M	O	V	B	J
O	Q	S	P	C	Z	S	Z	E	P	O	C	A	J	K	X	M	V	Z	A	Y	C	M	D	G	V	R	Z	H	L
B	R	M	F	Y	L	F	K	X	Q	W	Y	I	G	U	U	E	S	S	W	O	X	V	M	W	B	G	K	M	E
P	J	D	R	G	Y	N	D	J	D	P	E	A	A	V	Y	A	R	R	H	R	Y	O	G	L	X	L	D	W	A

BETWEEN-SUBJECTS DESIGN
BETWEEN-SUBJECTS FACTOR
CELL
COMPLETE FACTORIAL DESIGN

INTERACTION
MAIN EFFECT
MIXED DESIGN
SIMPLE MAIN EFFECT TESTS

TWO-WAY ANOVA
WITHIN-SUBJECTS DESIGN
WITHIN-SUBJECTS FACTOR

CROSSWORD PUZZLES

ACROSS

2   A statistical procedure used to test hypotheses concerning the variance of groups created by combining the levels of two factors. This test is used when the variance in any one population is unknown.

3   A research design for a two-way ANOVA, in which different participants are observed at each level of the between-subjects factor and are repeatedly observed across the levels of the within-subjects factor.

4   A research design for a two-way ANOVA, in which different participants are observed in each cell or at each level of both factors.

6   A research design for the two-way ANOVA, in which the same participants are observed in each cell or across the levels of both factors.

8   A type of factor for which different participants are observed at each level of the factor.

9   A hypothesis test used to analyze a significant interaction by comparing the mean differences or simple main effects of one factor at each level of a second factor.

10   A research design in which each level of one factor is combined or crossed with each level of the other factor, with participants observed in each cell or combination of levels.

11   A source of variation associated with the variance of group means across the combination of levels of two factors.

DOWN

1   A type of factor in which the same participants are observed across the levels of the factor.

5   A source of variation associated with mean differences across the levels of a single factor.

7   The combination of one level from each factor as presented in a table summary.

PRACTICE QUIZZES

LO 1: Describe how the complexity of the two-way ANOVA differs from that of the *t* tests and one-way ANOVAs.

1. The two-way ANOVA differs from the one-way ANOVA in that:
   a. the two way ANOVA is used when we observe more than two groups
   b. the one-way ANOVA is used when we observe the levels of two factors
   c. the two-way ANOVA is used when we observe the levels of two factors
   d. the one-way ANOVA is used when we observe more than two groups

2. Unlike the *t* tests, the two-way ANOVA can be used when:
   a. the same participants are observed across groups
   b. different participants are observed across groups
   c. two groups are observed in the same study
   d. the levels of two factors are combined

3. Which of the following is a common reason to include a second factor in a research design?
   a. a hypothesis may require that we observe two factors
   b. to ensure that enough participants are included in a study
   c. to control for threats to validity
   d. both a and c

LO 2: List the three types of factorial designs for the two-way ANOVA.

4. Researcher A measures intelligence scores among participants of different handedness (left-handed, right-handed). Researcher B measures characteristics of handwriting among participants asked to write with both their left and right hands. Which researcher included a within-subjects factor in the research design?
   a. Researcher A
   b. Researcher B
   c. none, because both factors were between-subjects factors
   d. both, because both factors were within-subjects factors

5. A researcher conducts a study in which a different group of participants is observed at each combination of levels for two factors. Which type of design is described for the two-way ANOVA?
   a. between-subjects design
   b. mixed design
   c. within-subjects design

6. A researcher conducts a study in which the same group of participants is observed at each combination of levels for two factors. Which type of design is described for the two-way ANOVA?

    a. between-subjects design

    b. mixed design

    c. within-subjects design

7. A mixed design has one between-subjects factor with two levels and one within-subjects factor with three levels. If 12 participants are observed at each level of the between-subjects factor, then how many total participants are observed in this study?

    a. 12 participants

    b. 24 participants

    c. 36 participants

    d. 72 participants

LO 3: Define and explain the following terms: *cell*, *main effect*, and *interaction*.

8. When we arrange the data in an ANOVA test in a table, the combination of one level from each factor is called a:

    a. cell

    b. design

    c. factor

    d. combo

9. When we arrange the data in an ANOVA test in a table, the number of cells represents the number of _____ in a study.

    a. participants

    b. factors

    c. researchers

    d. groups

10. A main effect is a source of variation associated with mean differences:

    a. in the cell means given in a table summary

    b. across the combination of levels of two factors

    c. across the levels of a single factor

    d. across the combination of levels of two or more factors

11. A source of variation associated with the variance of group means across the combination of levels of two factors is called a(n):

    a. main effect

    b. interaction

    c. cell mean

    d. variable

12. How many interactions are possible in the two-way between-subjects ANOVA?

    a. 0

    b. 1

    c. 2

    d. 3

LO 4: Identify the assumptions and list the order of interpretation for outcomes in the two-way between-subjects ANOVA.

13. The assumption that the population or populations being sampled from are normally distributed is particularly important when researchers select _____ samples.

    a. small

    b. independent

    c. random

    d. large

14. Which of the following is not an assumption of the two-way between-subjects ANOVA?

    a. normality

    b. random sampling

    c. homogeneity of variance

    d. homogeneity of covariance

15. In a two-way between-subjects ANOVA, which effect should be analyzed first when it is significant?

    a. the main effect of Factor A

    b. the main effect of Factor B

    c. the interaction

16. In a two-way between-subjects ANOVA, which effect is potentially the most informative when it is significant?

    a. the main effect of Factor A

    b. the main effect of Factor B

    c. the interaction

LO 5: Calculate the degrees of freedom for the two-way between-subjects ANOVA and locate critical values in the *F* table.

17. A researcher conducts a study in which 12 participants are observed at each combination of two factors, where Factor A has three levels and Factor B has two levels. What are the degrees of freedom for the A × B interaction?

    a. 1

    b. 2

    c. 6

    d. 66

18. A researcher conducts a study in which 12 participants are observed at each combination of two factors, where Factor A has three levels and Factor B has two levels. What are the degrees of freedom for error?

    a. 6

    b. 66

    c. 71

    d. 72

19. A researcher conducts a study in which six participants are observed in each group created by combining the levels of two factors, where Factor A has two levels and Factor B has three levels. What is the critical value for the main effect test of Factor A using a .05 level of significance?

    a. 4.17

    b. 3.32

    c. 7.56

    d. 2.42

20. What is the approximate critical value for the interaction test using the data given in the table at a .05 level of significance?

Source of Variation	SS	df	MS	F
Factor A	60	2	30	9.4*
Factor B	40	2	20	6.3*
A × B	80	4	20	6.3*
Error	200	63	3.2	
Total	380			

    a. 2.37

    b. 3.15

    c. 2.76

    d. 2.53

LO 6: Compute the two-way between-subjects ANOVA and interpret the results.

21. Using a two-way between-subjects ANOVA, Factor A has two levels, Factor B has two levels, and $n = 12$ per group. If $SS_{A \times B} = 15$ and $SS_E = 220$, then what was the decision for the interaction test at a .05 level of significance?

    a. reject the null hypothesis

    b. retain the null hypothesis

    c. not enough information

22. Using a two-way between-subjects ANOVA, Factor A has four levels, Factor B has three levels, and $n = 6$. If $SS_A = 300$ and $SS_E = 180$, then what was the decision for the main effect of Factor A at a .05 level of significance?

    a. reject the null hypothesis

    b. retain the null hypothesis

    c. not enough information

23. A researcher conducts two studies. In Study 1, $n = 8$, $p = 2$, and $q = 2$. In Study 2, $n = 8$, $p = 3$, and $q = 2$. If $F_{A \times B} = 4.06$ in both studies, then in which study will the decision be to reject the null hypothesis for the interaction test at a .05 level of significance?

    a. Study 1

    b. Study 2

    c. both

    d. none

24. A researcher computes the following two-way between-subjects ANOVA table. Which effect is significant at a .05 level of significance? (*Hint:* Complete the table first.)

Source of Variation	SS	df	MS	F
Factor A	54	2		
Factor B	32	4		
A × B	88	8		
Error	480	60		
Total	654	74		

    a. the main effect of Factor A only

    b. the main effect of Factor B only

    c. the main effect of Factor A and the interaction

    d. no effects were significant

25. A researcher computes the following one-way between-subjects ANOVA table. Which effect is significant at a .05 level of significance? (*Hint:* Complete the table first.)

Source of Variation	SS	df	MS	F
Factor A	10	1		
Factor B	32	2		
A × B	120	2		
Error	168	42		
Total	330	47		

    a. the main effect of Factor A and the interaction

    b. the main effect of Factor B and the interaction

    c. the interaction only

    d. all effects were significant

LO 7: Identify when it is appropriate to compute simple main effect tests and analyze a significant interaction.

26. Hypothesis tests used to analyze a significant interaction by comparing the mean differences of one factor at each level of a second factor are called:

    a. effect size tests

    b. two-way ANOVA tests

    c. 1-between 1-within tests

    d. simple main effect tests

27. Simple main effect tests are necessary to analyze:

    a. a significant main effect

    b. any significant effect

    c. a significant interaction

    d. the results of a one-way ANOVA

28. The table shows the group means for a two-way ANOVA. Which group means in the table would be analyzed using simple main effect tests?

		Factor A		
		A1	A2	
Factor B	B1	4	8	6
	B2	10	2	6
		7	5	

    a. row means (6, 6)

    b. column means (7, 5)

    c. cell means (2, 4, 8, 10)

LO 8: Compute proportion of variance for the two-way between-subjects ANOVA.

29. Which measure of proportion of variance for the two-way between-subjects ANOVA tends to overestimate the size of an effect?

    a. eta-squared

    b. omega-squared

30. A researcher conducts two studies. In Study 1, the main effect of Factor A was significant. In Study 2, the main effect of Factor A was not significant. If the value of eta-squared for Factor A was the same in both studies, then in which study was the effect size the largest?

    a. Study 1

    b. Study 2

    c. the value is the same in both studies

31. A researcher conducts a study using the two-way between-subjects ANOVA. He computes $SS_{A \times B} = 50$ and $SS_T = 600$. What is the proportion of variance for the interaction using eta-squared?

a. .08

b. .10

c. .12

d. .14

32. What is omega-squared for the significant effect using the values given in the F table for the two-way between-subjects ANOVA? (Hint: First determine the significant effect, and then compute omega-squared.)

Source of Variation	SS	df	MS	F
Factor A	12	1	12	2.0
Factor B	30	2	15	2.5
A × B	120	2	60	10.0
Error	252	42	6	
Total	414	47		

a. .20

b. .23

c. .26

d. .29

LO 9: Summarize the results of the two-way between-subjects ANOVA in APA format.

33. To report the results of the two-way between-subjects ANOVA and post hoc tests, which of the following is reported?

a. the test statistic for each significant main effect and interaction

b. the p value for each significant main effect and interaction

c. the post hoc tests used to analyze significant main effects

d. all of the above

34. A two-way between-subjects ANOVA showed a significant main effect of Factor A, $F(3, 180) = 6.09$, $p < .05$, and a significant main effect of Factor B, $F(4, 180) = 4.18$, $p < .05$. How many groups were observed in this study?

a. 4

b. 5

c. 20

d. 180

35. A researcher reports the following interaction: $F(2, 44) = 3.11$. Is the p value less than .05 for this test?

a. yes, because the critical value is larger than 3.11

b. no, because the critical value is larger than 3.11

c. no, because the critical value is smaller than 3.11

d. not enough information

SPSS IN FOCUS

The Two-Way Between-Subjects ANOVA

Follow the General Instructions Guidebook to complete this exercise. Also, an example for following these steps is provided in the SPSS in Focus section (Section 14.8) of the book. Complete and submit the SPSS grading template and a printout of the output file.

Exercise 14.1: Relationship Status, Sex, and Forgiveness

A hypothetical study investigated the extent to which heterosexual participants were willing to forgive an opposite-sex partner for transgressions in a relationship. Male and female participants completed a questionnaire where they read five different situations where an opposite-sex partner transgressed in a relationship. After each situation, participants rated their willingness to forgive on a scale from 1 (*not forgive at all*) to 9 (*definitely forgive*). Hence, total ratings could range from 5 (all 1s recorded) to 45 (all 9s recorded). Given the following data, test whether forgiveness varies by sex and/or relationship status at a .05 level of significance.

Sex		Relationship Status	
		Short Term	Long Term
Male		18	8
		24	22
		12	20
		9	11
		12	5
		29	21
		13	25
		9	30
		32	28
		36	28
Female		28	18
		34	32
		22	27
		19	21
		14	14
		27	32
		28	25
		28	24
		31	25
		20	25

With regard to the SPSS exercise, answer the following questions:

Based on the output shown in SPSS, complete the following *F* table (label each factor in the space provided in the first column):

Sources of Variation	SS	df	MS	F Statistic	Sig.
A					
B					
AB					
Error					
Total					

Based on the value of the test statistics, what is the decision for each factor in the two-way between-subjects ANOVA? (Circle one)

Factor A: Retain the null hypothesis   Reject the null hypothesis

Factor B: Retain the null hypothesis   Reject the null hypothesis

A × B interaction: Retain the null hypothesis   Reject the null hypothesis

Based on the *F* table you just completed, state the following values:

Total sample size   _____

Sample size per cell   _____

Number of levels for Factor A (*p*)   _____

Number of levels for Factor B (*q*)   _____

Significance for each test:

Factor A   _____

Factor B   _____

A × B interaction   _____

Based on your decision(s), what is the next appropriate step? *Note:* Simple main effect tests are necessary when the interaction is significant.

If the interaction is significant, then reorganize the data and compute a one-way ANOVA to analyze the simple main effects (or you can compute a *t* test if $k = 2$). Otherwise, compute post hoc tests on the main effects and state each pair of means that significantly differed.

Compute proportion of variance using eta-squared or omega-squared for each *significant* effect, and state the size of the effect as small, medium, or large. (Show your work.) In a sentence, also state the proportion of variance in the dependent variable that can be explained by the levels or combination of levels for each factor. *Note:* The table in SPSS gives you all the information you need to compute proportion of variance.

State the conclusion for this test in APA format. Make sure you summarize the test statistic, the effect size, and each significant simple main effect or post hoc comparison test. Provide an interpretation for the statistics you report.

CHAPTER SUMMARY ORGANIZED BY LEARNING OBJECTIVE

LO 1: Describe how the complexity of the two-way ANOVA differs from that of the *t* tests and one-way ANOVAs.

- A two-way ANOVA is more complex in that the levels of two factors (not one factor) are observed in a single study. Like the *t* tests and the one-way ANOVA, the two-way ANOVA can be used when different participants are observed in each group or at each level of one factor (between-subjects design), and when the same participants are observed in each group or across the levels of a factor (within-subjects design).
- Two common reasons for observing two factors in a single study are (1) the hypothesis requires the observation of two factors, and (2) to control or account for threats to validity.

LO 2: List the three types of factorial designs for the two-way ANOVA.

- A two-way ANOVA is a statistical procedure used to test hypotheses concerning the variance of row, column, and cell means, where the levels of two factors are combined. This test is used when the variance in any one population is unknown.
- The three designs for a two-way ANOVA are as follows:

  1. The 2-between or between-subjects design is where different participants are observed in each cell or group.

  2. The 1-between 1-within or mixed design is where different participants are observed at each level of the between-subjects factor and the same participants are observed at each level of the within-subjects factor.

  3. The 2-within or within-subjects design is where the same participants are observed in each cell or group.

LO 3: Define and explain the following terms: *cell*, **main effect**, and **interaction**.

- A cell is the combination of one level from each factor. Each cell is a group in a study.
- A main effect is a source of variation associated with mean differences across the levels of a single factor.
- An interaction is a source of variation associated with the variance of group means across the combination of levels for two factors. It is a measure of how cell means at each level of one factor change across the levels of a second factor.

LO 4: Identify the assumptions and list the order of interpretation for outcomes in the two-way between-subjects ANOVA.

- Four assumptions for the two-way between-subjects ANOVA are normality, random sampling, independence, and homogeneity of variance.
- In the two-way between-subjects ANOVA, there are three sources of between-groups variation and one source of error variation:

  1. Between-groups variation is a measure of the variance of the group means. Three sources of between-groups variation are the following:

Main effect of Factor A

Main effect of Factor B

Interaction of Factors A and B, called the A × B interaction

2. Within-groups (error) variation is a measure of the variance of scores in each group (or within the cells of a summary table). This source of error is the denominator for each hypothesis test.

- If significant, an interaction is typically analyzed first using the two-way between-subjects ANOVA.

LO 5: Calculate the degrees of freedom for the two-way between-subjects ANOVA and locate critical values in the *F* table.

- The degrees of freedom for a two-way between-subjects ANOVA are as follows:

Degrees of freedom for Factor A: $df_A = p - 1$.

Degrees of freedom for Factor B: $df_B = q - 1$.

Degrees of freedom for the A × B interaction: $df_{A \times B} = (p - 1)(q - 1)$.

Degrees of freedom error: $df_E = pq (n - 1)$.

Degrees of freedom total: $df_T = npq - 1$.

- To find the critical value for each hypothesis test, use the degrees of freedom for the factor or interaction that is being tested and the degrees of freedom error.

LO 6: Compute the two-way between-subjects ANOVA and interpret the results.

- The test statistics for the main effects and interaction are as follows:

Main effect for Factor A: $F_A = \frac{MS_A}{MS_E}$.

Main effect for Factor B: $F_B = \frac{MS_B}{MS_E}$.

A × B interaction: $F_{A \times B} = \frac{MS_{A \times B}}{MS_E}$.

- The steps for conducting a two-way between-subjects ANOVA are as follows:

Step 1: State the hypotheses.

Step 2: Set the criteria for a decision.

Step 3: Compute the test statistic.

Stage 1: Preliminary calculations.

Stage 2: Intermediate calculations.

Stage 3: Computing sums of squares (*SS*).

Stage 4: Completing the *F* table.

Step 4: Make a decision.

LO 7: Identify when it is appropriate to compute simple main effect tests and analyze a significant interaction.

- Simple main effect tests are appropriate to analyze a significant interaction. If an interaction is significant, then the interaction is analyzed first. To analyze a significant interaction, follow three steps:

Step 1: Choose how to describe the data.

Step 2: Compute simple main effect tests.

Step 3: Compute pairwise comparisons.

- Simple main effect tests are hypothesis tests used to analyze a significant interaction by comparing the mean differences or the simple main effects for one factor at each level of a second factor.

LO 8: Compute proportion of variance for the two-way between-subjects ANOVA.

- One measure of proportion of variance for the two-way between-subjects ANOVA is eta-squared:

Factor A: $\eta_A^2 = \frac{SS_A}{SS_T}$, Factor B: $\eta_B^2 = \frac{SS_B}{SS_T}$,

A × B interaction: $\eta_{A \times B}^2 = \frac{SS_{A \times B}}{SS_T}$.

- A second, more conservative measure is omega-squared:

Factor A: $\omega_A^2 = \frac{SS_A - df_A(MS_E)}{SS_T + MS_E}$,

Factor B: $\omega_B^2 = \frac{SS_B - df_B(MS_E)}{SS_T + MS_E}$,

A × B interaction: $\omega_{A \times B}^2 = \frac{SS_{A \times B} - df_{A \times B}(MS_E)}{SS_T + MS_E}$.

LO 9: Summarize the results of the two-way between-subjects ANOVA in APA format.

- To summarize any type of two-way ANOVA, we report the test statistic, the degrees of freedom, and the p value for each significant main effect and interaction. Effect size should also be reported for each significant hypothesis test and for the simple main effect tests. To report the results of a post hoc test, identify the name of post hoc test used and the p value for the test. Means and standard errors or standard deviations measured in a study can be summarized in a figure or a table, or in the main text.

LO 10: Compute the two-way between-subjects ANOVA using SPSS.

- SPSS can be used to compute the two-way between-subjects ANOVA using the Analyze, General Linear Model, and Univariate options in the menu bar. These actions will display a dialog box that allows you to identify the variables, choose an appropriate post hoc test for the main effects, and run the analysis. SPSS does not perform simple main effect tests by default. If a significant interaction is obtained, then you must reorganize the data and conduct these tests separately.

PART V

Making Inferences About Patterns, Frequencies, and Ordinal Data

15

Correlation

LEARNING OBJECTIVES

After reading this chapter, you should be able to:

1. Identify the direction and strength of a correlation between two factors.

2. Compute and interpret the Pearson correlation coefficient and test for significance.

3. Compute and interpret the coefficient of determination.

4. Define *homoscedasticity*, *linearity*, and *normality* and explain why each assumption is necessary to appropriately interpret a significant correlation coefficient.

5. Explain how causality, outliers, and restriction of range can limit the interpretation of a significant correlation coefficient.

6. Compute and interpret the Spearman correlation coefficient and test for significance.

7. Compute and interpret the point-biserial correlation coefficient and test for significance.

8. Compute and interpret the phi correlation coefficient and test for significance.

9. Convert the value of r to a t statistic and χ^2 statistic.

10. Summarize the results of a correlation coefficient in APA format.

11. Compute the Pearson, Spearman, point-biserial, and phi correlation coefficients using SPSS.

CHAPTER OUTLINE

15.1 The Structure of a Correlational Design

An alternative method to those introduced to this point, called the correlational method, is to treat each factor like a dependent variable and measure the relationship between each pair of variables.

- Four correlation coefficients were introduced in this chapter. Each correlation coefficient was derived from the Pearson correlation coefficient and is used to analyze data measured on different scales of measurement.

15.2 Describing a Correlation

A correlation is used to describe the pattern of change in the values of two factors and to determine whether the pattern observed in a sample is also present in the population from which the sample was selected. In behavioral research, we tend to describe the *linear* relationship between two variables.

- *Correlation:* A statistical procedure used to describe the strength and direction of a linear relationship between two factors.
- *Correlation coefficient (r):* A measure of the strength and direction of the linear relationship, or correlation, between two factors. The value of r ranges from -1.0 to $+1.0$.

The Direction of a Correlation

The sign of the correlation (+ or −) indicates the direction of the relationship between two factors. In a figure, a positive correlation (+) displays an ascending line from left to right, which indicates that as values of one factor increase, values of a second factor also increase. A negative correlation (−) displays a descending line from left to right in the figure, which indicates that as values of one factor increase, values of a second factor decrease.

The Strength of a Correlation

The value of a correlation coefficient indicates the strength of a correlation. The closer the correlation coefficient is to ± 1.0, the stronger the relationship between two factors. The closer the value is to ± 1.0, the closer that data points fall to the regression line on a graph. The closer the value is to 0, the farther that data points fall from the regression line on a graph and the weaker the correlation or relationship between two factors.

- *Regression line:* The best-fitting straight line to a set of data points that minimizes the distance that all data points fall from it.

- A common way to illustrate a correlation is using a graph called a *scatter plot*, which is used to illustrate the relationship between two variables, denoted (x, y). The x variable is plotted along the x-axis of a graph; the y variable is plotted along the y-axis of a graph.

15.3 Pearson Correlation Coefficient

The Pearson correlation coefficient is the most common correlation coefficient used to determine the strength and direction of a relationship between two factors. The Pearson formula is used when we measure data on an interval or ratio scale. To compute the Pearson correlation coefficient, first compute preliminary calculations, then compute the Pearson correlation coefficient (r).

- *Preliminary calculations:* These calculations are necessary to find the sum of squares (SS) needed to compute the Pearson formula. We make computations to find SS_{XY}, SS_X, and SS_Y.
  - Note that $SS_{XY} = SP$ (sum of products). SP is another way to refer to the estimate of the sum of squares for XY (SS_{XY}).
- Compute the Pearson correlation coefficient: $r = \dfrac{SS_{XY}}{\sqrt{SS_X SS_Y}}$.

  - The value in the numerator reflects the *covariance* of two factors (X and Y), which is the extent to which values on the x-axis (X) and the y-axis (Y) vary together.
  - The value in the denominator reflects the extent to which two factors (X and Y) vary independently.

Effect Size: The Coefficient of Determination

To compute proportion of variance, we compute the *coefficient of determination* by squaring the correlation coefficient r.

- r^2 or R^2 is used to measure the proportion of variance in one factor that can be explained by known values of a second factor.

Hypothesis Testing: Testing for Significance

We can use the following steps to test whether the correlation observed in a sample is also present in the population.

- *Step 1: State the hypotheses.* The null hypothesis states that there is no relationship between two factors; the alternative hypothesis states that there is a relationship between two factors in a population. The correlation coefficient for a population is symbolized by the Greek letter rho, ρ.

$$H_0: \rho = 0.$$

$$H_1: \rho \neq 0.$$

- *Step 2: Set the criteria for a decision.* Compute a one-tailed or two-tailed test at a specified level of significance (e.g., .05). The degrees of freedom are the number of scores that are free to vary for X and Y (*df: n* − 2). Locate the critical values in Table B.5 in Appendix B of the book (also reprinted in the appendix of this study guide): The levels of significance for one-tailed and two-tailed tests are listed in the columns; the degrees of freedom are listed in the rows.
- *Step 3: Compute the test statistic.* We follow the steps to compute the correlation coefficient *r*.
- *Step 4: Make a decision.* Compare the obtained value to the critical value to make a decision to retain or reject the null hypothesis. If *r* exceeds the critical value, then we reject the null hypothesis; otherwise, we retain the null hypothesis.

15.4 SPSS in Focus: Pearson Correlation Coefficient

SPSS can be used to compute the Pearson correlation coefficient using the Analyze, Correlate, and Bivariate options in the menu bar. These actions will display a dialog box that allows you to identify the variables and run the correlation.

15.5 Assumptions of Tests for Linear Correlations

Three key assumptions to test for the significance of a linear correlation are homoscedasticity, linearity, and normality.

- *Homoscedasticity* is the assumption that there is a constant or equal variance between the data points dispersed along the regression line.
- *Linearity* is the assumption that the best way to describe a set of data points is with a straight line.
- *Normality* is the assumption that the data points are normally distributed. This assumption requires that the population of X and Y scores for the two factors forms a bivariate normal distribution in which:
  - The population of X scores is normally distributed.
  - The population of Y scores is normally distributed.
  - For each X score, the distribution of Y scores is normally distributed.
  - For each Y score, the distribution of X scores is normally distributed.

15.6 Limitations in Interpretation: Causality, Outliers, and Restrictions of Range

Fundamental limitations using the correlational method require that a significant correlation be interpreted with caution. The considerations for interpreting a significant correlation include causality, outliers, and restrictions of range.

Causality

Because we do not manipulate an independent variable and make little effort to control for possible confound variables, a significant correlation cannot be interpreted as causal. Instead, a significant correlation informs us only about the *strength* and the *direction* of the relationship between two factors. We conclude that two factors are related and not that changes in one factor caused changes in a second factor.

- *Cofound variable:* An unanticipated variable not accounted for in a research study that could be causing or associated with observed changes in one or more measured variables.

Outliers

Outliers can change both the strength and the direction of a correlation and should therefore be considered when interpreting a significant correlation.

- *Outlier:* A score that falls substantially above or below most other scores in the data set.

Restriction of Range

It is also important to avoid making conclusions about relationships that fall beyond the range of data measured. The restriction of range problem occurs when the range of data measured in a sample is restricted or smaller than the range of data in the general population. To avoid the problem of restriction of range, we should not describe a correlation beyond the range of data observed.

15.7 Alternative to Pearson *r*: Spearman Correlation Coefficient

The Spearman rank-order correlation is a measure of the direction and strength of the linear relationship of two ranked factors on an ordinal scale of measurement.

$$\text{Spearman formula: } r_s = 1 - \frac{6 \Sigma D^2}{n(n^2 - 1)}.$$

- In the formula, D is the difference between the ranks of Factor X and Factor Y, and n is the number of pairs of ranks.

To compute the Spearman formula, we must rank the data. We follow three steps to compute the Spearman correlation coefficient.

- Step 1: Average tied ranks. Place the ranks in descending order. If two ranks are tied, sum the tied ranks and divide by 2. Assign the average value to both of the tied ranks in turn, and then shift the remaining ranks accordingly.

- Step 2: Compute preliminary calculations.
  - ○ Subtract X and Y scores to compute the difference (D) between ranks.
  - ○ Square and sum the deviation scores for X and Y.
- Step 3: Compute the Spearman correlation coefficient.

To make a decision, choose a one-tailed or two-tailed test, set the level of significance, and then find the critical values in Table B.6 in Appendix B of the book (also reprinted in the appendix of this study guide). In Table B.6, the levels of significance are listed in the columns, and the number of pairs (n) is listed in the rows.

15.8 SPSS in Focus: Spearman Correlation Coefficient

SPSS can be used to compute the Spearman correlation coefficient using the Analyze, Correlate, and Bivariate options in the menu bar. These actions will display a dialog box that allows you to identify the variables, select the option to compute a Spearman correlation, and run the correlation.

15.9 Alternative to Pearson r: Point-Biserial Correlation Coefficient

The *point-biserial correlation coefficient* (r_{pb}) is a measure of the direction and strength of the linear relationship of one factor that is continuous (on an interval or ratio scale of measurement) and a second factor that is dichotomous (on a nominal scale of measurement).

$$\text{Point-biserial formula: } r_{pb} = (\frac{M_{Y_1} - M_{Y_2}}{s_Y})(\sqrt{pq}), \text{ where } s_Y = \sqrt{\frac{SS_Y}{n}}.$$

- p and q are the proportions of scores at each level of the dichotomous variable, s_Y is the standard deviation of Y scores (scores for the continuous factor), and n is the number of pairs of scores measured.

We follow three steps to compute the point-biserial correlation coefficient.

- Step 1: Code the dichotomous variable. Code the levels of the dichotomous variable as 1 and 2.
- Step 2: Compute preliminary calculations.
  - ○ Compute the average Y score at each level of the dichotomous variable and overall.
  - ○ Subtract each Y score from the overall mean of Y (M_Y).
  - ○ Multiply and sum the deviation scores for Y.
- Step 3: Compute the point-biserial correlation coefficient.
  - ○ Note that because one of the factors is dichotomous, the direction of the correlation coefficient is not meaningful.

To test for significance, use the two-independent-sample t test by making each level of the dichotomous variable a different group and making values of Y the dependent variable measured in each group.

- To convert r to t: $t^2 = \dfrac{r^2}{(1-r^2)/df}$.

- To locate the critical values, look in Table B.2 in Appendix B of the book (also reprinted in the appendix of this study guide). The degrees of freedom will equal $n - 2$ (the same as a two-independent-sample t test) and set a level of significance.

15.10 SPSS in Focus: Point-Biserial Correlation Coefficient

There is no command in SPSS to compute a point-biserial correlation coefficient. To compute a point-biserial correlation coefficient using SPSS, first code the dichotomous variable, and then follow the directions for computing a Pearson correlation coefficient.

15.11 Alternative to Pearson r: Phi Correlation Coefficient

The phi correlation coefficient (r_ϕ) is a measure of the direction and strength of the linear relationship of two dichotomous factors on a nominal scale of measurement.

$$\text{Phi coefficient formula: } r_\phi = \frac{ad - bc}{\sqrt{ABCD}}.$$

- In the formula, a, b, c, and d refer to the cells, and A, B, C, and D refer to the column and row totals, as shown in the following 2×2 matrix. A positive correlation occurs when the values in cells a and d are larger than the values in cells b and c. A negative correlation occurs when the values in cells b and c are larger than the values in cells a and d.

		Variable X		
		X_1	X_2	
Variable Y	Y_1	a	b	A
	Y_2	c	d	B
		C	D	

- When the row and column totals in the 2×2 matrix are the same, we can use the following simplified formula to compute the phi correlation coefficient: $r_\phi = \dfrac{\text{matches} - \text{mismatches}}{\text{sample size}}$.

o Matches occur when the levels of each dichotomous factor are coded the same (e.g., both 1s or both 2s); mismatches occur when the levels of each dichotomous factor are different (e.g., 1, 2).

To test for the significance of a phi correlation coefficient, we convert r to a chi-square test statistic (χ^2) and then compute a chi-square test.

- To convert r to χ^2 : $\chi^2 = r_\phi^2 n$
- To locate the critical value, look in Table B.7 in Appendix B of the book (also reprinted in the appendix of this study guide). In this table, the levels of significance are listed in each column, and the degrees of freedom are listed in each row. For the phi correlation coefficient, the degrees of freedom for this test are always equal to 1.

15.12 SPSS in Focus: Phi Correlation Coefficient

There is no command in SPSS to compute a phi correlation coefficient. To compute a phi correlation coefficient using SPSS, first code each dichotomous variable, then weight each variable using the Weight cases . . . option in the menu bar, and finally follow the directions for computing a Pearson correlation coefficient.

15.13 APA in Focus: Reporting Correlations

To summarize correlations, we report the strength, the direction, and the p value for each correlation coefficient. Sample size and effect size should also be reported. The means and the standard error or the standard deviations measured in a study can be summarized in a figure, in a table, or in the main text. When we compute many correlations in a single study, we often report each correlation coefficient in a table called a *correlation matrix*.

CHAPTER FORMULAS

Correlation

Correlation Coefficients

$r = \dfrac{SS_{XY}}{\sqrt{SS_X SS_Y}}$ (Pearson correlation coefficient)

$r_s = 1 - \dfrac{6\sum D^2}{n(n^2 - 1)}$ (Spearman rank-order correlation coefficient)

$r_{pb} = (\dfrac{M_{Y_1} - M_{Y_2}}{s_Y})(\sqrt{pq})$ (Point-biserial correlation coefficient)

$r_\phi = \dfrac{ad - bc}{\sqrt{ABCD}}$ (Phi correlation coefficient)

Converting the Correlation Coefficient (r) to t and χ^2

$t^2 = \dfrac{r^2}{(1 - r^2)/df}$ (Formula for converting r to t)

$\chi^2 = r_\phi^2 n$ (Formula for converting r to χ^2)

Effect Size

$r^2 = \eta^2$ (The coefficient of determination)

TIPS AND CAUTIONS FOR STUDENTS

- *Direction of a correlation:* Keep in mind that a negative correlation indicates direction only. A negative correlation does not mean all the scores are negative or that two factors are not related. Instead, a negative correlation refers to the relationship between two factors such that as values for one factor increase, values for a second factor decrease. The closer a negative correlation is to -1.0, the stronger this relationship is between the two factors.

- *Sum of products:* The sum of products is similar to a sum of squares calculation in that it gives an estimate of variation. For reference, keep in mind that in terms of notation, $SS_{XY} = SP$.

- *Homoscedasticity:* The assumption of homoscedasticity is in many ways similar to the assumption of homogeneity of variance. Do not let the long name intimidate you: This is merely a way to state that the dispersion or variance of data points will be approximately the same along the regression line.

- *Correlation is not causation:* Causality cannot be inferred with correlational data. A correlation never demonstrates that changes in one factor cause changes in a second factor. Instead, always think of two factors as changing together but not necessarily due to one another—their relationship is associative, not causal.

KEY TERM WORD SEARCHES

```
Q Z K Q F P H I C O R R E L A T I O N C O E F F I C I E N T X U W J Z Q N J Q V
E F O F G W Z F Z C O N F O U N D V A R I A B L E Y Z I R W J T X R Q R C I P S
Y I C B K P O W B O Y H D R L M N J R Q A B Z Y N P B Y W S N N O N Q X E U O Q
K C H C X C Q F F E D T R Y R W I D O V N P A J B L S P B O H S U A G Y U X A K
Z W S R O U V Q W T O A G T D U C Y B L K A E R W L Y Q S S B L D D V Q X I U P
H P B T H Z G M B W L W W W P A Y R B V D V F Y D R D X D X M X T D U W C I H E
X S Q Y X T G W F O O C X Z W N R L K D P P V J I D K O C T C S S Q U I O F E A
Y L R G M O J B A N B G L I L F S H W C G Q U J S U L M V K G E N I N N R Y L R
I C G Z H D W M V H T G M Y N M Y N D O C Z M A C O Q T I N Y Y U N T J R E P S
H I Q M F Y E S O X I R A K Z J W M W V C E K Q J N Y X J Y T T P I W Q E F M O
P T O W J A H T L R M O Z L Q H N C L A W R H Y G A U T U E S I D T U W L G S N
H F U K X X O W L J K N C L B G L T N R F R M O C Q F P S J I U E O K O A F X C
Q M U J C U M Q K G R S R C S A G R P I G T C E F I F M C P F Y S W V I T V H O
S V P R X R O J N W B H Q U Y X U I M A U M G M E P R B E H Z V V T W S I O V R
Z O W L U S S M D F M V H B X O J O I N A G R Z Z V N C O A F N T B K C O V T R
P J R O A A C K F G X G B H L E O S H C E A O A X S E L X R S T W Y C U N U F E
R M G Q P T E O P V N T U J F I C X U E F O L Z K O D S N M A H Y M R Z C X F L
L B O K U M D I W R S D I M L U B H P F U R C R N X G C O O O G C J I C O B J A
I K K C C D A S W Z J B B G G Q X L F F D J A N O J U I C L A Y D I S R E X E T
N C R O J U S N N E A H P O S I T I V E C O R R E L A T I O N M H Y J R F E D I
E Z R I X V T S I U Q L Y K Y T N O S S N I O R U O N Z J I M A E C J U F Z J O
A B I Z J K I I T S J O C G H U S F Q I Q E M E C V Y L K W T M J P Q Y I J M N
R F T J Y F C X B F Y W D A S H Y L B E N E G Y N B X A M Z G A Z M I X C H N C
I M H J L O I C X W B I J E M N X N M K F O R A R L Y S X V E Z K V D K I U M O
T D S T Z C T A R A O R I N S C L A X S T V U V T K S R G S W Q N G T R E B U E
Y V S L C N Y A R X H J J D C O K X K Q Z R H H A I I V I U J B L P W Q N I P F
H M Q G U D Y C I H D Q I G P V C S K M O S D H E F V H V W U N N T Y D T L U F
K E N J G Q S P E A R M A N C O R R E L A T I O N C O E F F I C I E N T Y E R I
B S R M E L A Q G Z R E S T R I C T I O N O F R A N G E C U J B L N T Y I W D C
G O T P X J D D B S N X D J A C O N T F I H I K H X X O C O L I Q R F Y D H C I
C O R R E L A T I O N U C Y I N T Q I S S O G T O U Q V Y F R I I Z M P B Q J E
X F X K W U M T Q G Z U O U Y F F Z V R U V A K Z X Y U V Q J R H W K S C U H N
R M H U D K V E R O J T H P G Z P C F N K Y V R Y A W S X E B V E K X I I J Z T
R P P V G K K B J U A X U Q X H X S R P W D N C G N N O J J H X Q L P K P Y P K
S L H W Q C R A J K Y C Z Q R E G R E S S I O N L I N E N R T C N B A M O T W X
W R Z M D H F G H J I A G I Z N L K G D D Q G K R F W M W N L A Y O L T F Q P O
R E V E R S E C A U S A L I T Y Z T E E Q T R P L K C A Q C I P T G L P I V X K
S J U Y I B R X U W V W M Z Z A N S B U L K W W J R J V E U B T Q I L U V O V J
O C O E F F I C I E N T O F D E T E R M I N A T I O N C R U N I E V F V Q U N G
Y W U D Y I N X O Q S V S A U B F E N E E R J M Z Y B R B D W S B Y V E Z M K U
```

COEFFICIENT OF DETERMINATION

CONFOUND VARIABLE

CORRELATION

CORRELATION COEFFICIENT

COVARIANCE

HOMOSCEDASTICITY

LINEARITY

NEGATIVE CORRELATION

PEARSON CORRELATION COEFFICIENT

PHI CORRELATION COEFFICIENT

POSITIVE CORRELATION

REGRESSION LINE

RESTRICTION OF RANGE

REVERSE CAUSALITY

SPEARMAN CORRELATION COEFFICIENT

KEY TERM WORD SEARCHES

ACROSS

1 Used to measure the direction and strength of the linear relationship between two factors, where the data for both factors are measured on an interval or ratio scale of measurement.

2 Indicates that the values of two factors change in the same direction.

7 Used to measure the direction and strength of the linear relationship between two ranked factors on an ordinal scale of measurement.

8 The best-fitting straight line for a set of data points.

9 The assumption that there is an equal variance or scatter of data points dispersed along the regression line.

11 Indicates that the values of two factors change in different directions.

14 An unanticipated variable that is not accounted for in a research study and could be causing or associated with observed changes in one or more variables in the study.

16 Used to measure the strength and direction of the linear relationship, or correlation, between two factors.

DOWN

1 Used to measure the direction and strength of the linear relationship between one factor that is continuous (on an interval or ratio scale of measurement) and a second factor that is dichotomous (on a nominal scale of measurement).

3 Used to measure the proportion of variance in one factor (Y) that can be explained by known values of a second factor (X).

4 The sum of squares for two factors, X and Y. SP is the numerator for the Pearson correlation formula.

5 A problem that arises when the range of data for one or both correlated factors in a sample is limited or restricted, compared to the range of data in the population from which the sample was selected.

6 Used to measure the direction and strength of the linear relationship between two dichotomous factors on a nominal scale of measurement.

10 A problem that arises when the direction of causality between two factors can be in either direction.

12 A statistical procedure used to describe the strength and direction of the linear relationship between two factors.

13 The extent to which the values of two factors (X and Y) vary together.

15 The assumption that the best way to describe a pattern of data is using a straight line.

LO 1: Identify the direction and the strength of a correlation between two factors.

1. A statistical procedure used to describe the strength and direction of the linear relationship between two factors is called a:

   a. parameter

   b. factor

   c. correlation

   d. confound

2. The _____ of the correlation coefficient indicates the direction of a correlation.

   a. sign

   b. value

   c. strength

   d. linearity

3. Researcher A reported $r = -.86$. Researcher B reported $r = +.43$. Which researcher reported the stronger correlation?

   a. Researcher A

   b. Researcher B

4. Does the display of data points show a negative correlation or a positive correlation?

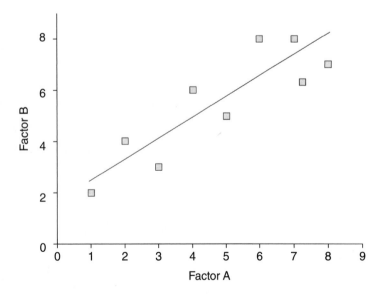

   a. negative correlation

   b. positive correlation

LO 2: Compute and interpret the Pearson correlation coefficient and the test for significance.

5. The correlation coefficient used to measure the direction and strength of the linear relationship of two factors, where the data for both factors are measured on an interval or ratio scale of measurement, is called the:

a. Pearson correlation coefficient

b. Spearman correlation coefficient

c. point-biserial correlation coefficient

d. phi correlation coefficient

6. If the covariance of two factors (X and Y) is $SS_{XY} = 450$, and the variability of X and Y separately is $(SS_X SS_Y) = 640{,}000$, then what is the value of the correlation coefficient?

a. less than .001

b. .01

c. .56

d. .59

7. A researcher measures the relationship between time spent playing video games (in hours) and cognitive performance. If $SS_{XY} = 40$, $SS_X = 200$, and $SS_Y = 100$, then what is the value of the correlation coefficient?

a. .002

b. .20

c. .25

d. .28

8. A researcher measures two correlations, A and B. Suppose the value of SS_{XY} is the same for each correlation, and $\sqrt{SS_X SS_Y}$ is larger for Correlation A. Which correlation will be larger?

a. Correlation A

b. Correlation B

c. none, the correlations will be equal

9. A researcher computes $r = .45$ using a sample of 18 participants. What is the decision for a Pearson correlation coefficient for a two-tailed test at a .05 level of significance?

a. retain the null hypothesis

b. reject the null hypothesis

c. not enough information

LO 3: Compute and interpret the coefficient of determination.

10. A measure of the proportion of variance in one factor (Y) that can be explained by known values of a second factor (X) is called the:

a. covariance

b. correlation coefficient

c. coefficient of determination

d. regression line

11. A researcher measures the following correlation: $r = +.38$. What is the value of the coefficient of determination?

a. .14

b. .38

c. .62

d. .76

12. A researcher measures the following correlation between the amount of fat consumed in a diet and general health: $r = -.62$. Which of the following gives an appropriate description of the relationship between these two factors?

a. as the amount of fat consumed in a diet increases, general health decreases

b. about 38% of the variability in general health can be explained by the amount of fat consumed in a diet

c. increasing the amount of fat consumed in a diet causes a decline in general health

d. both a and b

LO 4: Define *homoscedasticity*, *linearity*, and *normality* and explain why each assumption is necessary to appropriately interpret a significant correlation coefficient.

13. Which of the following is not an assumption to test for the significance of a linear correlation?

a. homoscedasticity

b. independence

c. normality

d. linearity

14. The assumption that there is an equal variance of data points dispersed along the regression line is called:

a. homoscedasticity

b. linearity

c. normality

d. correlation

15. What does the assumption of linearity refer to?

a. that the variance of data points is minimal

b. that all data points fall exactly on a straight line

c. that the distribution of data points is normal

d. that the best way to describe a pattern of data is using a straight line

16. To test for linear correlations, we assume that data points are _____ in general and at each point along the distribution of the other variable.

a. positively correlated

b. negatively correlated

c. normally distributed

d. positively skewed

LO 5: Explain how causality, outliers, and restriction of range can limit the interpretation of a significant correlation coefficient.

17. Which of the following is a limitation for interpreting a significant correlation coefficient?

    a. correlations do not show cause

    b. outliers can influence the value and sign of a correlation coefficient

    c. data should not be interpreted beyond the range of data measured

    d. all of the above

18. A significant correlation shows that two factors are _____, not that one factor _____ changes in a second factor.

    a. causal; is related to

    b. related; causes

19. Outliers can obscure the relationship between two factors by altering the:

    a. extent to which two correlations are related to a third factor

    b. extent to which changes in one factor cause changes in a second factor

    c. direction and strength of an observed correlation coefficient

    d. none of the above

20. What is the limitation in which the range of data for one or both factors in a sample is smaller than the range of data in the larger population?

    a. restriction of range

    b. outliers

    c. correlation

    d. causality

LO 6: Compute and interpret the Spearman correlation coefficient and the test for significance.

21. The correlation coefficient used to measure the direction and strength of the linear relationship of two ranked factors on an ordinal scale of measurement is called the:

    a. Pearson correlation coefficient

    b. Spearman correlation coefficient

    c. point-biserial correlation coefficient

    d. phi correlation coefficient

22. A researcher measures ranked data and computes $\sum D^2 = 105$ and $n = 20$. What is the value of the Spearman correlation coefficient?

a. .01

b. .08

c. .99

d. .92

23. A researcher measures the correlation between rankings of quality of service and how well employees are treated at a local business. If $\Sigma D = 230$ and $n = 12$, then what is the decision for this correlation test?

a. retain the null hypothesis

b. reject the null hypothesis

c. not enough information

LO 7: Compute and interpret the point-biserial correlation coefficient and the test for significance.

24. The correlation coefficient used to measure the direction and strength of the linear relationship of one factor that is continuous and a second factor that is dichotomous is called the:

a. Pearson correlation coefficient

b. Spearman correlation coefficient

c. point-biserial correlation coefficient

d. phi correlation coefficient

25. A researcher measures the relationship between how quickly patrons eat (slow, fast) and the number of calories they consume in their meal. Why is it obvious that a point-biserial correlation is appropriate to analyze these data?

a. because rate of eating is a dichotomous factor and calories consumed is continuous

b. because rate of eating measured on a nominal scale and calories consumed is a ratio scale measurement

c. because both factors are continuous and dichotomous

d. both a and b are correct

26. A researcher measures the correlation between crime rates (high, low) and price of housing in a sample of local neighborhoods. In the study, the same number of high- and low-crime-rate neighborhoods were sampled. If $s_Y = 23,000$ and $M_{Y_1} - M_{Y_2} = 11,000$, then what is the value of the correlation coefficient?

a. .12

b. .24

c. .48

d. .76

LO 8: Compute and interpret the phi correlation coefficient and test for significance.

27. The correlation coefficient used to measure the direction and strength of the linear relationship of two dichotomous factors on a nominal scale of measurement is called the:

a. Pearson correlation coefficient

b. Spearman correlation coefficient

c. point-biserial correlation coefficient

d. phi correlation coefficient

28. A researcher measures the relationship between reading level (poor, good) and self-confidence (low, high) in a sample of second-grade children. Why is it obvious that a phi correlation is appropriate to analyze these data?

a. because both factors are continuous and discrete

b. because reading level is dichotomous and self-confidence is continuous

c. because both factors are dichotomous

d. both a and c are correct

29. A researcher measures the relationship between reading level (poor, good) and self-confidence (low, high) in a sample of second-grade children. Compute the phi correlation coefficient using these data.

		Reading Level	
		Poor	Good
Self-Confidence	Low	12	38
	High	38	12

a. .08

b. .28

c. .52

d. 1.04

LO 9: Convert the value of r to a t statistic and a χ^2 statistic.

30. The correlation coefficient, r, can be converted to what values?

a. coefficient of determination

b. chi-square statistic

c. t statistic

d. all of the above

31. A researcher computes $r = .32$ using a sample of 40 participants. Convert this correlation coefficient to a t statistic value. What is the value of t?

a. 2.08

b. 4.34

c. 3.24

d. 5.00

32. A researcher computes $r = .24$ using a sample of 32 participants. Convert this correlation coefficient to a χ^2 statistic value. What is the value of χ^2?

    a. 3.24

    b. 1.84

    c. 2.43

    d. 0.05

LO 10: Summarize the results of a correlation coefficient in APA format.

33. Which of the following is reported for the results of a correlation coefficient?

    a. the sign and value of the correlation coefficient

    b. the p value of the hypothesis test

    c. the sample size

    d. all of the above

34. A researcher reports the following Pearson correlation coefficient, $r = .370$, using a sample of 28 participants. Is the p value less than .05 for this test?

    a. yes, because the critical value is equal to .361

    b. yes, because the critical value is smaller than .361

    c. no, because the critical value is equal to .374

    d. no, because the critical value is larger than .374

35. The correlation matrix summarizes the results of a study on the relationship between student performance on an exam and three demographic characteristics of students. Which correlation coefficient was significant based on the summary given in the correlation matrix?

Student Characteristics	Exam Scores		
	1	2	3
1. Study time			
2. Family support	.29*		
3. Loan debt	.08	−.24	

*Correlation significant at $p < .05$.

    a. family support and study time

    b. family support and loan debt

    c. study time and loan debt

    d. both a and b

SPSS IN FOCUS

Pearson Correlation Coefficient

Follow the General Instructions Guidebook to complete this exercise. Also, an example for following these steps is provided in the SPSS in Focus section (Section 15.4) of the book. Complete and submit the SPSS grading template and a printout of the output file.

Exercise 15.1: Notebook Computer Use and Grades

A professor notices that more and more students are using their notebook computers in class, presumably to take notes. He wonders if this may actually improve academic success. To test this, the professor records the number of times each student uses his or her computer during a class for one semester and the final grade in the class (out of 100 points). If notebook computer use during class is related to improved academic success, then a positive correlation should be evident. Given the following data, test whether notebook computer use and grades are related at a .05 level of significance.

Notebook Computer Use	Final Grade for Course
30	86
23	88
6	94
0	56
24	78
36	72
10	80
0	90
0	82
8	60
12	84
18	74
0	78
32	66
36	54
12	98
8	81
18	74
22	70
38	90
5	85
29	93
26	67
10	80

With regard to the SPSS exercise, answer the following questions:

Based on the value of the correlation coefficient, is there a significant relationship? (Circle one)

Yes, significant   No, insignificant

Based on the SPSS output, state the following values:

Pearson correlation   _____

Coefficient of determination   _____

Sample size   _____

Significance (2-tailed)   _____

State the conclusions for this test using APA format. First, describe the correlation coefficient in words and give the value of r. Then give the value of R^2 and describe (in words) the effect size using the coefficient of determination.

SPSS IN FOCUS

Spearman Correlation Coefficient

Follow the General Instructions Guidebook to complete this exercise. Also, an example for following these steps is provided in the SPSS in Focus section (Section 15.8) of the book. Complete and submit the SPSS grading template and a printout of the output file.

Exercise 15.2: Popularity and Being Picked for Games

A researcher noted that children who claim to "not fit in" often cite as evidence for this that they are picked last whenever games are played during recess. He wanted to see if there was any merit to this claim. To test this claim, he observed a pickup basketball game during recess at a local school. He recorded the order that students were picked (10 players were picked on each team). After the game, he gave the students a form with the name of each player listed and had them rank each player in order of how "popular" they were. All students ranked each other, and the overall rankings for each student were used to rank the popularity of each player. If the order of picking players and popularity rankings were related, then this was taken as evidence that there is merit to the idea that being picked last may reflect "fitting in" among children. Given the following data, test whether the order of being picked and popularity rankings are related at a .05 level of significance.

Order of Being Picked	Popularity Rankings
1	1
2	3
3	5
4	16
5	20
6	2
7	8
8	4
9	14
10	9
11	13
12	19
13	15
14	7
15	11
16	6
17	10
18	17
19	18
20	12

With regard to the SPSS exercise, answer the following questions:

Based on the value of the correlation coefficient, is there a significant relationship? (Circle one)

         Yes, significant   No, insignificant

Based on the SPSS output, state the following values:

Correlation coefficient   _____

Coefficient of determination   _____

Sample size   _____

Significance (2-tailed)   _____

State the conclusions for this test using APA format. First, describe the correlation coefficient in words and give the value of r. Then give the value of R^2 and describe (in words) the effect size using the coefficient of determination.

Follow the General Instructions Guidebook to complete this exercise. Also, an example for following these steps is provided in the SPSS in Focus section (Section 15.10) of the book. Complete and submit the SPSS grading template and a printout of the output file.

Exercise 15.3: Loneliness and Physical Activity

A health psychologist noticed that individuals with greater social support tend to be more physically active. She hypothesized that persons who are lonely are also less likely to be physically active. To test this, she had a sample of participants complete two surveys. To measure physical activity, participants completed the Minnesota Leisure Time Physical Activity (MLTPA) Questionnaire. This questionnaire was used to categorize participants as having engaged or not engaged in any of 14 exercises, sports, or physically active hobbies. Hence, physical activity (engaged, did not engage) was the dichotomous factor. These same participants also completed the R-UCLA Loneliness Scale (R-UCLA). Scores on this measure range from 20 to 80, with higher scores indicating greater loneliness. Given the following data, test whether loneliness and physical activity are related at a .05 level of significance.

Physical Activity	Loneliness
1	45
1	28
1	64
1	34
1	70
1	38
1	47
1	60
1	26
1	33
1	49
1	37
2	60
2	69
2	72
2	52
2	48
2	68
2	70
2	72
2	58
2	65

With regard to the SPSS exercise, answer the following questions:

Based on the value of the correlation coefficient, is there a significant relationship? (Circle one)

Yes, significant   No, insignificant

Based on the SPSS output, state the following values:

Correlation coefficient   _____

Coefficient of determination   _____

Sample size   _____

Significance (2-tailed)   _____

State the conclusions for this test using APA format. First, describe the correlation coefficient in words and give the value of r. Then give the value of R^2 and describe (in words) the effect size using the coefficient of determination.

Follow the General Instructions Guidebook to complete this exercise. Also, an example for following these steps is provided in the SPSS in Focus section (Section 15.12) of the book. Complete and submit the SPSS grading template and a printout of the output file.

Exercise 15.4: Racial Bias and Product Advertising

To test the extent to which racial bias influences how positively consumers view products advertised on television, a researcher first asked a sample of participants to complete a racial attitudes survey. Scores on this survey were used to categorize participants as being racially biased or unbiased. Then each participant watched two 30-second advertisement clips. Both advertisement clips were the same, except that a White actor was present in one clip and a Black actor was present in the other clip. Participants were then asked to choose which advertisement was more effective at selling the product (all participants had to choose one of the clips). The number of participants (by racial bias category) who chose the opposite-race actor versus the same-race actor clip is given below. Test whether the racial bias of participants and choice of advertisement clip were related at a .05 level of significance.

Racial Bias		Race of Actor in Advertisement Clip	
		Opposite-Race Actor	Same-Race Actor
	Low	46	42
	High	22	40

With regard to the SPSS exercise, answer the following questions:

Based on the value of the correlation coefficient, is there a significant relationship? (Circle one)

        Yes, significant   No, insignificant

Based on the SPSS output, state the following values:

    Correlation coefficient   _____

    Coefficient of determination   _____

    Sample size   _____

    Significance (2-tailed)   _____

State the conclusions for this test using APA format. First, describe the correlation coefficient in words and give the value of r. Then give the value of R^2 and describe (in words) the effect size using the coefficient of determination.

CHAPTER SUMMARY ORGANIZED BY LEARNING OBJECTIVE

LO 1: Identify the direction and strength of a correlation between two factors.

- A correlation is a statistical procedure used to describe the strength and direction of the linear relationship between two factors.
- The value of the correlation coefficient (r) is used to measure the strength and direction of the linear relationship between two factors. The value of r ranges from –1.0 to +1.0.

  (a) The direction of a correlation is indicated by the sign (+ or –) of r. When a correlation is positive (+), two factors change in the same direction; when a correlation is negative (–), two factors change in opposite directions.

  (b) The strength of the correlation is indicated by the value of r, with values closer to ±1.0 indicating stronger correlations and correlations closer to 0 indicating weaker correlations. The closer that data points fall to the regression line, the stronger the correlation.

LO 2–3: Compute and interpret the Pearson correlation coefficient and test for significance; compute and interpret the coefficient of determination.

- The Pearson correlation coefficient (r) is a measure of the direction and strength of the linear relationship between two factors in which the data for both factors are measured on an interval or ratio scale of measurement. The steps to compute the Pearson correlation coefficient are as follows:

  Step 1: Compute preliminary calculations.

  Step 2: Compute the Pearson correlation coefficient: $r = \dfrac{SS_{XY}}{\sqrt{SS_X SS_Y}}$.

- The coefficient of determination (r^2 or R^2) measures the extent to which changes in one factor (Y) can be explained by changes in a second factor (X).
- To test for the significance of a Pearson correlation coefficient, follow the four steps to hypothesis testing and use r as the test statistic. The critical values for the test are given in Table B.5 in Appendix B.

LO 4: Define *homoscedasticity*, *linearity*, and *normality* and explain why each assumption is necessary to appropriately interpret a significant correlation coefficient.

- Three assumptions for interpreting a significant correlation coefficient are homoscedasticity, linearity, and normality. Homoscedasticity is the assumption that the variance of data points dispersed along the regression line is equal. Linearity is the assumption that the best way to describe the pattern of data is using a straight line. Normality is the assumption that data points are normally distributed.

LO 5: Explain how causality, outliers, and restriction of range can limit the interpretation of a significant correlation coefficient.

- Three additional considerations that must be made to accurately interpret a significant correlation coefficient are that (1) correlations do not demonstrate cause, (2) outliers can change the direction and the strength of a correlation, and (3) never generalize the direction and the strength of a correlation beyond the range of data measured (restriction of range).

LO 6: Compute and interpret the Spearman correlation coefficient and test for significance.

- The Spearman rank-order correlation coefficient (r_s) is a measure of the direction and strength of the linear relationship between two ranked factors. The formula for the Spearman correlation coefficient is

$$r_s = 1 - \frac{6\sum D^2}{n(n^2 - 1)}.$$

- The steps to compute a Spearman correlation coefficient are as follows:

Step 1: Average tied ranks.

Step 2: Compute preliminary calculations.

Step 3: Compute the Spearman correlation coefficient (r_s).

- To test for significance, find the critical values for a Spearman correlation coefficient located in Table B.6 in Appendix B.

LO 7: Compute and interpret the point-biserial correlation coefficient and test for significance.

- The point-biserial correlation coefficient (r_{pb}) is a measure of the direction and strength of the linear relationship of one factor that is continuous (on an interval or ratio scale of measurement) and a second factor that is dichotomous (on a nominal scale of measurement). The formula for the point-biserial correlation coefficient is

$$r_{pb} = \left(\frac{M_{Y_1} - M_{Y_2}}{s_Y}\right)\left(\sqrt{pq}\right), \text{ where } s_Y = \sqrt{\frac{SS_Y}{n}}.$$

- The steps to compute a point-biserial correlation coefficient are as follows:

Step 1: Code the dichotomous factor.

Step 2: Compute preliminary calculations.

Step 3: Compute the point-biserial correlation coefficient (r_{pb}).

- To test for significance, convert a point-biserial correlation coefficient to a t statistic using the first equation given in the Learning Objective (LO) 9 summary and locate critical values in the t table given in Table B.2 in Appendix B.

LO 8: Compute and interpret the phi correlation coefficient and test for significance.

- The phi correlation coefficient (r_ϕ) is a measure of the direction and strength of the linear relationship between two dichotomous factors. The formula for the phi correlation coefficient is

$$r_\phi = \frac{ad - bc}{\sqrt{ABCD}}.$$

- To test for significance, convert a phi correlation coefficient to a chi-square (χ^2) statistic using the second equation given in the LO 9 summary and locate critical values in the chi-square table given in Table B.7 in Appendix B.

LO 9: Convert the value of r to a t statistic and χ^2 statistic.

- Equation to convert the value of r to a t statistic: $t^2 = \frac{r^2}{(1 - r^2)/df}$.

- Equation to convert the value of r to a χ^2 statistic: $\chi^2 = r_\phi^2 N$.

LO 10: Summarize the results of a correlation coefficient in APA format.

- To summarize correlations, report the strength and direction of each correlation coefficient and the p value for each correlation. The sample size and the effect size should also be reported. The means and the standard error or standard deviations measured in a study can be summarized in a figure or table or in the main text. To report many correlations in a single study, use a correlation matrix.

LO 11: Compute the Pearson, Spearman, point-biserial, and phi correlation coefficients using SPSS.

- SPSS can be used to compute the Pearson correlation coefficient using the Analyze, Correlate, and Bivariate options in the menu bar. These actions will display a dialog box that allows you to identify the variables and to run the correlation.

- SPSS can be used to compute the Spearman correlation coefficient using the Analyze, Correlate, and Bivariate options in the menu bar. These actions will display a dialog box that allows you to identify the variables, to select the option to compute a Spearman correlation, and to run the correlation.

- There is no command in SPSS to compute a point-biserial correlation coefficient. To compute a point-biserial correlation coefficient using SPSS, first code the dichotomous factor, and then follow the directions for computing a Pearson correlation coefficient.

- There is no command in SPSS to compute a phi correlation coefficient. To compute a phi correlation coefficient using SPSS, first code each dichotomous factor, then weight each variable using the Weight Cases . . . option in the menu bar, and finally follow the directions for computing a Pearson correlation coefficient.

16

Linear Regression and Multiple Regression

LEARNING OBJECTIVES

After reading this chapter, you should be able to:

1. Define linear regression and describe the relationship between a predictor variable and a criterion variable.

2. Compute and interpret the method of least squares.

3. Identify each source of variation in an analysis of regression.

4. Compute an analysis of regression and interpret the results.

5. Compute and interpret the standard error of estimate.

6. Define multiple regression, and compute and interpret an analysis of multiple regression.

7. Delineate the unstandardized and standardized β coefficients.

8. Compute the relative contribution of each predictor variable and interpret the results.

9. Summarize the results of an analysis of regression and multiple regression in APA format.

10. Compute an analysis of regression and an analysis of multiple regression using SPSS.

CHAPTER OUTLINE

16.1 From Relationships to Predictions

We can use the information provided by the correlation coefficient r (introduced in Chapter 15 of the book) to predict values of one factor, given known values of a second factor. Specifically, we use the value of r to compute the equation of a regression line and then use this equation to predict values of one factor, given known values of a second factor in a population—this statistical procedure is called linear regression.

- *Linear regression:* A statistical procedure used to determine the equation of a regression line to a set of data points and to determine the extent to which the regression equation can be used to predict values of one factor, given known values of a second factor in a population.

16.2 Fundamentals of Linear Regression

To use linear regression, we need to identify the predictor variable and the criterion variable.

- *Predictor variable (X):* The variable with values that are known and can be used to predict values of another variable.
- *Criterion variable (Y):* The variable with unknown values that can be predicted or estimated, given known values of the predictor variable.

Three questions can be answered using linear regression:

1. Is a linear pattern evident in a set of data points?
   o To identify a pattern, graph the data.

2. Which equation of a straight line can best describe this pattern?
   o The equation of the best-fitting straight line is called a *regression equation.*

3. Are the predictions made from this equation significant?
   o To determine significance, we use a statistical test called an *analysis of regression.*

16.3 What Makes the Regression Line the Best-Fitting Line?

To find the equation of a regression line, we calculate the sum of the squared distances of data points from a regression line. The regression line is associated with the smallest total value of the sum of squares (*SS*).

- *The method of least squares:* A statistical procedure used to compute the slope (*b*) and *y*-intercept (*a*) of the best-fitting straight line to a set of data points.

16.4 The Slope and *y*-Intercept of a Straight Line

- The equation of a straight line is $Y = bX + a$.
  - *Y* is a value of the criterion variable.
  - *X* is a value of the predictor variable.
  - *b* is the slope of a straight line.
  - *a* is the *y*-intercept, which is the value of *Y* when $X = 0$.

The Slope

The slope of a straight line is used to measure the change in *Y* relative to the change in *X*. When *X* and *Y* change in the same direction, the slope is positive. When *X* and *Y* change in opposite directions, the slope is negative.

$$\text{slope } (b) = \frac{\text{change in } Y}{\text{change in } X}.$$

The *y*-Intercept

The *y*-intercept of a straight line is the value of the criterion variable (*Y*) when the predictor variable (*X*) is 0.

16.5 Using the Method of Least Squares to Find the Best Fit

We use the *method of least squares* to find the equation of the regression line to a set of data points. We follow three steps to compute the method of least squares.

1. Compute preliminary calculations. The preliminary calculations are used to find SP, SS_X, M_X, and M_Y.

2. Calculate the slope: $b = \dfrac{\text{change in } Y}{\text{change in } X} = \dfrac{SS_{XY}}{SS_X}$.

3. Calculate the *y*-intercept: $a = M_Y - bM_X$.

Once we find the slope and *y*-intercept, we can solve for each predicted value of *Y* by substituting each value *X* into the regression equation. The predicted value of *Y* is symbolized as $\hat{Y}$.

$$\text{Regression equation: } \hat{Y} = bX + a.$$

16.6 Using Analysis of Regression to Determine Significance

Analysis of regression is a statistical procedure used to test hypotheses for one or more predictor variables to determine whether the regression equation for a sample of data points can be used to predict values of the criterion variable (Y) given known values of the predictor variable (X) in the population.

We use the four steps of hypothesis testing to conduct an analysis of regression.

Step 1. State the hypotheses. The null hypothesis is that the variance in Y is not related to changes in X. The alternative hypothesis is that the variance in Y is related to changes in X.

The variance in Y that is related to changes in X is called regression variation.

The variance in Y that is not related to changes in X is called residual variation.

Step 2: Set the criteria for a decision. The level of significance is typically equal to .05. Refer to the F table in Table B.3 in Appendix B of the book (also reprinted in the appendix of this study guide) to find the critical values. To find the critical values, we need to know the degrees of freedom regression (1) and the degrees of freedom residual ($n - 2$).

Step 3: Compute the test statistic: $F = \dfrac{MS_{\text{regression}}}{MS_{\text{residual}}}$.

To compute the SS for the regression variation, multiply SS_Y by the *coefficient of determination* (r^2).

$$SS_{\text{regression}} = r^2 SS_Y, \text{ where } r = \frac{SS_{XY}}{\sqrt{SS_X SS_Y}}.$$

To compute the SS for residual variation, multiply SS_Y by the remaining proportion of variance ($1 - r^2$).

$$SS_{\text{residual}} = (1 - r^2) SS_Y.$$

The following table lists the formulas for completing the F table.

Source of Variation	SS	df	MS	F_{obt}
Regression	$r^2 SS_Y$	1	$\dfrac{SS_{\text{regression}}}{df_{\text{regression}}}$	$\dfrac{MS_{\text{regression}}}{MS_{\text{residual}}}$
Residual (error)	$(1 - r^2) SS_Y$	$n - 2$	$\dfrac{SS_{\text{residual}}}{df_{\text{residual}}}$	
Total	$SS_{\text{regression}} + SS_{\text{residual}}$	$n - 1$		

Step 4: Make a decision. Compare the obtained value to the critical value to make a decision to retain or reject the null hypothesis.

16.7 SPSS in Focus: Analysis of Regression

SPSS can be used to compute an analysis of regression using the Analyze, Regression, and Linear options in the menu bar. These actions will display a dialog box that allows you to identify the variables and run the analysis.

16.8 Using the Standard Error of Estimate to Measure Accuracy

When even one data point fails to fall exactly on the regression line, there is error in how accurately the line will predict values of the criterion variable. This error is measured by the standard error of estimate.

- *Standard error of estimate* (s$_e$): An estimate of the standard deviation or the distance that a set of data points deviates from the regression line.

$$s_e = \sqrt{MS_{residual}} \, .$$

The standard error of estimate is used as a measure of the accuracy of predictions. The smaller the standard error of estimate, the more accurate the regression line will be to make predictions of Y values, given values of X.

16.9 Introduction to Multiple Regression

It is often necessary to consider multiple predictor variables in a single equation of a regression line. This type of analysis is called multiple regression. To use multiple regression, we add the slope, b, and the predictor variable, X, for each additional predictor variable. An advantage of this test is that it allows us to detect the extent to which two or more predictor variables interact. The linear equations with one, two, and three predictor variables are as follows.

One predictor variable: $\hat{Y} = bX + a$.

Two predictor variables: $\hat{Y} = b_1X_1 + b_2X_2 + a$.

Three predictor variables: $\hat{Y} = b_1X_1 + b_2X_2 + b_3X_3 + a$.

16.10 Computing and Evaluating Significance for Multiple Regression

The computation for multiple regression is similar to our computation with a single predictor variable, but we need a few added computations to account for the added predictor variable. To make the calculations with two predictor variables, we compute preliminary calculations to identify variability, then use those calculations to find the multiple regression equation. To evaluate the significance of the multiple regression equation, follow the four steps of hypothesis testing. For details regarding the calculations needed, and setting the criteria for a decision, refer to Chapter 16 of the book. The formula for the multiple regression test statistic is

$$F_{obt} = \frac{MS_{regression}}{MS_{residual}}.$$

16.11 The β Coefficient for Multiple Regression

In addition to evaluating the significance of a multiple regression equation, we can consider the relative contribution of each factor. In other words, we can identify if one of the predictor variables is a better predictor. The standardized beta coefficient, β, reflects the distinctive contribution of each predictor variable. The equation for the standardized regression equation is

$$Z_{\hat{Y}} = \beta_1(Z_{X_1}) + \beta_2(Z_{X_2}).$$

For linear regression with one predictor variable, β will equal r. That is, the standardized beta coefficient will be equal to the correlation coefficient. For multiple regression, however, β is usually smaller than r because the ability of each predictor variable to predict values of Y usually overlaps. Thus, the standardized beta coefficient accounts for the unique, distinctive contribution of each predictor variable, excluding any overlap with other predictor variables.

16.12 Evaluating Significance for the Relative Contribution of Each Predictor Variable

We can further evaluate the relative contribution of each predictor variable by evaluating the significance of the added contribution of each factor. To evaluate the significance of the relative contribution of each factor, we can follow three steps,

Step 1: Find r^2 for the "other" predictor variable.

Step 2: Identify SS accounted for by the predictor variable of interest.

Step 3: Complete the F table and make a decision.

16.13 SPSS in Focus: Multiple Regression Analysis

SPSS can be used to compute an analysis of multiple regression using the Analyze, Regression, and Linear options in the menu bar. These actions will display a dialog box that allows you to identify the variables and run the analysis.

16.14 APA in Focus: Reporting Regression Analysis

To summarize linear regression involving a single predictor variable, we report the test statistic, the degrees of freedom, and the p value for the regression analysis. The data points often are summarized in a scatter plot or a figure displaying the regression line. To summarize the results of multiple regression, we typically add the standardized β coefficient for each factor that significantly contributes to a prediction.

CHAPTER FORMULAS

Linear Regression

Method of Least Squares

$Y = bX + a$ (Linear equation for a straight line)

$b = \dfrac{SS_{XY}}{SS_X}$ (Slope of a straight line)

$a = M_Y - bM_X$ (y-intercept for a straight line)

Analysis of Regression

$F_{\text{obt}} = \dfrac{MS_{\text{regression}}}{MS_{\text{residual}}}$ (Test statistic for analysis of regression and multiple regression)

$df_{\text{regression}} = 1$ (Degrees of freedom regression with one predictor variable)

$df_{\text{residual}} = n - 2$ (Degrees of freedom residual)

$s_e = \sqrt{MS_{\text{residual}}}$ (Standard error of estimate)

TIPS AND CAUTIONS FOR STUDENTS

- *Predictions:* Describing the correlational relationship between two factors is useful because it allows us to use procedures to predict changes in the values of one factor given known values of a second factor. This is the key distinction between correlation and regression: Correlation strictly shows the relationship between two factors (described by the correlation coefficient, r), and regression is used to predict changes in one factor, given known values of a second related factor.

- *The linear regression and straight lines:* The formulas for regression are similar to those used for an analysis of variance (ANOVA), so do not be intimidated. The typical relationship between two factors is described using a straight line. The equation of a straight line, $Y = bX + a$, is used to describe the relationship between two related factors. If you can find the equation of a straight line, then you can calculate a regression line and perform an analysis of regression.

- *Multiple regression:* When we use multiple predictor variables to predict changes in a criterion variable, we use an analysis called multiple regression. To accommodate more predictor variables in the equation of a regression line, we add the slope, b, and the predictor variable, X, for each additional variable. Hence, we simply add a bX for each predictor variable. While the computations will get more involved in order to identify the variability predicted by each factor, the basic model for how to accommodate additional predictor variables is fairly straightforward.

KEY TERM WORD SEARCHES

```
Q Z B T T Q C V Q I Y K X J W H W J A T X C K D F B F L C E
A M S C S J E J L I N E A R R E G R E S S I O N B N I H V T
E E G E M D Y R E S I D U A L V A R I A T I O N X S B T R W
L N D N R O Y N S L Q T Q H M R V Z S G J A T X E Y F W E B
X R S T L A L D A P Y W P D Z Q R E G R E S S I O N W E G Z
T E T U P M I Y Z S J W Z P Y P J B M U D X T Z E L M W R D
D G A J S Y M L M E T H O D O F L E A S T S Q U A R E S E J
M R N S U E E I C O P J T F C H I Q A H G C N W T G G T S S
U E D A A L V W S Z M V W U K A Y X E U E N X X D V W V S X
L S A W E N D S L O P E L Y K P T O E N W M C U M T G W I F
T S R Q S S Z C S W V F E O Z Y S D Z S L V Z K F J Z G O I
I I D V R C R C Q Y R X G U E J F O U O J Q N X U Y V T N I
P O E X X T V X G S S U R A T O C X A H U W E O B Q L Q A R
L N R J P S O K G W G X U G B W Z Z C L P N N B Z H S M N Q
E V R C O R F L G T C R I T E R I O N V A R I A B L E R A L
R A O G R H E A E J L E M R H R Z L V X B C L D X P R S L Q
E R R T C H U D R O N N P R T S T L F C J O I Z B N E E Y E
G I O C U U P O I O U O S U Q E K W Z T D J U B F I R G S B
R A F A O J S P J C P A C P A P T X B B F D B R P Y Y S I J
E T E X U E K O Z P T K M O O A P F W C C B B V W K A G S I
S I S W T B G P I D I O I I A M S N E Z P S E E J B L Z A G
S O T O Y O W D V N F N R V T R G X A K X K K H E K K O W B
I N I D A F V W H H T V T V L A C G L M B G A R N T R S T H
O A M Q M E V W O A S E Y V A T V K V O J J C S Z U D Z V D
N D A N A L Y S I S O F R E G R E S S I O N R G J W I I O L
E L T X N R D B Y T K K L C U C I W L F D E J O Z U M V Q I
R S E E M J M K G H W X X F E E F A O I K S L A V H E T E Y
Z M R B C A U K F O G B Y D O P A C B F S Y B K Z G C C F I
V L Z K E O K U Q U V X K X Y L T J T L I T M V G X N F W P
M K Z Z V M O U O W W K S T K F L I N D E O Y Z T J W V A E
```

ANALYSIS OF REGRESSION

CRITERION VARIABLE

LINEAR REGRESSION

METHOD OF LEAST SQUARES

MULTIPLE REGRESSION

PREDICTOR VARIABLE

REGRESSION

REGRESSION ANALYSIS

REGRESSION VARIATION

RESIDUAL VARIATION

SLOPE

STANDARD ERROR OF ESTIMATE

Y-INTERCEPT

CROSSWORD PUZZLES

ACROSS

1 Used to measure the change in Y relative to the change in X.

3 A statistical procedure used to test hypotheses for one or more predictor variables to determine whether the regression equation for a sample of data points can be used to predict values of the criterion variable (Y) given values of the predictor variable (X) in a population.

5 A statistical method that includes two or more predictor variables in the equation of a regression line to predict changes in a criterion variable.

6 The variable with values that are known and can be used to predict values of another variable.

7 The variance in Y that is not related to changes in X.

8 A statistical procedure used to determine the equation of a regression line to a set of data points and the extent to which the regression equation can be used to predict values of one factor, given known values of a second factor in a population.

9 A statistical procedure used to compute the slope (b) and y-intercept (a) of the best-fitting straight line to a set of data points.

10 The variable with unknown values that can be predicted or estimated, given known values of the predictor variable.

DOWN

1 An estimate of the standard deviation or distance that a set of data points falls from the regression line.

2 The value of the criterion variable (Y) when the predictor variable (X) equals 0.

4 The variance in Y that is related to or associated with changes in X.

PRACTICE QUIZZES

LO 1: Define linear regression and describe the relationship between a predictor variable and a criterion variable.

1. _____ is a statistical procedure used to determine the equation of the regression line to a set of data points and to determine the extent to which the regression equation can be used to predict values of one factor, given known values of a second factor in a population.

   a. Linear regression

   b. Evaluation

   c. Predictor testing

   d. Criterion testing

2. A researcher tests the extent to which the timing of a stimulus presentation, X, can be used to predict the frequency of a behavioral response, Y. Which factor is the predictor variable?

   a. the frequency of a behavioral response

   b. the timing of a stimulus presentation

   c. both factors are predictor variables in this example

3. A researcher tests the extent to which the wealth of a country can be used to predict the unemployment rate of a nation. Which factor is the criterion variable?

   a. the wealth of a country

   b. the unemployment rate of a nation

   c. both factors are criterion variables in this example

4. Values of the _____ are known and can be used to predict values of the _____.

   a. predictor variable; predictor variable

   b. criterion variable; criterion variable

   c. predictor variable; criterion variable

   d. criterion variable; predictor variable

LO 2: Compute and interpret the method of least squares.

5. A statistical procedure used to compute the slope (b) and y-intercept (a) of the best-fitting straight line to a set of data points is called:

   a. the method of least squares

   b. the method of most squares

   c. the method of common squares

   d. the method of data squares

6. When pairs of scores for two factors move in the opposite directions, the slope of the regression is _____.

   a. nonlinear

   b. positive

   c. negative

   d. minimal

7. What is the value of the y-intercept for the regression line in the figure?

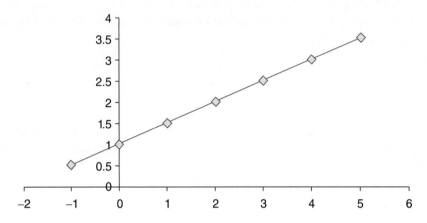

   a. −2

   b. −1

   c. 0

   d. +1

8. If $SS_{XY} = -26.02$ and $SS_X = 48.00$, then what is the value of the slope for the best-fitting regression line?

   a. 0.54

   b. −0.54

   c. 1.84

   d. −1.84

9. If $b = 0.54$, $M_Y = 3.25$, and $M_X = 5.85$, then what is the value of the y-intercept for the best-fitting regression line?

   a. 0.09

   b. 4.07

   c. 10.27

   d. −18.47

LO 3: Identify each source of variation in an analysis of regression.

10. The _____ is a statistical procedure used to test hypotheses for one or more predictor variables to determine whether the regression equation for a sample of data points can be used to predict values of the criterion variable, given values of the predictor variable in the population.

    a. analysis of regression

    b. method of least squares

    c. coefficient of determination

    d. regression line

11. The more variance in Y, the criterion variable, that we attribute to changes in X, the predictor variable, the larger the:

    a. error variation

    b. total variation

    c. residual variation

    d. regression variation

12. The farther that data points fall from the regression line, the larger the value of:

    a. predictive variation

    b. total variation

    c. residual variation

    d. regression variation

LO 4: Compute an analysis of regression and interpret the results.

13. An analysis of regression measures only the variance in ____ because it is the value we want to predict.

    a. X

    b. the predictor variable

    c. Y

    d. both a and b

14. An analysis of regression for one predictor variable is computed using a sample of 28 participants. What are the degrees of freedom associated with regression variation?

    a. 1

    b. 26

    c. 27

    d. 28

15. If the coefficient of determination is 0.60 and $SS_Y = 280$, then what is the sum of squares regression for an analysis of regression?

    a. 60

    b. 112

    c. 168

    d. 280

16. If the coefficient of determination is 0.32 and $SS_Y = 400$, then what is the sum of squares residual for an analysis of regression?

    a. 32

    b. 128

    c. 272

    d. 400

17. A researcher computes an analysis of regression for one predictor variable using a sample of 28 participants. Using the data given in the table, what is the decision at a .05 level of significance? (*Hint:* Complete the table first.)

Source of Variation	SS	df	MS	F
Regression				
Residual	260			
Total	290			

    a. reject the null hypothesis; X significantly predicts changes in Y

    b. retain the null hypothesis; X does not significantly predict changes in Y

    c. reject the null hypothesis; X does not significantly predict changes in Y

    d. retain the null hypothesis; X significantly predicts changes in Y

LO 5: Compute and interpret the standard error of estimate.

18. An estimate of the standard deviation or distance that a set of data points falls from the regression line is called:

    a. the criterion estimate

    b. the predictor estimate

    c. the standard error of the mean

    d. the standard error of estimate

19. A researcher computes a mean square residual equal to 4.29. What is the value of the standard error of estimate?

    a. 2.07

    b. 4.29

    c. 18.40

    d. not enough information

20. A researcher computes the following table for an analysis of regression. What is the value of the standard error of estimate?

Source of Variation	SS	df	MS	F
Regression	18	1	18	6.0*
Residual	54	18	3	
Total	72			

a. 3

b. 1.73

c. 4.24

d. 7.35

21. The standard error of estimate is a measure of:

a. the accuracy of predictions made using the equation of a regression line

b. the square root of the mean square residual

c. the distance that data points fall from the regression line

d. all of the above

LO 6: Define multiple regression, and compute and interpret an analysis of multiple regression.

22. A statistical method that includes two or more predictor variables in the equation of a regression line to predict changes in a criterion variable is called:

a. standard regression

b. estimate regression

c. multiple regression

d. two-way regression

23. Including multiple predictors in the regression equation can allow researchers to detect the extent to which two or more predictor variables _____.

a. interact

b. distribute

c. consolidate

d. equate

24. To accommodate more predictor variables in the equation of a regression line, we add the _____ and the _____ to the equation of the regression line for each additional variable.

a. slope; predictor variable

b. criterion variable; predictor variable

c. coefficient of determination; sample size

d. slope; coefficient of determination

LO 7: Delineate the unstandardized and standardized β coefficients.

25. A researcher asks if one predictor variable can significantly increase the prediction of Y beyond that already predicted by another predictor variable. Which value can allow the researcher to answer this question?

    a. the slope

    b. the proportion of variance

    c. the y-intercept

    d. the standardized beta coefficient

26. The standardized beta coefficient equals the value of the unstandardized beta coefficient when we analyze:

    a. one criterion variable

    b. one predictor variable

    c. more than one predictor variable

    d. any number of criterion and predictor variables

27. The standardized beta coefficient is used to analyze:

    a. the extent to which one predictor variable is a better predictor of variance in Y

    b. the method of least squares

    c. the formula for a regression line

    d. the residual variable left over by alpha

LO 8: Compute the relative contribution of each predictor variable and interpret the results.

28. What is the null hypothesis for a test of the relative contribution of each predictor variable in multiple regression?

    a. the variance in Y is not related to changes in X

    b. the variance in Y is related to changes in X

    c. adding X_1 does not improve prediction of variance in Y beyond that already predicted by X_2

    d. adding X_1 improves prediction of variance in Y beyond that already predicted by X_2

29. How do we convert an F statistic into a t statistic?

    a. square the F statistic

    b. take the square root of the F statistic

    c. take the ratio of the F statistic

    d. conduct a hypothesis test

30. We can evaluate the significance of the relative contribution of each factor by first determining the SS_Y predicted by each factor alone.

    a. false, it is not possible to find the relative contribution of each factor

    b. false, it is not possible to identify the regression equation for a set of data points

    c. true, but the significance of the relative contribution of each factor is not meaningful

    d. true, this is exactly how we can evaluate the significance of the relative contribution of each factor

LO 9: Summarize the results of an analysis of regression and multiple regression in APA format.

31. Which of the following is reported for the results of an analysis of regression?

    a. the test statistic value

    b. the p value of the hypothesis test

    c. the degrees of freedom

    d. all of the above

32. A researcher reports the following for an analysis of regression: $F(1, 28) = 4.12$. What is the decision for this test?

    a. reject the null hypothesis

    b. retain the null hypothesis

    c. not enough information to make a decision

33. A researcher reports the following for an analysis of regression: $F(2, 32) = 3.42, p < .05$. If this was an analysis of regression using one predictor variable, then which value must be wrong in the summary for this test?

    a. the test statistic

    b. the degrees of freedom for the criterion variable

    c. the degrees of freedom for the predictor variable

    d. the p value

34. To report the results of multiple regression, we typically add what value that is generally not required to be reported for an analysis of regression with one predictor variable?

    a. the standardized β coefficient for each factor that significantly contributes to a prediction

    b. the p value for the hypothesis test

    c. the degrees of freedom for the hypothesis test

    c. the test statistic for the hypothesis test

Follow the General Instructions Guidebook to complete this exercise. Also, an example for following these steps is provided in the SPSS in Focus section (Section 16.7) of the book. Complete and submit the SPSS grading template and a printout of the output file.

Exercise 16.1: Attitudes and Eco-Friendly Behaviors

A researcher notes that many individuals who eat organic foods also tend to behave in ways that benefit the planet (referred to as eco-friendly behaviors). She wanted to see if the attitudes people have toward organic food consumption could be used to predict eco-friendly behaviors among college students. To test this, she had college students complete two surveys. The organic attitudes survey assessed participant attitudes toward organic foods in general and toward the people who consume organic foods. This survey was scored between 0 and 50, with higher scores indicating more positive attitudes toward organic food consumption. The eco-friendly behaviors survey assessed the extent to which participants recycled, reused, and conserved energy. This survey was also scored between 0 and 50, with higher scores indicating greater eco-friendly behaviors. Compute an analysis of regression to determine the extent to which attitudes toward organic food consumption can predict eco-friendly behaviors at a .05 level of significance.

Attitudes Toward Organic Food	Eco-Friendly Behaviors
38	40
50	46
28	30
16	12
10	19
13	20
34	38
45	40
42	10
30	36
26	28
28	21
32	32
18	20
22	28
40	31
29	40
14	48
44	42
12	20

With regard to the SPSS exercise, answer the following questions:

Based on the output shown in SPSS, complete the following regression table:

Sources of Variation	SS	df	MS	F-Statistic	Sig.
Regression					
Residual (error)					
Total					

Based on the value of the test statistic, what is the decision for the analysis of regression? (Circle one)

Retain the null hypothesis　　　　　　　　　　Reject the null hypothesis

Based on the regression table you just completed, state the following values:

Sample size　　　　　　　　　　　　　　　_____

Standard error of estimate　　　　　　　　　_____

Proportion of variance　　　　　　　　　　　_____

Significance　　　　　　　　　　　　　　　_____

State the results of the analysis of regression using APA format. Then give the value of R^2 and describe (in words) the effect size using the coefficient of determination.

SPSS IN FOCUS

Analysis of Multiple Regression

Follow the General Instructions Guidebook to complete this exercise. Also, an example for following these steps is provided in the SPSS in Focus section (Section 16.13) of the book. Complete and submit the SPSS grading template and a printout of the output file.

Exercise 16.2: Napping to Calm Children

A researcher tests the extent to which the number and length of naps for a child can predict how calm the child is during the day. To make this test, a researcher records the number of naps and the total length of naps among 15 children, and records how long they cry during the day (less crying = more calm). Compute an analysis of multiple regression to determine the extent to which napping can predict calmness among the children at a .05 level of significance.

Variables		
Number of Naps	Length of Naps (minutes)	Cry Time During Day (minutes)
3	80	6
1	65	1
2	90	3
1	50	2
1	45	0
2	60	9
4	90	5
0	0	6
2	40	4
1	30	0
3	45	3
3	85	6
2	60	8
1	20	7
1	25	2

With regard to the SPSS exercise, answer the following questions:

Sample size   _____

Standard error of estimate   _____

Proportion of variance (R^2)   _____

Based on the output shown in SPSS, complete the following regression table:

Sources of Variation	SS	df	MS	F-Statistic	Sig.
Regression					
Residual (error)					
Total					

Based on the value of the test statistic, what is the decision for the analysis of regression? (Circle one)

Retain the null hypothesis   Reject the null hypothesis

To identify the standardized β coefficients, state the following values:

Standardized β for number of naps   _____

Standardized β for length of naps   _____

Significance for test of number of naps   _____

Significance for test of length of naps   _____

State the results of the analysis of multiple regression using APA format. Refer to the standardized β coefficient to identify the relative significance of each factor.

CHAPTER SUMMARY ORGANIZED BY LEARNING OBJECTIVE

LO 1: Define linear regression and describe the relationship between a predictor variable and a criterion variable.

- Linear regression is a statistical procedure used to determine the equation of a regression line to a set of data points and the extent to which the regression equation can be used to predict values of one factor, given known values of a second factor in a population.

- We can use regression to answer these questions:

    1. Is a linear pattern evident for a set of data points?

    2. Which equation of a straight line can best describe this pattern?

    3. Are the predictions made from this equation significant?

LO 2: Compute and interpret the method of least squares.

- The method of least squares is a statistical procedure used to compute the slope (b) and y-intercept (a) of the best-fitting straight line to a set of data points, called the regression line. The three steps needed to find the equation of the regression line are as follows:

    Step 1: Compute preliminary calculations.

    Step 2: Calculate the slope (b).

    Step 3: Calculate the y-intercept (a).

- The equation of a straight line is $Y = bX + a$.

    o The slope (b) of a straight line is a measure of the change in Y relative to the change in X. When X and Y change in the same direction, the slope is positive. When X and Y change in opposite directions, the slope is negative. The formula for the slope is

    $$b = \frac{\text{change in } Y}{\text{change in } X} = \frac{SS_{XY}}{SS_X}.$$

    o The y-intercept (a) of a straight line indicates the value of Y when X equals 0. The formula for the y-intercept is

    $$a = M_Y - bM_X.$$

LO 3–4: Identify each source of variation in an analysis of regression; compute an analysis of regression and interpret the results.

- An analysis of regression is a statistical procedure used to test hypotheses for one or more predictor variables to determine whether the regression equation for a sample of data points can be used to predict values of the criterion variable (Y) given values of the predictor variable (X) in the population.

- An analysis of regression for one predictor variable includes two sources of variation:

    1. Regression variation is a measure of the variance in Y that is related to changes in X. The closer that data points fall to the regression line, the larger the value of regression variation. The formula for regression variation is

    $$SS_{\text{regression}} = r^2 SS_Y.$$

    2. Residual variation is a measure of the variance in Y that is not related to changes in X. This is the variance

in Y that is residual, left over, or remaining. The farther that data points fall from the regression line, the larger the value of residual variation. The formula for regression variation is

$$SS_{\text{residual}} = (1 - r^2)SS_Y.$$

- To make a decision, we compare the F statistic value to the critical value. When the F statistic is larger than the critical value, we reject the null hypothesis; otherwise, we retain the null hypothesis.

LO 5: Compute and interpret the standard error of estimate.

- The standard error of estimate (s_e) is an estimate of the standard deviation or distance that a set of data points falls from the regression line. The standard error of estimate equals the square root of the mean square residual:

$$s_e = \sqrt{MS_{\text{residual}}}.$$

- The standard error of estimate uses the standard deviation of data points as an estimate of the error in predictions made by a regression line. The smaller the standard error of estimate, the closer values of Y will be to their predicted values, $\hat{Y}$, on the regression line and the more accurate the predictions of Y will be using known values of X.

LO 6: Define multiple regression, and compute and interpret an analysis of multiple regression.

- Multiple regression is a statistical method that includes two or more predictor variables in the equation of a regression line to predict changes in a criterion variable. One advantage of including multiple predictors in the

regression equation is that we can detect the extent to which two or more predictor variables interact.

- To compute an analysis of multiple regression, first compute the multiple regression equation, then follow the four steps of hypothesis testing to evaluate the significance of the equation. To evaluate if a regression equation can significantly predict variance in Y, we measure the variance in Y that is (regression variation) and is not (residual variation) related to changes in the predictor variables (X_1, X_2).

- To compute the test statistic, we measure variance as a mean square, same as we did for ANOVA tests and for simple linear regression. We place the variance or mean square (MS) attributed to regression variation in the numerator and the variance or mean square attributed to residual variation in the denominator:

$$F_{\text{obt}} = \frac{MS_{\text{regression}}}{MS_{\text{residual}}}.$$

LO 7: Delineate the unstandardized and standardized β **coefficients.**

- With two predictor variables, the values of b_1 and b_2 are referred to as unstandardized beta coefficients. The value of the unstandardized beta coefficients can be unreliable due to many factors that can influence or bias the value of b. We can correct for this problem by standardizing the coefficients. When we standardize the beta coefficients, we can identify the relative contribution of each factor to predict values of Y. We represent each standardized beta coefficient as β.

- For linear regression with one predictor variable, the standardized beta coefficient equals the correlation coefficient. For multiple regression, however, β is usually smaller than r because the ability of each predictor variable to predict values of Y usually overlaps. Thus, the standardized beta coefficient accounts for the unique, distinctive contribution of each predictor variable, excluding any overlap with other predictor variables.

LO 8: Compute the relative contribution of each predictor variable and interpret the results.

- We can also evaluate the relative contribution of each predictor variable. To evaluate the significance of the relative contribution of each factor, we can follow three steps:

  Step 1: Find r^2 for the "other" predictor variable.

  Step 2: Identify SS accounted for by the predictor variable of interest.

  Step 3: Complete the F table and make a decision.

LO 9: Summarize the results of an analysis of regression and multiple regression in APA format.

- To summarize an analysis of regression involving a single predictor variable, we report the test statistic, the degrees of freedom, and the p value for the regression analysis. The data points for each pair of scores are often summarized in a scatter plot or figure displaying the regression line. The regression equation can be stated in the scatter plot.

- To summarize the results of multiple regression, we typically add the standardized β coefficient for each factor that significantly contributes to a prediction.

LO 10: Compute an analysis of regression and an analysis of multiple regression using SPSS.

- SPSS can be used to compute an analysis of regression using the Analyze, Regression, and Linear options in the menu bar. These actions will display a dialog box that allows you to identify the variables and run the analysis.

- SPSS can also be used to compute an analysis of multiple regression using the Analyze, Regression, and Linear options in the menu bar. These actions will display a dialog box that allows you to identify the variables and run the analysis.

17

Nonparametric Tests

Chi-Square Tests

LEARNING OBJECTIVES

After reading this chapter, you should be able to:

1. Distinguish between nonparametric and parametric tests.

2. Explain how the test statistic is computed for a chi-square test.

3. Calculate the degrees of freedom for the chi-square goodness-of-fit test and locate critical values in the chi-square table.

4. Compute the chi-square goodness-of-fit test and interpret the results.

5. Identify the assumption and the restriction of expected frequency size for the chi-square test.

6. Calculate the degrees of freedom for the chi-square test for independence and locate critical values in the chi-square table.

7. Compute the chi-square test for independence and interpret the results.

8. Compute effect size for the chi-square test for independence.

9. Summarize the results of a chi-square test in APA format.

10. Compute the chi-square goodness-of-fit test and the chi-square test for independence using SPSS.

CHAPTER OUTLINE

17.1 Tests for Nominal Data

When data are measured on an interval or ratio scale of measurement, the test statistic used for each hypothesis test can measure variance in the formula. These tests, called parametric tests, include the z test, t tests, and analyses of variance (ANOVAs).

- *Parametric tests:* Hypothesis tests used to test hypotheses about parameters in a population in which the data are normally distributed and are measured on an interval or ratio scale of measurement.

However, the variance can only meaningfully convey differences when data are measured on a scale in which the distance that scores deviate from their mean is meaningful. Although data on interval and ratio scales do meaningfully convey distance, data on nominal and ordinal scales do not. Hence, when we measure data on a nominal or ordinal scale, we require tests called nonparametric tests that use test statistics that do not analyze the variance of the data. Chapter 17 of the book introduces nonparametric tests for nominal data.

There are three characteristics of nonparametric tests:

1. Nonparametric tests can be used even when we do not make inferences about parameters in a population, although they can be used to test hypothesized relationships in a population.

2. Nonparametric tests do not require that the data in the population be normally distributed. Because the data can have any type of distribution, nonparametric tests are often called distribution-free tests.

3. Nonparametric tests can be used to analyze data on a nominal or ordinal scale of measurement.

17.2 The Chi-Square Goodness-of-Fit Test

The chi-square goodness-of-fit test is a statistical procedure used to determine whether observed frequencies at each level of one categorical variable are similar to or different from the frequencies we expected at each level of the categorical variable. This type of test is typically organized in a table with two rows, one that lists the observed frequencies for each category and the other that lists the expected frequencies for each category.

- Frequency observed (f_o): The count or frequency of participants recorded in each category or at each level of the categorical variable.

- Frequency expected (f_e): The count or frequency of participants in each category or at each level of the categorical variable, as determined by the proportion expected in each category.
  - We multiply the total sample size (**N**) by the proportion expected in each category (**p**) to find the frequency expected in each category.

The Test Statistic

The test statistic compares the discrepancy between the observed frequencies and the expected frequencies. The larger the discrepancy between observed and expected frequencies, the larger the value of the test statistic.

$$\text{Chi-square formula: } \chi^2_{\text{obt}} = \Sigma \frac{(f_o - f_e)^2}{f_e}.$$

The Degrees of Freedom

The chi-square distribution is a positively skewed distribution of test statistic values for all possible samples when the null hypothesis is true. The degrees of freedom are equal to the number of levels of the categorical variable minus 1 ($df = k - 1$).

Hypothesis Testing for Goodness of Fit

We use the four steps of hypothesis testing to compute the chi-square goodness-of-fit test.

- *Step 1: State the hypotheses.* The null hypothesis states that expected frequencies are correct. The alternative hypothesis states that the expected frequencies are not correct (i.e., the expected frequencies are not a "good fit").
- *Step 2: State the criteria for a decision.* The level of significance is typically equal to .05. To find the critical values, refer to the chi-square table in Table B.7 in Appendix B of the book (also reprinted in the appendix of this study guide). Find the intersection of the level of significance and the *df* for the test.
- *Step 3: Compute the test statistic.* Substitute the observed and expected frequencies into the chi-square formula for each level of the categorical variable, and sum across the levels.
- *Step 4: Make a decision.* Compare the obtained value to the critical value to make a decision to retain or reject the null hypothesis.

17.3 SPSS in Focus: The Chi-Square Goodness-of-Fit Test

The chi-square goodness-of-fit test can be computed in SPSS by using the Analyze, Nonparametric tests, and Chi-square options in the menu bar. These actions will display a dialog box that allows you to identify the groups and run the test. A Weight cases option must also be selected from the menu bar.

17.4 Interpreting the Chi-Square Goodness-of-Fit Test

Interpreting the chi-square goodness-of-fit test is different from interpreting any other test taught in this book in two ways: The chi-square test (1) is not interpreted in terms of differences between categories and (2) can be used to confirm that a null hypothesis is correct. Using the chi-square goodness-of-fit test, we compare the discrepancy between observed and expected frequencies *at each level* of the categorical variable, thereby making a total of k comparisons.

17.5 Independent Observations and Expected Frequency Size

Assumption: A key assumption for the chi-square test is that the observed frequencies are recorded independently, meaning that each observed frequency must come from different and unrelated participants.

Restriction: One restriction on using a chi-square test is that the size of an expected frequency should never be smaller than 5 in a given category. There are two ways to overcome this limitation:

1. Increase the sample size so that it is five times larger than the number of levels of the categorical variable.

2. Increase the number of levels of the categorical variable, which will increase k and the critical value for the hypothesis test.

17.6 The Chi-Square Test for Independence

The chi-square test for independence is a statistical procedure used to determine whether frequencies observed at the combination of levels of two categorical variables are similar to frequencies expected.

Determining Expected Frequencies

To determine the expected frequencies:

1. Identify the row and column totals.

2. Compute the following formula for each cell:

$$f_e = \frac{\text{row total} \times \text{column total}}{N}.$$

The Test Statistic

The test statistic for the chi-square test for independence is the same as that used with the chi-square goodness-of-fit test. The test statistic measures the discrepancy between the observed frequency and the expected frequency in each cell.

$$\text{Chi-square formula: } \chi^2_{\text{obt}} = \Sigma \frac{(f_o - f_e)}{f_e}.$$

The Degrees of Freedom

The degrees of freedom for a chi-square test for independence are the product of the degrees of freedom for each categorical variable: $df = (k_1 - 1)(k_2 - 1)$.

Hypothesis Testing for Independence

We use the four steps of hypothesis testing to compute the chi-square test for independence.

Step 1: State the hypotheses. The null hypothesis states that the two categorical variables are independent. The alternative hypothesis states that the two categorical variables are related.

Step 2: Set the criteria for a decision. The level of significance is typically equal to .05. To find the critical values, refer to the chi-square table in Table B.7 in Appendix B of the book (also reprinted in the appendix of this study guide). Find the intersection of the level of significance and the *df* for the test.

Step 3: Compute the test statistic. Substitute the observed and expected frequencies into the chi-square formula for each cell or combination of levels of the categorical variables, and sum across the levels.

Step 4: Make a decision. Compare the obtained value to the critical value to make a decision to retain or reject the null hypothesis.

17.7 The Relationship Between Chi-Square and the Phi Coefficient

The phi correlation coefficient and the 2×2 chi-square test for independence are used for the same type of data. In Chapter 15 of the book, we converted the phi correlation coefficient into a chi-square test statistic using the following equation:

$$\chi^2 = r_\phi^2 n.$$

Thus, the phi correlation coefficient and the chi-square test statistic are related. This relationship allows us to use the phi correlation coefficient to estimate effect size for the chi-square test for independence.

17.8 Measures of Effect Size

We use one of three measures of effect size for the chi-square test for independence: the proportion of variance, the phi coefficient, and Cramer's V.

Effect Size Using Proportion of Variance

The proportion of variance (ϕ^2) is a measure of effect size where the r term for the correlation coefficient is replaced with ϕ.

$$\phi^2 = \frac{\chi^2}{N}.$$

Effect Size Using the Phi Coefficient

The square root of the proportion of variance can also be reported as an estimate of effect size. The square root of the proportion of variance is the phi coefficient.

$$\phi = \sqrt{\frac{\chi^2}{N}}.$$

Effect Size Using Cramer's V

When the levels of one or both categorical variables are greater than two, we use Cramer's V (or Cramer's phi) to estimate effect size.

$$V = \sqrt{\frac{\chi^2}{N \times df_{\text{smaller}}}}.$$

- The term df_{smaller} is the smaller of the two degrees of freedom for each of the categorical variables.

17.9 SPSS in Focus: The Chi-Square Test for Independence

The chi-square test for independence is computed in SPSS using the Analyze, Descriptive Statistics, and Crosstabs options in the menu bar. These actions will display a dialog box that allows you to identify the groups and run the test. A Weight cases option must also be selected from the menu bar.

17.10 APA in Focus: Reporting the Chi-Square Test

To summarize any chi-square test, we report the test statistic, the degrees of freedom, and the p value. The observed frequencies can be summarized in a figure, in a table, or in the main text. To summarize the chi-square test for independence, we also report effect size.

CHAPTER FORMULAS

Chi-Square Tests

Chi-Square Tests

$$\chi^2_{obt} = \Sigma \frac{(f_o - f_e)^2}{f_e}$$ (Test statistic for the chi-square goodness-of-fit test and the chi-square test for independence)

$$df = k - 1$$ (Degrees of freedom for the chi-square goodness-of-fit test)

$$df = (k_1 - 1)(k_2 - 1)$$ (Degrees of freedom for the chi-square test for independence)

Effect Size (Chi-Square Test for Independence)

$$\phi^2 = \frac{\chi^2}{N}$$ (Effect size using the proportion of variance)

$$\phi = \sqrt{\frac{\chi^2}{N}}$$ (Effect size using the phi coefficient)

$$V = \sqrt{\frac{\chi^2}{N \times df_{smaller}}}$$ (Effect size using Cramer's V)

TIPS AND CAUTIONS FOR STUDENTS

- *Nonparametric tests:* Nonparametric tests are used as alternatives for data that do not fit the assumption of *normality* and for data that are not on an interval or ratio scale of measurement. Keep in mind that hypothesis tests can only be computed when the assumptions for computing those tests are satisfied or met. Therefore, if the data violate an assumption for a hypothesis test, then nonparametric tests provide an appropriate alternative because they are not restricted by assumptions of normality and can be used when the data are on a nominal or ordinal scale of measurement.

- *Chi-square:* Both chi-square tests use the same test statistic. Keep in mind that the test statistic measures the discrepancy between observed and expected frequencies. It does not measure differences between group means. For this reason, the chi-square tests are only appropriate when we count the frequency of people or objects. Any other use of this test is inappropriate.

KEY TERM WORD SEARCHES

D	E	G	U	J	O	C	O	Y	U	F	G	R	S	E	M	L	O	E	Z	Y	B	A	W	N	O	W	T	K	R
R	F	Y	M	F	J	W	G	V	O	A	D	H	U	O	D	D	F	Z	A	O	Y	X	S	K	B	D	J	H	U
S	I	E	H	D	Z	H	E	M	F	R	E	Q	U	E	N	C	Y	O	B	S	E	R	V	E	D	O	V	P	F
S	P	Y	U	U	G	I	J	L	R	U	K	C	S	H	F	C	D	G	M	Z	B	W	R	Y	A	R	P	V	Y
S	D	K	J	F	C	I	U	P	H	W	B	X	I	A	O	U	E	K	R	C	C	J	P	C	G	R	S	G	V
T	P	T	O	M	R	Y	Q	Z	T	M	Z	L	M	W	J	L	B	S	W	D	E	V	G	X	T	W	J	O	I
D	O	P	N	U	A	N	G	I	J	W	B	Y	V	L	X	S	Q	P	M	F	R	E	Z	W	D	R	Y	J	V
U	Q	P	C	R	M	Q	Y	J	Y	S	J	C	C	R	W	U	E	J	K	I	F	C	G	X	J	Q	Y	P	T
K	D	P	X	M	E	O	F	M	W	D	V	Z	I	S	X	C	C	O	M	D	C	Y	I	N	A	G	P	R	J
N	O	N	P	A	R	A	M	E	T	R	I	C	T	E	S	T	S	C	E	C	S	T	A	R	I	O	Q	O	P
U	E	P	D	Q	S	H	I	F	P	I	X	K	J	U	G	C	L	M	D	R	F	Q	L	U	B	O	X	W	W
W	U	D	D	D	V	Q	R	E	I	I	X	Z	J	M	U	Q	C	Y	T	A	R	S	S	H	A	D	X	M	Y
G	W	A	C	U	R	S	H	S	G	T	N	F	C	L	R	F	G	A	E	M	E	L	I	D	C	N	Z	W	V
S	D	F	E	C	H	I	S	Q	U	A	R	E	T	E	S	T	C	Y	S	E	Q	P	W	W	Q	E	E	X	U
R	P	A	R	A	M	E	T	R	I	C	T	E	S	T	S	P	B	O	T	R	U	Q	Q	G	C	S	S	H	K
A	M	A	M	A	Z	M	E	V	D	X	D	H	B	P	C	O	R	X	F	S	E	R	P	X	O	S	X	O	F
M	V	S	W	Z	G	P	K	R	Q	E	R	O	W	K	M	J	T	W	O	P	N	N	T	M	A	O	O	R	L
V	P	V	C	X	C	Y	V	N	Q	M	Y	E	R	O	W	K	Z	X	R	H	C	X	C	A	H	F	D	O	V
B	A	L	Z	V	D	E	N	K	Z	P	O	S	C	S	S	J	T	Z	I	I	Y	K	O	F	Y	F	W	C	B
Q	U	I	V	I	S	O	C	B	X	K	O	V	I	T	R	G	P	H	N	J	E	V	G	V	E	I	K	Q	N
D	D	G	V	B	O	W	U	N	J	E	P	Q	X	Z	Q	A	U	I	D	V	X	X	R	Q	X	T	Z	J	P
H	U	V	Q	Y	E	U	P	L	V	F	V	V	R	B	U	J	M	Q	E	Z	P	K	V	Q	U	T	J	B	V
Q	L	M	J	W	S	Y	P	Z	R	T	G	L	V	I	O	U	U	Z	P	M	E	E	V	W	G	E	L	I	K
F	L	E	A	H	W	I	E	D	Y	M	I	D	W	B	C	C	Q	F	E	E	C	D	B	G	V	S	Z	K	P
R	V	O	F	X	O	I	T	E	U	R	L	J	D	Q	E	Q	I	M	N	V	T	P	C	T	T	T	Q	F	E
G	D	E	J	A	X	H	R	J	P	S	O	U	V	D	X	H	L	E	D	W	E	B	M	X	Q	A	N	N	O
Z	O	B	U	P	S	J	B	P	Z	L	Q	O	B	M	H	P	X	T	E	R	D	A	M	F	L	X	I	L	I
D	T	G	O	V	M	I	I	D	H	U	D	W	K	T	N	Y	V	U	N	Q	T	V	P	F	I	F	T	T	W
O	M	I	Q	M	E	J	G	I	J	L	P	D	G	S	I	A	V	T	C	W	G	G	Y	H	P	N	V	N	O
O	Y	U	C	Q	T	V	U	R	H	Z	N	D	L	E	M	F	R	J	E	C	G	E	M	Z	W	P	I	O	A

CHI-SQUARE TEST

CRAMER'S PHI

CRAMER'S *V*

FREQUENCY EXPECTED

FREQUENCY OBSERVED

GOODNESS-OF-FIT TEST

NONPARAMETRIC TESTS

PARAMETRIC TESTS

TEST FOR INDEPENDENCE

373

CROSSWORD PUZZLES

ACROSS

3 Hypothesis tests that are used to test hypotheses about parameters in a population in which the data are normally distributed and measured on an interval or ratio scale of measurement.

5 Hypothesis tests that are used to test hypotheses that do not make inferences about parameters in a population, to test hypotheses about data that can have any type of distribution, and to analyze data on a nominal or ordinal scale of measurement.

6 A positively skewed distribution of chi-square test statistic values for all possible samples when the null hypothesis is true.

7 The count or frequency of participants recorded in each category or at each level of the categorical variable.

8 An estimate of effect size for the chi-square test for independence for two categorical variables with any number of levels.

9 A type of chi-square test that is used to determine whether frequencies observed at the combination of levels of two categorical variables are similar to frequencies expected.

DOWN

1 The count or frequency of participants in each category, or at each level of the categorical variable, as determined by the proportion expected in each category.

2 A type of chi-square test that is used to determine whether observed frequencies at each level of one categorical variable are similar to or different from the frequencies we expected at each level of the categorical variable.

4 A statistical procedure used to test hypotheses about the discrepancy between the observed and expected proportion of counts or frequencies in different nominal categories.

PRACTICE QUIZZES

LO 1: Distinguish between nonparametric and parametric tests.

1. _____ are hypothesis tests that are used (1) to test hypotheses that do not make inferences about parameters in a population, (2) to test hypotheses about data that can have any type of distribution, and (3) to analyze data on a nominal or ordinal scale of measurement.

   a. Parametric tests

   b. Nonparametric tests

   c. both a and b

2. _____ are hypothesis tests that are used to test hypotheses about parameters in a population in which the data in the population are normally distributed and measured on an interval or ratio scale of measurement.

   a. Parametric tests

   b. Nonparametric tests

   c. both a and b

3. Nonparametric tests are alternatives to parametric tests that are used to analyze data on which scales of measurement?

   a. nominal and ratio

   b. ordinal and interval

   c. interval and ratio

   d. nominal and ordinal

4. When we measure data on a nominal or ordinal scale, we require hypothesis tests that use test statistics that do not analyze the _____ of the data.

   a. effect size

   b. significance

   c. variance

   d. meaning

LO 2: Explain how the test statistic is computed for a chi-square test.

5. The count or frequency of participants recorded in each category or at each level of the categorical variable is called:

   a. frequency observed

   b. frequency expected

   c. both a and b

6. The count or frequency of participants in each category, or at each level of the categorical variable, as determined by the proportion expected in each category, is called:

   a. the frequency observed

   b. the frequency expected

   c. both a and b

7. The test statistic compares the _____ between observed and expected frequencies.

   a. frequency

   b. outcome

   c. discrepancy

   d. effect size

8. The test statistic equals _____ when the observed and expected frequencies are the same.

   a. 0

   b. 1

   c. a negative value

   d. a positive value

9. The _____ of the chi-square test statistic accounts for the relative size of a discrepancy between observed and expected frequencies.

   a. numerator

   b. frequency

   c. square root

   d. denominator

LO 3: Calculate the degrees of freedom for the chi-square goodness-of-fit test and locate critical values in the chi-square table.

10. What are the degrees of freedom for a chi-square goodness-of-fit test with $k = 3$?

    a. 1

    b. 2

    c. 3

    d. 4

11. A researcher counts the number of students who agree, disagree, or are indifferent concerning a recent school policy change. What are the degrees of freedom for this chi-square goodness-of-fit test?

    a. 1

    b. 2

    c. 3

    d. 4

12. What is the critical value for a chi-square goodness-of-fit test at a .05 level of significance when $k = 4$?

    a. 3.84

    b. 5.99

    c. 7.81

    d. 9.49

13. A researcher had participants rank the importance of five economic issues. The frequency of times that a category or an economic issue was ranked first was recorded. What is the critical value for this chi-square goodness-of-fit test at a .05 level of significance?

    a. 11.07

    b. 5.99

    c. 7.81

    d. 9.49

LO 4: Compute the chi-square goodness-of-fit test and interpret the results.

14 The frequency observed of individuals preferring Product A is 32, and the number preferring Product B is 40. If the frequency expected is based on the null hypothesis that $p = .50$ for each product, then what is the value of the test statistic?

    a. 1.90

    b. 2.28

    c. 2.50

    d. 0.89

15. The frequency observed in each of four categories is 28, 30, 26, and 20. If the frequency expected is based on the null hypothesis that $p = .25$ for each category, then what is the value of the test statistic?

    a. 1.95

    b. 2.15

    c. 2.95

    d. 3.05

16. What is the value of the test statistic for a chi-square goodness-of-fit test using the following data?

	Category			
	A	**B**	**C**	**D**
f_o	40	34	32	44
f_e	45	30	30	45

    a. 1.24

    b. 1.53

    c. 3.52

    d. 6.00

17. To interpret a significant chi-square goodness-of-fit test, we compare observed and expected frequencies:

    a. across the levels of the categorical variable

    b. between the levels of the categorical variable

    c. at each level of the categorical variable

    d. all of the above

LO 5: Identify the assumption and the restriction of expected frequency size for the chi-square test.

18. Which of the following is a key assumption for the chi-square test?

    a. the data in the population are normally distributed

    b. the data are measured on an interval or ratio scale

    c. observed frequencies are recorded independently

    d. both a and c

19. The size of an expected frequency should never be smaller than ____ in a given category.

    a. 5

    b. 6

    c. 9

    d. 10

20. Which of the following is a strategy that can be used when the size of an expected frequency is smaller than 5 in a given category?

    a. increase the sample size so that it is five times larger than the number of levels of the categorical variable

    b. increase the number of levels of the categorical variable so that k is greater than 4

    c. reduce the standard error

    d. both a and b

LO 6: Calculate the degrees of freedom for the chi-square test for independence and locate critical values in the chi-square table.

21. What are the degrees of freedom for a chi-square test for independence with $k_1 = 3$ and $k_2 = 4$?

    a. 3

    b. 4

    c. 6

    d. 12

22. A researcher tests for the relationship between attendance for an exam (absent, tardy, on time) and living arrangement (on campus, commuter). What are the degrees of freedom for this chi-square test for independence?

   a. 1

   b. 2

   c. 6

   d. not enough information

23. What is the critical value for a chi-square test for independence at a .05 level of significance when $k_1 = 2$ and $k_2 = 4$?

   a. 3.84

   b. 7.81

   c. 12.59

   d. 15.51

24. A researcher tests for the relationship between grades on an exam (passing, failing) and whether students took all prerequisite courses (yes, no). What is the critical value for this chi-square test for independence at a .05 level of significance?

   a. 3.84

   b. 5.99

   c. 7.81

   d. 9.49

LO 7: Compute the chi-square test for independence and interpret the results.

25. The test statistic for the chi-square test for independence is the same as that for what other hypothesis test?

   a. analysis of regression

   b. chi-square goodness-of-fit

   c. Pearson correlation

   d. analysis of variance

26. The frequencies observed for two categorical factors are given in the table. What is the expected frequency in cell BD?

		Category 1	
		A	B
Category 2	C	14	10
	D	12	20

   a. 11.14

   b. 12.86

   c. 14.86

   d. 17.14

27. The frequencies observed for the number of participants working full- or part-time and eating a good or poor diet are given in the table. What is the value of the test statistic for a chi-square test for independence?

		Health of Diet	
		Poor	Good
Work Schedule	Part-Time	18	30
	Full-Time	28	16

   a. 4.58

   b. 4.70

   c. 6.27

   d. 6.91

28. The null hypothesis for a chi-square test for independence is that:

   a. two categorical variables are dependent or related

   b. two categorical variables are independent or unrelated

   c. the observed and expected frequencies have minimal variance

   d. both b and c

LO 8: Compute effect size for the chi-square test for independence.

29. When the levels of one or more categorical variables are greater than two, we use _____ to estimate effect size?

   a. the proportion of variance

   b. the phi coefficient

   c. Cramer's V

   d. all of the above

30. Using a sample of 80 participants, a researcher computes the following test statistic for a chi-square test for independence: $\chi^2(1) = 4.05$. What is the effect size using the phi coefficient?

   a. 4.05

   b. .23

   c. .05

   d. 1.00

31. Using a sample of 120 participants, a researcher computes the following test statistic for a chi-square test for independence: $\chi^2(4) = 23.28$. If the smaller degrees of freedom are 2, then what is the effect size using Cramer's V?

a. .31

b. .44

c. .23

d. .28

32. Cramer's $V = .25$. If the degrees of freedom smaller are 2, then what is the size of this effect?

a. small

b. medium

c. large

LO 9: Summarize the results of a chi-square test in APA format.

33. Which of the following is reported for the results of a chi-square test?

a. the test statistic value

b. the p value of the hypothesis test

c. the degrees of freedom

d. all of the above

34. A researcher reports the following for a chi-square goodness-of-fit test: $\chi^2(3) = 9.12$. What is the decision for this test?

a. reject the null hypothesis

b. retain the null hypothesis

c. not enough information to make a decision

35. A researcher reports the following for a chi-square test for independence: $\chi^2(4) = 6.02$, $p < .05$ ($\phi = .18$). Assuming that both categorical factors had three levels, which value is not possible in this summary?

a. the test statistic value

b. the degrees of freedom

c. the estimate of effect size

d. the p value

Follow the General Instructions Guidebook to complete this exercise. Also, an example for following these steps is provided in the SPSS in Focus section (Section 17.3) of the book. Complete and submit the SPSS grading template and a printout of the output file.

Exercise 17.1: Stress Disorders Following Deployment

Many men and women in the U.S. military are required to make multiple deployments to war zones. Each deployment can last up to a year or longer, having lasting effects on stress to soldiers and their families. To better understand the extent to which multiple deployments may increase the hardships on those serving in war zones, a researcher asked a group of soldiers who had served four deployments in a war zone to indicate whether their first, second, third, or fourth military deployment was the most stressful. Frequencies were expected to be the same in each category. The frequency of soldiers choosing one of four categories is given in the table. Test whether the frequencies observed are different from frequencies expected at a .05 level of significance (assume equal frequencies).

	Number of Deployments to War			
	1	2	3	4+
Frequency observed	22	36	34	36

With regard to the SPSS exercise, answer the following questions:

Based on the value of the test statistic, what is the decision for the chi-square goodness-of-fit test? (Circle one)

Retain the null hypothesis   Reject the null hypothesis

Based on the data given in the SPSS output, state the frequency observed and the frequency expected for each level of the categorical factor. Make sure you label a group name for each level of the categorical variable.

Level of Factor (k)   Frequency Observed   Frequency Expected

_____   _____   _____

_____   _____   _____

_____   _____   _____

_____   _____   _____

Based on the SPSS output, state the following values for the test statistic:

Total sample size   _____

Chi-square test statistic   _____

Degrees of freedom   _____

Significance   _____

State the conclusions for this test using APA format. Provide an interpretation for your conclusion.

Follow the General Instructions Guidebook to complete this exercise. Also, an example for following these steps is provided in the SPSS in Focus section (Section 17.9) of the book. Complete and submit the SPSS grading template and a printout of the output file.

Exercise 17.2: Making the Grade With New Books

A professor hypothesized that students who read used books with highlighting in them would retain the least information from the book. To test this hypothesis, she recorded whether students in a large classroom used books that were new, used with minimal highlighting (MH), or used with substantial highlighting (SH). At the end of the course, she recorded whether or not each student passed the course. Test whether the type of book used (new, used with MH, used with SH) is related to the outcome in the class (pass, fail) at a .05 level of significance.

		Type of Book		
		New	Used With MH	Used With SH
Outcome	Pass	78	72	62
	Fail	8	16	19

With regard to the SPSS exercise, answer the following questions:

Based on the value of the test statistic, what is the decision for the chi-square test for independence? (Circle one)

Retain the null hypothesis   Reject the null hypothesis

Based on the data given in the SPSS output, draw the frequency expected table and fill in the frequencies expected in each cell, row, column, and total.

Based on the SPSS output, state the following values for the test statistic:

Total sample size   _____

Chi-square test statistic   _____

Degrees of freedom   _____

Significance   _____

What is the effect size using Cramer's *V*? (Show your work.) *Note:* The value that you compute should match that given in the SPSS output table.

State the conclusions for this test using APA format. Make sure you state the value of the test statistic, the degrees of freedom, the *p* value, and the effect size. Provide an interpretation for your conclusion.

CHAPTER SUMMARY ORGANIZED BY LEARNING OBJECTIVE

LO 1: Distinguish between nonparametric and parametric tests.

- Parametric tests are hypothesis tests that are used to test hypotheses about parameters in a population in which the data are normally distributed and measured on an interval or ratio scale of measurement.
- Nonparametric tests are hypothesis tests that are used (1) to test hypotheses that do not make inferences about parameters in a population, (2) to test hypotheses about data that can have any type of distribution, and (3) to analyze data on a nominal or ordinal scale of measurement.

LO 2: Explain how the test statistic is computed for a chi-square test.

- The test statistic for a chi-square test is

$$\chi^2_{obt} = \sum \frac{(f_o - f_e)^2}{f_e}.$$

- The test statistic compares the discrepancy between observed frequencies and the expected frequencies stated in a null hypothesis. The larger the discrepancy between observed and expected frequencies, the larger the value of the test statistic.

LO 3–4: Calculate the degrees of freedom for the chi-square goodness-of-fit test and locate critical values in the chi-square table; compute the chi-square goodness-of-fit test and interpret the results.

- The chi-square goodness-of-fit test is a statistical procedure used to determine whether observed frequencies at each

level of one categorical variable are similar to or different from the frequencies we expected at each level of the categorical variable. The degrees of freedom for this test are $k - 1$.

- There is no statistical basis for interpreting which discrepancies are significant. The more discrepancies we add, or the larger k is, the more difficult it is to interpret a significant test. One strategy is to identify the largest discrepancies, which tend to be the focus of a significant result, with smaller discrepancies tending to be ignored.

LO 5: Identify the assumption and the restriction of expected frequency size for the chi-square test.

- An assumption for the chi-square test is that observed frequencies are independently recorded in each category. A restriction of this test is that expected frequencies should be greater than 5 in each category. This restriction can be overcome when we increase the sample size such that it is five times larger than the number of levels of the categorical variable or increase the number of levels of the categorical variable.

LO 6–7: Calculate the degrees of freedom for the chi-square test for independence and locate critical values in the chi-square table; compute the chi-square test for independence and interpret the results.

- The chi-square test for independence is a statistical procedure used to determine whether frequencies observed at the combination of levels of two categorical variables are similar to expected frequencies.

- To find the expected frequency in each cell of a frequency table for a chi-square test for independence, first find the row and the column totals for each cell, then calculate the following formula for each cell:

$$f_e = \frac{\text{row total} \times \text{column total}}{N}.$$

- The test statistic is the same as that for the chi-square goodness-of-fit test. The degrees of freedom are $(k_1 - 1)(k_2 - 1)$. A significant outcome indicates that two categorical variables are related or dependent.

LO 8: Compute effect size for the chi-square test for independence.

- Effect size for a chi-square test for independence measures the size of an observed effect. Three measures of effect size are as follows:

Effect size using proportion of

variance: $\phi^2 = \frac{\chi^2}{N}$.

Effect size using the phi coefficient: $\phi = \sqrt{\frac{\chi^2}{N}}$.

Effect size using Cramer's *V*:

$$V = \sqrt{\frac{\chi^2}{N \times df_{\text{smaller}}}}.$$

LO 9: Summarize the results of a chi-square test in APA format.

- To summarize the chi-square goodness-of-fit test, report the test statistic, the degrees of freedom, and the *p* value. The observed frequencies can be summarized in a figure or table or in the main text. For the chi-square test for independence, an estimate for effect size should also be reported.

LO 10: Compute the chi-square goodness-of-fit test and the chi-square test for independence using SPSS.

- The chi-square goodness-of-fit test is computed using the Analyze, Nonparametric tests, and Chi-square options in the menu bar. These actions will display a dialog box that allows you to identify the groups and run the test. A Weight cases option must also be selected from the menu bar.
- The chi-square test for independence is computed using the Analyze, Descriptive statistics, and Crosstabs options in the menu bar. These actions will display a dialog box that allows you to identify the groups and run the test. A Weight cases option must also be selected from the menu bar.

18

Nonparametric Tests

Tests for Ordinal Data

LEARNING OBJECTIVES

After reading this chapter, you should be able to:

1. Explain why ordinal data are computed using nonparametric tests.

2. Compute the one-sample and related-samples sign tests and interpret the results.

3. Compute the normal approximation for the sign test.

4. Compute the Wilcoxon signed-ranks T test and interpret the results.

5. Compute the normal approximation for the Wilcoxon signed-ranks T test.

6. Compute the Mann-Whitney U test and interpret the results.

7. Compute the normal approximation for the Mann-Whitney U test.

8. Compute the Kruskal-Wallis H test and interpret the results.

9. Compute the Friedman test and interpret the results.

10. Summarize the results of nonparametric tests for ordinal data in APA format.

11. Compute the related-samples sign test, the Wilcoxon signed-ranks T test, the Mann-Whitney U test, the Kruskal-Wallis H test, and the Friedman test using SPSS.

18.1 Tests for Ordinal Data

Nonparametric tests have been adapted to analyze ordinal data. Also, when interval or ratio data are skewed, the skewed data can be converted to ranks and analyzed using a nonparametric test.

Scales of Measurement and Variance

Ordinal data do not convey the distance between scores, so the variance cannot be used in the formula of the test statistic to analyze ordinal data. The advantage of using ranked data is that it eliminates large variance due to outliers. Because measuring ranked data minimizes variability, a test for ordinal data can actually increase the power to detect an effect when data are skewed with outliers.

Minimizing Bias: Tied Ranks

When tied ranks are present in ordinal data, it can lead to bias when making a decision to reject or retain the null hypothesis. To avoid bias, we average the tied ranks, same as we did using the Spearman correlation coefficient in Chapter 15 of the book. To average tied ranks, we treat tied ranks as sequential (e.g., 1 and 1 become 1 and 2) and then assign each the average of the two sequential ranks.

18.2 The Sign Test

The *sign test* is a statistical procedure used to determine the binomial probability that an observed number of scores fall above and below the median (one sample) or are positive and negative (related samples). The sign test is used as a nonparametric alternative to the one-sample *t* test and the related-samples *t* test.

One-Sample Sign Test

To perform the one-sample sign test, all data must be converted to either a plus (+) sign or a minus (−) sign: + if above the median and − if below the median. Hence, the two signs (+ and −) are binomial ordinal data. To perform the one-sample sign test, we follow the four steps of hypothesis testing.

- *Step 1: State the hypotheses.* The null hypothesis states that the number of scores above and below the median is equal. The alternative hypothesis states that there are more scores either above or below the median.

- *Step 2: Set the criteria for a decision.* Set a level of significance, and then refer to the distribution of binomial probabilities for the sample size (*n*) in Table B.8 in Appendix B of the book.
- *Step 3: Compute the test statistic.* Assign a plus or a minus sign to each value depending on if it is above or below the median and discard any values that equal the median. The test statistic, *x*, is the number of pluses or minuses, whichever occurs most often.
- *Step 4: Make a decision.* To make a decision, we use the binomial probability table in Table B.8 to find the probability of obtaining at least the number of scores above or below the median for a given sample size *n*.

Related-Samples Sign Test

The related-samples sign test is used to compare differences between two related or matched samples and can be used as an alternative to the related-samples *t* test. This test is computed the same as a one-sample sign test with the following exception:

- The null hypothesis states that the number of positive difference scores and negative difference scores is equal. The alternative hypothesis states that the number of positive and negative difference scores is not equal. To find the test statistic, we compute difference scores. The value of the test statistic is the number of positive or negative difference scores, whichever occurs most often.

The Normal Approximation for the Sign Test

For larger samples, a binomial distribution approximates a normal distribution. Hence, we can use the *z* statistic to make this test as well. When we have a large sample size, we can use the following formula in place of the sign test:

$$z = \frac{x - np}{\sqrt{np(1-p)}},$$

where

- x = the value of the text statistic,
- n = the sample size, and
- p = .50, which is the probability that we will obtain scores above or below the median when the null hypothesis is true.

18.3 SPSS in Focus: The Related-Samples Sign Test

SPSS can be used to compute the related-samples sign test using the Analyze, Nonparametric tests, and 2 Related Samples . . . options in the menu bar. These actions will display a dialog box that allows you to choose the sign test, identify the groups, and run the test.

18.4 The Wilcoxon Signed-Ranks *T* Test

The Wilcoxon signed-ranks *T* test is a statistical procedure used to determine whether the total ranks in two related groups are significantly different. The Wilcoxon signed-ranks *T* test is used as a nonparametric alternative to the related-samples *t* test. We follow three steps to compute this test.

- Step 1: Rank each difference score regardless of the sign.
- Step 2: Separate the ranks into two groups: those associated with positive differences (+) and those associated with negative differences (−).
- Step 3: Sum the ranks in each group. The smaller total is the test statistic.

The null hypothesis for the Wilcoxon signed-ranks *T* test is that there is no difference in ranks between groups. The alternative hypothesis is that there is a difference in ranks between groups.

To determine whether a result is significant, compare the value of *T* to the critical value listed in Table B.9 in Appendix B of the book. The table is organized with the level of significance for one- and two-tailed tests listed in the columns and the sample size listed in the rows. When the test statistic, *T*, is equal to or less than the critical value, we reject the null hypothesis.

The Normal Approximation for the Wilcoxon *T*

With large samples, we can use a normal approximation of the Wilcoxon signed-ranks *T* test. Hence, we can use the *z* statistic to make this test as well. The test statistic for the Wilcoxon signed-ranks *T* test corresponds to a *z* distribution and takes the basic form of the following *z* transformation formula:

$$z = \frac{T - \mu_T}{\sigma_T}.$$

$$\mu_T = \frac{n(n+1)}{4} \quad \text{(Mean when the null hypothesis is true)}$$

$$\sigma_T = \sqrt{\frac{n(n+1)(2n+1)}{24}} \quad \text{(Standard deviation when the null hypothesis is true)}$$

18.5 SPSS in Focus: The Wilcoxon Signed-Ranks *T* Test

SPSS can be used to compute the Wilcoxon signed-ranks *T* test using the Analyze, Nonparametric tests, and 2 Related Samples . . . options in the menu bar. These actions will display a dialog box that allows you to identify the groups and run the test.

18.6 The Mann-Whitney U Test

The Mann-Whitney U test is a statistical procedure used to determine whether the dispersion of ranks in two independent groups is equal. The Mann-Whitney U test is used as a nonparametric alternative to the two-independent-sample t test. We follow three steps to compute this test.

- Step 1: Combine scores from both samples (keeping track of which scores came from which sample) and rank them.
- Step 2: Assign points when a score in one group outranks scores in another group. The number of points assigned is equal to the number of scores that it outranks in the other group.
- Step 3: Sum the points in each group to find the test statistic (U). The smaller total is the test statistic.

The null hypothesis for the Mann-Whitney U test is that the ranks in two groups are equally dispersed. The alternative hypothesis is that the ranks in two groups are not equally dispersed.

To determine whether a result is significant, we compare the value of the test statistic to the critical value found in Table B.10 in Appendix B of the book. The critical value is located at the intersection of the sample sizes for each group. If the test statistic is equal to or less than the critical value, we decide to reject the null hypothesis.

Computing the Test Statistic U

When the sample size is large, the test statistic for two independent groups (A and B) can be computed using the following formulas for each group:

$$\text{Group A: } U_A = n_A n_B + \frac{n_A(n_A + 1)}{2} - \sum R_A.$$

$$\text{Group B: } U_B = n_A n_B + \frac{n_B(n_B + 1)}{2} - \sum R_B.$$

- n_A, n_B = the sample size for each group.
- R is the rank for each group.

Once U_A and U_B are calculated, the smaller value is the test statistic. Compare the test statistic to the same critical value given in Table B.10 in Appendix B of the book. If the test statistic is equal to or less than the critical value, we decide to reject the null hypothesis.

The Normal Approximation for U

When samples are large enough, we can use the normal approximation for the Mann-Whitney U test. The normal approximation formula is

$$z = \frac{U - \mu_U}{\sigma_U}.$$

$\mu_U = \frac{n_A n_B}{2}$ (Mean when the null hypothesis is true)

$\sigma_U = \sqrt{\frac{n_A n_B (n_A + n_B + 1)}{12}}$ (Standard deviation when the null hypothesis is true)

18.7 SPSS in Focus: The Mann-Whitney U Test

SPSS can be used to compute the Mann-Whitney U test using the Analyze, Nonparametric Tests, and 2 Independent Samples options in the menu bar. These actions will display a dialog box that allows you to identify the groups and run the test.

18.8 The Kruskal-Wallis H Test

The Kruskal-Wallis H test is a statistical procedure used to determine whether the total ranks in two or more independent groups are significantly different. The Kruskal-Wallis H test is used as a nonparametric alternative to the one-way between-subjects analysis of variance (ANOVA). We follow three steps to compute the test statistic.

- Step 1: Combine scores from each group (keeping track of which scores came from which sample) and rank them in numerical order.
- Step 2: Sum the ranks for each group.
- Step 3: Compute the test statistic H.

$$H = \frac{12}{N(N+1)} \left(\sum \frac{R^2}{n} \right) - 3(N+1),$$

where

- o N = total number of participants observed,
- o n = the number of participants per group, and
- o R = the total rank in each group.

The null hypothesis for this test is that the sum of ranks in each group does not differ between groups. The alternative hypothesis is that the sum of ranks in each group differs between groups.

When the null hypothesis is true, the test statistic H will be distributed as a chi-square distribution with $(k - 1)$ degrees of freedom. To determine whether a result is significant, we compare the value of the test statistic to the critical value found in the chi-square table in Table B.7 in Appendix B of the book (also reprinted in the appendix of this study guide). If the test statistic exceeds the critical value, we decide to reject the null hypothesis.

18.9 SPSS in Focus: The Kruskal-Wallis H Test

SPSS can be used to compute the Kruskal-Wallis H test using the Analyze, Nonparametric Tests, and k Independent Samples options in the menu bar. These actions will display a dialog box that allows you to identify the groups and run the test.

18.10 The Friedman Test

The Friedman test is a statistical procedure used to determine whether the total ranks in two or more groups are significantly different when the same participants are observed in each group. The Friedman test is used as a nonparametric alternative to the one-way within-subjects ANOVA. We follow three steps to compute this test.

- Step 1: Rank scores across each row for each individual participant.
- Step 2: Sum the ranks for each group.
- Step 3: Compute the test statistic (χ^2_R).

$$\chi^2_R = \frac{12}{nk(k + 1)} \sum R^2 - 3n(k + 1),$$

where

- R = the total ranks in each group,
- n = the number of participants in each group; n will be the same for each group because the same participants are observed in each group, and
- k = the number of groups.

The null hypothesis for the Friedman test is that the sum of ranks in each group does not differ between groups. The alternative hypothesis is that the sum of ranks in each group differs between groups. When the null hypothesis is true, the test statistic will be distributed as a chi-square distribution with $(k - 1)$ degrees of freedom. To determine the critical value, we look in the chi-square table in Table B.7 in Appendix B of the book (also reprinted in the appendix of this study guide). If the test statistic exceeds the critical value, we decide to reject the null hypothesis.

18.11 SPSS in Focus: The Friedman Test

SPSS can be used to compute the Friedman test using the Analyze, Nonparametric Tests, and k Related Samples options in the menu bar. These actions will display a dialog box that allows you to identify the groups and run the test.

18.12 APA in Focus: Reporting Nonparametric Tests

To summarize any nonparametric test, report the test statistic, the degrees of freedom (if applicable), and the p value for the test. The degrees of freedom would be applicable for the Friedman test and the Kruskal-Wallis H test because both tests use the chi-square distribution to set the criteria for a decision. The sign test, Wilcoxon signed-ranks T test, and Mann-Whitney U test can be computed in two ways because each test has a normal approximation alternative with large samples. For each test, you can report the original test statistic value (x for the sign test, T for the Wilcoxon signed-ranks T test, or U for the Mann-Whitney U test) or the z score for the normal approximation of these tests.

Tests for Ordinal Data

The Sign Test

$$z = \frac{x - np}{\sqrt{np(1-p)}}$$ (Test statistic for the normal approximation of the sign test)

Wilcoxon Signed-Ranks T Test

$$z = \frac{T - \mu_T}{\sigma_T}$$ (Test statistic for the normal approximation of the Wilcoxon T)

$$\mu_T = \frac{n(n+1)}{4}$$ (The mean for the test statistic T)

$$\sigma_T = \sqrt{\frac{n(n+1)(2n+1)}{24}}$$ (The standard deviation for the test statistic T)

Mann-Whitney U Test

$$z = \frac{U - \mu_U}{\sigma_U}$$ (Test statistic for the normal approximation of the Mann-Whitney U)

$$\mu_U = \frac{n_A n_B}{2}$$ (The mean for the test statistic U)

$$\sigma_U = \sqrt{\frac{n_A n_B (n_A + n_B + 1)}{12}}$$ (The standard deviation for the test statistic U)

The Kruskal-Wallis H Test

$$H = \frac{12}{N(N+1)} \left(\sum \frac{R^2}{n} \right) - 3(N+1)$$ (Test statistic for the Kruskal-Wallis H test)

The Friedman Test

$$\chi_R^2 = \frac{12}{nk(k+1)} \sum R^2 - 3n(k+1)$$ (Test statistic for the Friedman test)

TIPS AND CAUTIONS FOR STUDENTS

- *Ordinal scale and variance:* Ordinal data do not convey information regarding the distance between scores. Thus, nonparametric tests are needed to analyze differences between groups where ordinal data are measured. Parametric tests are used to analyze variability, or the distance that scores deviate from their mean. Because the mean and the distance that scores fall from it have no meaning using ordinal data, parametric tests are inappropriate. For this reason, nonparametric tests are used to analyze ordinal data.

- *Tied ranks:* Keep in mind that when you have two or more equal ranks, you must average the tied ranks before computing a nonparametric test. When we average the tied ranks, we assign the average rank to all tied ranks. If necessary, do not forget to shift all other ranks accordingly. The last rank should be equal to the number of ranked scores.

- *The sign test:* For the sign test, assigning a + or − sign to each value ensures that all the data are converted to binomial data—data with only two outcomes (+ and − signs). This is crucial for conducting this test because a distribution of binomial probabilities is used to make a decision for this test.

- *The Wilcoxon signed-ranks* T *test:* Note that to perform this test, you must first compute difference scores. The difference scores are the scores you rank, not the original values of the two related samples.

KEY TERM WORD SEARCHES

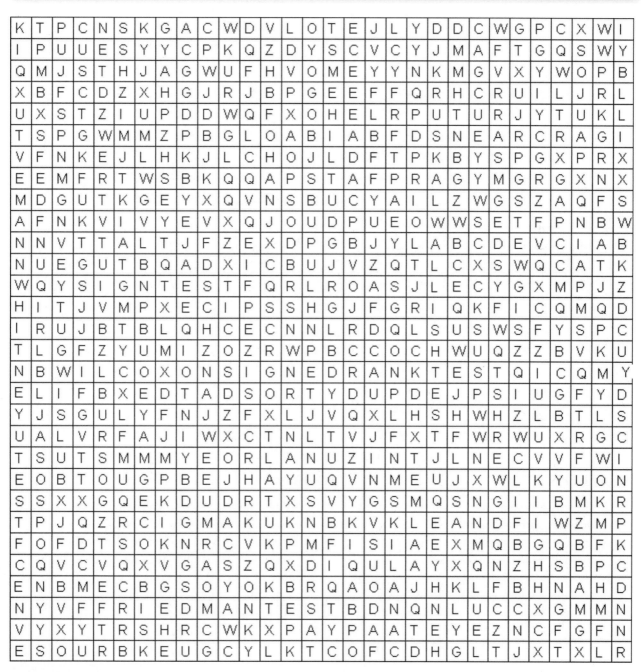

K	T	P	C	N	S	K	G	A	C	W	D	V	L	O	T	E	J	L	Y	D	D	C	W	G	P	C	X	W	I
I	P	U	U	E	S	Y	Y	C	P	K	Q	Z	D	Y	S	C	V	C	Y	J	M	A	F	T	G	Q	S	W	Y
Q	M	J	S	T	H	J	A	G	W	U	F	H	V	O	M	E	Y	Y	N	K	M	G	V	X	Y	W	O	P	B
X	B	F	C	D	Z	X	H	G	J	R	J	B	P	G	E	E	F	F	Q	R	H	C	R	U	I	L	J	R	L
U	X	S	T	Z	I	U	P	D	D	W	Q	F	X	O	H	E	L	R	P	U	T	U	R	J	Y	T	U	K	L
T	S	P	G	W	M	M	Z	P	B	G	L	O	A	B	I	A	B	F	D	S	N	E	A	R	C	R	A	G	I
V	F	N	K	E	J	L	H	K	J	L	C	H	O	J	L	D	F	T	P	K	B	Y	S	P	G	X	P	R	X
E	E	M	F	R	T	W	S	B	K	Q	Q	A	P	S	T	A	F	P	R	A	G	Y	M	G	R	G	X	N	X
M	D	G	U	T	K	G	E	Y	X	Q	V	N	S	B	U	C	Y	A	I	L	Z	W	G	S	Z	A	Q	F	S
A	F	N	K	V	I	V	Y	E	V	X	Q	J	O	U	D	P	U	E	O	W	W	S	E	T	F	P	N	B	W
N	N	V	T	T	A	L	T	J	F	Z	E	X	D	P	G	B	J	Y	L	A	B	C	D	E	V	C	I	A	B
N	U	E	G	U	T	B	Q	A	D	X	I	C	B	U	J	V	Z	Q	T	L	C	X	S	W	Q	C	A	T	K
W	Q	Y	S	I	G	N	T	E	S	T	F	Q	R	L	R	O	A	S	J	L	E	C	Y	G	X	M	P	J	Z
H	I	T	J	V	M	P	X	E	C	I	P	S	S	H	G	J	F	G	R	I	Q	K	F	I	C	Q	M	Q	D
I	R	U	J	B	T	B	L	Q	H	C	E	C	N	N	L	R	D	Q	L	S	U	S	W	S	F	Y	S	P	C
T	L	G	F	Z	Y	U	M	I	Z	O	Z	R	W	P	B	C	C	O	C	H	W	U	Q	Z	Z	B	V	K	U
N	B	W	I	L	C	O	X	O	N	S	I	G	N	E	D	R	A	N	K	T	E	S	T	Q	I	C	Q	M	Y
E	L	I	F	B	X	E	D	T	A	D	S	O	R	T	Y	D	U	P	D	E	J	P	S	I	U	G	F	Y	D
Y	J	S	G	U	L	Y	F	N	J	Z	F	X	L	J	V	Q	X	L	H	S	H	W	H	Z	L	B	T	L	S
U	A	L	V	R	F	A	J	I	W	X	C	T	N	L	T	V	J	F	X	T	F	W	R	W	U	X	R	G	C
T	S	U	T	S	M	M	M	Y	E	O	R	L	A	N	U	Z	I	N	T	J	L	N	E	C	V	V	F	W	I
E	O	B	T	O	U	G	P	B	E	J	H	A	Y	U	Q	V	N	M	E	U	J	X	W	L	K	Y	U	O	N
S	S	X	X	G	Q	E	K	D	U	D	R	T	X	S	V	Y	G	S	M	Q	S	N	G	I	I	B	M	K	R
T	P	J	Q	Z	R	C	I	G	M	A	K	U	K	N	B	K	V	K	L	E	A	N	D	F	I	W	Z	M	P
F	O	F	D	T	S	O	K	N	R	C	V	K	P	M	F	I	S	I	A	E	X	M	Q	B	G	Q	B	F	K
C	Q	V	C	V	Q	X	V	G	A	S	Z	Q	X	D	I	Q	U	L	A	Y	X	Q	N	Z	H	S	B	P	C
E	N	B	M	E	C	B	G	S	O	Y	O	K	B	R	Q	A	O	A	J	H	K	L	F	B	H	N	A	H	D
N	Y	V	F	F	R	I	E	D	M	A	N	T	E	S	T	B	D	N	Q	N	L	U	C	C	X	G	M	M	N
V	Y	X	Y	T	R	S	H	R	C	W	K	X	P	A	Y	P	A	A	T	E	Y	E	Z	N	C	F	G	F	N
E	S	O	U	R	B	K	E	U	G	C	Y	L	K	T	C	O	F	C	D	H	G	L	T	J	X	T	X	L	R

FRIEDMAN TEST

KRUSKAL-WALLIS *H* TEST

MANN-WHITNEY *U* TEST

SIGN TEST

WILCOXON SIGNED-RANKS *T* TEST

CROSSWORD PUZZLES

ACROSS

2 Used as a nonparametric alternative to the one-way within-subjects ANOVA.

3 Used as a nonparametric alternative to the two-independent-sample t test.

5 Used as a nonparametric alternative to the related-samples t test by determining whether the total ranks in two related groups are significantly different.

DOWN

1 Used as a nonparametric alternative to the one-way between-subjects ANOVA.

4 A statistical procedure used to determine the binomial probability that an observed number of scores fall above and below the median (one sample) or are positive and negative (related samples).

PRACTICE QUIZZES

LO 1: Explain why ordinal data are computed using nonparametric tests.

1. Ordinal data do not convey distance, which is why analyzing the _____ of ordinal data is meaningless.
   a. difference
   b. variance
   c. value
   d. significance

2. The variance cannot be used to analyze ranked data because ordinal data do not convey _____.
   a. order
   b. ranks
   c. distance
   d. value

3. How does measuring ranked data increase the power to detect an effect for skewed data sets?
   a. converting data to ranks minimizes variability caused by outliers
   b. converting data to ranks increases how skewed the data are
   c. converting data to ranks increases how variable the data are
   d. ranked data are more accurate than original scores

LO 2: Compute the one-sample and related-samples sign tests and interpret the results.

4. The _____ is a statistical procedure used to determine the binomial probability that an observed number of scores fall above and below the median (one sample) or are positive and negative (related samples).
   a. sign test
   b. positive test
   c. absolute test
   d. negative test

5. A researcher finds that 15 scores fall above the median, 1 equals the median, and 4 fall below the median. What is the value of the test statistic for a one-sample sign test?
   a. 1
   b. 4
   c. 15
   d. 20

6. A researcher finds that 8 scores fall above the median, 1 equals the median, and 1 falls below the median. What is the p value for a one-sample sign test?

   a. .044

   b. .010

   c. .001

   d. .055

7. A researcher compares differences in aptitude scores before and after a treatment. He subtracts pairs of scores from each group and finds that 12 difference scores are positive, 2 equal zero, and 1 is negative. What is the value of the test statistic for a related-samples sign test?

   a. 0

   b. 1

   c. 2

   d. 12

8. A researcher compares differences in ratings for two types of toys. She subtracts pairs of ratings given by each participant and finds that 10 difference scores are positive, 2 equal zero, and 2 are negative. What is the decision for a related-samples sign test at a .05 level of significance?

   a. retain the null hypothesis

   b. reject the null hypothesis

   c. not enough information

LO 3: Compute the normal approximation for the sign test.

9. With smaller sample sizes, we make a decision for the sign test using probabilities for outcomes in a _____ distribution.

   a. skewed

   b. normal

   c. binominal

   d. bimodal

10. With larger samples, a binominal distribution approximates a _____ distribution.

    a. skewed

    b. normal

    c. modal

    d. bimodal

11. Which test statistic do we use to compute the normal approximation for the sign test?

    a. z statistic

    b. t statistic

   c. *F* statistic

   d. χ^2 statistic

12. Why is the value of *p* equal to .50 in the formula for the normal approximation for the sign test, $z = \dfrac{x - np}{\sqrt{np(1 - p)}}$?

   a. half the outcomes in a normal distribution are equal to the mean

   b. there is a 50% chance of rejecting the null hypothesis

   c. that is the approximate probability in the rejection region

   d. it is the value stated by the null hypothesis

LO 4: Compute the Wilcoxon signed-ranks *T* test and interpret the results.

13. A statistical procedure used to determine whether the total ranks in two related groups are significantly different is called the:

   a. Mann-Whitney *U* test

   b. Wilcoxon signed-ranks *T* test

   c. Kruskal-Wallis *H* test

   d. Friedman test

14. The table shows the amount of time participants attended to an easy cognitive task and a difficult cognitive task. What is the value of the test statistic for the Wilcoxon signed-ranks *T* test?

Time (seconds)	
Easy Task	**Difficult Task**
23	20
12	16
11	10
15	0
25	5
20	8

   a. 1

   b. 3

   c. 5

   d. 18

15. The test statistic for a Wilcoxon signed-ranks *T* test is *T* = 71 using a sample of 24 participants. What is the decision for a two-tailed test at a .05 level of significance?

   a. reject the null hypothesis

   b. retain the null hypothesis

   c. not enough information

16. Using the Wilcoxon signed-ranks T test, the _____ the value of the test statistic, the more likely the decision will be to reject the null hypothesis.

    a. smaller

    b. larger

LO 5: Compute the normal approximation for the Wilcoxon signed-ranks T test.

17. The null hypothesis for the normal approximation for the Wilcoxon signed-ranks T test is that:

    a. the variance of positive scores is greater than the variance of negative scores

    b. the mean rank of positive scores is greater than the mean rank of negative scores

    c. positive and negative difference scores are associated with equal ranks

    d. there are more positive than negative difference scores between groups

18. Using a two-tailed test at a .05 level of significance, what are the critical values for the normal approximation for the Wilcoxon signed-ranks T test?

    a. it depends on the sample size

    b. it depends on the number of groups

    c. ±1.645

    d. ±1.96

19. Which test statistic do we use to compute the normal approximation for the Wilcoxon signed-ranks T test?

    a. z statistic

    b. t statistic

    c. F statistic

    d. χ^2 statistic

LO 6: Compute the Mann-Whitney U test and interpret the results.

20. A statistical procedure used to determine whether the dispersion of ranks in two independent groups is equal is called the:

    a. Mann-Whitney U test

    b. Wilcoxon signed-ranks T test

    c. Kruskal-Wallis H test

    d. Friedman test

21. The Mann-Whitney U test is a nonparametric alternative to which hypothesis test?

    a. related-samples t test

    b. two-independent-sample t test

    c. one-way between-subjects ANOVA

    d. one-way within-subjects ANOVA

22. The table shows the distance that participants in two cities commute to work. What is the value of the test statistic for the Mann-Whitney U test?

Distance (miles)	
City A	City B
40	22
32	30
12	10
38	9
24	15
20	18

a. 4

b. 6

c. 7

d. 29

23. The test statistic for a Mann-Whitney U test is $U = 37$ using a sample of 11 participants in each group. What is the decision for a two-tailed test at a .05 level of significance?

a. reject the null hypothesis

b. retain the null hypothesis

c. not enough information

24. Using the Mann-Whitney U test, the _____ the value of the test statistic, the more likely the decision will be to reject the null hypothesis.

a. smaller

b. larger

LO 7: Compute the normal approximation for the Mann-Whitney U test.

25. The null hypothesis for the normal approximation for the Mann-Whitney U test is that:

a. scores are evenly dispersed between groups

b. the mean rank of positive scores is greater than the mean rank of negative scores

c. the variance of positive scores is greater than the variance of negative scores

d. there are more positive than negative difference scores between groups

26. What is the value of the test statistic for the normal approximation for the Mann-Whitney U test if $U = 16$, $\mu_U = 10.50$, and $\sigma_U = 2.80$?

a. 1.06

b. 1.14

c. 1.96

d. 2.28

27. Which test statistic do we use to compute the normal approximation for the Mann-Whitney U test?

    a. z statistic

    b. t statistic

    c. F statistic

    d. χ^2 statistic

LO 8: Compute the Kruskal-Wallis H test and interpret the results.

28. A statistical procedure used to determine whether the total ranks in two or more independent groups are significantly different is called the:

    a. Mann-Whitney U test

    b. Wilcoxon signed-ranks T test

    c. Kruskal-Wallis H test

    d. Friedman test

29. The Kruskal-Wallis H test is a nonparametric alternative to which hypothesis test?

    a. related-samples t test

    b. two-independent-sample t test

    c. one-way between-subjects ANOVA

    d. one-way within-subjects ANOVA

30. What is the value of the test statistic for the Kruskal-Wallis H test if the ranks in each of three groups are 18, 50, and 52 and the sample size in each group is $n = 5$?

    a. 3.42

    b. 6.35

    c. 6.91

    d. 7.28

31. A researcher tests for differences between four groups with 10 participants observed in each group ($N = 40$). The test statistic for the Kruskal-Wallis H test is $H = 8.33$. What is the decision using a .05 level of significance?

    a. reject the null hypothesis

    b. retain the null hypothesis

    c. not enough information

LO 9: Compute the Friedman test and interpret the results.

32. A statistical procedure used to determine whether the total ranks in two or more groups are significantly different when the same participants are observed in each group is called the:

    a. Mann-Whitney U test

    b. Wilcoxon signed-ranks T test

    c. Kruskal-Wallis H test

    d. Friedman test

33. The Friedman test is a nonparametric alternative to which hypothesis test?

    a. related-samples t test

    b. two-independent-sample t test

    c. one-way between-subjects ANOVA

    d. one-way within-subjects ANOVA

34. What is the value of the test statistic for the Friedman test if the ranks in each of three related groups are 11, 14, and 17 and the sample size in each group is $n = 7$?

    a. 1.98

    b. 2.22

    c. 2.66

    d. 4.28

35. A researcher tests for differences between three related groups with 10 participants observed in each group ($N = 30$). The test statistic for the Friedman test is $\chi^2_R = 5.62$. What is the decision using a .05 level of significance?

    a. reject the null hypothesis

    b. retain the null hypothesis

    c. not enough information

LO 10: Summarize the results of nonparametric tests for ordinal data in APA format.

36. Which of the following is reported for a Friedman test but not for a Mann-Whitney U test?

    a. the test statistic value

    b. the p value of the test

    c. the degrees of freedom

    d. none of the above

37. Using a sample of eight participants, a researcher reports the following for a Wilcoxon signed-ranks T test, $T = 6$. What is the decision for this test?

    a. reject the null hypothesis

    b. retain the null hypothesis

    c. not enough information to make a decision

38. Which of the following tests can be reported using the z statistic?

    a. the related-samples sign test

    b. the Wilcoxon signed-ranks T test

    c. the Mann-Whitney U test

    d. all of the above

SPSS IN FOCUS

The Related-Samples Sign Test

Follow the General Instructions Guidebook to complete this exercise. Also, an example for following these steps is provided in the SPSS in Focus section (Section 18.3) of the book. Complete and submit the SPSS grading template and a printout of the output file.

Exercise 18.1: Quitting Caffeine Following Pregnancy

Many women who drink caffeinated drinks stop drinking them during pregnancy but often return to drinking caffeine following the pregnancy. One researcher asked whether the tendency to go back to drinking caffeine following pregnancy is different for women who are pregnant for the first time versus the second time. To test this, she selected a sample of identical twins who were both pregnant. One twin was pregnant for the first time; the second twin was pregnant for the second time. Six months following the participants' respective pregnancies, the researcher recorded the number of caffeinated drinks that each twin drank for 1 week. The data are given below. Test whether these two groups significantly differed at a .05 level of significance.

First-Time Pregnancy	Second-Time Pregnancy
12	24
8	18
0	4
0	7
20	28
0	0
8	20
8	22
11	12
10	19
0	8
12	0
0	16
26	23
9	12
4	6
8	12
14	0
15	4
12	14
8	10
22	2

With regard to the SPSS exercise, answer the following questions:

Based on the value of the test statistic, what is the decision for the related-samples sign test? (Circle one)

Retain the null hypothesis   Reject the null hypothesis

Based on the data given in the SPSS output, state the following frequencies:

Negative differences   _____

Positive differences   _____

Ties   _____

Total   _____

Significance   _____

State the conclusions for this test using APA format. Provide an interpretation for your conclusion.

SPSS IN FOCUS

The Wilcoxon Signed-Ranks *T* Test

Follow the General Instructions Guidebook to complete this exercise. Also, an example for following these steps is provided in the SPSS in Focus section (Section 18.5) of the book. Complete and submit the SPSS grading template and a printout of the output file.

Exercise 18.2: Early Childhood Traits Among Illicit Drug Users

Research suggests that people with serious substance use disorders had delinquent traits before ever using illicit drugs. To test this, a researcher selected pairs of siblings, where one sibling was diagnosed as alcohol dependent and the other sibling was not diagnosed as alcohol dependent. All siblings took a retrospective survey, called the Self-Report Early Delinquency (SRED) Scale, which is used to identify differences in antisocial and delinquent behavior among siblings during their childhood (presumably before any substance abuse). Higher scores on the SRED Scale indicate greater expression of delinquent traits in childhood. Given the following data, test whether alcohol-dependent siblings expressed greater delinquent traits in childhood at a .05 level of significance.

Alcohol-Dependent Sibling	Non-Alcohol-Dependent Sibling
12	12
38	8
23	13
27	8
38	5
17	18
30	9
27	19
22	8
29	10
39	7
36	10
18	20
8	2
40	29
38	10
40	8
26	6

With regard to the SPSS exercise, answer the following questions:

Based on the value of the test statistic, what is the decision for the Wilcoxon signed-ranks T test? (Circle one)

      Retain the null hypothesis   Reject the null hypothesis

Based on the data given in the SPSS output, state the following frequencies:

    Negative differences   _____

    Positive differences   _____

    Ties   _____

    Total   _____

Based on the SPSS output, state the following values for the test statistic:

    z _____

    Asymp. Sig. (2-tailed)   _____

State the conclusions for this test using APA format. Provide an interpretation for your conclusion.

SPSS IN FOCUS

The Mann-Whitney *U* Test

Follow the General Instructions Guidebook to complete this exercise. Also, an example for following these steps is provided in the SPSS in Focus section (Section 18.7) of the book. Complete and submit the SPSS grading template and a printout of the output file.

Exercise 18.3: Educating Students With Disabilities

Federal laws mandate the inclusion of students with disabilities into regular classrooms. The challenge for educators is that students with disabilities are included in classrooms with general educators (those without advanced special education training). This may lead general education teachers to have much different attitudes regarding the inclusion of students with disabilities into the regular classroom. To test this, a researcher gave special education teachers (those with advanced special education training) and general education teachers an inclusion survey. This survey was used to determine how positively teachers viewed the inclusion of students with disabilities in regular classrooms. Scores could range from 0 to 40, with higher scores indicating more positive attitudes. Given the following data, test whether these two groups of teachers significantly differ at a .05 level of significance.

General Education Teachers	Special Education Teachers
32	23
29	28
12	29
16	17
24	13
38	18
12	38
30	32
23	30
28	28
24	34
8	26
26	29
20	31

With regard to the SPSS exercise, answer the following questions:

Based on the value of the test statistic, what is the decision for the Mann-Whitney U test? (Circle one)

Retain the null hypothesis   Reject the null hypothesis

Based on the data given in the SPSS output, state the following values for each group. Make sure you label a group name for each group in each column in the space provided.

	Group 1:	Group 2:
	_____	_____
Sample size	_____	_____
Mean rank	_____	_____
Sum of ranks	_____	_____

Based on the SPSS output, state the following values for the test statistic:

Mann-Whitney U _____

z _____

Asymp. Sig. (2-tailed)   _____

State the conclusions for this test using APA format. Provide an interpretation for your conclusion.

SPSS IN FOCUS

The Kruskal-Wallis *H* Test

Follow the General Instructions Guidebook to complete this exercise. Also, an example for following these steps is provided in the SPSS in Focus section (Section 18.9) of the book. Complete and submit the SPSS grading template and a printout of the output file.

Exercise 18.4: Convenience and Visibility of Vegetables

Studies have shown that when candy is convenient and visible, people will eat more of it. To test whether this would also be true with vegetables, a researcher asked participants to sit at a desk where a bowl of carrots and celery was placed either on the desk (convenient and visible), in the desk drawer (convenient but not visible), in a cabinet 10 feet away from the desk (inconvenient but visible), or in another section of the room separated by a partition (inconvenient and not visible). Participants were seated at the desk and told they could eat the vegetables available in the room while they waited to be called upon. All participants sat at the desk for 10 minutes. The number of carrots and celery consumed was recorded. Given the following data, test whether differences between groups were significant at a .05 level of significance.

Convenience–Visibility			
Yes–Yes	Yes–No	No–Yes	No–No
8	0	1	2
6	4	5	5
4	2	2	6
5	3	4	3
2	2	0	0
8	5	0	2
3	2	1	5
7	5	5	3
5	3	4	6
8	8	0	4
4	5	6	5
2	0	9	5
6	2	3	1
4	5	6	2
5	4	8	2
1	8	0	0

With regard to the SPSS exercise, answer the following questions:

Based on the value of the test statistic, what is the decision for the Kruskal-Wallis H test? (Circle one)

Retain the null hypothesis   Reject the null hypothesis

Based on the data given in the SPSS output, state the sample size and the mean rank for each group. Make sure you label a group name for each group in the first column.

Group Name	Sample Size	Mean Rank
_____	_____	_____
_____	_____	_____
_____	_____	_____
_____	_____	_____

Based on the SPSS output, state the following values for the test statistic:

Chi-square   _____

Degrees of freedom   _____

Asymp. Sig.   _____

State the conclusions for this test using APA format. Provide an interpretation for your conclusion.

SPSS IN FOCUS

The Friedman Test

Follow the General Instructions Guidebook to complete this exercise. Also, an example for following these steps is provided in the SPSS in Focus section (Section 18.11) of the book. Complete and submit the SPSS grading template and a printout of the output file.

Exercise 18.5: Canine Aggression According to Their Owners

Canine aggression can pose a serious public health and animal welfare concern. On the basis of this knowledge, a researcher wanted to determine who is at greatest risk of encountering canine aggression in a local community where animal welfare funds had been cut. He asked dog owners in a community to complete a canine behavioral assessment survey, which consisted of three subscales (aggression toward strangers, owners, and other dogs). Each subscale was scored out of 30 points, with higher scores indicating a greater risk of encountering canine aggression. Owners of a similar number of different dog breeds were represented in this sample. Scores on each subscale were compared to test for differences in canine aggression directed toward strangers, owners, and dogs. Test whether these differences were significant at a .05 level of significance.

Participant	Subscale		
	Strangers	Owners	Other Dogs
A	11	10	20
B	14	14	18
C	10	12	19
D	8	16	18
E	28	29	17
F	26	20	20
G	7	12	20
H	19	9	17
I	12	11	16
J	14	19	19
K	10	13	15
L	16	12	12
M	9	10	16
N	11	9	13

With regard to the SPSS exercise, answer the following questions:

Based on the value of the test statistic, what is the decision for the Friedman test? (Circle one)

Retain the null hypothesis   Reject the null hypothesis

Based on the data given in the SPSS output, state the mean rank for each group. Make sure you label a group name for each group in the first column:

Group Name	Sample Size	Mean Rank
_____	_____	_____
_____	_____	_____
_____	_____	_____
_____	_____	_____

Based on the SPSS output, state the following values for the test statistic:

N _____

Chi-square   _____

Degrees of freedom   _____

Asymp. Sig.   _____

State the conclusions for this test using APA format. Provide an interpretation for your conclusion.

CHAPTER SUMMARY ORGANIZED BY LEARNING OBJECTIVE

LO 1: Explain why ordinal data are computed using nonparametric tests.

- Variance can only meaningfully convey the distance that scores deviate from the mean when data are measured on an interval or ratio scale. Ordinal data do not meaningfully convey the distance that scores deviate from their mean. For this reason, nonparametric tests are most appropriate for analyzing ordinal data.

LO 2–3: Compute the one-sample and related-samples sign tests and interpret the results; compute the normal approximation for the sign test.

- The sign test is a statistical procedure used to determine the binomial probability that an observed number of scores fall above and below the median (one sample) or are positive and negative (related samples). This test is used as a nonparametric alternative to the one-sample t test and the related-samples t test.
- For the one-sample sign test, count the number of scores above and below the median. Assign a plus sign to each value above the median, assign a negative sign to each value below the median, and discard values that equal the median. When the null hypothesis is true, the number of pluses and minuses will be the same; the larger the discrepancy between pluses and minuses, the more likely we are to reject the null hypothesis.
- For the related-samples sign test, subtract pairs of scores for each participant. Count the number of difference scores that are positive and negative, and discard values that equal 0. When the null hypothesis is true, the number of positive and negative difference scores will be the same; the larger the discrepancy between positive and negative difference scores, the more likely we are to reject the null hypothesis.
- The formula for the normal approximation of the sign test is

$$z = \frac{x - np}{\sqrt{np(1-p)}}, \text{ where } p = .50.$$

LO 4–5: Compute the Wilcoxon signed-ranks T test and interpret the results; compute the normal approximation for the Wilcoxon signed-ranks T test.

- The Wilcoxon signed-ranks T test is a statistical procedure used to determine whether the total ranks in two related groups are significantly different. This test is used as a nonparametric alternative to the related-samples t test.
- The steps for completing the Wilcoxon signed-ranks T test are as follows:
    - **Step 1:** Rank each difference score regardless of the sign.
    - **Step 2:** Separate the ranks into two groups: those associated with positive differences (+) and those associated with negative differences (–).
    - **Step 3:** Sum the ranks in each group. The smaller total is the test statistic.
- The null hypothesis for this test is that there is no difference in ranks between groups. The alternative hypothesis is that there is a difference in ranks

between groups. The smaller the value of the test statistic, the more likely we are to reject the null hypothesis.

- The formula for the normal approximation of the Wilcoxon signed-ranks T test is

$$z = \frac{T - \mu_T}{\sigma_T}, \text{ where } \mu_T = \frac{n(n+1)}{4},$$

$$\text{and } \sigma_T = \sqrt{\frac{n(n+1)(2n+1)}{24}}.$$

LO 6–7: Compute the Mann-Whitney U test and interpret the results; compute the normal approximation for the Mann-Whitney U test.

- The Mann-Whitney U test is a statistical procedure used to determine whether the dispersion of ranks in two independent groups is equal. This test is used as a nonparametric alternative to the two-independent-sample t test.
- The steps for completing this test are as follows:

  ○ **Step 1:** Combine scores from both samples and rank them in numerical order. (Keep track of the group that scores came from.)

  ○ **Step 2:** Assign points when a score in one group outranks scores in another group.

  ○ **Step 3:** Sum the points in each group to find the test statistic (U). The smaller total is the test statistic.

- The null hypothesis for this test is that the ranks in two groups are equally dispersed. The alternative hypothesis is that the ranks in two groups are not equally dispersed. The smaller the value for the test statistic, the more likely we are to reject the null hypothesis.
- The formula for the normal approximation of the Mann-Whitney U test is

$$z = \frac{U - \mu_U}{\sigma_U}, \text{ where } \mu_U = \frac{n_A n_B}{2};$$

$$\sigma_U = \sqrt{\frac{n_A n_B (n_A + n_B + 1)}{12}}.$$

LO 8: Compute the Kruskal-Wallis H test and interpret the results.

- The Kruskal-Wallis H test is a statistical procedure used to determine whether the total ranks in two or more independent groups are significantly different. This test is used as a nonparametric alternative to the one-way between-subjects ANOVA.
- The steps for completing this test are as follows:

  ○ **Step 1:** Combine scores from each group and rank them in numerical order. (Keep track of the group that scores came from.)

  ○ **Step 2:** Sum the ranks for each group.

  ○ **Step 3:** Compute the test statistic (H):

$$H = \frac{12}{N(N+1)} \left(\sum \frac{R^2}{n} \right) - 3(N + 1).$$

- The null hypothesis for this test is that the sum of ranks in each group does not differ. The alternative hypothesis is that the sum of ranks in each group differs. When the null hypothesis is true and n is greater than or equal to 5 per group, the test statistic H is approximately distributed as a chi-square distribution. For this reason, we use the chi-square distribution to make a decision for this test.

LO 9: Compute the Friedman test and interpret the results.

- The Friedman test is a statistical procedure used to determine whether the total ranks in two or more groups are significantly different when the same participants are observed in each group. This test is used as a nonparametric alternative to the one-way within-subjects ANOVA.

- The steps for completing this test are as follows:

  o **Step 1:** Rank scores across each row for each individual participant.

  o **Step 2:** Sum the ranks for each group.

  o **Step 3:** Compute the test statistic $\left(\chi_R^2\right)$:

$$\chi_R^2 = \frac{12}{nk(k+1)}\sum R^2 - 3n(k+1).$$

- The null hypothesis for this test is that the sum of ranks in each group does not differ. The alternative hypothesis is that the sum of ranks in each group differs. When the null hypothesis is true and n is greater than or equal to 5 per group, the test statistic χ_R^2 is approximately distributed as a chi-square distribution. For this reason, we use the chi-square distribution to make a decision for this test.

LO 10: Summarize the results of nonparametric tests for ordinal data in APA format.

- To summarize any nonparametric test, report the test statistic and the p value for the test. The degrees of freedom for the chi-square distribution are also reported for the Friedman and the Kruskal-Wallis H tests.

LO 11: Compute the related-samples sign test, the Wilcoxon signed-ranks T test, the Mann-Whitney U test, the Kruskal-Wallis H test, and the Friedman test using SPSS.

- SPSS can be used to compute the related-samples sign test by selecting the Analyze, then Nonparametric tests and 2 Related Samples . . . , options in the menu bar. These actions will display a dialog box that allows you to choose the sign test, identify the groups, and run the test.

- SPSS can be used to compute the Wilcoxon signed-ranks T test by selecting the Analyze, then Nonparametric tests and 2 Related Samples . . . , options in the menu bar. These actions will display a dialog box that allows you to identify the groups and run the test.

- SPSS can be used to compute the Mann-Whitney U test by selecting the Analyze, then Nonparametric Tests and 2 Independent Samples, options in the menu bar. These actions will display a dialog box that allows you to identify the groups and run the test.

- SPSS can be used to compute the Kruskal-Wallis H test by selecting the Analyze, then Nonparametric Tests and k Independent Samples, options in the menu bar. These actions will display a dialog box that allows you to identify the groups and run the test.

- SPSS can be used to compute the Friedman test by selecting the Analyze, then Nonparametric Tests and k Related Samples, options in the menu bar. These actions will display a dialog box that allows you to identify the groups and run the test.

Appendix

General Instruction Guidebook for Using SPSS

The General Instructions Guidebook (GIG) for using SPSS provides standardized instructions for using SPSS to enter and analyze data. The instructions provided in the GIG are also given in the *Statistics for the Behavioral Sciences* textbook. Each chapter, except Chapter 8, gives at least one step-by-step SPSS in Focus section. These sections provide step-by-step instructions for using SPSS to enter data and compute the statistics taught in each chapter. On the other hand, this guidebook provides general instructions without the context of a specific example. You can use these instructions to complete each exercise and refer to the SPSS examples in the textbook to clear up any points of confusion.

The instructions here are organized by exercise in this guidebook to make it easier for you to find the appropriate instructions to complete each SPSS exercise. The instructions for each exercise are given with a reference for which SPSS in Focus section provides an example for following the steps. Note that the term *factor* is used in this guidebook to describe an independent variable and a quasi-independent variable. This guidebook does not distinguish between these types of variables because both can be entered and analyzed using SPSS.

Exercise 1.1: Entering and Defining Variables

This exercise is illustrated in Chapter 1, Section 1.7 (SPSS in Focus).

Enter data by column:

1. Open the Variable View tab. In the Name column, enter each variable name (one variable per row).

2. Go to the Decimals column and reduce the value to the degree of accuracy of the data.

3. Open the Data View tab. You will see that the each variable is now the title for each column. Enter the data for each variable in the appropriate column.

Enter data by row (this requires *coding* the grouped data):

1. Open the Variable View tab. Enter the variable name in the first row and a name of the dependent variable in the second row.

2. Go to the Decimals column and reduce the value to 0 for the first row because values in this column will be coded using whole numbers. Reduce the Decimals column value in the second row to the degree of accuracy of the data.

3. Go to the Values column in the first row and click on the small gray box with three dots. In the dialog box, enter a number in the Values cell and the name of each level of the factor in the Label cell. After each entry, select Add. Repeat these steps for each level of the factor, and then select OK. The data are now coded as numbers.

4. Open the Data View tab. In the first column, enter each code *n* times. For example, if you measure five scores at each level of the factor, then you will enter each number (or code) five times in the first column. In the second column, enter the values of the dependent variable. These values should match up with the levels of the factor you coded.

Exercise 2.1: Frequency Distributions for Quantitative Data

This exercise is illustrated in Chapter 2, Section 2.4 (SPSS in Focus).

1. Click on the Variable View tab and enter the variable name in the first row of the Name column. Reduce the Decimals column value in the first row to the degree of accuracy of the data.

2. Click on the Data View tab and enter the values of the variable in the first column. Enter the data in any order you wish, but make sure all the data are entered correctly.

3. Go to the menu bar and click Analyze, then Descriptive Statistics and Frequencies, to display a dialog box.

4. In the dialog box, select the variable name and click the arrow in the center to move the variable into the Variable(s): box to the right. Make sure the option to display frequency tables is selected.

5. Select OK, or select Paste and click the Run command.

Exercise 2.2: Frequency Distributions for Categorical Data

This exercise is illustrated in Chapter 2, Section 2.7 (SPSS in Focus).

1. Click on the Variable View tab and enter the variable name in the first row of the Name column. In the second row, enter *frequencies*. In the Decimals column, reduce the value to 0 in the first row and reduce it to the degree of accuracy of the data in the second row.

2. Code the data for the variable listed in the first row (refer to the instructions given in Exercise 1.1).

3. Click on the Data View tab and enter each numeric code one time in the first column. In the second column, enter the frequency across from the appropriate numeric code.

4. Go to Data, then Weight cases . . . to display a dialog box. Select Weight cases by and move *frequencies* into the Frequency Variable: box. Now each frequency is linked to each level of the variable.

5. Go to the menu bar and click Analyze, then Descriptive Statistics and Frequencies, to display a dialog box.

6. In the dialog box, select the variable and click the arrow in the center to move it into the box labeled Variable(s): to the right. Make sure the option to display frequency tables is selected.

7. Select OK, or select Paste and click the Run command.

Exercise 2.3: Histograms, Bar Charts, and Pie Charts

This exercise is illustrated in Chapter 2, Section 2.12 (SPSS in Focus).

1. Click on the Variable View tab and enter the variable name in the Name column. In the Decimals column, reduce the value to the degree of accuracy of the data.

2. Click on the Data View tab and enter the values for the variable in the first column. Enter the data in any order you wish, but make sure all the data are entered correctly.

3. Go to the menu bar and click Analyze, then Descriptive Statistics and Frequencies, to display a dialog box.

4. In the dialog box, select the variable name and click the arrow in the center to move it into the box labeled Variable(s): to the right. Because we only want the graphs and charts in this example, make sure the option to display frequency tables is not selected.

5. Click on the Charts option in the dialog box. Here you have the option to select bar charts, pie charts, or histograms. You can select only one at a time. Once you select a graph, select Continue.

6. Select OK, or select Paste and click the Run command.

Exercise 3.1: Mean, Median, and Mode

This exercise is illustrated in Chapter 3, Section 3.6 (SPSS in Focus).

1. Click on the Variable View tab and enter the variable name in the Name column. In the Decimals column, reduce the value to the degree of accuracy of the data.

2. Click on the Data View tab and enter the values for the variable in the first column.

3. Go to the menu bar and click Analyze, then Descriptive Statistics and Frequencies, to display a dialog box.

4. In the dialog box, select the variable name and click the arrow in the center, which will move it into the box labeled Variable(s): to the right. Make sure the option to display frequency tables is not selected, and then select Statistics to display another dialog box.

5. In this dialog box, select Mean, Median, and Mode to the right; then select Continue.

6. Select OK, or select Paste and click the Run command.

Exercise 4.1: Range, Variance, and Standard Deviation

This exercise is illustrated in Chapter 4, Section 4.11 (SPSS in Focus).

1. Click on the Variable View tab and enter the variable name in the Name column. In the Decimals column, reduce the value to the degree of accuracy of the data.

2. Click on the Data View tab and enter the values for the variable in the first column.

3. Go to the menu bar and click Analyze, then Descriptive Statistics and Frequencies, to display a dialog box.

4. In the dialog box, select the variable name and click the arrow in the center, which will move it into the box labeled Variable(s): to the right. Make sure the option to display frequency tables is not selected, and then select Statistics to display another dialog box.

5. In this dialog box, select Std. deviation, Variance, and Range; then select Continue.

6. Select OK, or select Paste and click the Run command.

Exercise 5.1: Probability Tables

This exercise is illustrated in Chapter 5, Section 5.6 (SPSS in Focus).

Construct a probability table:

1. Click on the Variable View tab and enter the first variable in the Name column. Below that enter the second variable name in the same column. Because the variables will be coded, reduce the value in the Decimals column to 0 for both rows. In the third row, enter *frequencies* in the Name column and reduce the Decimals column value to 0.

2. Code the levels of the variables listed in the first two rows (refer to the instructions given in Exercise 1.1).

3. Go to the Data View and enter the numeric codes in the first and second columns. For example, for a 2 × 2 contingency table, enter 1, 1, 2, 2 down the first column, and enter 1,

2, 1, 2 down the second column. In the third column, enter the corresponding frequencies for each coded cell.

4. Go to Data, then Weight cases ... to display a dialog box. Select Weight cases by and move *frequencies* into the Frequency Variable: box. Now each frequency is linked to each cell.

5. Go to the menu bar and click Analyze, then Descriptive Statistics and Crosstabs, to display a dialog box.

6. In the dialog box, select the first coded variable and click the top arrow to move it into the Row(s): box to the right. Next, select the second coded variable and click the arrow to move it into the Column(s): box to the right.

7. Select OK, or select Paste and click the Run command.

Construct a conditional probability table:

1. Follow Steps 1 to 7 for constructing a probability table.

2. Next, click Cells ... to display another dialog box. Select the Row, Column, and Total options under the Percentages heading to the left and select Continue.

3. Select OK, or select Paste and click the Run command.

Exercise 6.1: Converting Raw Scores to Standard z Scores

This exercise is illustrated in Chapter 6, Section 6.8 (SPSS in Focus).

1. Click on the Variable View tab and enter the variable name in the Name column. In the Decimals column, reduce the value to the degree of accuracy of the data.

2. Click on the Data View tab and enter the values for the variable in the first column.

3. Go to the menu bar and click Analyze, then Descriptive Statistics and Descriptives, to display a dialog box.

4. In the dialog box, select the variable name and click the arrow to move it into the Variable(s): box. Select the "Save standardized values as variables" box.

5. Select OK, or select Paste and click the Run command.

Exercise 7.1: Estimating the Standard Error of the Mean

This exercise is illustrated in Chapter 7, Section 7.7 (SPSS in Focus).

1. Click on the Variable View tab and enter the variable name in the Name column. In the Decimals column, reduce the value to the degree of accuracy of the data.

2. Click on the Data View tab and enter the values for the variable in the first column.

3. Go to the menu bar and click Analyze, then Descriptive Statistics and Descriptives, to display a dialog box.

4. In the dialog box, select the variable name and click the arrow to move it into the box labeled Variable(s): to the right. Click the Options . . . tab to display a new dialog box.

5. In the new dialog box, select S.E. mean in the Dispersion box and click Continue.

6. Select OK, or select Paste and click the Run command.

Exercise 9.1: One-Sample *t* Test

This exercise is illustrated in Chapter 9, Section 9.6 (SPSS in Focus).

1. Click on the Variable View tab and enter the variable name in the Name column. In the Decimals column, reduce the value to the degree of accuracy of the data.

2. Click on the Data View tab and enter the values for the variable in the first column.

3. Go to the menu bar and click Analyze, then Compare Means and One-Sample T Test, to display a dialog box.

4. In the dialog box, select the variable name and click the arrow in the middle to move it to the Test Variable(s): box.

5. Enter the value stated in the null hypothesis in the Test Value: box. The value in SPSS is 0 by default.

6. Select OK, or select Paste and click the Run command.

Exercise 9.2: Two-Independent-Sample *t* Test

This exercise is illustrated in Chapter 9, Section 9.9 (SPSS in Focus).

1. Click on the Variable View tab and enter the factor in the Name column. In the second row, enter the name of the dependent variable in the Name column. Reduce the value to 0 in the Decimals column in the first row and to the degree of accuracy of the data in the second row.

2. In the Values column, code the levels of the factor listed in the first row (refer to the instructions given in Exercise 1.1).

3. In the Data View tab, enter each code *n* times in the first column. For example, if you measure five scores in each group (or at each level of the factor), then enter each numeric code five times in the first column. In the second column, enter the values for the dependent variable so that they correspond with the code for each group.

4. Go to the menu bar and click Analyze, then Compare Means and Independent-Samples T Test, to display a dialog box.

5. Using the arrows to move the variables, select the dependent variable and place it in the Test Variable(s): box; select the factor and move it into the Grouping Variable: box. Two question marks will appear in the Grouping Variable: box.

6. Click Define Groups . . . to display a new dialog box. Place the numeric code for each group in the spaces provided and then click Continue. The numeric codes should now appear in the Grouping Variable: box (instead of question marks).

7. Select OK, or select Paste and click the Run command.

Exercise 10.1: The Related-Samples *t* Test

This exercise is illustrated in Chapter 10, Section 10.4 (SPSS in Focus).

1. Click on the Variable View tab and enter the name of the first group in the Name column in the first row; enter the name of the second group in the second row. Reduce the Decimals column value in both rows to the degree of accuracy of the data.

2. Click on the Data View tab. Enter the data for each group. Each pair of scores should line up in each row.

3. Go to the menu bar and click Analyze, then Compare Means and Paired-Samples T Test, to display a dialog box.

4. In the dialog box, select each group in the left box and move them to the right box using the arrow in the middle. The groups should be side by side in the box to the right.

5. Select OK, or select Paste and click the Run command.

Exercise 11.1: Confidence Intervals for the One-Sample *t* Test

This exercise is illustrated in Chapter 11, Section 11.5 (SPSS in Focus).

1. Follow Steps 1 to 5 in Exercise 9.1. Select Options . . . to change the level of confidence for a confidence interval. By default, the level of confidence is set at 95%. Then select Continue.

2. Select OK, or select Paste and click the Run command.

Exercise 11.2: Confidence Intervals for the Two-Independent-Sample *t* Test

This exercise is illustrated in Chapter 11, Section 11.7 (SPSS in Focus).

1. Follow Steps 1 to 6 in Exercise 9.2. Select Options . . . to change the level of confidence for a confidence interval. By default, the level of confidence is set at 95%. Then select Continue.

2. Select OK, or select Paste and click the Run command.

Exercise 11.3: Confidence Intervals for the Related-Samples *t* Test

This exercise is illustrated in Chapter 11, Section 11.9 (SPSS in Focus).

1. Follow Steps 1 to 4 in Exercise 10.1. Select Options . . . to change the level of confidence for a confidence interval. By default, the level of confidence is set at 95%. Then select Continue.

2. Select OK, or select Paste and click the Run command.

Exercise 12.1: The One-Way Between-Subjects ANOVA

This exercise is illustrated in Chapter 12, Section 12.8 (SPSS in Focus).

Compute this test using the One-Way ANOVA command:

1. Click on the Variable View tab and enter the name of the factor in the Name column. Go to the Decimals column for this row and reduce the value to 0 (because this variable will be coded). In the second row, enter the name of the dependent variable in the Name column. Reduce the Decimals column value in the second row to the degree of accuracy of the data.

2. In the Values column, code the levels of the factor listed in the first row (refer to the instructions given in Exercise 1.1).

3. In the Data View tab, enter each code *n* times in the first column. For example, if you measure five scores in each group (or level), then enter each numeric code five times in the first column. In the second column, enter the values for the dependent variable so that they correspond with the codes for each group.

4. Go to the menu bar and click Analyze, then Compare Means and One-Way ANOVA, to display a dialog box.

5. Using the appropriate arrows, move the factor into the Factor: box. Move the dependent variable into the Dependent List: box.

6. Click the Post Hoc option to display a new dialog box. Select an appropriate post hoc test and click Continue.

7. Select OK, or select Paste and click the Run command.

Compute this test using the GLM Univariate command:

1. Follow Steps 1 to 3 for using the One-Way ANOVA command.

2. Go to the menu bar and click Analyze, then General Linear Model and Univariate, to display a dialog box.

3. Using the appropriate arrows, move the factor into the Fixed Factor(s): box. Move the dependent variable into the Dependent Variable: box.

4. Select the Post Hoc . . . option to display a new dialog box, which will give you the option to perform post hoc comparisons so long as you move the factor into the Post Hoc Tests for: box. Select an appropriate post hoc test and click Continue.

5. Select OK, or select Paste and click the Run command.

Exercise 13.1: The One-Way Within-Subjects ANOVA

This exercise is illustrated in Chapter 13, Section 13.6 (SPSS in Focus).

1. Click on the Variable View tab and enter the name of each group (or level of the factor) in the Name column. One group should be entered in each row. Go to the Decimals column and reduce the value to the degree of accuracy of the data for each row.

2. Click on the Data View tab. Each group is now listed in each column. Enter the data for each respective column.

3. Go to the menu bar and click Analyze, then General Linear Model and Repeated Measures, to display a dialog box.

4. In the Within-Subject Factor Name box, enter a name for the repeated-measures factor. In the Number of Levels box, SPSS is asking for the number of levels of the factor (or the number of groups). Enter the number, and the Add option will illuminate. Click Add, and the factor (with the number of levels in parentheses) will appear in the box below. Click Define to display a new dialog box.

5. In the dialog box, use the appropriate arrows to move each column into the Within-Subjects Variables (cues) box.

6. Then select Options to display a new dialog box. To compute effect size, use the arrow to move the factor into the Display Means for: box. Then check the Compare main effects option. Using the drop-down arrow under the Confidence interval adjustment heading, select an appropriate post hoc test. Then select Continue.

7. Select OK, or select Paste and click the Run command.

Exercise 14.1: The Two-Way Between-Subjects ANOVA

This exercise is illustrated in Chapter 14, Section 14.8 (SPSS in Focus).

1. Click on the Variable View tab and enter the name of each factor (one in each row) in the Name column; in the third row, enter a name of the dependent variable in the Name column. Reduce the value to 0 in the Decimals column for the first two rows (for both factors). Reduce the value to the degree of accuracy of the data in the third row.

2. In the Values column, code the levels of both factors listed in the first two rows (refer to the instructions given in Exercise 1.1).

3. In the Data View tab, enter each code for the first factor n times in the first column. Enter each code for the second factor n times in the second column. The two columns create the cells. In the second column, enter the values for the dependent variable such that the data in each cell are listed across from the corresponding codes for each cell.

4. Go to the menu bar and click Analyze, then General Linear Model and Univariate, to display a dialog box.

5. Use the appropriate arrows to move the factors into the Fixed Factor(s): box. Move the dependent variable into the Dependent Variable: box.

6. Finally, click Options to display a new dialog box. In the Factor(s) and Factor Interactions box, move the main effects and interaction into the Display Means for: box by using the arrow. Then click Continue.

7. Select Post Hoc . . . to display another dialog box. Use the arrow to bring both main effects from the Factor(s) box into the Post Hoc Tests for: box. Select an appropriate pairwise comparison for the main effects. (*Note:* SPSS does not perform simple effect tests. If you get a significant interaction, you will have to conduct these tests separately.) To obtain an estimate of the power for each hypothesis test, select Observed power and click Continue.

8. Select OK, or select Paste and click the Run command.

Exercise 15.1: Pearson Correlation Coefficient

This exercise is illustrated in Chapter 15, Section 15.4 (SPSS in Focus).

1. Click on the Variable View tab and enter the first variable name in the Name column; enter the second variable name in the Name column below it. Go to the Decimals column and reduce the value to the degree of accuracy of the data for each row.

2. Click on the Data View tab. Enter the data for each variable in the appropriate columns.

3. Go to the menu bar and click Analyze, then Correlate and Bivariate, to display a dialog box.

4. Using the arrows, move both variables into the Variables box.

5. Select OK, or select Paste and click the Run command.

Exercise 15.2: Spearman Correlation Coefficient

This exercise is illustrated in Chapter 15, Section 15.8 (SPSS in Focus).

1. Click on the Variable View tab and enter the first variable name in the Name column; enter the second variable name in the Name column below it. Go to the Decimals column and reduce the value to the degree of accuracy of the data for each row.

2. Click on the Data View tab. Enter the original scores or ranks (including tied ranks) for each variable in the appropriate columns.

3. Go to the menu bar and click Analyze, then Correlate and Bivariate, to display a dialog box.

4. Using the arrows, move both variables into the Variables: box. Uncheck the Pearson box and check the Spearman box in the Correlation Coefficients portion of the dialog box.

5. Select OK, or select Paste and click the Run command.

Exercise 15.3: Point-Biserial Correlation Coefficient

This exercise is illustrated in Chapter 15, Section 15.10 (SPSS in Focus).

1. Click on the Variable View tab and enter the name of the dichotomous factor in the Name column; enter the name of the continuous factor in the Name column below it. Go to the Decimals column and reduce the value to 0 for the dichotomous factor and to the degree of accuracy of the data for the continuous factor.

2. In the Values column, code the levels of the dichotomous factor listed in the first row (refer to the instructions given in Exercise 1.1).

3. Click on the Data View tab. In the first column, enter each code n times such that the number of codes entered for each level of the dichotomous factor is equal to the number of scores at each level of the dichotomous factor. In the second column, enter the values of the continuous factor as they correspond with the levels of the dichotomous variable.

4. Go to the menu bar and click Analyze, then Correlate and Bivariate, to display a dialog box.

5. Using the arrows, move both factors into the Variables: box.

6. Select OK, or select Paste and click the Run command.

Exercise 15.4: Phi Correlation Coefficient

This exercise is illustrated in Chapter 15, Section 15.12 (SPSS in Focus).

1. Click on the Variable View tab and enter the name of the first dichotomous factor in the Name column. Below that enter the name of the second dichotomous factor in the same column. Because these factors will be coded, go to the Decimals column and reduce the value to 0 for both rows. In the third row, enter *frequencies* in the Name column and reduce the Decimals column value to 0.

2. In the Values column, code the levels of the dichotomous factors listed in the first two rows (refer to the instructions given in Exercise 1.1).

3. Go to the Data View and enter the numeric codes in the first and second columns. For a phi correlation coefficient, always enter 1, 1, 2, and 2 in the first column and enter 1, 2, 1, and

2 in the second column. In the third column, enter the corresponding frequencies for each coded cell.

4. Go to the menu bar and click Data, then Weight Cases . . . , to display a new dialog box. Select Weight cases by and move the *frequencies* column into the Frequency Variable: box, and then select OK.

5. Again, go to the menu bar and click Analyze, then Correlate and Bivariate, to display a dialog box. Use the arrows to move both dichotomous factors into the Variables: box.

6. Select OK, or select Paste and click the Run command.

Exercise 16.1: Analysis of Regression

This exercise is illustrated in Chapter 16, Section 16.7 (SPSS in Focus).

1. Click on the Variable View tab and enter the predictor variable name in the Name column; enter the criterion variable name in the Name column below it. Go to the Decimals column and reduce the value in both rows to the degree of accuracy for the data.

2. Click on the Data View tab. Enter the data for the predictor variable (X) in the first column. Enter the data for the criterion variable (Y) in the second column.

3. Go to the menu bar and click Analyze, then Regression and Linear, to display a dialog box.

4. Use the arrows to move the predictor variable into the Independent(s) box; move the criterion variable into the Dependent box.

5. Select OK, or select Paste and click the Run command.

Exercise 16.2: Multiple Regression Analysis

This exercise is illustrated in Chapter 16, Section 16.13 (SPSS in Focus).

1. Click on the Variable View tab and enter each predictor variable and the criterion variable in a separate cell in the Name column. In the Decimals column, reduce the value in each row to the degree of accuracy for the data.

2. Click on the Data View tab. Enter the data for each predictor variable and the criterion variable in the corresponding columns.

3. Go to the menu bar and click Analyze, then Regression and Linear, to display the dialog box.

4. Using the arrows, move each predictor variable into the box labeled Independent(s); move the criterion variable into the box labeled Dependent.

5. Select OK, or select Paste and click the Run command.

Exercise 17.1: The Chi-Square Goodness-of-Fit Test

This exercise is illustrated in Chapter 17, Section 17.3 (SPSS in Focus).

1. Click on the Variable View tab and enter the nominal variable name in the Name column in the first row; enter *frequencies* in the Name column below it. Go to the Decimals column and reduce the value to 0 for both rows.

2. In the Values column, code the levels of the nominal variable listed in the first row (refer to the instructions given in Exercise 1.1).

3. Click on the Data View tab. In the first column, enter each coded value one time. In the second column, enter the observed frequencies that correspond to each coded value.

4. Go to the menu bar and click Data, then Weight Cases by, to display a dialog box. In the new dialog box, click Weight cases by and move *frequencies* into the Frequency Variable cell. Select OK.

5. Go to the menu bar and click Analyze, then Nonparametric Tests and Chi-square, to display a new dialog box.

6. Using the arrows, move the nominal variable into the Test Variable List: box. In the Expected Values box, notice that we have two options: We can assume that all expected frequencies are equal, or we can enter the frequencies for each cell. If the expected frequencies are equal, then leave this alone; if they are not equal, then enter the expected frequencies one at a time and click Add to move them into the cell.

7. Select OK, or select Paste and click the Run command.

Exercise 17.2: The Chi-Square Test for Independence

This exercise is illustrated in Chapter 17, Section 17.9 (SPSS in Focus).

1. To organize the data, write out the contingency table on a separate piece of paper such that one variable is listed in the row and a second variable is listed in the column. Click on the Variable View tab, and in the Name column, enter the name of the *row* variable in the first row and the name of the *column* variable in the second row. In the third row, enter *frequencies* in the Name column. Reduce the value to 0 in each row in the Decimals column.

2. In the Values column, code the levels of both nominal variables listed in the first two rows (refer to the instructions given in Exercise 1.1).

3. In the Data View tab, set up the cells by row and column. Enter the codes for the row and column variable in the appropriately labeled column. For example, if the *row* variable has two levels and the *column* variable has three levels, then enter 1, 1, 1, 2, 2, and 2 in the first column of the Data View. Set up the cells in the second column by entering the levels in numeric order across from each level of the *row* variable. Using the same example, enter 1,

2, 3, 1, 2, and 3 in the second column. The two columns create the cells. Enter the corresponding observed frequencies for each cell in the third column.

4. Go to the menu bar and click Data, then Weight Cases by, to display a dialog box. In the new dialog box, click Weight cases by and move *frequencies* into the Frequency Variable: cell. This tells SPSS that the frequencies you enter are those for each row–column combination. Select OK.

5. Go to the menu bar and click Analyze, then Descriptive Statistics and Crosstabs, to display a dialog box.

6. Using the arrows, move the *row* variable into the Row(s) box and move the *column* variable into the Column(s) box. Click Statistics . . . to open a new dialog box.

7. Select Chi-square in the top left. To compute effect size, select Phi and Cramer's V in the box labeled Nominal. Click Continue.

8. Select OK, or select Paste and click the Run command.

Exercise 18.1: The Related-Samples Sign Test

This exercise is illustrated in Chapter 18, Section 18.3 (SPSS in Focus).

1. Click on the Variable View tab and enter the name of the first level of the factor in the Name column in the first row; enter the name of the second level of the factor in the second row. Reduce the Decimals column value in both rows to the degree of accuracy of the data.

2. Click on the Data View tab. Enter the data for each level of the factor. Make sure the scores for each related pair are matched in each row.

3. Go to the menu bar and click Analyze, then Nonparametric Tests and 2 Related Samples . . . , to display a dialog box.

4. In the dialog box, select each level of the factor in the left box and move them to the right box using the arrow in the middle. The variables should be side by side in the box to the right. In the Test Type box, make sure that only the box next to Sign is checked.

5. Select OK, or select Paste and click the Run command.

Exercise 18.2: The Wilcoxon Signed-Ranks *T* Test

This exercise is illustrated in Chapter 18, Section 18.5 (SPSS in Focus).

1. Click on the Variable View tab and enter the name of the first level of the factor in the Name column in the first row; enter the name of the second level of the factor in the second row. Reduce the Decimals column value in both rows to the degree of accuracy of the data.

2. Click on the Data View tab. Enter the data for each level of the factor. Make sure the scores for each related pair are matched in each row.

3. Go to the menu bar and click Analyze, then Nonparametric Tests and 2 Related Samples . . . , to display a dialog box.

4. In the dialog box, select each level of the factor in the left box and move them to the right box using the arrow in the middle. The variables should be side by side in the box to the right. In the Test Type box, make sure that only the box next to Wilcoxon is checked.

5. Select OK, or select Paste and click the Run command.

Exercise 18.3: The Mann-Whitney U Test

This exercise is illustrated in Chapter 18, Section 18.7 (SPSS in Focus).

1. Click on the Variable View tab and enter the factor in the Name column. In the second row, enter the name of the dependent variable in the Name column. Reduce the value to 0 in the Decimals column in the first row and to the degree of accuracy of the data in the second row.

2. In the Values column, code the levels of the factor listed in the first row (refer to the instructions given in Exercise 1.1).

3. In the Data View tab, enter each code n times in the first column. For example, if you measure five scores in each group (or level), then enter each numeric code five times in the first column. In the second column, enter the values for the dependent variable so that they correspond with the code for each group.

4. Go to the menu bar and click Analyze, then Nonparametric Tests and 2 Independent Samples, to display a dialog box.

5. Notice that Mann-Whitney U is selected by default. Using the arrows, move the dependent variable into the Test Variable List box and the factor into the Grouping Variable box. Click Define Groups . . . to open a new dialog box. Place the numeric code for each group in the spaces provided and then click Continue.

6. Select OK, or select Paste and click the Run command.

Exercise 18.4: The Kruskal-Wallis H Test

This exercise is illustrated in Chapter 18, Section 18.9 (SPSS in Focus).

1. Click on the Variable View tab and enter the name of the factor in the Name column. Go to the Decimals column for this row and reduce the value to 0 (because this variable will be coded). In the second row, enter the name of the dependent variable in the Name column. Reduce the Decimals column value in the second row to the degree of accuracy of the data.

2. In the Values column, code the levels of the factor listed in the first row (refer to the instructions given in Exercise 1.1).

3. In the Data View tab, enter each code *n* times in the first column. For example, if you measure five scores in each group (or level), then enter each numeric code five times in the first column. In the second column, enter the values for the dependent variable so that they correspond with the codes for each group.

4. Go to the menu bar and click Analyze, then Nonparametric Tests and k Independent Samples, to display a dialog box.

5. Notice that Kruskal-Wallis *H* is selected by default. Using the arrows, move the dependent variable into the Test Variable List box and the factor into the Grouping Variable box. Click Define Groups . . . to open a new dialog box. Enter the range of codes entered. Select Continue.

6. Select OK, or select Paste and click the Run command.

Exercise 18.5: The Friedman Test

This exercise is illustrated in Chapter 18, Section 18.11 (SPSS in Focus).

1. Click on the Variable View tab and enter the name of each level of the factor in the Name column. One level (or group) should be listed in each row. Go to the Decimals column and reduce the value to the degree of accuracy of the data.

2. Click on the Data View tab. Each column is now labeled with each level of the factor. Enter the data for each respective column.

3. Go to the menu bar and click Analyze, then Nonparametric Tests and k Related Samples, to display a dialog box.

4. Notice that Friedman is selected by default. Use the arrows to move each column into the Test Variables box.

5. Select OK, or select Paste and click the Run command.

Answers to Key Term Word Searches and Crossword Puzzles

Chapter 1

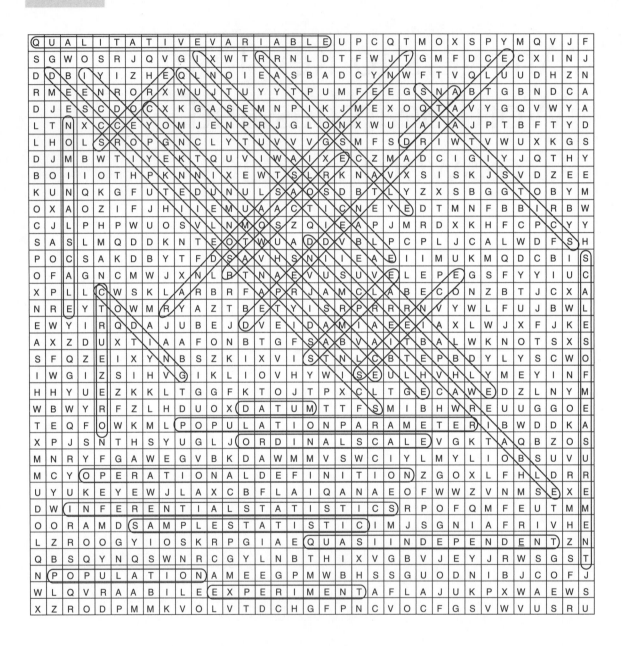

Chapter 1

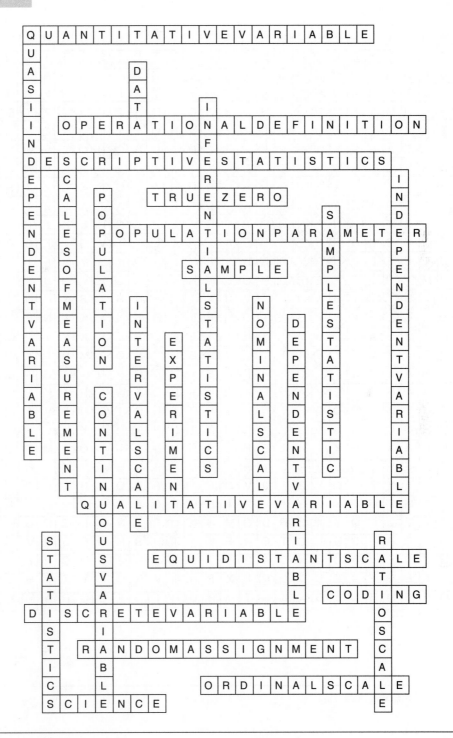

Chapter 2

```
K Q M D D Y Q K B R J R E L A T I V E P E R C E N T B B Q U E
S I M P L E F R E Q U E N C Y D I S T R I B U T I O N D L O M
N B D X O H Y Q G Z U O P E N C L A S S E S C X A Q S V W G N
K J L I T M M J Q R C L A S S W I D T H P C F N X R D G E J P
G P F N U M K E C D O K H M B Q Q Z U N Z F J Y Z T D R K S M
S H T R X P Z O Z U L U S T Y V Y H O I T C C N O B G C R Z A
Y H G J E A G E Y W M P P A R C D I U R Q N O L V W X T K T M
X A Q F V Q D A W M T U R E N Y T S A O E R P N V W I N N P X
X Y U M F K U E X R P B L E D R D H W U U F S L X X S I G A I
O T O A D R A E A U M E U A O D C E Q G A T A R Z I O O Q E B
K R N S Z F H N A N O R P T R A E P E C H L K S P Y P I V S
O C Z T Y S C O R C E G O C A I R T L T V G I E B E E Y C U
G X U I E E L G U R Y R R B E F V D A D K D Y L E I Z N R U K
I I O M I R O T F E P D N O E N N E I K L F I N J R Y I E M P
V Z V P U T V I H N N L I V U A T W R G R T S I G H S N A U C
E O E K C L F A H P B C I S M P L I H E N X K A N B L T L L I
N B K I Z G A V L U M T Y E T A E C L E L X X Y Y H O E R A Q
F P P G J Y M T Y B A T T P V R B D C E O A M B P X W R A T J
S Y S N A C Y Z I L O S A R O S I R D G R W T A H W E V N I A
B T H W W R R U E V A U E K W L E B O A W A R I K E R A G V P
C K E W Y W T R Q Q E N L V P Y E U Q T G N P V T B L E E R
C K O M O D N A U D N P X D G B T G R T R A Y K L E O S R F M
H M L G A X K G Y I K T E R A S N M O A I I O A M S U B O R Y
W H N M F R E Q U E N C Y R J R U A B N S O V K J H N X O E U
E K V K F Y Z F Q X G I J V C F I C P P Q R N V E C D Y Q Q C
I Q W A M T M T K G U I V X I E D E G A E N V R R O A K D U M
Q E E X B C U O T X Z H D Q M A N Q S T N Z L C Q G R O F E T
U L U Y G B L C D L O T Q N F V I T N S H V C B P V Y R W N C
A L U P P E R B O U N D A R Y I S I S V S S M C H P V B T C P
R C X P E G F S E C T O R F X P H T V B O F Y Z F H L N K Y W
X Q O H F M H N L G X K W T M H D H I S T O G R A M X T J X Y
```

SOURCE: www.variety-games.com.

Chapter 2

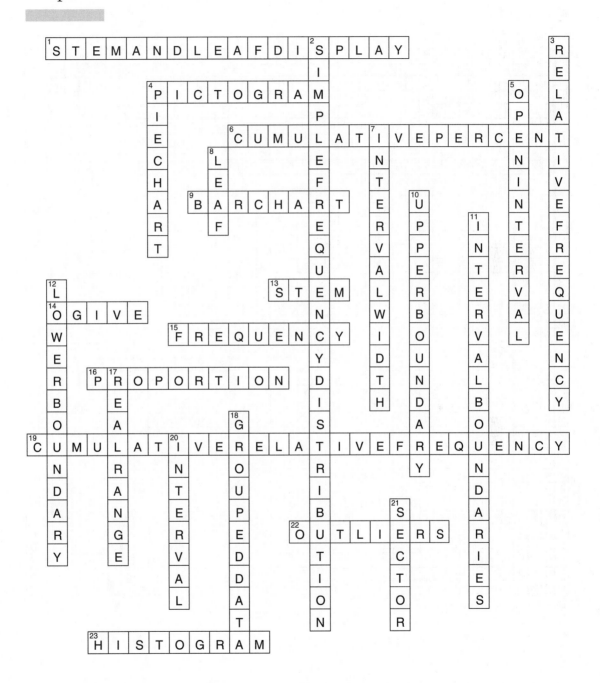

SOURCE: www.variety-games.com.

Chapter 3

G	U	Z	N	K	Z	F	Z	K	R	K	X	J	A	C	X	M	Z	R	O	L	Q	L	Y	M	Y	J	X	L	I	Z	E	M	L	P	E	V	Y	O	V
N	N	D	S	M	P	E	R	W	Z	Y	G	P	X	Q	N	K	N	X	A	B	M	Q	H	O	B	S	F	K	Y	K	X	C	O	K	W	K	S	D	W
O	I	U	G	A	U	S	S	I	A	N	D	I	S	T	R	I	B	U	T	I	O	N	J	U	B	K	Y	E	T	B	O	Z	A	C	M	H	U	X	B
R	M	E	V	E	K	W	Y	H	Y	O	A	D	B	N	T	C	S	J	A	G	H	K	G	J	J	I	R	R	L	X	H	P	I	R	O	J	R	P	N
M	O	A	V	E	R	A	G	E	T	Z	V	N	D	V	Y	A	R	O	U	W	I	S	G	N	P	Q	Y	M	U	B	F	H	V	A	D	H	K	U	K
A	D	D	C	N	F	Q	B	L	T	H	L	K	J	Q	B	I	M	O	D	A	L	D	I	S	T	R	I	B	U	T	I	O	N	H	A	C	X	M	O
L	A	P	P	J	V	B	S	T	C	S	R	T	N	R	D	O	N	F	H	K	S	J	D	C	F	C	V	J	N	B	L	L	C	K	L	H	L	U	R
D	L	B	Z	J	L	I	K	M	Z	H	X	C	D	W	X	D	J	S	F	E	M	M	D	T	F	I	F	A	G	G	Q	D	J	R	D	W	M	L	G
I	D	X	Y	J	Y	Q	D	X	E	T	P	O	S	I	T	I	V	E	L	Y	S	K	E	W	E	D	R	F	Q	E	I	B	K	F	I	D	Z	T	F
S	I	X	G	W	E	C	D	J	S	Y	M	M	E	T	R	I	C	A	L	D	I	S	T	R	I	B	U	T	I	O	N	E	F	T	S	R	T	I	T
T	S	M	A	K	E	X	L	T	W	F	V	J	G	O	M	D	O	W	X	E	G	Y	G	S	R	O	Z	T	W	F	O	K	J	G	T	L	Z	M	T
R	T	Q	T	L	Q	I	Q	J	X	E	V	R	S	R	Z	O	N	H	O	K	V	N	T	J	W	X	R	X	Q	R	K	Z	A	D	R	M	J	O	Y
I	R	C	M	O	Q	P	G	I	O	V	X	G	B	W	R	A	C	V	V	P	M	Z	G	X	N	Y	S	S	G	T	V	Q	P	F	I	P	Q	D	P
B	I	L	C	V	H	A	U	H	G	E	F	N	P	Y	Q	P	B	Z	Q	H	E	F	N	Z	J	S	E	Y	Q	X	W	C	U	A	B	O	G	A	R
U	B	W	E	G	B	B	O	H	T	U	A	J	I	O	T	T	Y	W	I	R	T	Q	M	Q	L	B	G	G	X	H	X	K	W	J	U	P	B	L	L
T	U	M	N	S	Z	T	E	V	X	E	B	A	J	E	P	E	Q	Q	Z	F	B	H	G	C	M	I	J	V	P	P	Z	E	H	K	T	U	K	D	D
I	T	Z	T	R	G	I	G	L	G	X	D	O	V	V	O	U	L	G	H	X	P	Q	Y	B	V	C	Q	G	P	D	C	W	J	D	I	L	V	I	T
O	I	T	R	E	Q	Z	A	A	L	F	K	M	H	S	Z	E	L	T	K	H	X	W	D	N	S	A	J	F	F	O	I	N	S	R	O	A	F	S	D
N	O	J	A	C	N	K	Z	R	B	S	V	V	E	H	H	S	F	A	I	F	C	R	J	F	Z	S	G	Z	J	R	D	M	O	O	N	T	B	T	R
M	N	M	L	T	T	C	P	P	Q	H	I	K	A	F	C	A	V	G	A	V	B	A	C	X	Z	H	S	Y	Y	D	A	W	F	I	G	R	N
N	T	G	T	A	U	Q	U	F	L	T	F	A	Q	N	N	A	A	V	T	Q	G	D	C	R	I	L	N	L	D	R	F	T	U	E	O	L	I	P
T	B	X	E	N	R	V	G	F	M	U	H	P	V	K	P	P	W	Z	M	O	Y	I	S	Z	X	F	Y	C	Z	V	R	Y	O	L	N	R	B	A
E	X	H	N	G	Y	Y	B	U	Z	Y	Q	M	W	E	Y	P	D	V	G	S	T	N	V	M	M	L	R	N	D	U	S	A	P	G	X	U	J	U	S
V	F	R	D	U	P	A	N	N	W	N	S	B	E	H	D	J	S	K	E	W	E	D	D	S	T	R	I	B	U	T	I	O	N	O	S	A	T	N
W	Z	K	E	L	F	V	Q	E	F	O	S	M	G	T	T	D	V	D	J	U	K	S	S	M	N	G	U	Y	D	R	R	F	Y	Y	U	I	K	I	K
E	C	H	N	A	W	A	E	A	G	C	S	M	E	H	I	M	I	L	V	F	K	N	T	H	E	I	O	V	T	T	X	W	T	N	P	Z	S	O	H
T	I	W	C	R	P	S	W	N	U	A	G	R	Q	A	U	C	T	S	M	L	S	V	M	V	L	A	F	M	B	V	I	J	O	Y	D	E	L	N	M
M	A	F	Y	D	N	E	O	G	N	N	N	T	Z	Y	A	N	R	M	X	T	A	Z	G	M	E	X	B	N	U	H	B	G	G	A	G	I	I	P	Z	Q
V	E	E	T	I	U	O	Z	H	D	P	Y	I	H	M	G	M	J	E	Y	R	H	J	H	L	Z	N	K	S	S	D	G	Y	O	Z	E	F	J	I	F
N	S	G	L	S	G	S	F	B	I	D	M	V	V	U	W	C	Y	A	Z	A	D	R	I	T	M	B	K	S	J	P	P	U	C	C	Y	G	W
F	B	Y	A	T	G	A	Y	E	H	F	X	I	L	E	B	L	B	F	F	N	F	B	Q	X	T	G	E	B	N	W	M	S	J	K	S	X	O	Z	X
X	A	Z	X	R	S	M	D	L	H	E	C	H	H	D	O	O	W	X	H	E	J	U	C	Y	X	X	M	K	M	L	Y	U	E	K	X	B	N	E
E	F	I	Y	I	T	P	I	Z	Z	Z	G	O	I	E	U	N	V	Q	E	X	Y	Z	T	D	M	M	G	R	N	M	Z	R	J	G	Q	K	K	R
O	I	P	U	B	Z	L	X	Y	G	W	D	H	D	H	J	U	S	S	E	O	E	B	S	V	S	C	U	M	A	I	W	I	S	U	K	W	G	H
P	C	Y	C	U	F	E	G	Q	C	J	J	E	P	W	R	B	B	K	G	J	Y	T	Q	N	Z	O	N	W	Q	J	N	M	M	L	N	T	L	C	N
D	B	Q	C	T	V	S	M	F	P	S	L	I	K	L	F	G	R	O	E	B	X	N	Q	B	D	L	N	F	P	W	C	O	E	Q	W	P	T	M	I
N	A	K	E	I	N	I	M	O	B	U	N	F	M	E	E	H	U	Z	R	W	O	P	X	B	Y	E	W	Y	G	P	C	D	D	Z	V	V	O	X	D
R	G	G	K	O	O	Z	L	Z	P	H	P	G	T	L	R	V	W	X	X	F	X	K	M	C	G	H	H	W	L	C	E	I	Z	R	Q	O	A	N
A	N	P	D	N	C	E	Q	I	S	A	M	P	L	E	M	E	A	N	I	U	I	D	Y	D	U	X	G	C	Y	X	J	A	A	S	F	E	A	C	G
O	N	M	I	G	X	O	Q	F	K	E	V	I	I	U	C	G	B	R	T	H	E	M	U	Y	E	Z	A	U	G	N	H	I	N	W	N	M	X	O	C

Chapter 3

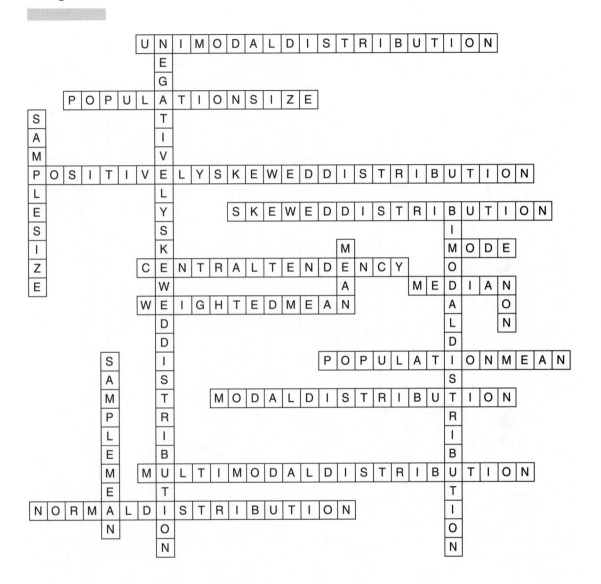

Chapter 4

```
U O V P E Q Q J O P B O P C Y J F Y S B V D I P O Q V X Q G R J D S E H F T L T
X J O E G F X C X Q R D L I C I R G G B O U T S I X R K K V S Q T E E U R H Z B
J Q N Y G Y C F B B W Q Z M K F D P V V I N N S C X B J H O K B S M E W L A W N
U F R Q I O E S D J Y R C L D T V D V V I X S Y N R U X V Q Z F G I C A P Q X E
S T A N D A R D D E V I A T I O N X D P X F X Z I W H P O L A H F I B E W N T D
Q T H X N E K T K A L N C Y Y R X D Z O S P Q K F J K P R A F X D N C X U N S J
Q H K P P M L H E B I C J N D B X U E P M G O X N X T S F C H K E T D K H G A V
P D Z E C P A I B M M I D R A N G E H U N C W G I T H H V T U M W E X G E X M Q
D Z Z F W I F H Q E I E M O P L L L F L D G A C L V D M N B D H C R X Y D R P X
N I H F Q R Z R O Z C H E D I B K R D A X X O S D V S I D E J B K Q F I L X L O
X C X X Q I A K W W A F D K T C W L U T A F D F K N P W N V I N O U X N V F E U
D I T F H C W E V G V M I Y J B M Q Q I E F U I P M P I B D F B J A I T D J V E
Z Y O R O A T J Z J E R A C X D T W W O Y S Q L O L Q S L E E Q C R M E Y S A C
U K D X Z L B L V U Z I N X F D Z L F N N K K S P S M O H V F K P T S R W X R F
Z A D S P R Q B Y X W G Q L V Q L H V S G A E E U X Z E O H J B V I D Q V C I T
R W C Y C U U U D X F A U O Q G V G P T N E X C L C Z A D Z J L N L E U Z Y A R
S Q B X U L A N W D E K A W U S S J E A X B A X A I Q J A C M Z E G A S W N B
U I K O Z E R B E L F O R E A Y J B K N M J T E T J T U D Y A I N R R E I C O
R P D C E Z T I X V J W T R R Z E P T D F T R M I C N G G W R N J A E T H P E Z
B X W Z X J I A Q P U P I Q T L W E F A E P V C O R M T A P O B L N E I L G Z A
Y B R A G W L S M F W X L U I N W R C R U C A P N A Z C B F I C R G S L T E P H
A K A L K T E E X L P X E A L U J C O D K A R I V W R P Q R F N Y E O E C C J K
A R V K Y V S D Q O M U M R E W L E D D C F I D A S J N S F S M V S F R H H U Z
D E N Y C M M E Y C Z S F T D Q E N Z E Y T A E R C A X F L G M N G F A L E W Z
G E X Q Y F K S A L T H R I E M Z T I V Y J B C I O D K A S I S G Z R N L B X C
I S V R A M F T N F A L B L V N V I P I T F I I A R R B O Y X N X J E G D Y L D
Q N Q Q M H I H R S C H E I F G L M A C X L L N E X B W F C P N P E E Y S X Z
E U V I A X A M C W S K V C A P F E N T Y B I E C S D J V I M V Q A D A I H G G
A B A B S T O A I D W W T J T E D S Q I K M T S E M B L R S E O J F O D P E N J
D V A R U B T U S J D B X I J B E J O A R Y E W E W L E Y R W P O M V N V Q V
P Z U U S B T O S J C V R D O Y K T I N D J A F L T L R X Z A W D C W F G S F H
B N O B C P I R N C P H H B N A T A V T Z L V F S H D Q Q D N N D W N R T T E Q
S U M O F S Q U A R E S S P R Q D W A D O Q P K I O Q T V G G K X E J A Q H E Y
W R G A N D L X K X U P P E R Q U A R T I L E O Y D T P X Z E Q E F M C D E L P
D F M W X G S Z E N R U I Y K C I L I E R Z U R A U G I K G Z D E B N T H O O B
O Q G F F L J L B U P B G B W B Y U A P J N M Q O M V L Z A J Q H A K I J R O S
E Z L O K F Y L T I A X G C C T R F N O C A R J U M I C K N P R X N E L W E Z I
B Y H N E U N L B T G N N I E U M S C N P R B C D N Y E R C K C G C L E Q M H G
O V X W J K O W X Z G M C B M J K Q E Z V E Z G Q W I R R Z K C S X O S X X Q T
I R O G Q Y Y E Z I Q W S A M P L E S T A N D A R D D E V I A T I O N K I S U Q
```

Chapter 4

Chapter 5

```
Q G Q R Z Y W U R U G J D H F V Q N C E A T H S N W G Q J Y B W L B I V J R T C
H W O H R R K R R H D I C H O T O M O U S V A R I A B L E Q N Z N C A X Z X E D
S F K T S K X C Y J L Z U Z X E F Z M U L T I P L I C A T I V E R U L E J A W L
P Z B K C J J J B L W L N Q K B L U P H T I S H W O E N E V R Z W H R D G J J Q A
O A M N Z M E P V T L K T C D W S F W X V E F U W P F Y H V B K Y H F H G T W B
A X J C G O D E O G O E N T E J V S Q K G F I Z R A L L X V Q Y I U W X U C N H
L A K A H X X F C V L N D L O V V P K L F D R H S P R O B A B I L I T Y Q Q V T
W G P S E I Z G U I S T D F J U C K C U X Z A I K R H E T T S J R C E I V F S I
U M P B H S R C X I E I N V Y U T W Y E B W E F M B B A Y E S T H E O R E M F
Y A R Y W N W R S A M P L E S P A C E R U A K J Z B S A F G K O D K V W D K M X
B R L P G C Z I R Z D A V H R T U N O K W W M A R X V Y R D E N E O K P Q V Z I
K E H A S B A B G P G T C B Q A P A P M Q T S L E H F M L P Q A P F M R R K K J
C W D K A Q R F R Y A D X O V P G I O S E S D S N O P L P K U D E B R O Q G X S
W E Q D A F M J E J N A V P G J V S Q Z E S Q W L E B V X X J D N M R B R C S B
R L R N R J J F B K U U N R V Y Q Y O G I F P Y Y J O M U W W I D J S A W E R K
A C H U H Q J T G B K F O O B S N M T M M S D A C X O J F B C T E X I B A L X N
Q T Z R V E S I E G G H V Q E K L F X I Z F X S C H E S E D B I N E D I R O C U
N B Q H A U X Q H B J K X N W V N O N L V G J Q M E N F D C D V T P H L O K W J
O P H E H H K F U H H Q E J P C A R Y G S A V N P U P O E M C E O W M I Q N C G
X H J D O W D W E G O Y S N M G X F I X E D E V E N T S P M Q L U R O T B U O U
O M T G B A Y E S S L A W O T R L U Z R C S V Q N J K O E Q H A T A W Y I V M Q
Z W Y A A V S D N U Q V P K E T L O H P X V R P J C F D K D N W C O Q D N X P P
T V M U Z V J O I W W O U D Z X V L P G V E G P X U S I Z A D O G A I O X L A
Q I G Q P L F H I T M O K Z K G R C B R U L X P X X F D B O I Q M W R S M U E M
R R E W D A N Z M C J J T Y T I D Y F F F S I P T K I E S A D P E W Q T I M M S
O M F X R G L C V N V J C V Z M X L O G Y I L M E V W V Y J M M S S G R A F E F
B R N O M W A L V D J L T R Z B U X I O N W X B O C Z U Q N G O G Y B I L X N B
Q R L C F U F B T B V K M T I A C D X P C O W X P M T I V E Y X U Y X B D S T U
B Q A L Z V E Z T O H X E F L V E H Y C V N N S L J W E V E A M P A O U I Z A L
C L Q H J X E A F L R Z M C Q Q Y Q Z N D I A P Y J U S D C R X Q G Z T S S R S
R R S X J M N A S X I C K V R J O L I U L A I A C L Y N O A S M J X I T Z Y G
X B E R U Z X B A R I Z M A T H E M A T I C A L E X P E C T A T I O N O R G O A
N B V R Y H Q J S V Y O Z M R E W T M V L L N G R Z L D G Z K D R N N I A U Z
X A D D I T I V E R U L E O U K Q I W F G G D U N F W D Y W K P U C N U B O T A
Y V N C S K U W S V M U T U A L L Y E X C L U S I V E O U T C O M E S M U L C S
H B M U L T I P L I C A T I V E L A W V I V M R A N D O M E V E N T S C T O O F
H A N F Y Y K W M G H Y Y M I T L V V T N V L G H B N P B P A X A W G O I M M T
W P S W X O P O I N D E P E N D E N T O U T C O M E S N N G Z I X Z R U O S E L
O H X W K V U X F J X C G C O N D I T I O N A L O U T C O M E S W T H S N Y S F
B R Y X R T O H P T S A G G R A N D O M V A R I A B L E S B E U Z F V Z V E N X
```

Chapter 5

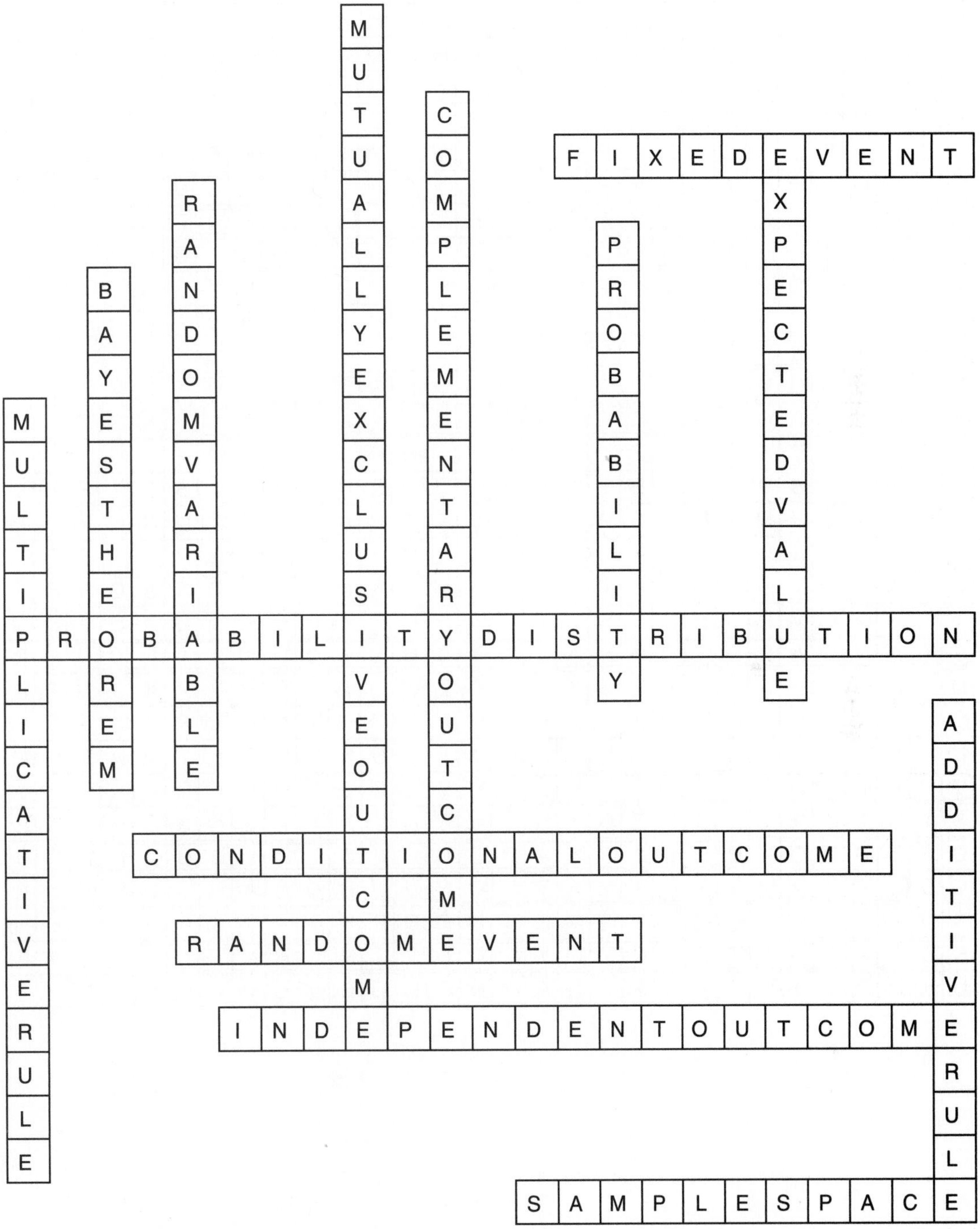
MUTUALLYEXCLUSIVEOUTCOM
COMPLEMENTARYOUTCOM
FIXEDEVENT
RANDOMVARIABLE
PROBABILITY
EXPECTEDVALUE
BAYESTHEOREM
MULTIPLICATIVERULE
PROBABILITYDISTRIBUTION
ADDITIVERULE
CONDITIONALOUTCOME
RANDOMEVENT
INDEPENDENTOUTCOME
SAMPLESPACE

SOURCE: www.variety-games.com.

Chapter 6

```
G U I S B G G H U A G D I R Z J R O K F M M C O M S C Z C Z
J T B E Q G B Y A O Y W D E N P H B Q G Q R Z Y W U R U G J
D H F V Q N C E A T H S N W G Q J Y B W L B I V J R T C H W
O H R R K R R H N Z N C A X Z X E D S F K T S K X C Y J L Z
U Z X E F Z A W L P Z B K C J J B L W L N Q K B L U P H T I
S H W O E N E V R Z W H R D G J J Q A O A M N Z M E P V T L
K T C D W S F W X V E F U W P F Y H V Z T A B L E N B K Y H
F H G T W N O R M A L D I S T R I B U T I O N I B A X J C G
O D E O G O E N T E J V S Q K G F I Z R A L L X V Q Y I U W
X U C N H S Y M M E T R I C A L D I S T R I B U T I O N L L
A K A H X R E A L L I M I T S G X F C V L N D L V V P K L F
D R H S Q Q V T W G P S E I Z G U I S Z S C O R E S V T D F
J C K C U X G A U S S I A N D I S T R I B U T I O N S Z A I
K R H E T T S J R C E I V F S I U M P B H S R C X I E I N V
Y U W Y E B W E F M B Y A R Y W N W R U A K J Z B S A F G K
O K V W D K M X B R L P G C Z I R Z D A V H R T U N K W W M
A R X V Y R D E N O K Q V Z I K E H A S B A B G P G T C B Q
A P A P Q T S L E H F M L P Q F M R K K J C W D K A Q R F R
Y A D X O V P G I O S S D S N O P L P K U B R Q G X S W E Q
S T A N D A R D N O R M A L T R A N S F O R M A T I O N F R
D A F M J E J N A V P G J V S Q Z E Q W L E B V X X J M R R
C S B R L R N R J J F B K U U N R V Y Q Y O G I F Y Y J O M
U W W J S W E R K A C H U H Q J T G B K F O O B S N M T M M
U N I T N O R M A L T A B L E H V S D C X O J F B C X I A L
X N Q T Z R V E S I E G G H V Q E K L F X I Z F X S H E S E
D B E D R O R B E L L S H A P E D D I S T R I B U T I O N J
C D Z T R A N S F O R M A T I O N U N B Q H A U X Q H B J K
X N W V N O N L V G J Q M N F D C D P H O K W J O P H E H H
K S T A N D A R D N O R M A L D I S T R I B U T I O N B J F
U H H Q E J P C A R Y G S A V N P U O E M C W M Q N G X H J
```

Chapter 6

Chapter 7

S	A	M	P	L	E	D	E	S	I	G	N	X	J	L	E	K	H	M	D	C	X	D	S	P	A	D	X	J	U
J	Z	C	O	M	L	H	R	T	E	H	X	S	W	L	R	M	L	N	Z	A	Z	X	T	F	D	X	V	N	X
K	E	U	A	U	I	L	A	W	O	F	L	A	R	G	E	N	U	M	B	E	R	S	A	S	K	R	L	J	R
P	X	D	N	R	D	E	G	K	A	S	A	D	O	J	J	T	K	B	I	I	I	Q	T	A	I	I	Z	S	M
W	Y	O	Z	H	V	W	P	W	N	H	U	O	Y	T	U	V	W	H	P	K	R	A	Y	M	A	R	I	A	G
H	K	T	I	D	E	R	J	M	L	S	T	H	S	U	N	F	C	G	U	K	P	V	X	P	B	P	J	M	C
F	X	Q	O	G	M	C	Q	H	L	U	Z	Q	X	P	G	J	C	C	Z	X	Q	D	U	L	D	Q	G	P	Y
Q	U	M	M	V	H	U	E	P	E	O	V	E	M	V	B	M	B	L	D	Q	W	U	I	I	V	R	U	L	C
M	N	Q	L	B	C	U	L	N	Z	O	Z	V	Y	Z	R	W	H	K	S	O	Y	P	E	N	D	I	C	I	J
S	B	N	B	K	D	I	A	R	T	A	F	I	D	C	M	A	S	N	G	B	R	C	L	G	U	R	P	N	K
Q	I	X	W	F	X	Q	H	Z	R	S	B	Y	P	L	R	U	H	Z	M	O	D	H	W	N	P	F	G	C
Y	A	U	M	Z	A	Y	G	S	U	S	A	R	C	V	V	H	S	W	D	T	Y	U	X	I	K	Q	W	E	V
M	S	Z	G	L	C	S	K	K	Q	C	Z	L	W	V	A	U	U	F	U	S	A	S	M	T	E	R	V	R	H
E	E	N	O	L	F	D	E	J	Q	D	L	H	L	M	I	Q	H	S	E	T	I	W	A	H	Y	I	D	R	P
C	D	B	K	E	J	I	U	D	K	E	Y	X	V	I	F	W	W	M	F	X	J	N	S	O	C	R	S	O	Z
H	E	K	W	Z	G	B	O	L	E	W	D	B	Z	L	M	T	D	M	C	E	S	K	X	U	W	P	M	R	J
V	S	F	P	Q	W	Q	Z	R	E	S	B	X	Y	K	X	I	W	I	K	J	T	U	M	T	D	Q	F	T	A
P	T	H	K	I	C	I	O	K	P	K	T	W	Z	U	Z	M	T	C	I	G	S	F	O	R	G	R	V	C	M
P	I	C	R	X	C	C	J	P	G	J	O	I	J	C	S	J	N	T	U	N	A	I	P	E	H	T	S	D	M
K	M	A	L	X	A	O	G	P	S	L	S	S	M	I	U	P	F	S	H	D	N	Z	E	P	V	C	B	X	T
V	A	T	X	F	V	Z	T	Q	R	I	E	J	I	A	A	D	M	A	X	E	U	C	E	L	S	D	K	R	D
E	T	E	H	L	E	K	A	G	T	M	S	M	Q	T	T	Y	S	C	H	A	O	J	V	A	V	A	S	Z	Y
G	O	V	O	P	A	N	O	S	U	P	I	F	D	U	I	O	B	G	Q	U	N	R	H	C	D	C	M	D	L
J	R	I	I	R	I	O	M	G	D	E	R	D	M	E	Y	X	R	Y	J	J	X	D	E	E	A	X	T	G	F
Y	F	L	Q	A	P	Y	S	T	A	N	D	A	R	D	E	R	R	O	R	O	F	T	H	M	E	A	N	X	A
F	S	C	M	O	E	F	J	D	G	T	T	X	Q	E	K	D	E	P	O	J	C	U	D	E	M	D	I	C	I
P	K	D	Q	A	P	Y	M	P	R	X	A	T	N	V	C	P	D	G	Q	V	I	C	B	N	X	B	H	C	Y
Z	G	G	B	X	U	S	D	D	S	H	S	R	U	M	G	P	V	V	H	R	N	C	C	T	M	C	G	I	B
H	C	I	V	O	S	A	M	P	L	I	N	G	D	I	S	T	R	I	B	U	T	I	O	N	X	Q	K	R	Y
W	T	C	Z	T	C	S	A	M	P	L	I	N	G	W	I	T	H	R	E	P	L	A	C	E	M	E	N	T	M

Chapter 7

```
S A M P L I N G W I T H R E P L A C E M E N T
A
M
P
L                       S
I                       A
N         S A M P L I N G E R R O R
G                       P   A
W                       L   W
I     S         U       I   O
T     A         N       N   F
H     M         B       G   L
O     P         I       D   A
U     L         A       I   R
T     E         S       S   G
R     D         E       T   E
E     E         D       R   N
P     S         E       I   U
L     I         S       B   M
A     G         T       U   B
C E N T R A L L I M I T T H E O R E M
E               M       I   R
M               A       O   S
E               T       N
N               O
T   S T A N D A R D E R R O R O F T H E M E A N
```

Chapter 8

Chapter 8

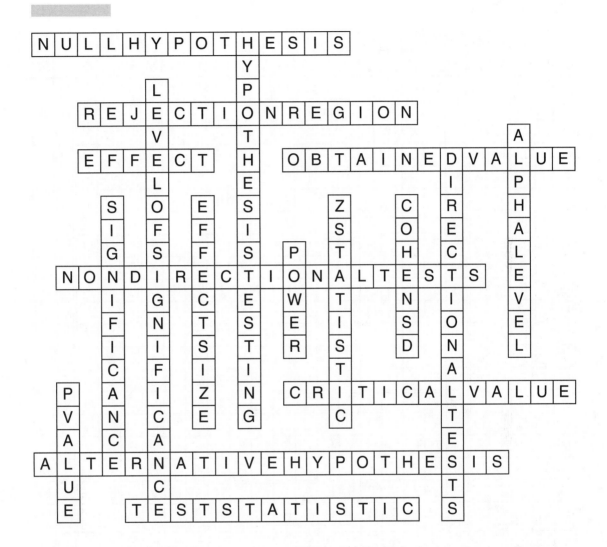

Chapter 9

I	S	D	F	V	F	D	E	G	R	E	E	S	O	F	F	R	E	E	D	O	M	X	M	I
I	J	J	U	E	E	B	M	A	S	O	C	E	G	W	N	S	F	J	M	W	X	G	J	B
B	V	O	S	S	P	S	N	Z	A	E	T	J	D	X	Q	Y	E	Y	A	Y	K	O	M	V
E	F	A	C	T	P	M	T	T	S	Z	H	C	Z	I	H	Z	N	U	K	T	E	O	K	B
A	M	M	K	I	U	P	K	I	I	X	X	V	V	G	W	Q	O	P	A	D	B	F	P	H
E	K	M	H	M	E	P	J	Z	M	Q	E	P	G	Z	T	E	S	N	S	I	U	W	O	I
K	T	B	K	A	H	D	C	K	I	A	Z	E	K	D	I	T	V	A	F	S	G	F	O	B
G	O	L	R	T	S	H	P	W	M	S	T	X	A	X	F	E	X	X	C	T	B	Z	L	T
A	B	N	Y	E	Q	Q	A	F	C	Q	Z	E	I	S	I	L	P	Q	X	R	S	J	E	O
D	S	S	H	D	P	R	L	Z	H	F	Z	L	D	W	S	Z	F	F	R	I	H	U	D	B
B	E	S	C	S	M	F	M	J	F	R	L	P	O	C	Z	E	T	X	G	B	T	X	S	T
G	R	F	R	T	S	Z	C	F	D	P	S	C	F	X	O	I	D	R	Q	U	B	F	A	A
B	V	C	H	A	G	H	V	P	L	M	R	Z	B	Z	M	H	U	A	P	T	J	A	M	I
C	E	K	A	N	J	U	M	P	F	S	F	W	N	D	W	B	E	R	U	I	Z	Y	P	N
J	D	W	K	D	R	T	L	Q	Q	D	T	D	H	N	H	Q	Z	N	V	O	B	T	L	E
N	T	S	Q	A	X	F	P	D	V	F	X	V	Z	B	Q	Z	D	S	S	N	S	H	E	D
X	D	V	L	R	X	T	S	T	A	T	I	S	T	I	C	M	P	Y	I	D	F	N	V	X
G	P	B	L	D	E	R	G	M	M	D	H	U	L	F	Y	E	F	X	I	M	Q	G	A	C
U	V	J	Y	E	G	D	I	G	H	Y	I	I	R	F	X	Q	M	I	W	F	G	X	R	D
Q	I	K	F	R	N	K	S	L	X	A	Q	D	V	G	B	G	K	C	E	F	V	J	I	M
D	O	T	G	R	P	L	Z	Q	T	R	E	A	T	M	E	N	T	B	V	Q	E	B	A	N
B	P	X	O	O	W	A	I	R	N	J	R	O	F	X	T	A	B	I	G	W	H	R	N	U
E	D	Z	X	R	J	P	I	E	B	A	S	J	M	H	Q	Z	I	E	L	B	J	P	C	A
F	C	W	A	Z	T	I	X	E	G	K	V	S	K	W	C	Y	C	E	E	P	O	M	E	O
G	T	K	J	C	Y	S	W	Q	L	P	C	U	V	M	O	P	W	D	V	M	Y	R	O	F

Chapter 9

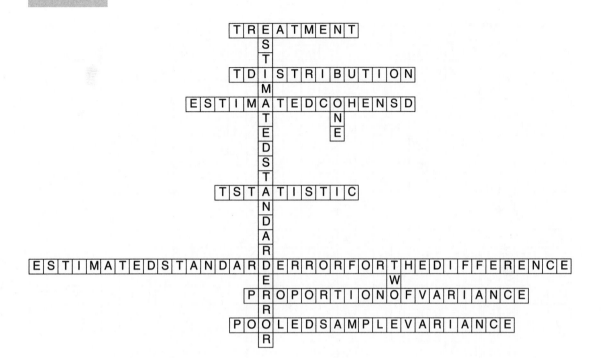

Chapter 10

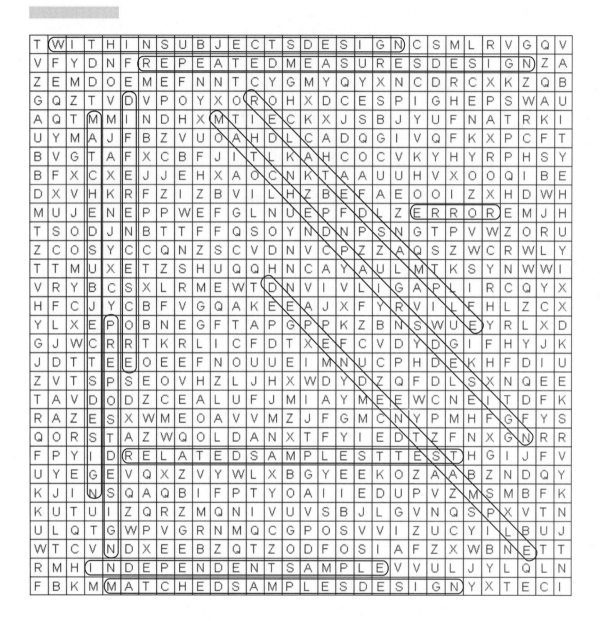

Chapter 10

```
        R                       D                       W
        E               R       I               P       I
        L   M   I       E       F               R       T
        A   A   N       L       F               E       H
        T   T   D       A       E               P       I
        E   C   E       T       R               O       N
        D   H   P       E       E               S       S
    E   S   E   E       D       N               T       U
    R   A   M   P       A       C               D       B
R E P E A T E D M E A S U R E S D E S I G N
    O   L   I   N       P       C               I       C
    R   E   R   T       L       O               G       T
        S   S   S       E       R               N       S
        T   D   A               E                       D
        T   E   M               S                       E
        E   S   P                                       S
        S   I   L                                       I
        T   G   E                                       G
            N                                           N
```

Chapter 11

R	W	O	P	T	U	H	N	T	Y	U	O	M	K	E	U	Y	A	M	V	W	V	B	E	R
O	Y	J	D	P	U	U	A	T	S	X	O	G	K	U	V	I	G	U	Q	Q	K	G	J	G
L	F	E	S	T	I	M	A	T	I	O	N	X	E	Q	R	N	Z	I	V	V	J	X	E	W
Y	J	D	E	A	N	S	R	G	F	R	P	U	L	R	Z	T	P	A	K	C	O	H	H	O
C	S	R	K	E	C	A	L	W	B	E	J	P	O	F	Y	E	X	X	Q	O	M	P	W	O
R	K	C	Z	F	N	A	Z	A	S	V	L	P	W	V	Q	R	X	P	H	N	V	R	T	A
X	L	O	M	G	V	E	B	I	J	T	C	E	E	S	J	V	X	O	Y	F	K	S	X	C
L	E	N	X	D	D	A	T	A	Q	J	S	R	R	I	R	A	B	I	F	I	X	M	R	J
I	V	F	W	U	E	F	Q	G	X	A	M	C	C	N	W	L	G	N	E	D	K	T	F	W
W	E	I	U	M	M	U	O	R	Q	B	B	O	O	A	M	E	L	T	K	E	G	B	K	A
H	L	D	H	S	N	W	C	T	O	C	N	N	N	M	E	S	G	E	I	N	A	B	Q	X
X	O	E	V	C	G	N	O	P	E	X	N	F	F	A	C	T	P	E	E	C	T	K	L	Y
E	F	N	I	Y	J	T	G	L	E	E	W	I	I	V	S	I	M	S	K	E	U	J	E	O
X	C	C	B	U	D	X	R	F	F	N	A	D	D	Y	H	M	K	T	W	I	W	C	X	H
Z	O	E	N	B	W	V	J	K	T	J	F	E	E	A	Q	A	I	I	F	N	A	E	M	K
D	N	L	A	L	G	D	N	S	L	F	W	N	N	L	Y	T	V	M	K	T	M	N	K	Q
N	F	I	B	F	L	S	E	I	A	E	W	C	C	R	S	I	G	A	G	E	K	M	Y	W
W	I	M	S	K	O	D	J	D	N	H	K	E	E	J	Q	O	D	T	U	R	U	K	R	K
E	D	I	S	I	G	Y	D	I	V	T	N	L	L	Q	F	N	O	I	J	V	M	Q	Q	R
G	E	T	Y	X	W	H	E	X	X	Q	O	I	I	T	W	B	X	O	W	A	O	Z	H	F
N	N	S	P	U	G	F	I	Q	Q	X	B	M	M	W	A	E	N	N	E	L	C	E	S	M
I	C	Z	K	D	J	A	M	U	C	W	P	I	I	T	Q	O	B	G	C	E	B	X	Z	T
P	E	F	R	H	V	B	P	K	G	S	U	T	T	S	V	N	Z	U	K	G	U	U	L	G
U	B	E	K	I	Z	X	K	D	F	E	Z	K	U	X	C	T	W	N	Y	W	J	V	D	U
A	V	C	O	N	F	I	D	E	N	C	E	B	O	U	N	D	A	R	I	E	S	J	A	B

Chapter 11

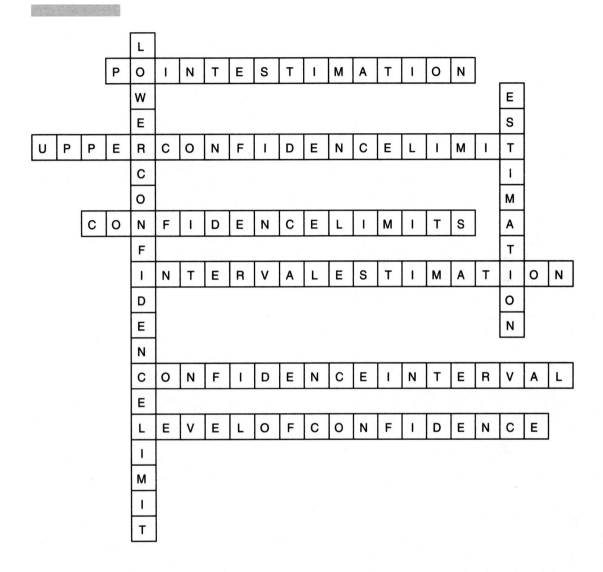

Chapter 12

K	B	P	N	U	A	E	Z	O	Z	W	A	V	K	G	E	Z	Q	Z	T	G	A	B	L	E	P	E	Y	K	D
X	E	X	F	B	O	Z	Z	N	U	I	E	H	Q	E	K	F	L	A	V	F	F	I	F	U	L	J	D	N	Y
K	T	Y	Q	C	U	W	B	E	Z	V	U	V	G	E	F	I	V	M	P	W	Q	F	T	O	I	S	E	U	R
S	W	D	U	R	L	M	A	W	J	J	O	E	V	H	J	G	Q	G	Z	Y	B	D	X	Z	Z	U	G	W	T
O	E	R	K	H	K	Q	C	A	J	W	A	C	K	U	D	V	Y	G	I	T	P	H	Z	C	H	I	U	T	C
U	E	R	T	D	Q	V	X	Y	E	Y	P	H	R	Z	G	T	F	E	Z	K	Q	D	P	O	E	Y	P	H	Z
R	N	S	R	A	H	R	P	B	U	P	U	D	C	K	U	V	Y	G	I	T	P	B	S	Z	I	P	A	Z	R
C	S	N	L	P	W	S	F	E	S	F	G	A	E	F	D	I	S	T	R	I	B	U	T	I	O	N	I	P	E
E	U	J	U	L	I	E	X	T	N	T	A	N	N	C	W	G	C	S	T	J	R	K	U	Y	I	Z	R	C	D
O	B	B	R	C	T	M	G	W	H	F	A	D	Z	A	F	B	J	C	V	G	B	I	D	T	E	H	W	B	C
F	J	U	L	W	H	R	Y	E	X	B	F	T	L	P	L	B	F	T	U	B	K	G	E	S	I	Z	I	X	B
V	E	A	I	R	I	N	L	E	J	Q	P	U	I	V	C	Y	Y	X	Q	P	P	I	N	I	B	T	S	U	M
A	C	I	W	C	N	M	Z	N	X	M	L	Z	C	S	F	S	S	L	N	Z	K	M	T	S	P	V	E	U	G
R	T	D	U	W	G	K	V	S	Q	J	Z	X	D	G	T	O	A	U	L	Y	J	I	S	C	I	C	V	Z
I	S	T	E	F	R	C	P	U	Y	W	J	E	Y	R	B	T	I	S	Q	P	C	Z	V	B	Z	O	F	B
A	D	M	W	M	O	F	Z	B	Z	N	J	W	T	L	K	D	C	A	S	O	F	S	E	B	L	D	M	O	Z
T	E	H	W	Y	U	B	C	J	U	I	U	Q	G	H	V	U	S	R	J	P	F	K	D	Y	I	Z	P	I	F
I	S	F	Q	Q	P	H	X	E	P	J	J	U	Q	W	Q	C	F	Z	O	D	W	V	R	F	O	F	A	M	E
O	I	P	I	I	V	A	V	C	O	D	Q	N	V	O	Q	B	R	H	L	V	K	K	A	H	M	Q	R	Z	E
N	G	P	M	J	A	B	G	T	S	B	D	K	C	T	B	B	H	Z	X	O	G	D	N	R	C	B	I	C	L
G	N	D	I	G	R	S	B	S	T	U	E	Y	F	F	O	B	T	A	I	N	E	D	G	Z	I	N	S	P	E
N	A	S	N	M	I	B	J	A	H	M	R	D	O	I	Q	G	D	V	N	W	A	I	E	O	Y	A	O	B	E
J	A	A	V	O	A	Z	I	N	O	G	E	T	N	L	D	H	J	B	F	T	Q	J	Z	X	V	S	N	Z	O
G	H	I	X	R	B	Z	R	O	C	O	B	S	E	R	V	E	D	P	O	W	E	R	J	C	O	E	S	C	L
G	V	M	J	X	I	J	O	V	T	C	U	A	O	D	U	V	O	X	P	C	H	O	I	V	Z	T	A	X	E
G	C	N	U	A	L	S	F	A	E	Q	Y	Y	E	Z	C	N	G	P	E	O	R	E	N	C	C	B	B	A	H
Q	C	K	W	T	I	J	Z	L	S	D	L	P	A	Z	V	X	E	W	Q	T	Q	A	T	H	S	Q	L	B	V
K	E	A	M	S	T	A	L	S	T	P	N	O	C	L	P	D	K	V	A	E	O	W	H	J	F	L	H	L	A
N	I	K	T	L	Y	R	O	T	S	O	Y	K	D	I	Z	J	I	R	I	O	I	A	X	J	L	S	M	W	E
O	B	Z	O	E	G	A	Y	R	G	D	V	R	T	B	O	L	K	X	W	P	N	Y	R	X	X	Z	L	C	D

SOURCE: www.variety-games.com.

Chapter 12

LEVELSOFTHEFACTOR

POSTHOCTEST

BETWEENGROUPSVARIATION

DEGREESOFFREEDOMNUMERATOR

SOURCEOFVARIATION

ANALYSISOFVARIANCE

Chapter 13

```
L J U C G J E U G Y A W D Q K S T J H O E U F H C E E R E K M H B U Y Y
R Y I H A J Y Z M I D Q B H Z L L C L T R D N Z T B E N P V M T E C F S
T U K C H F F U S Z Z O C J F Z A E I E G N L I E F V V J D A P T A K J
N F A J V G N W K O A M C D K W M O U A M G J C S W L J W R S K W Z D T
W Z Z Q J B Q K D W I S T S Y H O A G J X H W Y T N J W Q F R D E B J J
G K W V O F S J B C M T D S R Y K E J T T W P D W B C A F A E L E T H J
K L N K S N W N Z V E J E K R E S V N U I P N Q I G V T E N J X N R T M
T I F K Z L E M F T A L T W S J A H J X Y Z T X S U G O Z S Z Q P Y M Q
S Q J Z H V B W H C V M F M Z A U N C N T U M Z E L K D L M U F E D C Z
C D C A B A O V A Q X Y K P T O Y X M N K S W F A Q X O D J P M R W S J
F K V Y U L C Y X Y D P B A V J W O X S P S G G L X L C M W F G S E A F
B J J T A C A L L U W S Q O X S T M B P D C R Z P D X M S Z F T O R Z P
V Y L Z D N U R D G L I N H X E U C S F O W D K H K G V N J B F N S D T
B S Z H U I N U L Y L N T R Q P O F D B L K S S A O B T I A L Q S X O I
U G E E M I J S T K E Y W H R F Y U W C Q R I I Q A K G A A M J V V B W
F U J K J S V S S R H N P E I C C B Q T V X Q M X E U G H I F K A P D C
R W V O L E G Y Z R B M V B Y N L L S C F Z O I M G P L N J M G R S K N
M G H N F O O Z R V V R Y E J L S U S M X C D N J H V S S P M K I J C H
O S Q Y M N Q A X N Q P Q H E X S U Q F M K J S Y F K W W J E K A M P Q
P R U W F Z H C F A S S E L O R T W B E P X F Z S S C R U Q S C T E Z Z
R N D W I G F I D R F N F K I S L N H J Z T K R C D C H M M N Y I N S E
U A O X N Y K P B I M F W G M X H P X A E G G W A S G Y S V Q T O R U B
Q H E O Z J P E J I P Y F A A O G I Q S Y C N E N E H A R T K P N V K V
Q E T S P N K B X N K U A X R G K K A C C D T C Q J S J X L Y T Y U N J
K W V N T C H X Q R D J G C Z M A E U I S M B S D J X E N P Y U S Q H Q
M V L W R Y V F M L N A L G Y Y Y O A E R X U R A E V X U H S W M B P Q
M S B E T W E E N P E R S O N S P G D A D N W N N N A Q Q I L Y O R Z G
Q D Z O B U S V A A Y T O A Y V Q U X U A D Q D X D O B V J Z F P S Q W
Y P B B G L R W M P G B P J Q H U T E F M M W R X S W V M A V I A Y D A
G O S R J I H E O Q C L L T R L W O K K M T K E N O F V A R G F D M J K
T B C V W E I H A V H K S I J L M N T O M E O D U D L M H Z L Z Y C J Y
K U T O F E M K I F E M N H V T P T V X O M Y A T T V Z P V Z I I J J Z
R T Z N K A T F X Q R Y F M R J F G L J X V S U M I M V N X V H C D H D
S S B E T W E E N P E R S O N S M H Z Q F L X V G A J C V Q N X B M D B
X Z C V A E A B N Y S A U O U X I S T Z V N O Q V I S R S Y X A U T E E
F I Z M F K K W N Z P U D F B E T W E E N P E R S O N S J N A S E F S D
```

Chapter 13

The crossword answers are:

- DEGREESOFFREEDOMBETWEENPERSONS (down)
- MEANSQUAREBETWEENPERSON (down)
- BETWEENPERSONSVARIATION (down)
- TESTWISEALPHA (across)
- SUMOFSQUARESBETWEENPERSONS (across)

SOURCE: www.variety-games.com.

Chapter 14

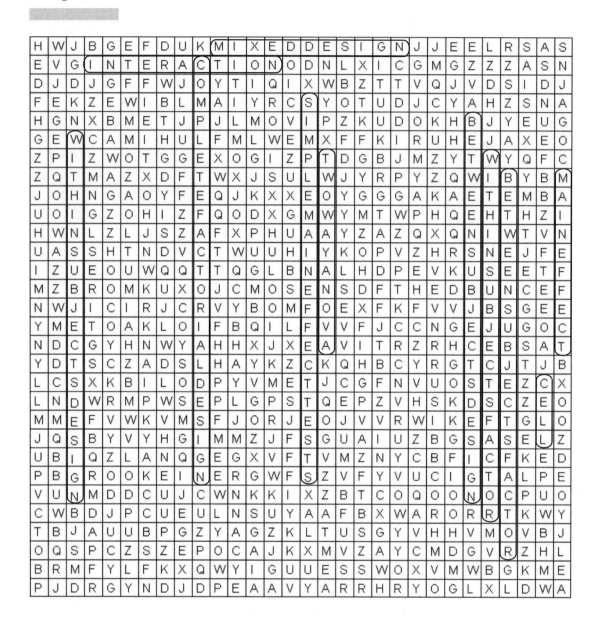

Chapter 14

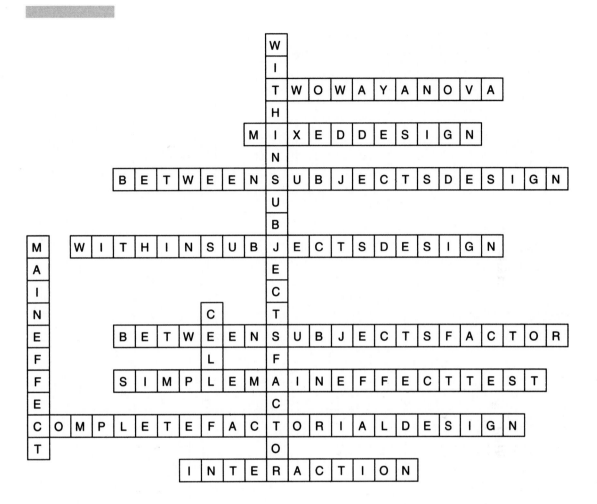

Chapter 15

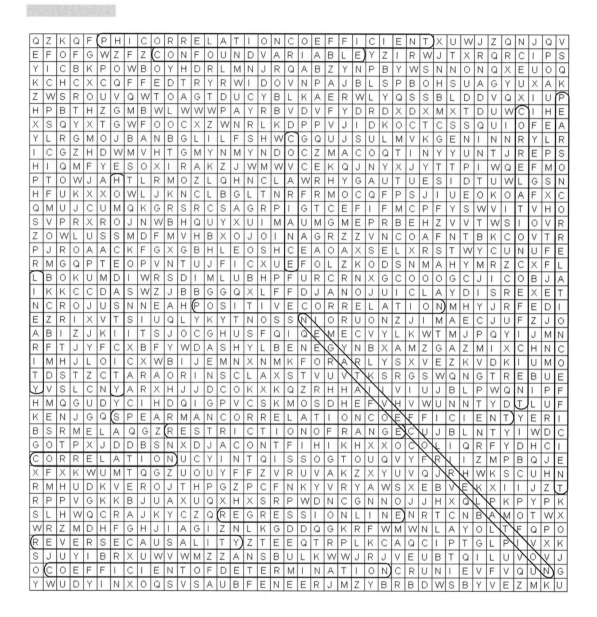

Chapter 15

PEARSONCORRELATIONCOEFFICIENT
POINTBISERIALCORRELATIONCOEFFICIENT
POSITIVECORRELATION
COEFFICIENTOFDETERMINATION
SUMOFPRODUCTS
PHICORRELATIONCOEFFICIENT
RESTRICTIONOFRANGE
SPEARMANCORRELATIONCOEFFICIENT
REGRESSIONLINE
HOMOSCEDASTICITY
REVERSECAUSALITY
NEGATIVECORRELATION
CORRELATION
COVARIANCE
CONFOUNDVARIABLE
LINEARITY
CORRELATIONCOEFFICIENT

SOURCE: www.variety-games.com.

Chapter 16

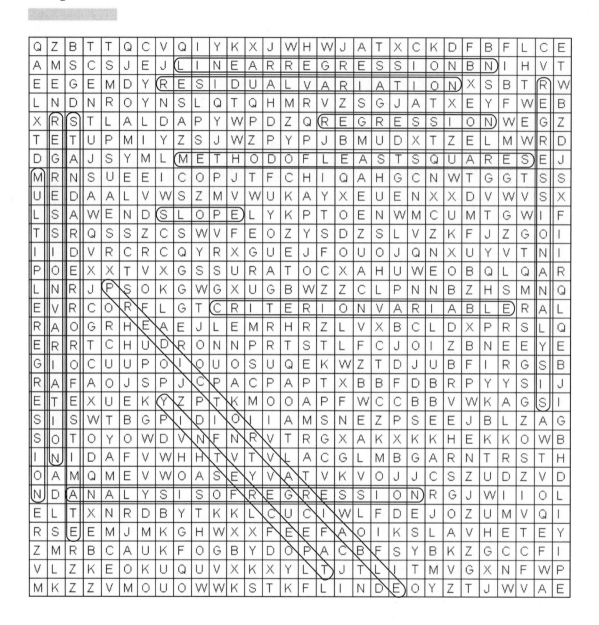

Chapter 16

```
S L O P E
T           Y
A           I
N           N
D           T
A N A L Y S I S O F R E G R E S S I O N
R         E     R
D         G     C
E   M U L T I P L E R E G R E S S I O N
R         E     P
R         S     T
O         S
R         I
O     P R E D I C T O R V A R I A B L E
F         N
E   R E S I D U A L V A R I A T I O N
S         A
T     L I N E A R R E G R E S S I O N
I         I
M E T H O D O F L E A S T S Q U A R E S
A         T
T         I
E     C R I T E R I O N V A R I A B L E
          N
```

SOURCE: www.variety-games.com.

Chapter 17

D	E	G	U	J	O	C	O	Y	U	F	G	R	S	E	M	L	O	E	Z	Y	B	A	W	N	O	W	T	K	R
R	F	Y	M	F	J	W	G	V	O	A	D	H	U	O	D	D	F	Z	A	O	Y	X	S	K	B	D	J	H	U
S	I	E	H	D	Z	H	E	M	F	R	E	Q	U	E	N	C	Y	O	B	S	E	R	V	E	D	O	V	P	F
S	P	Y	U	U	G	I	J	L	R	U	K	C	S	H	F	C	D	G	M	Z	B	W	R	Y	A	R	P	V	Y
S	D	K	J	F	C	I	U	P	H	W	B	X	I	A	O	U	E	K	R	C	C	J	P	C	G	R	S	G	V
T	P	T	O	M	R	Y	Q	Z	T	M	Z	L	M	W	J	L	B	S	W	D	E	V	G	X	T	W	J	O	I
D	O	P	N	U	A	N	G	I	J	W	B	Y	V	L	X	S	Q	P	M	F	R	E	Z	W	D	R	Y	J	V
U	Q	P	C	R	M	Q	Y	J	Y	S	J	C	C	R	W	U	E	J	K	I	F	C	G	X	J	Q	Y	P	T
K	D	P	X	M	E	O	F	M	W	D	V	Z	I	S	X	C	C	O	M	D	C	Y	I	N	A	G	P	R	J
N	O	N	P	A	R	A	M	E	T	R	I	C	T	E	S	T	S	C	E	C	S	T	A	R	I	O	Q	O	P
U	E	P	D	Q	S	H	I	F	P	I	X	K	J	U	G	C	L	M	D	R	F	Q	L	U	B	O	X	W	W
W	U	D	D	D	V	Q	R	E	I	I	X	Z	J	M	U	Q	C	Y	T	A	R	S	S	H	A	D	X	M	Y
G	W	A	C	U	R	S	H	S	G	T	N	F	C	L	R	F	G	A	E	M	E	L	I	D	C	N	Z	W	V
S	D	F	E	C	H	I	S	Q	U	A	R	E	T	E	S	T	C	Y	S	E	Q	P	W	W	Q	E	E	X	U
R	P	A	R	A	M	E	T	R	I	C	T	E	S	T	S	P	B	O	T	R	U	Q	Q	G	C	S	S	H	K
A	M	A	M	A	Z	M	E	V	D	X	D	H	B	P	C	O	R	X	F	S	E	R	P	X	O	S	X	O	F
M	V	S	W	Z	G	P	K	R	Q	E	R	O	W	K	M	J	T	W	O	P	N	N	T	M	A	O	O	R	L
V	P	V	C	X	C	Y	V	N	Q	M	Y	E	R	O	W	K	Z	X	R	H	C	X	C	A	H	F	D	O	V
B	A	L	Z	V	D	E	N	K	Z	P	O	S	C	S	S	J	T	Z	I	I	Y	K	O	F	Y	F	W	C	B
Q	U	I	V	I	S	O	C	B	X	K	O	V	I	T	R	G	P	H	N	J	E	V	G	V	E	I	K	Q	N
D	D	G	V	B	O	W	U	N	J	E	P	Q	X	Z	Q	A	U	I	D	V	X	X	R	Q	X	T	Z	J	P
H	U	V	Q	Y	E	U	P	L	V	F	V	V	R	B	U	J	M	Q	E	Z	P	K	V	Q	U	T	J	B	V
Q	L	M	J	W	S	Y	P	Z	R	T	G	L	V	I	O	U	U	Z	P	M	E	E	V	W	G	E	L	I	K
F	L	E	A	H	W	I	E	D	Y	M	I	D	W	B	C	C	Q	F	E	E	C	D	B	G	V	S	Z	K	P
R	V	O	F	X	O	I	T	E	U	R	L	J	D	Q	E	Q	I	M	N	V	T	P	C	T	T	T	Q	F	E
G	D	E	J	A	X	H	R	J	P	S	O	U	V	D	X	H	L	E	D	W	E	B	M	X	Q	A	N	N	O
Z	O	B	U	P	S	J	B	P	Z	L	Q	O	B	M	H	P	X	T	E	R	D	A	M	F	L	X	I	L	I
D	T	G	O	V	M	I	I	D	H	U	D	W	K	T	N	Y	V	U	N	Q	T	V	P	F	I	F	T	T	W
O	M	I	Q	M	E	J	G	I	J	L	P	D	G	S	I	A	V	T	C	W	G	G	Y	H	P	N	V	N	O
O	Y	U	C	Q	T	V	U	R	H	Z	N	D	L	E	M	F	R	J	E	C	G	E	M	Z	W	P	I	O	A

Chapter 17

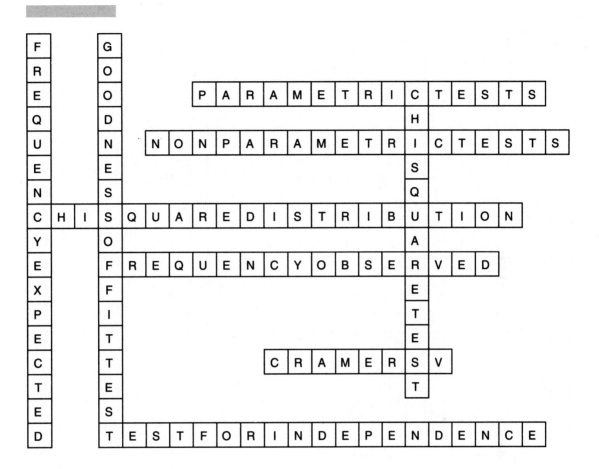

Chapter 18

```
K T P C N S K G A C W D V L O T E J L Y D D C W G P C X W I
I P U U E S Y Y C P K Q Z D Y S C V C Y J M A F T G Q S W Y
Q M J S T H J A G W U F H V O M E Y Y N K M G V X Y W O P B
X B F C D Z X H G J R J B P G E E F F Q R H C R U I L J R L
U X S T Z I U P D D W Q F X O H E L R P U T U R J Y T U K L
T S P G W M M Z P B G L O A B I A B F D S N E A R C R A G I
V F N K E J L H K J L C H O J L D F T P K B Y S P G X P R X
E E M F R T W S B K Q Q A P S T A F P R A G Y M G R G X N X
M D G U T K G E Y X Q V N S B U C Y A I L Z W G S Z A Q F S
A F N K V I V Y E V X Q J O U D P U E O W S E T F P N B W
N N V T T A L T J F Z E X D P G B J Y L A B C D E V C I A B
N U E G U T B Q A D X I C B U J V Z Q T L C X S W Q C A T K
W Q Y S I G N T E S T F Q R L R O A S J L E C Y G X M P J Z
H I T J V M P X E C I P S S H G J F G R I Q K F I C Q M Q D
I R U J B T B L Q H C E C N N L R D Q L S U S W S F Y S P C
T L G F Z Y U M I Z O Z R W P B C C O C H W U Q Z Z B V K U
N B W I L C O X O N S I G N E D R A N K T E S T Q I C Q M Y
E L I F B X E D T A D S O R T Y D U P D E J P S I U G F Y D
Y J S G U L Y F N J Z F X L J V Q X L H S H W H Z L B T L S
U A L V R F A J I W X C T N L T V J F X T F W R W U X R G C
T S U T S M M M Y E O R L A N U Z I N T J L N E C V V F W I
E O B T O U G P B E J H A Y U Q V N M E U J X W L K Y U O N
S S X X G Q E K D U D R T X S V Y G S M Q S N G I I B M K R
T P J Q Z R C I G M A K U K N B K V K L E A N D F I W Z M P
F O F D T S O K N R C V K P M F I S I A E X M Q B G Q B F K
C Q V C V Q X V G A S Z Q X D I Q U L A Y X Q N Z H S B P C
E N B M E C B G S O Y O K B R Q A O A J H K L F B H N A H D
N Y V F R I E D M A N T E S T B D N Q N L U C C X G M M N
V Y X Y T R S H R C W K X P A Y P A A T E Y E Z N C F G F N
E S O U R B K E U G C Y L K T C O F C D H G L T J X T X L R
```

SOURCE: www.variety-games.com.

Chapter 18

Answers to Practice Quizzes

Chapter 1

1. b	8. b	15. d	22. d
2. a	9. a	16. d	23. a
3. c	10. c	17. c	24. c
4. a	11. b	18. a	25. b
5. d	12. c	19. a	
6. c	13. b	20. d	
7. a	14. b	21. b	

Chapter 2

1. a	8. a	15. b	22. b
2. d	9. b	16. d	23. d
3. c	10. c	17. b	
4. c	11. d	18. a	
5. c	12. d	19. d	
6. d	13. b	20. c	
7. a	14. a	21. b	

Chapter 3

1. b	7. c	13. c	19. b
2. a	8. a	14. b	20. c
3. c	9. b	15. b	21. a
4. b	10. d	16. a	
5. c	11. a	17. d	
6. d	12. a	18. a	

Chapter 4

1. b	6. d	11. b	16. a
2. a	7. b	12. b	17. a
3. c	8. c	13. a	18. b
4. b	9. d	14. d	19. c
5. a	10. c	15. b	20. b

Chapter 5

1. a	8. c	15. d	22. c
2. c	9. d	16. c	23. d
3. a	10. b	17. d	24. c
4. d	11. d	18. a	25. b
5. d	12. c	19. a	
6. b	13. a	20. c	
7. a	14. b	21. b	

Chapter 6

1. a	6. c	11. a	16. d
2. b	7. b	12. c	17. b
3. d	8. b	13. a	18. c
4. c	9. b	14. d	19. a
5. d	10. c	15. c	20. b

Chapter 7

1. b	8. b	15. a	22. b
2. c	9. a	16. b	23. a
3. d	10. b	17. d	24. d
4. a	11. d	18. d	25. d
5. d	12. a	19. d	26. c
6. c	13. b	20. a	27. a
7. c	14. c	21. b	

Chapter 8

1. d	11. b	21. a	31. d
2. a	12. a	22. d	32. a
3. b	13. d	23. b	33. b
4. d	14. a	24. d	
5. c	15. a	25. a	
6. a	16. b	26. c	
7. c	17. d	27. d	
8. d	18. c	28. a	
9. c	19. c	29. b	
10. a	20. b	30. b	

Chapter 9

1. b	10. b	19. c	28. b
2. d	11. d	20. b	29. b
3. a	12. a	21. b	30. a
4. b	13. a	22. d	31. d
5. b	14. d	23. b	32. a
6. a	15. c	24. a	33. d
7. c	16. d	25. a	
8. d	17. b	26. d	
9. a	18. a	27. c	

Chapter 10

1. a	8. c	15. b	22. d
2. b	9. c	16. a	23. c
3. d	10. b	17. b	24. a
4. a	11. c	18. c	25. d
5. c	12. a	19. c	26. d
6. d	13. a	20. c	27. b
7. b	14. a	21. a	

Chapter 11

1. c	8. b	15. d	22. c
2. d	9. a	16. b	23. a
3. b	10. c	17. c	24. b
4. a	11. d	18. c	25. d
5. c	12. b	19. b	26. d
6. a	13. b	20. d	27. b
7. a	14. a	21. a	

Chapter 12

1. b	8. b	15. b	22. b
2. c	9. d	16. b	23. b
3. c	10. b	17. a	24. d
4. a	11. d	18. b	25. c
5. d	12. d	19. c	26. d
6. a	13. a	20. b	27. d
7. c	14. c	21. d	28. d

Chapter 13

1. a	9. a	17. b	25. c
2. c	10. a	18. c	26. b
3. b	11. d	19. a	27. d
4. b	12. b	20. a	28. b
5. d	13. a	21. a	29. c
6. c	14. a	22. a	30. c
7. b	15. b	23. c	31. a
8. b	16. a	24. d	

Chapter 14

1. c	6. c	11. b	16. c
2. d	7. b	12. b	17. b
3. d	8. a	13. a	18. b
4. b	9. d	14. d	19. a
5. a	10. c	15. c	20. d

21. b	25. b	29. a	33. d
22. a	26. d	30. c	34. c
23. b	27. c	31. a	35. b
24. a	28. c	32. c	

Chapter 15

1. c	10. c	19. c	28. c
2. a	11. a	20. a	29. c
3. a	12. d	21. b	30. d
4. b	13. b	22. d	31. a
5. a	14. a	23. a	32. b
6. c	15. d	24. c	33. d
7. d	16. c	25. d	34. c
8. b	17. d	26. b	35. a
9. a	18. b	27. d	

Chapter 16

1. a	11. d	21. d	31. d
2. b	12. c	22. c	32. b
3. b	13. c	23. a	33. c
4. c	14. a	24. a	34. a
5. a	15. c	25. d	
6. c	16. c	26. b	
7. d	17. b	27. a	
8. b	18. d	28. c	
9. a	19. a	29. b	
10. a	20. b	30. d	

Chapter 17

1. b	10. b	19. a	28. b
2. a	11. b	20. d	29. c
3. d	12. c	21. c	30. b
4. c	13. d	22. b	31. a
5. a	14. d	23. b	32. b
6. b	15. b	24. a	33. d
7. c	16. a	25. b	34. a
8. a	17. c	26. d	35. c
9. d	18. c	27. c	

Chapter 18

1. b	11. a	21. b	31. a
2. c	12. d	22. c	32. d
3. a	13. b	23. b	33. d
4. a	14. b	24. a	34. c
5. c	15. a	25. a	35. b
6. d	16. a	26. c	36. c
7. d	17. c	27. a	37. b
8. a	18. d	28. c	38. d
9. c	19. a	29. c	
10. b	20. a	30. d	

Statistical Tables

TABLE B.1   The unit normal table.

Column (A) lists z-score values. Column (B) lists the proportion of the area between the mean and the z-score value. Column (C) lists the proportion of the area beyond the z score in the tail of the distribution. (Note: Because the normal distribution is symmetrical, areas for negative z scores are the same as those for positive z scores.)

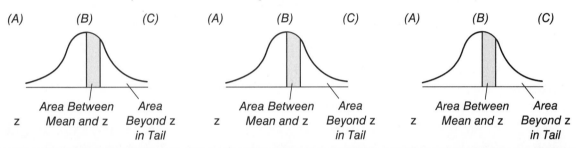

(A) z	(B) Area Between Mean and z	(C) Area Beyond z in Tail	(A) z	(B) Area Between Mean and z	(C) Area Beyond z in Tail	(A) z	(B) Area Between Mean and z	(C) Area Beyond z in Tail
0.00	.0000	.5000	0.15	.0596	.4404	0.30	.1179	.3821
0.01	.0040	.4960	0.16	.0636	.4364	0.31	.1217	.3783
0.02	.0080	.4920	0.17	.0675	.4325	0.32	.1255	.3745
0.03	.0120	.4880	0.18	.0714	.4286	0.33	.1293	.3707
0.04	.0160	.4840	0.19	.0753	.4247	0.34	.1331	.3669
0.05	.0199	.4801	0.20	.0793	.4207	0.35	.1368	.3632
0.06	.0239	.4761	0.21	.0832	.4168	0.36	.1406	.3594
0.07	.0279	.4721	0.22	.0871	.4129	0.37	.1443	.3557
0.08	.0319	.4681	0.23	.0910	.4090	0.38	.1480	.3520
0.09	.0359	.4641	0.24	.0948	.4052	0.39	.1517	.3483
0.10	.0398	.4602	0.25	.0987	.4013	0.40	.1554	.3446
0.11	.0438	.4562	0.26	.1026	.3974	0.41	.1591	.3409
0.12	.0478	.4522	0.27	.1064	.3936	0.42	.1628	.3372
0.13	.0517	.4483	0.28	.1103	.3897	0.43	.1664	.3336
0.14	.0557	.4443	0.29	.1141	.3859	0.44	.1700	.3300

(A) z	(B) Area Between Mean and z	(C) Area Beyond z in Tail	(A) z	(B) Area Between Mean and z	(C) Area Beyond z in Tail	(A) z	(B) Area Between Mean and z	(C) Area Beyond z in Tail
0.45	.1736	.3264	0.78	.2823	.2177	1.11	.3665	.1335
0.46	.1772	.3228	0.79	.2852	.2148	1.12	.3686	.1314
0.47	.1808	.3192	0.80	.2881	.2119	1.13	.3708	.1292
0.48	.1844	.3156	0.81	.2910	.2090	1.14	.3729	.1271
0.49	.1879	.3121	0.82	.2939	.2061	1.15	.3749	.1251
0.50	.1915	.3085	0.83	.2967	.2033	1.16	.3770	.1230
0.51	.1950	.3050	0.84	.2995	.2005	1.17	.3790	.1210
0.52	.1985	.3015	0.85	.3023	.1977	1.18	.3810	.1190
0.53	.2019	.2981	0.86	.3051	.1949	1.19	.3830	.1170
0.54	.2054	.2946	0.87	.3078	.1922	1.20	.3849	.1151
0.55	.2088	.2912	0.88	.3106	.1894	1.21	.3869	.1131
0.56	.2123	.2877	0.89	.3133	.1867	1.22	.3888	.1112
0.57	.2157	.2843	0.90	.3159	.1841	1.23	.3907	.1093
0.58	.2190	.2810	0.91	.3186	.1814	1.24	.3925	.1075
0.59	.2224	.2776	0.92	.3212	.1788	1.25	.3944	.1056
0.60	.2257	.2743	0.93	.3238	.1762	1.26	.3962	.1038
0.61	.2391	.2709	0.94	.3264	.1736	1.27	.3980	1020
0.62	.2324	.2676	0.95	.3289	.1711	1.28	.3997	.1003
0.63	.2357	.2643	0.96	.3315	.1685	1.29	.4015	.0985
0.64	.2389	.2611	0.97	.3340	.1660	1.30	.4032	.0968
0.65	.2422	.2578	0.98	.3365	.1635	1.31	.4049	.0951
0.66	.2454	.2546	0.99	.3389	.1611	1.32	.4066	.0934
0.67	.2486	.2514	1.00	.3413	.1587	1.33	.4082	.0918
0.68	.2517	.2483	1.01	.3438	.1562	1.34	.4099	.0901
0.69	.2549	.2451	1.02	.3461	.1539	1.35	.4115	.0885
0.70	.2580	.2420	1.03	.3485	.1515	1.36	.4131	.0869
0.71	.2611	.2389	1.04	.3508	.1492	1.37	.4147	.0853
0.72	.2642	.2358	1.05	.3531	.1469	1.38	.4162	.0838
0.73	.2673	.2327	1.06	.3554	.1446	1.39	.4177	.0823
0.74	.2704	.2296	1.07	.3577	.1423	1.40	.4192	.0808
0.75	.2734	.2266	1.08	.3599	.1401	1.41	.4207	.0793
0.76	.2764	.2236	1.09	.3621	.1379	1.42	.4222	.0778
0.77	.2794	.2206	1.10	.3643	.1357	1.43	.4236	.0764

(A) z	(B) Area Between Mean and z	(C) Area Beyond z in Tail	(A) z	(B) Area Between Mean and z	(C) Area Beyond z in Tail	(A) z	(B) Area Between Mean and z	(C) Area Beyond z in Tail
1.44	.4251	.0749	1.77	.4616	.0384	2.10	.4821	.0179
1.45	.4265	.0735	1.78	.4625	.0375	2.11	.4826	.0174
1.46	.4279	.0721	1.79	.4633	.0367	2.12	.4830	.0170
1.47	.4292	.0708	1.80	.4641	.0359	2.13	.4834	.0166
1.48	.4306	.0694	1.81	.4649	.0351	2.14	.4838	.0162
1.49	.4319	.0681	1.82	.4656	.0344	2.15	.4842	.0158
1.50	.4332	.0668	1.83	.4664	.0336	2.16	.4846	.0154
1.51	.4345	.0655	1.84	.4671	.0329	2.17	.4850	.0150
1.52	.4357	.0643	1.85	.4678	.0322	2.18	.4854	.0146
1.53	.4370	.0630	1.86	.4686	.0314	2.19	.4857	.0143
1.54	.4382	.0618	1.87	.4693	.0307	2.20	.4861	.0139
1.55	.4394	.0606	1.88	.4699	.0301	2.21	.4864	.0136
1.56	.4406	.0594	1.89	.4706	.0294	2.22	.4868	.0132
1.57	.4418	.0582	1.90	.4713	.0287	2.23	.4871	.0129
1.58	.4429	.0571	1.91	.4719	.0281	2.24	.4875	.0125
1.59	.4441	.0559	1.92	.4726	.0274	2.25	.4878	.0122
1.60	.4452	.0548	1.93	.4732	.0268	2.26	.4881	.0119
1.61	.4463	.0537	1.94	.4738	.0262	2.27	.4884	.0116
1.62	.4474	.0526	1.95	.4744	.0256	2.28	.4887	.0113
1.63	.4484	.0516	1.96	.4750	.0250	2.29	.4890	.0110
1.64	.4495	.0505	1.97	.4756	.0244	2.30	.4893	.0107
1.65	.4505	.0495	1.98	.4761	.0239	2.31	.4896	.0104
1.66	.4515	.0485	1.99	.4767	.0233	2.32	.4898	.0102
1.67	.4525	.0475	2.00	.4772	.0228	2.33	.4901	.0099
1.68	.4535	.0465	2.01	.4778	.0222	2.34	.4904	.0096
1.69	.4545	.0455	2.02	.4783	.0217	2.35	.4906	.0094
1.70	.4554	.0446	2.03	.4788	.0212	2.36	.4909	.0091
1.71	.4564	.0436	2.04	.4793	.0207	2.37	.4911	.0089
1.72	.4573	.0427	2.05	.4798	.0202	2.38	.4913	.0087
1.73	.4582	.0418	2.06	.4803	.0197	2.39	.4916	.0084
1.74	.4591	.0409	2.07	.4808	.0192	2.40	.4918	.0082
1.75	.4599	.0401	2.08	.4812	.0188	2.41	.4920	.0080
1.76	.4608	.0392	2.09	.4817	.0183	2.42	.4922	.0078

(A) z	(B) Area Between Mean and z	(C) Area Beyond z in Tail	(A) z	(B) Area Between Mean and z	(C) Area Beyond z in Tail	(A) z	(B) Area Between Mean and z	(C) Area Beyond z in Tail
2.43	.4925	.0075	2.74	.4969	.0031	3.05	.4989	.0011
2.44	.4927	.0073	2.75	.4970	.0030	3.06	.4989	.0011
2.45	.4929	.0071	2.76	.4971	.0029	3.07	.4989	.0011
2.46	.4931	.0069	2.77	.4972	.0028	3.08	.4990	.0010
2.47	.4932	.0068	2.78	.4973	.0027	3.09	.4990	.0010
2.48	.4934	.0066	2.79	.4974	.0026	3.10	.4990	.0010
2.49	.4936	.0064	2.80	.4974	.0026	3.11	.4991	.0009
2.50	.4938	.0062	2.81	.4975	.0025	3.12	.4991	.0009
2.51	.4940	.0060	2.82	.4976	.0024	3.13	.4991	.0009
2.52	.4941	.0059	2.83	.4977	.0023	3.14	.4992	.0008
2.53	.4943	.0057	2.84	.4977	.0023	3.15	.4992	.0008
2.54	.4945	.0055	2.85	.4978	.0022	3.16	.4992	.0008
2.55	.4946	.0054	2.86	.4979	.0021	3.17	.4992	.0008
2.56	.4948	.0052	2.87	.4979	.0021	3.18	.4993	.0007
2.57	.4949	.0051	2.88	.4980	.0020	3.19	.4993	.0007
2.58	.4951	.0049	2.89	.4981	.0019	3.20	.4993	.0007
2.59	.4952	.0048	2.90	.4981	.0019	3.21	.4993	.0007
2.60	.4953	.0047	2.91	.4982	.0018	3.22	.4994	.0006
2.61	.4955	.0045	2.92	.4982	.0018	3.23	.4994	.0006
2.62	.4956	.0044	2.93	.4983	.0017	3.24	.4994	.0006
2.63	.4957	.0043	2.94	.4984	.0016	3.25	.4994	.0006
2.64	.4959	.0041	2.95	.4984	.0016	3.30	.4995	.0005
2.65	.4960	.0040	2.96	.4985	.0015	3.35	.4996	.0004
2.66	.4961	.0039	2.97	.4985	.0015	3.40	.4997	.0003
2.67	.4962	.0038	2.98	.4986	.0014	3.45	.4997	.0003
2.68	.4963	.0037	2.99	.4986	.0014	3.50	.4998	.0002
2.69	.4964	.0036	3.00	.4987	.0013	3.60	.4998	.0002
2.70	.4965	.0035	3.01	.4987	.0013	3.70	.4999	.0001
2.71	.4966	.0034	3.02	.4987	.0013	3.80	.4999	.0001
2.72	.4967	.0033	3.03	.4988	.0012	3.90	.49995	.00005
2.73	.4968	.0032	3.04	.4988	.0012	4.00	.49997	.00003

SOURCE: Based on J. E. Freund, *Modern Elementary Statistics* (11th edition). Pearson Prentice Hall, 2004.

TABLE B.2 The *t* distribution.

Table entries are values of *t* corresponding to proportions in one tail or in two tails combined.

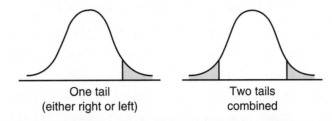

One tail
(either right or left)

Two tails
combined

	Proportion in One Tail					
	.25	.10	.05	.025	.01	.005
	Proportion in Two Tails Combined					
df	.50	.20	.10	.05	.02	.01
1	1.000	3.078	6.314	12.706	31.821	63.657
2	0.816	1.886	2.920	4.303	6.965	9.925
3	0.765	1.638	2.353	3.182	4.541	5.841
4	0.741	1.533	2.132	2.776	3.747	4.604
5	0.727	1.476	2.015	2.571	3.365	4.032
6	0.718	1.440	1.943	2.447	3.143	3.707
7	0.711	1.415	1.895	2.365	2.998	3.499
8	0.706	1.397	1.860	2.306	2.896	3.355
9	0.703	1.383	1.833	2.282	2.821	3.250
10	0.700	1.372	1.812	2.228	2.764	3.169
11	0.697	1.363	1.796	2.201	2.718	3.106
12	0.695	1.356	1.782	2.179	2.681	3.055
13	0.694	1.350	1.771	2.160	2.650	3.012
14	0.692	1.345	1.761	2.145	2.624	2.977
15	0.691	1.341	1.753	2.131	2.602	2.947
16	0.690	1.337	1.746	2.120	2.583	2.921
17	0.689	1.333	1.740	2.110	2.567	2.898
18	0.688	1.330	1.734	2.101	2.552	2.878
19	0.688	1.328	1.729	2.093	2.539	2.861
20	0.687	1.325	1.725	2.086	2.528	2.845
21	0.686	1.323	1.721	2.080	2.518	2.831
22	0.686	1.321	1.717	2.074	2.508	2.819
23	0.685	1.319	1.714	2.069	2.500	2.807

	Proportion in One Tail					
	.25	.10	.05	.025	.01	.005
	Proportion in Two Tails Combined					
df	.50	.20	.10	.05	.02	.01
24	0.685	1.318	1.711	2.064	2.492	2.797
25	0.684	1.316	1.708	2.060	2.485	2.787
26	0.684	1.315	1.706	2.056	2.479	2.779
27	0.684	1.314	1.703	2.052	2.473	2.771
28	0.683	1.313	1.701	2.048	2.467	2.763
29	0.683	1.311	1.699	2.045	2.462	2.756
30	0.683	1.310	1.697	2.042	2.457	2.750
40	0.681	1.303	1.684	2.021	2.423	2.704
60	0.679	1.296	1.671	2.000	2.390	2.660
120	0.677	1.289	1.658	1.980	2.358	2.617
∞	0.674	1.282	1.645	1.960	2.326	2.576

SOURCE: Table III of R.A. Fisher and F. Yates, *Statistical Tables for Biological, Agricultural and Medical Research,* 6th ed. London: Longman Group Ltd., 1974 (previously published by Oliver and Boyd Ltd., Edinburgh). Adapted and reprinted with permission of Addison Wesley Longman.

TABLE B.3 Critical values for the F distribution.

Critical values at a .05 level of significance are given in lightface type.

Critical values at a .01 level of significance are given in boldface type.

		Degrees of Freedom Numerator											
		1	2	3	4	5	6	7	8	9	10	20	∞
Degrees of Freedom Denominator	1	161 **4052**	200 **5000**	216 **5403**	225 **5625**	230 **5764**	234 **5859**	237 **5928**	239 **5928**	241 **6023**	242 **6056**	248 **6209**	254 **6366**
	2	18.51 **98.49**	19.00 **99.00**	19.16 **99.17**	19.25 **99.25**	19.30 **99.30**	19.33 **99.33**	19.36 **99.34**	19.37 **99.36**	19.38 **99.38**	19.39 **99.40**	19.44 **99.45**	19.5 **99.5**
	3	10.13 **34.12**	9.55 **30.92**	9.28 **29.46**	9.12 **28.71**	9.01 **28.24**	8.94 **27.91**	8.88 **27.67**	8.84 **27.49**	8.81 **27.34**	8.78 **27.23**	8.66 **26.69**	8.5 **26.1**
	4	7.71 **21.20**	6.94 **18.00**	6.59 **16.69**	6.39 **15.98**	6.26 **15.52**	6.16 **15.21**	6.09 **14.98**	6.04 **14.80**	6.00 **14.66**	5.96 **14.54**	5.80 **14.02**	5.6 **13.5**
	5	6.61 **16.26**	5.79 **13.27**	5.41 **12.06**	5.19 **11.39**	5.05 **10.97**	4.95 **10.67**	4.88 **10.45**	4.82 **10.27**	4.78 **10.15**	4.74 **10.05**	4.56 **9.55**	4.37 **9.02**
	6	5.99 **13.74**	5.14 **10.92**	4.76 **9.78**	4.53 **9.15**	4.39 **8.75**	4.28 **8.47**	4.21 **8.26**	4.15 **8.10**	4.10 **7.98**	4.06 **7.87**	3.87 **7.39**	3.67 **6.88**
	7	5.59 **13.74**	4.74 **9.55**	4.35 **8.45**	4.12 **7.85**	3.97 **7.46**	3.87 **7.19**	3.79 **7.00**	3.73 **6.84**	3.68 **6.71**	3.63 **6.62**	3.44 **6.15**	3.23 **5.65**
	8	5.32 **11.26**	4.46 **8.65**	4.07 **7.59**	3.84 **7.01**	3.69 **6.63**	3.58 **6.37**	3.50 **6.19**	3.44 **6.03**	3.39 **5.91**	3.34 **5.82**	3.15 **5.36**	2.93 **4.86**
	9	5.12 **10.56**	4.26 **8.02**	3.86 **6.99**	3.63 **6.42**	3.48 **6.06**	3.37 **5.80**	3.29 **5.62**	3.23 **5.47**	3.18 **5.35**	3.13 **5.26**	2.93 **4.80**	2.71 **4.31**
	10	4.96 **10.04**	4.10 **7.56**	3.71 **6.55**	3.48 **5.99**	3.33 **5.64**	3.22 **5.39**	3.14 **5.21**	3.07 **5.06**	3.02 **4.95**	2.97 **4.85**	2.77 **4.41**	2.54 **3.91**
	11	4.84 **9.65**	3.98 **7.20**	3.59 **6.22**	3.36 **5.67**	3.20 **5.32**	3.09 **5.07**	3.01 **4.88**	2.95 **4.74**	2.90 **4.63**	2.86 **4.54**	2.65 **4.10**	2.40 **3.60**
	12	4.75 **9.33**	3.89 **6.93**	3.49 **5.95**	3.26 **5.41**	3.11 **5.06**	3.00 **4.82**	2.92 **4.65**	2.85 **4.50**	2.80 **4.39**	2.76 **4.30**	2.54 **3.86**	2.30 **3.36**
	13	4.67 **9.07**	3.80 **6.70**	3.41 **5.74**	3.18 **5.20**	3.02 **4.86**	2.92 **4.62**	2.84 **4.44**	2.77 **4.30**	2.72 **4.19**	2.67 **4.10**	2.46 **3.67**	2.21 **3.17**
	14	4.60 **8.86**	3.74 **6.51**	3.34 **5.56**	3.11 **5.03**	2.96 **4.69**	2.85 **4.46**	2.77 **4.28**	2.70 **4.14**	2.65 **4.03**	2.60 **3.94**	2.39 **3.51**	2.13 **3.00**
	15	4.54 **8.68**	3.68 **6.36**	3.29 **5.42**	3.06 **4.89**	2.90 **4.56**	2.79 **4.32**	2.70 **4.14**	2.64 **4.00**	2.59 **3.89**	2.55 **3.80**	2.33 **3.36**	2.07 **2.87**

	Degrees of Freedom Numerator											
	1	**2**	**3**	**4**	**5**	**6**	**7**	**8**	**9**	**10**	**20**	**∞**
16	4.49 **8.53**	3.63 **6.23**	3.24 **5.29**	3.01 **4.77**	2.85 **4.44**	2.74 **4.20**	2.66 **4.03**	2.59 **3.89**	2.54 **3.78**	2.49 **3.69**	2.28 **3.25**	2.01 **2.75**
17	4.45 **8.40**	3.59 **6.11**	3.20 **5.18**	2.96 **4.67**	2.81 **4.34**	2.70 **4.10**	2.62 **3.93**	2.55 **3.79**	2.50 **3.68**	2.45 **3.59**	2.23 **3.16**	1.96 **2.65**
18	4.41 **8.28**	3.55 **6.01**	3.16 **5.09**	2.93 **4.58**	2.77 **4.25**	2.66 **4.01**	2.58 **3.85**	2.51 **3.71**	2.46 **3.60**	2.41 **3.51**	2.19 **3.07**	1.92 **2.57**
19	4.38 **8.18**	3.52 **5.93**	3.13 **5.01**	2.90 **4.50**	2.74 **4.17**	2.63 **3.94**	2.55 **3.77**	2.48 **3.63**	2.43 **3.52**	2.38 **3.43**	2.15 **3.00**	1.88 **2.49**
20	4.35 **8.10**	3.49 **5.85**	3.10 **4.94**	2.87 **4.43**	2.71 **4.10**	2.60 **3.87**	2.52 **3.71**	2.45 **3.56**	2.40 **3.45**	2.35 **3.37**	2.12 **2.94**	1.84 **2.42**
21	4.32 **8.02**	3.47 **5.78**	3.07 **4.87**	2.84 **4.37**	2.68 **4.04**	2.57 **3.81**	2.49 **3.65**	2.42 **3.51**	2.37 **3.40**	2.32 **3.31**	2.09 **2.88**	1.81 **2.36**
22	4.30 **7.94**	3.44 **5.72**	3.05 **4.82**	2.82 **4.31**	2.66 **3.99**	2.55 **3.76**	2.47 **3.59**	2.40 **3.45**	2.35 **3.35**	2.30 **3.26**	2.07 **2.83**	1.78 **2.31**
23	4.28 **7.88**	3.42 **5.66**	3.03 **4.76**	2.80 **4.26**	2.64 **3.94**	2.53 **3.71**	2.45 **3.54**	2.38 **3.41**	2.32 **3.30**	2.28 **3.21**	2.04 **2.78**	1.76 **2.26**
24	4.26 **7.82**	3.40 **5.61**	3.01 **4.72**	2.78 **4.22**	2.62 **3.90**	2.51 **3.67**	2.43 **3.50**	2.36 **3.36**	2.30 **3.25**	2.26 **3.17**	2.02 **2.74**	1.73 **2.21**
25	4.24 **7.77**	3.38 **5.57**	2.99 **4.68**	2.76 **4.18**	2.60 **3.86**	2.49 **3.63**	2.41 **3.46**	2.34 **3.32**	2.28 **3.21**	2.24 **3.13**	2.00 **2.70**	1.71 **2.17**
26	4.22 **7.72**	3.37 **5.53**	2.98 **4.64**	2.74 **4.14**	2.59 **3.82**	2.47 **3.59**	2.39 **3.42**	2.32 **3.29**	2.27 **3.17**	2.22 **3.09**	1.99 **2.66**	1.69 **2.13**
27	4.21 **7.68**	3.35 **5.49**	2.96 **4.60**	2.73 **4.11**	2.57 **3.79**	2.46 **3.56**	2.37 **3.39**	2.30 **3.26**	2.25 **3.14**	2.20 **3.06**	1.97 **2.63**	1.67 **2.10**
28	4.20 **7.64**	3.34 **5.45**	2.95 **4.57**	2.71 **4.07**	2.56 **3.76**	2.44 **3.53**	2.36 **3.36**	2.29 **3.23**	2.24 **3.11**	2.19 **3.03**	1.96 **2.60**	1.65 **2.07**
29	4.18 **7.60**	3.33 **5.42**	2.93 **4.54**	2.70 **4.04**	2.54 **3.73**	2.43 **3.50**	2.35 **3.33**	2.28 **3.20**	2.22 **3.08**	2.18 **3.00**	1.94 **2.57**	1.63 **2.04**
30	4.17 **7.56**	3.32 **5.39**	2.92 **4.51**	2.69 **4.02**	2.53 **3.70**	2.42 **3.47**	2.34 **3.30**	2.27 **3.17**	2.21 **3.06**	2.16 **2.98**	1.93 **2.55**	1.61 **2.01**
31	4.16 **7.53**	3.30 **5.36**	2.91 **4.48**	2.68 **3.99**	2.52 **3.67**	2.41 **3.45**	2.32 **3.28**	2.25 **3.15**	2.20 **3.04**	2.15 **2.96**	1.92 **2.53**	1.60 **1.89**
32	4.15 **7.50**	3.29 **5.34**	2.90 **4.46**	2.67 **3.97**	2.51 **3.65**	2.40 **3.43**	2.31 **3.26**	2.24 **3.13**	2.19 **3.02**	2.14 **2.93**	1.91 **2.51**	1.59 **1.88**

Degrees of Freedom Denominator (row labels at left)

		Degrees of Freedom Numerator											
		1	**2**	**3**	**4**	**5**	**6**	**7**	**8**	**9**	**10**	**20**	**∞**
	33	4.14	3.28	2.89	2.66	2.50	2.39	2.30	2.23	2.18	2.13	1.90	1.58
		7.47	**5.31**	**4.44**	**3.95**	**3.63**	**3.41**	**3.24**	**3.11**	**3.00**	**2.91**	**2.49**	**1.87**
	34	4.13	3.28	2.88	2.65	2.49	2.38	2.29	2.23	2.17	2.12	1.89	1.57
		7.44	**5.29**	**4.42**	**3.93**	**3.61**	**3.39**	**3.22**	**3.09**	**2.98**	**2.89**	**2.47**	**1.86**
	35	4.12	3.27	2.87	2.64	2.49	2.37	2.29	2.22	2.16	2.11	1.88	1.56
		7.42	**5.27**	**4.40**	**3.91**	**3.59**	**3.37**	**3.20**	**3.07**	**2.96**	**2.88**	**2.45**	**1.85**
	36	4.11	3.26	2.87	2.63	2.48	2.36	2.28	2.21	2.15	2.11	1.87	1.55
		7.40	**5.25**	**4.38**	**3.89**	**3.57**	**3.35**	**3.18**	**3.05**	**2.95**	**2.86**	**2.43**	**1.84**
	37	4.11	3.25	2.86	2.63	2.47	2.36	2.27	2.20	2.14	2.10	1.86	1.54
		7.37	**5.23**	**4.36**	**3.87**	**3.56**	**3.33**	**3.17**	**3.04**	**2.93**	**2.84**	**2.42**	**1.83**
	38	4.10	3.24	2.85	2.62	2.46	2.35	2.26	2.19	2.14	2.09	1.85	1.53
		7.35	**5.21**	**4.34**	**3.86**	**3.54**	**3.32**	**3.15**	**3.02**	**2.92**	**2.83**	**2.40**	**1.82**
	39	4.09	3.24	2.85	2.61	2.46	2.34	2.26	2.19	2.13	2.08	1.84	1.52
		7.33	**5.19**	**4.33**	**3.84**	**3.53**	**3.30**	**3.14**	**3.01**	**2.90**	**2.81**	**2.39**	**1.81**
	40	4.08	3.23	2.84	2.61	2.45	2.34	2.25	2.18	2.12	2.07	1.84	1.51
		7.31	**5.18**	**4.31**	**3.83**	**3.51**	**3.29**	**3.12**	**2.99**	**2.88**	**2.80**	**2.37**	**1.80**
	42	4.07	3.22	2.83	2.59	2.44	2.32	2.24	2.17	2.11	2.06	1.82	1.50
		7.27	**5.15**	**4.29**	**3.80**	**3.49**	**3.26**	**3.10**	**2.96**	**2.86**	**2.77**	**2.35**	**1.78**
	44	4.06	3.21	2.82	2.58	2.43	2.31	2.23	2.16	2.10	2.05	1.81	1.49
		7.24	**5.12**	**4.26**	**3.78**	**3.46**	**3.24**	**3.07**	**2.94**	**2.84**	**2.75**	**2.32**	**1.76**
	60	4.00	3.15	2.76	2.53	2.37	2.25	2.17	2.10	2.04	1.99	1.75	1.39
		7.08	**4.98**	**4.13**	**3.65**	**3.34**	**3.12**	**2.95**	**2.82**	**2.72**	**2.63**	**2.20**	**1.60**
	120	3.92	3.07	2.68	2.45	2.29	2.18	2.09	2.02	1.96	1.91	1.66	1.25
		6.85	**4.79**	**3.95**	**3.48**	**3.17**	**2.96**	**2.79**	**2.66**	**2.56**	**2.47**	**2.03**	**1.38**
	∞	3.84	3.00	2.60	2.37	2.21	2.10	2.01	1.94	1.88	1.83	1.57	1.00
		6.63	**4.61**	**3.78**	**3.32**	**3.02**	**2.80**	**2.64**	**2.51**	**2.41**	**2.32**	**1.88**	**1.00**

Degrees of Freedom Denominator

SOURCE: The entries in this table were computed by the author.

TABLE B.4 The studentized range statistic (q).

The critical values for q correspond to alpha = .05 (lightface type) and alpha = .01 (boldface type).

df_E	Range								
	2	3	4	5	6	7	8	9	10
6	3.46 **5.24**	4.34 **6.32**	4.90 **7.02**	5.30 **7.55**	5.63 **7.98**	5.91 **8.33**	6.13 **8.62**	6.32 **8.87**	6.50 **9.10**
7	3.34 **4.95**	4.17 **5.91**	4.68 **6.54**	5.06 **7.00**	5.36 **7.38**	5.60 **7.69**	5.82 **7.94**	5.99 **8.17**	6.15 **8.38**
8	3.26 **4.75**	4.05 **5.64**	4.53 **6.21**	4.89 **6.63**	5.17 **6.97**	5.41 **7.26**	5.60 **7.47**	5.78 **7.70**	5.93 **7.89**
9	3.20 **4.60**	3.95 **5.43**	4.42 **5.95**	4.76 **6.34**	5.03 **6.67**	5.24 **6.91**	5.43 **7.13**	5.60 **7.33**	5.74 **7.50**
10	3.15 **4.48**	3.88 **5.27**	4.33 **5.77**	4.66 **6.14**	4.92 **6.43**	5.12 **6.67**	5.30 **6.89**	5.46 **7.06**	5.60 **7.22**
11	3.11 **4.38**	3.82 **5.16**	4.27 **5.63**	4.59 **5.98**	4.83 **6.25**	5.03 **6.48**	5.21 **6.69**	5.36 **6.85**	5.49 **7.01**
12	3.08 **4.32**	3.78 **5.05**	4.20 **5.50**	4.51 **5.84**	4.75 **6.10**	4.96 **6.32**	5.12 **6.52**	5.26 **6.67**	5.39 **6.82**
13	3.05 **4.26**	3.73 **4.97**	4.15 **5.41**	4.47 **5.74**	4.69 **5.98**	4.88 **6.19**	5.06 **6.39**	5.21 **6.53**	5.33 **6.68**
14	3.03 **4.21**	3.70 **4.90**	4.11 **5.33**	4.41 **5.64**	4.64 **5.88**	4.83 **6.10**	4.99 **6.28**	5.13 **6.41**	5.25 **6.56**
15	3.01 **4.17**	3.68 **4.84**	4.09 **5.26**	4.38 **5.56**	4.59 **5.80**	4.79 **6.01**	4.95 **6.18**	5.09 **6.31**	5.21 **6.46**
16	2.99 **4.13**	3.65 **4.79**	4.05 **5.19**	4.33 **5.50**	4.56 **5.72**	4.74 **5.94**	4.89 **6.10**	5.03 **6.23**	5.15 **6.37**
17	2.98 **4.10**	3.63 **4.75**	4.02 **5.15**	4.30 **5.44**	4.52 **5.66**	4.70 **5.86**	4.85 **6.02**	4.99 **6.14**	5.11 **6.28**
18	2.97 **4.07**	3.62 **4.71**	4.01 **5.10**	4.29 **5.39**	4.49 **5.60**	4.68 **5.80**	4.84 **5.95**	4.97 **6.08**	5.08 **6.21**
19	2.96 **4.05**	3.59 **4.68**	3.98 **5.05**	4.26 **5.35**	4.47 **5.56**	4.65 **5.75**	4.80 **5.91**	4.93 **6.03**	5.04 **6.15**
20	2.95 **4.02**	3.58 **4.64**	3.96 **5.02**	4.24 **5.31**	4.45 **5.51**	4.63 **5.71**	4.78 **5.86**	4.91 **5.98**	5.01 **6.09**
22	2.94 **3.99**	3.55 **4.59**	3.93 **4.96**	4.20 **5.27**	4.41 **5.44**	4.58 **5.62**	4.72 **5.76**	4.85 **5.87**	4.96 **6.00**
24	2.92 **3.96**	3.53 **4.55**	3.91 **4.92**	4.17 **5.17**	4.37 **5.37**	4.54 **5.55**	4.69 **5.70**	4.81 **5.81**	4.92 **5.93**

df$_E$	Range								
	2	3	4	5	6	7	8	9	10
26	2.91 **3.94**	3.52 **4.51**	3.89 **4.87**	4.15 **5.13**	4.36 **5.33**	4.53 **5.49**	4.67 **5.63**	4.79 **5.74**	4.90 **5.86**
28	2.90 **3.91**	3.50 **4.48**	3.87 **4.83**	4.12 **5.09**	4.33 **5.28**	4.49 **5.45**	4.63 **5.58**	4.75 **5.69**	4.86 **5.81**
30	2.89 **3.89**	3.49 **4.45**	3.85 **4.80**	4.10 **5.05**	4.30 **5.24**	4.47 **5.40**	0.60 **5.54**	4.73 **5.64**	4.84 **5.76**
40	2.86 **3.82**	3.45 **4.37**	3.79 **4.70**	4.05 **4.93**	4.23 **5.11**	4.39 **5.26**	4.52 **5.39**	4.65 **5.49**	4.73 **5.60**
60	2.83 **3.76**	3.41 **4.28**	3.75 **4.60**	3.98 **4.82**	4.16 **4.99**	4.31 **5.13**	4.44 **5.25**	4.56 **5.36**	4.65 **5.45**
100	2.81 **3.72**	3.36 **4.22**	3.70 **4.52**	3.93 **4.74**	4.11 **4.90**	4.26 **5.04**	4.39 **5.15**	4.50 **5.23**	4.59 **5.34**
∞	2.77 **3.64**	3.31 **4.12**	3.63 **4.40**	3.86 **4.60**	4.03 **4.76**	4.17 **4.88**	4.28 **4.99**	4.39 **5.08**	4.47 **5.16**

SOURCE: The entries in this table were computed by the author.

TABLE B.5   Critical values for the Pearson correlation*.

*To be significant, the sample correlation, *r*, must be greater than or equal to the critical value in the table.

df = n − 2	Level of Significance for One-Tailed Test			
	.05	.025	.01	.005
	Level of Significance for Two-Tailed Test			
	.10	.05	.02	.01
1	.988	.997	.9995	.99999
2	.900	.950	.980	.990
3	.805	.878	.934	.959
4	.729	.811	.882	.917
5	.669	.754	.833	.874
6	.622	.707	.789	.834
7	.582	.666	.750	.798
8	.549	.632	.716	.765
9	.521	.602	.685	.735
10	.497	.576	.658	.708
11	.476	.553	.634	.684
12	.458	.532	.612	.661
13	.441	.514	.592	.641
14	.426	.497	.574	.623
15	.412	.482	.558	.606
16	.400	.468	.542	.590
17	.389	.456	.528	.575
18	.378	.444	.516	.561
19	.369	.433	.503	.549
20	.360	.423	.492	.537
21	.352	.413	.482	.526
22	.344	.404	.472	.515
23	.337	.396	.462	.505
24	.330	.388	.453	.496

df = n − 2	Level of Significance for One-Tailed Test			
	.05	.025	.01	.005
	Level of Significance for Two-Tailed Test			
	.10	.05	.02	.01
25	.323	.381	.445	.487
26	.317	.374	.437	.479
27	.311	.367	.430	.471
28	.306	.361	.423	.463
29	.301	.355	.416	.456
30	.296	.349	.409	.449
35	.275	.325	.381	.418
40	.257	.304	.358	.393
45	.243	.288	.338	.372
50	.231	.273	.322	.354
60	.211	.250	.295	.325
70	.195	.232	.274	.302
80	.183	.217	.256	.283
90	.173	.205	.242	.267
100	.164	.195	.230	.254

SOURCE: Table VI of R. A. Fisher and F. Yates, *Statistical Tables for Biological, Agricultural and Medical Research*, 6th ed. London: Longman Group Ltd., 1974 (previously published by Oliver and Boyd Ltd., Edinburgh). Adapted and reprinted with permission of Addison Wesley Longman.

TABLE B.6   Critical values for the Spearman correlation*.

*To be significant, the sample correlation, *r*, must be greater than or equal to the critical value in the table.

	Level of Significance for One-Tailed Test			
	.05	.025	.01	.005
	Level of Significance for Two-Tailed Test			
n	.10	.05	.02	.01
4	1.000			
5	.900	1.000	1.000	
6	.829	.886	.943	1.000
7	.714	.786	.893	.929
8	.643	.738	.833	.881
9	.600	.700	.783	.833
10	.564	.648	.745	.794
11	.536	.618	.709	.755
12	.503	.587	.671	.727
13	.484	.560	.648	.703
14	.464	.538	.622	.675
15	.443	.521	.604	.654
16	.429	.503	.582	.635
17	.414	.485	.566	.615
18	.401	.472	.550	.600
19	.391	.460	.535	.584
20	.380	.447	.520	.570
21	.370	.435	.508	.556
22	.361	.425	.496	.544
23	.353	.415	.486	.532
24	.344	.406	.476	.521
25	.337	.398	.466	.511
26	.331	.390	.457	.501
27	.324	.382	.448	.491

	Level of Significance for One-Tailed Test			
	.05	.025	.01	.005
	Level of Significance for Two-Tailed Test			
n	.10	.05	.02	.01
28	.317	.375	.440	.483
29	.312	.368	.433	.475
30	.306	.362	.425	.467
35	.283	.335	.394	.433
40	.264	.313	.368	.405
45	.248	.294	.347	.382
50	.235	.279	.329	.363
60	.214	.255	.300	.331
70	.190	.235	.278	.307
80	.185	.220	.260	.287
90	.174	.207	.245	.271
100	.165	.197	.233	.257

TABLE B.7   Critical values of chi-square (χ^2).

	Level of Significance	
df	.05	.01
1	3.84	6.64
2	5.99	9.21
3	7.81	11.34
4	9.49	13.28
5	11.07	15.09
6	12.59	16.81
7	14.07	18.48
8	15.51	20.09
9	16.92	21.67
10	18.31	23.21
11	19.68	24.72
12	21.03	26.22
13	22.36	27.69
14	23.68	29.14
15	25.00	30.58
16	26.30	32.00
17	27.59	33.41
18	28.87	34.80
19	30.14	36.19
20	31.41	37.47
21	32.67	38.93
22	33.92	40.29
23	35.17	41.64
24	36.42	42.98
25	37.65	44.31
26	38.88	45.64
27	40.11	46.96
28	41.34	48.28
29	42.56	49.59
30	43.77	50.89
40	55.76	63.69
50	67.50	76.15
60	79.08	88.38
70	90.53	100.42

SOURCE: From Table IV of R. A. Fisher and F. Yates, *Statistical Tables for Biological, Agricultural and Medical Research*, 6th ed. London: Longman Group Ltd., 1974 (previously published by Oliver and Boyd Ltd., Edinburgh). Reprinted with permission of Addison Wesley Longman Ltd.

DECISION TREES

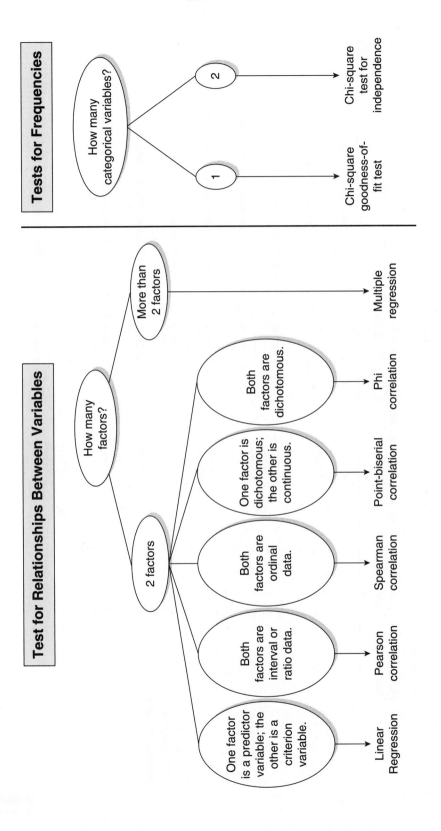

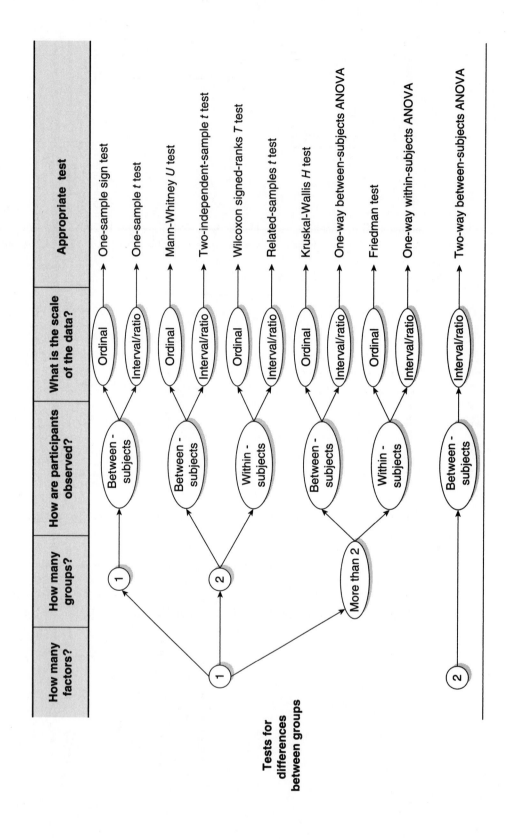

References

Agrawal, A., Madden, P. A. F., Buchholz, K. K., Heath, A. C., & Lynskey, M. T. (2008). Transitions to regular smoking and to nicotine dependence in women using cannabis. *Drug and Alcohol Dependence, 95,* 107–114.

American Psychological Association. (2009). *Publication manual of the American Psychological Association* (6th ed.). Washington, DC: Author.

Bernstein, P. L. (1998). *Against the Gods: The remarkable story of risk.* New York: Wiley.

Bradley, M. M., & Lang, P. J. (1994). Measuring emotion: The Self-Assessment Manikin and the semantic differential. *Journal of Behavior Therapy & Experimental Psychiatry, 25,* 49–59.

Edenborough, M., Jackson, D., Mannix, J., & Wilkes, L. M. (2008). Living in the red zone: The experience of child-to-mother violence. *Child and Family Social Work, 13,* 464–473.

Elias, S. M. (2007). Influence in the ivory tower: Examining the appropriate use of social power in the university classroom. *Journal of Applied Social Psychology, 37*(11), 2532–2548.

Gulledge, A. K., Stahmann, R. F., & Wilson, C. M. (2004). Seven types of nonsexual romantic physical affection among Brigham Young University students. *Psychological Reports, 95,* 609–614.

Hollands, J. G., & Spence, I. (1992). Judgments of change and proportion in graphical perception. *Human Factors, 34,* 313–334.

Hollands, J. G., & Spence, I. (1998). Judging proportions with graphs: The summation model. *Applied Cognitive Psychology, 12,* 173–190.

Jones, N., Blackey, H., Fitzgibbon, K., & Chew, E. (2010). Get out of MySpace! *Computers & Education, 54,* 776–782.

Kruger, J., & Savitsky, K. (2006). *The persuasiveness of one- vs. two-tailed tests of significance: When weak results are preferred over strong* [Abstract]. Retrieved from http://ssrn .com/abstract=946199

National Institute on Alcohol Abuse and Alcoholism. (2000). *Tenth special report to the U.S. Congress on alcohol and health* (NIH Pub. No. 00-1583). Washington, DC: National Institutes of Health.

Privitera, G. J. (2014). *Research methods for the behavioral sciences.* Thousand Oaks, CA: Sage.